Islamic Leadership and the State in Eurasia

Islamic Leadership and the State in Eurasia

Galina M. Yemelianova

ANTHEM PRESS

Anthem Press
An imprint of Wimbledon Publishing Company
www.anthempress.com

This edition first published in UK and USA 2025
by ANTHEM PRESS
75–76 Blackfriars Road, London SE1 8HA, UK
or PO Box 9779, London SW19 7ZG, UK
and
244 Madison Ave #116, New York, NY 10016, USA

First published in the UK and USA by Anthem Press in 2022

British Library Cataloguing-in-Publication Data
A catalogue record for this book is available from the British Library.

Library of Congress Control Number: 2024943702

ISBN-13: 978-1-83999-371-8 (Pbk)
ISBN-10: 1-83999-371-5 (Pbk)

Cover Image: Moscow Cathedral Mosque
(photograph by author, Moscow, 4 August 2018)

This title is also available as an e-book.

In memory of my father,
Mikhail Pavlovich Yemelianov
(1933–2021)

CONTENTS

List of Figures ix
Glossary xi
Note on Transliteration, Place Names and Calendars xvii
Additional Signs Used xix

Introduction 1

Part I Islam, Islamic Authority and Leadership before and during the Russian Rule 9

Chapter One Authority and Leadership in Islam: A Historical and Comparative Perspective 11
Chapter Two Islamic Leadership among Tatars and Other Turkic Peoples prior to and during Russian Rule 27
Chapter Three Islam and Islamic Leadership in the Caucasus 43
Chapter Four Islam, Islamic Authority and Leadership in Central Asia 55

Part II Islamic Authority and Leadership in the USSR 71

Chapter Five The Volga-Urals 73
Chapter Six The North Caucasus 87
Chapter Seven The South Caucasus 101
Chapter Eight Central Asia and Kazakhstan 113

Part III Islamic Authority and Leadership in Post-Soviet Lands 125

Chapter Nine Belarus, Ukraine and Lithuania 127
Chapter Ten European Russia 139
Chapter Eleven The Caucasus 157
Chapter Twelve Central Asia 179
Chapter Thirteen Eurasian Islamic Leadership within the Global Context 197

Notes 217
Bibliography 249
Index 259

FIGURES

2.1	Suyumbike Tower (Khān mosque), Kazan, Tatarstan	41
5.1	Map of the USSR	86
10.1	Mosque 'Yardam' and its leaders, Moscow	151
10.2	Muftī A'lbir Krganov, Moscow	152
10.3	Rashida-Abystai, Kazan, Tatarstan	153
10.4	Mosque 'Taubah', Naberezhnye Chelny, Tatarstan	154
10.5	Inside the Moscow Cathedral mosque	155
11.1	Cathedral mosque, Makhachkala, Dagestan	172
11.2	At the entrance of the Cathedral mosque, Makhachkala	172
11.3	Cathedral mosque, Babugent, Kabardino-Balkaria	173
11.4	Inside the Babugent Cathedral mosque, Babugent, Kabardino-Balkaria	173
11.5	Cathedral mosque, Cherkessk, Karachaevo-Cherkessia	174
11.6	Imām of the Gubden mosque, Gubden, Dagestan	174
11.7	Inside the Cathedral mosque, Makhachkala	175
11.8	Ismail Bostanov, Sharafutdin Chochayev and Akhmad-ḥajjee Tagaev	176
11.9	Juma mosque, Shemakhi, Azerbaijan	177
12.1	Remains of the 'Old mosque', Isfana, Batken region, Kyrgyzstan	192
12.2	Central mosque, Khujand, Tajikistan	193
12.3	At the Naqshbandī khānqāh, Qushi-Ata, Kazakhstan	193
12.4	Madrasah's teachers and the author, Karakol, Kyrgyzstan	194
12.5	Imām of the Central mosque, Karakol, Kyrgyzstan	194
12.6	Hazrat Sultan mosque, Nur-Sultan, Kazakhstan	195

GLOSSARY

abystai	a female Islamic authority among the Tatars and Bashkirs
abyz	a knowledgeable member of a Tatar local community
adab	rules of good Islamic behaviour
'adat	a customary law
Ahl al-Bayt	lit. 'People of the House'. Members of Prophet Muḥammad's family
akhund/akhun	a senior Islamic cleric in Azerbaijan; a leading imām among Tatars
aksakal	an elder
al-uṣūl al-jadīd	lit. 'a new method' in Arabic. A new way of madrasah teaching, based on phonetization, see also *jadīdism*
'ālim (pl. *'ulamā'*)	an Islamic scholar
alym	a blood price among some peoples of the Caucasus
amīr/emir	lit. 'ruler' in Arabic
'aqīdah	the Islamic creed
arkān al-Islām	pillars of Islam
asharshylyk	lit. 'famine' in Kazakh
'Āshūrā'	the tenth day of Muḥarram, when Ḥusayn ibn 'Ālī was killed
ataliq	a *vezīr* in the Bukhara Khānate
aul	a mountainous village in the North Caucasus; a village among Kazakhs and Kyrgyz
awlāt	a sacralized tribal formation among Turkmen
'awliyā'	a cult of saints in Ṣūfism
Bāb al-Abwāb	lit. 'Gate of All Gates' in Arabic. Arabic name of Darband/Derbent
barakah	a blessing in Islam
bay'ah	an oath of allegiance in Islam
baylarbay/beglerbeg	a governor in the Safawid Empire
baylarbaylik/beglerbeglik	a province of the Safawid Empire
beg/bek/bey	a chieftain among various Turkic nomads
bibi-otun/bibi-khalfa	a female religious authority among Central Asian Muslims
bid'ah	an unlawful innovation in Islam
caravan-sarai	a merchant station
chachvon	a face veil among women in Central Asia
Dā'ish/Daesh	'Islamic State of Iraq and al-Sham' (ISIS)
da'wah	Salafī Islamic proselytism
Dār al-Ḥarb	lit. 'Abode of War' in Arabic. A territory where warfare is legitimate

Dār al-Islām	lit. 'Abode of Islam' in Arabic. A territory where warfare is not permitted
Dasht-i-Qipchaq	Qipchaq Steppe, synonymous to Kazakh Steppe
dhikr	lit. 'remembrance' in Arabic. In Ṣūfīsm, a ritual prayer
dhikr-i khāfī	lit. 'silent *dhikr*'
dhikr-i jahrī	lit. 'loud *dhikr*'
dhimmī	non-Muslim population in the caliphate
dibir	Muslim religious functionary in Dagestan
divān	an advisory council
du'ā'	the possibility of supplication to the Prophet Muḥammad
dzhien	a local assembly among Volga Bulgars and Tatars; from the eighteenth century also a fair among Tatars and Bashkirs
eyalet	a province of the Ottoman Empire, see also *pashalyk*
faqīh	(pl. *fuqahā'*) an Islamic jurist
fatwā	a legal opinion, issued by a *muftī*
firqah	an Islamic group
fiqh	Islamic jurisprudence
ghazawāt	an Islamized war against the Russian invasion of the North Caucasus
guberniia	a province of the Russian Empire
Ḥadīth	account of Prophet Muḥammad's sayings
ḥāfiẓ	a professional reader of the Qur'ān
ḥajj	an Islamic pilgrimage to Mecca and Medina
ḥalāl	lit. 'permissible' in Arabic, opposite of ḥarām ('forbidden')
ḥalaqah	lit. 'cell' in Arabic
ḥaqīqah	lit. 'truth' in Arabic. The highest stage of Ṣūfī experience
ḥarām	lit. 'forbidden' in Arabic, opposite of *ḥalāl* ('permissible')
ḥijāb	a woman's veil covering the head and chest
ḥijrah	emigration to the land of Islam
Ḥijrī	Islamic lunar calendar
'Īd al-Aḍḥā	Feast of Sacrifice, see *Kurban-Bayram*
'Īd al-Fiṭr	Festival of Breaking Islamic Fast, see *Uraza-Bayram*
ijāzah	a Ṣūfī permission
ijmā'	consensus in *fiqh*
ijtihād	an independent judgement in Islam
inak	a prime minister in the Khiva Khānate
'ishā'/iastu	the fifth mandatory daily Islamic prayer
ishān	a Ṣūfī mentor
'iṣmah	lit. 'protection' in Arabic. A moral infallibility
istiḥsān	juristic preference
jadīdism	an Islamic and sociopolitical reformist movement among Tatars and Central Asian Muslims, see *al-uṣūl al-jadīd*
jāhilīyyah	lit. 'ignorance' in Arabic
jamā'ah/jamā'at	lit. 'group' in Arabic. A neighbourhood or Islamic community
janāzah	an Islamic burial

jihād	an Islamized war
jihādī	an Islamist militant
jizyah	an Islamic per capita yearly tax
kāfir	an infidel
kalām	Islamic scholastic theology
kalym	bride price
kānūn	a law among Turks
karachai	a low noble of Bulgar origins in the Kazan Khānate
Kavburo	Bolshevik party's department in charge of the Caucasus
khalīfah	a representative of a Ṣūfī sheikh
khānqāh	a Ṣūfī lodge
kharāj	an Islamic land tax
khojah/khwājah	lit. 'master' in Arabic. A honorific title of Ṣūfī sheikh
khums	one-fifth of the booty gained by early Muslims from their opponents
korenizatsiia	lit. 'nativization' in Russian. Bolsheviks' policy of putting non-Russian indigenous people in key government positions
kniazhestvo	a principality in Kievan Rus
krai	a province in the Russian Empire/Russia
kufr	disbelief
Kurban(Gurban)-Bayram(i)/Kurban-Ait	see *'Id al-Aḍhā*
kurultai	a legislative assembly among various Turkic peoples
madhhab	a school of Sunnī jurisprudence
madrasah/ medrese	an Islamic school
mahalla	a neighbourhood community in Central Asia
mālik/melik	a king
marja'-i taqlīd	lit. 'source of emulation'. The supreme Shī'ī leader
marthiah	a mourning song, performed during *'Āshūrā'*
maslahat/masliiat	a practice of *'adat*-based mediation in the North Caucasus
mawlā (pl. *mawālī*)	clients of Muslim Arab tribes
mawlīd	observance of the birth of the Prophet Muḥammad
mazār	a sacred place of popular veneration
ma'zūn	head of district in Shamil's imāmate
miḥrāb	a prayer niche in the *qiblah* wall
millet	a nation among Turks and other Turkic people
mir'āj	Prophet Muḥammad's spiritual journey
mollah-khana	a prayer-house in Azerbaijan
mu'athin/mu'azzin	a caller for Islamic prayer
mudarris	a madrasah teacher
mudīr	superintendent tasked by imām Shamīl to watch *nāib*s
muftī	lit. 'a *fatwā*-giver' in Arabic. A head of the Spiritual Directorate of Muslims in the Russian Empire/USSR/Russia

muftīate/muftīlik/ müftilik	an office of *muftī*
muḥaddith	a scholar of Ḥadīth
muhājir (pl. *muhājirūn*)	a re-settler from the Caucasus to Turkey in the nineteenth century
muḥtasib	lit. 'auditor' in Arabic. A member of the secret police in Shamīl's imāmate
mujāhid (pl. *mujāhidūn*)	a fighter for Islam
mujtahid (pl. *mujtahidūn*)	a Shīʿī jurist
mullah/mollah	an Islamic authority, usually a head of the mosque
mul'k	private land
mamlūk	a military slave
munāfiq (pl. *munāfiqūn*)	a hypocrite in Islam
murīdism	Ṣūfīsm-related anti-Russian movement in the North Caucasus
murshid	Ṣūfī master
murtad	an apostate from Islam
murtaziqah	lit. 'mercenaries' in Arabic. The privileged cavalry in Shamil's imāmate
murza	a Tatar noble
mustaftī	a petitioner of *fatwā*
mutakallim	a scholar of *kalām*
mutavalliiat	a muftīate's department in charge of local mullahs
nāib	lit. 'deputy' in Arabic. A governor in Shamil's imāmate
namāz	an Islamic prayer
namestnichestvo	a viceroyalty in the Russian Empire
niqah/kebin	an Islamic marriage
niẓām	lit. 'order' in Arabic. A legal or administrative ruling in Shamil's imāmate
Nowruz	lit. 'New Day' in Persian. A celebration of the vernal equinox
oblast'	a region in the Russian Empire/USSR/Russia
oglan	a Genghizid of lower ancestral lineage
oikoumene	a cultural habitat
okrug	a district in the Russian Empire
otpadenie	a return to Islam by forcibly baptized Muslims
paranja	a Muslim robe covering a woman's head and body
pashalyk	a province of the Ottoman Empire, see *eyalet*
pīr	a Ṣūfī master, a Ṣūfī visitation
purdah	women's seclusion
qāḍī/qāzī	an Islamic judge
qāḍī-ʿasker	a chief judge in the Ottoman Empire and some other Turkic polities
qadīmīsm	Islamic traditionalism among Tatars
qiblah	the orientation towards Mecca

qiyās	deductive analogy in *fiqh*
Qizilbash	lit. 'Red-headed' in Turkish. A member of the Turkic tribal confederation at the service of the Safawids
qurultai	parliament, or assembly among Turkic peoples
raion	a district in the USSR/Russia
Ramaḍān/Ramazan	the ninth month of the Islamic calendar, a month of fasting
ribāṭ	an Islamized frontier fortress, or Ṣūfī lodge
sabantui	the advent of spring among Volga Bulgars and Tatars
sayyīd	a member of *Ahl-al-Bayt* via imām Ḥusayn
ṣabr	lit. 'patience' in Arabic
ṣadaqah	a voluntary payment in Islam
Ṣaḥābī (pl. *Ṣaḥābah*)	Prophet Muḥammad's Companion
ṣalāh	an obligatory prayer
ṣawm	a self-purification/fasting
shahādah	the Islamic testimony of the oneness of God
shakhei-vakhsei	self-flagellation during *'Āshūrā'*, see *taṭbīr*
shakird	a medrese student among Tatars and Bashkirs
sharī'ah	Islamic law
sharīf	a member of *Ahl al-Bayt* via imām Ḥasan
shirk	polytheism
sīrah	Prophet Muḥammad's biography
shūrā	an Islamic council
skhod	rural council
stanitsa	a Cossack settlement
Sunnah	precedents based on Prophet Muḥammad's behaviour and sayings
sunnet	male circumcision
taip/teip	a clan, or neighbourhood-based community among Vainakhs
tafsīr	an exegesis of the Qur'ān
taj	a red twelve-pleated hat worn by a Qizilbash
tajwīd	rules of recitation of the Qur'ān
ṭalāq	a divorce in Islam
tarkhan	a small landowner in the Kazan Khānate
ṭarīqah/ṭarīqat	a Ṣūfī path and Ṣūfī brotherhood
takfīr	excommunication
taqīyyah	lit. 'prudence'. The practice of concealing Islamic faith under persecution
taqlīd	Islamic traditionalism
taṭbīr	self-flagellation among the Shī'ah, see *shaksei-vakhsey*
tukhum	a rural commune in the northern Caucasus
tura	a Ṣūfī sheikh; a member of *Ahl al-Bayt*
ulus	a Genghizid principality
ummah	Muslim community
'umrah	a minor *ḥajj*

Uraza-Bayram	see *ʿĪd al-Fiṭr*
ʿurf	local customs
ʿushr	a tithe
uṣūl al-dīn	key principles of the Islamic religion
uṣūl al-fiqh	Islamic jurisprudence
vezīr	prime minister in the Seljūq and Ottoman Empires
voevoda	a military commander/governor in medieval Russia
waqf	Islamic endowment
wilāyah/wilāyat	lit. 'guardianship' in Arabic. A caliphal province
wird	a branch of Ṣūfī *ṭarīqah*
Yasa	Genghizid legal code
yasak	a tribute among Genghizids and their followers
zakāh/zakāt	alms tax in Islam
zakāt al-fiṭr	a payment during Ramaḍān
zhenotdel	women's department within the Communist Party
ziyārat/ziyōrat	Ṣūfī visitation

NOTE ON TRANSLITERATION, PLACE NAMES AND CALENDARS

The use of a consistent system of transliteration has been problematic due to the many different alphabets and the several script changes that have occurred during the lengthy historical period covered in the book. Due to the centrality of the Arabic-based Islamic terminology I have used the Library of Congress system of transliteration from Arabic to English. The only exceptions are well-known terms such as, for example, 'Abbasid', rather than 'al-'Abāsīyah', or 'Daesh', rather than 'Dā'ish'. Most terms in Persian, Ottoman Turkish and other Turkic languages are transcribed in English by using a simplified version of transliteration which is most commonly used in English language publications, thus omitting diacritical characters, for example, 'Sadr al-Azam' instead of 'Ṣadr-i A'ẓam', or 'Astrakhan', rather than 'Hājītarkhān'. For transliteration from Russian I have similarly employed the Library of Congress system of transliteration. In most cases I have rendered plural forms of foreign words by adding an 's', instead of the form used in the language of origin; thus 'ṭarīqahs' instead of 'ṭuruq', or 'raions' instead of 'raiony'. Among the few exceptions are those words which are better known in their plural form, such as 'fuqahā' instead of 'faqīhs', or 'mujāhidīn' instead of mujāhids'. Due to the multitude of cultural traditions of place name and ethnonym spellings which existed in different historical periods I have favoured their simplified and most known versions in English by also providing other names in parenthesis, as *Bāb al-Abwāb* (Darband) or Jurzān (Georgia). For the purposes of simplicity I have mostly used the Gregorian calendar, although I have employed the *Hijrī* (HA) calendar (with the Gregorian calendar in parenthesis) for some critical dates during the times of Prophet Muḥammad and *Rāshidīn*. When discussing events during the imperial Russian period I have employed the Julian calendar, which was 12 days behind the Gregorian calendar in the nineteenth century and 13 days in the twentieth century. Dates after February 1918 have been rendered in accordance with the Gregorian calendar.

ADDITIONAL SIGNS USED

Ā, ā	as in	jihād
ə	as in	Məxmüt
Č, č	as in	Račius
Ḍ, ḍ	as in	qāḍī
ğ	as in	Hanlığı
Ḥ, ḥ	as in	Muḥammad
Ḫ, ḫ	as in	şeyḫülislām
Ī, ī	as in	al-Mahdī
Ṭ, ṭ	as in	ṭarīqah
Ṣ, ṣ	as in	Anṣār
Ū, ū	as in	Manṣūr
Ǜǘ	as in	şeyḫülislām
ű	as in	Yelű
Ẓ, ẓ	as in	ẓāhir
’	as in	fuqahā’
‘	as in	‘urf

INTRODUCTION

The idea for this book was born out of my awareness of the globalization-driven shifts in the nature and representation of Islamic religious authority and leadership and of state–Muslim relations worldwide. At the same time, my many years of research into Islam in ex-Soviet Muslim Eurasia convinced me of its distinctively Eurasian characteristics and dynamics, as well as of its particular responses to external Islamic, non-Islamic and anti-Islamic influences.[1] I was also aware of the continuing divergence between the post-Soviet Eurasian and the Western scholarship on Islam (and other historical and contemporary matters related to Eurasia), which led me to attempt the merging of their distinct academic approaches. I should emphasize that I use the term 'Eurasia' in its narrow geopolitical meaning in relation to post-Soviet Central Asia, the Caucasus, Russia and parts of Eastern Europe, while recognizing Eurasia's physiographic expanse from the Arctic Ocean in the north, the Mediterranean Sea and the Indian Ocean in the south, the Atlantic Ocean in the west and the Pacific Ocean in the east. My focus here is on Islamic authorities and leadership, exploring how throughout history they have sought to safeguard Islam despite politically and culturally adverse conditions and external domination. Conceptually, I make a nuanced distinction between Islamic authority that is primarily of a moral, religious and legal nature, and Islamic leadership which combines these characteristics with political engagement. I am particularly concerned with the historical evolution of the triangular relationship between the Islamic authorities/leadership; the state and Muslim grassroots communities across the territory corresponding to post-Soviet Eurasia; and how it compares with that relationship in the Islamic heartlands as well as in Europe. I also discuss the implications for this relationship of the end of the Cold War and the ensuing globalization. As in my other works, I treat the researched region as an integrated sociocultural area with its specific historical, cultural, socio-economic and political characteristics. My choice of the Muslim Middle East and Muslim communities in Europe for comparative purposes is defined by post-Soviet Eurasia's geographical, historical, cultural and political entanglement with these regions. For this reason I have left Indonesia, Malaysia, India, Nigeria and other Muslim-majority and Muslim-minority parts of the world out of my analysis.

The book's main thesis is that historically the nature and forms of Islamic leadership and authority, as well as their relations with the state and grassroots Muslim communities across most of the researched region, were defined by four main factors. One is the early arrival of Islam in the region and the inclusion of most of the Caucasus and Central Asia in the Umayyad and Abbasid Caliphates. The second is the region's lengthy domination by Turco-Mongol nomads who channelled state formation in the region along the lines of loose polyethnic and polyconfessional empires run by militarily strong Islamized rulers. Among other Turco-Mongol legacies is the persistence of strong localized and genealogical networks and communal identities, as well as the merger of Islam with customary and tribal norms, resulting in the emergence of a variety of distinctive 'Eurasian Islams'. The third factor relates to the inclusion in the nineteenth century of most of the researched region into the autocratic Russian Empire and the establishment of the distinctively Russian model of state–Muslim relations based on the institution of the *muftīate*. The fourth is the region's comprehensive Sovietization and atheization, which accounted for an elevated level of societal secularization and the evolution of most Eurasian Muslims into 'Soviet Muslims' who perceived Islam as part of their cultural tradition. Since the break-up of the USSR in 1991 and the subsequent transformation of its 15 constituent republics into independent states, the Islamic dynamic, including the outlook of the Islamic leadership and authorities and the nature of state–Muslim relations across post-Soviet Eurasia, has been shaped by a particular state's political orientation and the extent of its Muslim community's material and digitalized reintegration into the global *ummah* (Islamic community). An important factor has been the increased presence in the region of Fethullah Gülen's *Hizmet* (Service), *Tablīghī Jamā'ah* (Society of Preachers), *Ḥizb al-Taḥrīr al-Islāmī* (Party of Islamic Liberation) and other transnational Islamic and Islamist organizations, as well as the involvement of al-Azhar, the Islamic University of Medina and other Middle Eastern Islamic educational centres in the training of future Muslim clerics across post-Soviet Eurasia. In the 2000s the state–Muslims relations in the region were affected by the varying degrees of engagement of Eurasia's political and official Islamic leadership in the US-spearheaded 'War on Terror' triggered by the *jihādist*[2] attacks on New York and Washington in September 2001. In the post-Soviet period the emergence of considerable Muslim communities of labour migrants from Central Asia and the Caucasus – and in the case of Ukraine, also from the Middle East – in the historically largely Christian big cities of Russia, Ukraine, Belarus and Lithuania has also been significant.

The book argues that, in the three decades following the dissolution of the Soviet Union, the majority of Eurasian states have retained the de facto Soviet model of state–Muslim relations centred on the institution of the muftīate as the major agency for government's management of Islam and Muslims. This has been largely due to their remoulding of Soviet totalitarianism into authoritarian governances which have continued to prioritize the Eurasian/Soviet 'power vertical', societal secularism and communal and other group solidarities over civic and individual rights. It is significant that Eurasian authoritarian states have differed considerably from various autocratic and authoritarian regimes in the Middle East, including Turkey, where, historically, societal secularization was either superficial or incomplete. In the case of post-independence Lithuania, and to some extent Ukraine and Georgia – all of which had relatively small autochthonous Muslim populations – the political leaderships have departed from the Eurasian/Soviet model of political and social organization in favour of liberal democracy, the centrality of individual rights over collective rights and, internationally, have turned towards the European Union (EU) and the North Atlantic Treaty Organization (NATO). Consequently, in these cases the state's tight control over the Muslim community has been replaced by non-interference into the Islamic domain, leading to the gradual 'churchification'[3] of Islam and Muslims' transformation into an ethnic minority subjected to gradual assimilation within a predominantly Christian host society. A decline in Islamic self-identification has been particularly evident among the historically Muslim Adjarians in modern Georgia due to Tbilisi's national discourse centred on Georgian (Kartlian) ethnonationalism intertwined with Georgian Orthodox Christianity. These divergent political and societal trends across Eurasia have affected the Muslim communities' responses to the globalized and de-territorialized *Salafī* Islam[4] which has become dominant online.

I employ a transdisciplinary theoretical approach by drawing on history, theology/ religious studies, cultural anthropology and political science. The book is largely based on my numerous semi-structured interviews with muftīs and other high-ranking Muslim clergy;[5] with Ṣūfī sheikhs and representatives of 'unofficial Islam';[6] with leaders of Islamic and Islamo-national parties and organizations and relevant government officials and Islamologists, all of which were conducted in Tatarstan, Bashkortostan, Dagestan, Kabardino-Balkaria, Azerbaijan, Kazakhstan, Kyrgyzstan, Uzbekistan and Moscow between 1997 and 2020. The interviews formed part of 14 international research projects funded by the UK-based British Academy, the Economic and Social Research Council (ESRC), the Leverhulme Trust and the Nuffield Foundation. The book's other primary sources include official documents and statistics from muftīates and state departments dealing with religious issues. In order to achieve as balanced and multifaceted a perspective on the researched region as possible I have consulted a diverse range of secondary sources, drawing equally on relevant works by scholars from the West and from post-Soviet Eurasia. My discussion of the interrelationship of *'ulamā'* (Islamic scholars) and political leadership in the early Islamic period benefits from Hugh N. Kennedy's *The Prophet and the Age of the Caliphates* (2016) and *Muslim Spain and Portugal* (1996), Michael Chamberlain's *Knowledge and Social Practice in Medieval Damascus* (1994) and *Islamic Legal Interpretations*, edited by Muhammad K. Masud, Brinkley Messick and David Powers (1996). The comparative analysis of the office of muftī in the Ottoman and imperial Russian contexts is informed by Richard Repp's research on muftīs in the Ottoman Empire (1986) and Egdūnas Račius and Antonina Zhelyazkova's work on Islamic leadership in the former Ottoman and Russian Empires (2017). My analysis of Ṣūfī leadership in the North Caucasus and other parts of Muslim Eurasia benefitted from the work of Alexandre Bennigsen and S. Enders Wimbush (1985), Rustam T. Shodiyev (1993), Moshe Gammer (2006), Vahit Akaev (2010, 2011), Kaflan Khanbabaev (2010) and Shamil Shikhaliev (2017). The discussion of the implications of imperial Russian and Soviet rule for Islamic authorities and leadership across Eurasia draws on the writing of Dmitrii Arapov (2001, 2010, 2011), Rafik Mukhametshin (2003, 2010), Renat Bekkin (2020) and Yaacov Ro'i (2000), as well as edited volumes by Ashirbek Muminov (2008) and Anastasiya Ganich (2013) on Islamic authorities in Central Asia and Transcaucasia respectively. My take on Islamic leadership in Western and Eastern Europe is informed by the publications of Jorgen Nielsen (1999, 2004), Egdūnas Račius (2017, 2018, 2020) and Jocelyne Cesari (2004). The examination of the 'Al-Azharization' of some of the post-Soviet official Islamic leadership makes use of research on the global role of Al-Azhar Islamic University by Jacob Skovgaard-Petersen and Bettina Gräf (2009), Indira Falk Gesink (2010) and Masooda Bano and Keiko Sakurai (2015). The discussion of Islamist and jihādist[7] leadership draws on *Muslim Politics* by Dale F. Eickelman and James Piscatori (1996), *Islamic Fundamentalism* by Youssef Choueiri (2010), Faisal Devji's *Landscapes of the Jihad* (2005), Gilles Kepel's *Jihad: The Trail of Political Islam* (2002), Peter Mandaville's *Islam and Politics* (2014) and Olivier Roy's *Globalized Islam* (2004). The analysis of the implications of the digitalization of Islam for established Islamic authorities is informed by Gary Bunt's *Islam in the Digital Age* (2003), and the discussion of Moscow-driven secularization in Soviet Eurasia draws on the writing of Talal Asad (2003), Peter Berger (1999), Steve Bruce (2002), Jose Casanova (1994), Ernest Gellner (1992), John Esposito and Azzam Tamimi (2000), Olivier Roy (2007) and Bryan Turner (2011). I want to thank the University of Texas Libraries for permitting me to reproduce the map of the USSR. I am also grateful to the book's anonymous reviewers for their constructive comments and the Anthem Press editorial and production team for their excellent work.

The book's overreaching argument defines its structure. It is divided into three parts, corresponding to the researched region's medieval and modern history,[8] the Soviet era and the post-Soviet period. Each part consists of four chapters organized along chronological and regional lines. The introductory chapter in Part I outlines the key stages in the formation of Islamic authorities and their relationship with political leadership from the times of the Prophet Muḥammad till the nineteenth century, when Muslim Eurasia was absorbed within the Orthodox Christian Russian Empire. Its inclusion is justified by the early Islamization of most of Eurasia by either the Prophet Muḥammad's Companions or their immediate successors and the inclusion of parts of the Caucasus and Central Asia into the Arab Caliphate and the ensuing involvement of Eurasian 'ulamā' and *fuqahā'* (Islamic jurists) in the formative theological and legalist debates of the Islamic Golden Age. The chapter begins by examining the role of Prophet Muḥammad and the four righteous caliphs in defining the reference points of leadership in Islam. It touches upon the theological and political implications of the establishment of the Umayyad Caliphate with its centre in Damascus. For comparative purposes the chapter pays special attention to the Umayyad Córdoban Caliphate and *Mulūk al-Ṭawā'if* (Kings of the Territorial Divisions) in al-Andalus (Andalusia) of the Iberian Peninsula, which presented another model of the early non-Middle Eastern self-sufficient Islamic polity. It then discusses the Abbasid period which was responsible for the emergence of 'ulamā', fuqahā', *qāḍīs* (Islamic judges), muftīs, *imāms*, *Ṣūfī* (mystical Islamic) sheikhs and other representatives of Islamic authority in Eurasia. It explores the factors which determined the relationship between caliphal rule, regional political and Islamic authorities and local popular religious expression. It explains the reasons behind the proliferation of the *Ḥanafī* school of *Sunnī* Islam in most of Central Asia and the Volga-Urals on the one hand, and of the *Shāfi'ī* school of Sunnī Islam among various Caucasian peoples in the north-eastern Caucasus on the other. It proceeds to trace the link between Fāṭimid Egypt and the proliferation of *Ismā'īlī Shī'ism* in the Pamir mountains in contemporary Tajikistan. The final section examines the evolution of religious and political authorities in the Ottoman Empire (1299–1923) and Safawid Iran (1501–1736), both of which laid the foundation either of Ḥanafīsm-centred

Islamic theology, culture and politics, as in the Crimea and the north-western Caucasus, or of *Ithnā ʿAsharīyah* (Twelver)-based Islam and Muslim-ness, as in present-day Azerbaijan.

Chapter 2 deals with the Islamic leadership and grassroots Muslim communities among the Tatars and Bashkirs of the Volga-Urals region and among the Crimean Tatars in the Crimea. It examines the implications for Muslim clerics and ordinary Muslims of the Russian conquest of Kazan and other Genghizid khānates and the Tsarist assault on Islam and Muslims. It pays special attention to the emergence of the Tatar community on the territory of modern Lithuania. It then discusses the Islamic policy of Catherine II (Catherine the Great, r. 1729–96), resulting in the establishment of the state-controlled muftīate which laid the foundation for Russian, Soviet and post-Soviet state–Muslim relations, and the emergence of so-called 'Russian Islam'. The chapter analyses the distinctive characteristics of the Russian muftīate and compares it to the muftīship in Istanbul and other parts of the Muslim Middle East. Its final section examines the specifically Russian form of Islamic reformism – *jadīdīsm* – and its relationship with the Islamic reformist movement in the Middle East. Both the more immediate and the more far-reaching implications of jadīdism for the Islamic leadership among the Tatars and other Muslims of the Russian Empire are also addressed.

Chapter 3 deals with Islam and Islamic leadership in the Caucasus. It begins by discussing the theological, linguistic and ethnocultural implications of the north-eastern Caucasus' inclusion into the Abbasid Caliphate. It proceeds to examine the interplay in the region between *sharīʿah* (Islamic law) and *ʿadat*s (customary norms) and the correlation between the religious and political authority of qāḍīs and community elders. It addresses the pro-sharīʿah policies of *imām* Shamīl, the founder of the imāmate (1840–59) and its effects on the Islamic beliefs of Chechens and other Muslim highlanders. In the southern Caucasus, it discusses the intricacies of the Shīʿīzation of local Muslims under the influence of the Safawids, the specifics of Shīʿī religious and legal practices and the relationship between local Shīʿī authorities and those in Shīʿī Iran and Iraq with their Sunnī counterparts in the Ottoman Empire and in other parts of the Muslim Caucasus and Central Asia.[9] Chapter 4 is about the Islamization of Central Asia and the specifics of Islam among its various sedentary and nomadic peoples. It discusses the political and religious relations between the caliphal centre and its Central Asian province of *Mawarannahr* (lit. 'What Is beyond the River', with 'River' referring to Amu Darya), and pays special attention to the interplay between Arabized Islamic theology and regional Persianized culture. It is also concerned with the commonalities and specifics in state–Muslim relations in Central Asia compared to those in the Islamic heartland. In particular, it examines the complex relationship between ʿadats, tribal norms and sharīʿah and their respective roles in the legitimization of power among the Kazakhs and other Central Asian nomads on the one side, and various urbanites and sedentary peoples on the other. It then proceeds to discuss the religious and political role of ʿulamāʾ, qāḍīs and Ṣūfī sheikhs in the Bukhara Emīrate and the Khānates of Khiva and Kokand. The final section explores how the Russian conquest and the ensuing political and ideational separation of Central Asia from the *ummah* affected its religious and political leaders and authorities and various Muslim peoples.

Part II discusses the profound implications for the Islamic leadership and state–Muslim relations in Eurasia of the 70 years of atheistic Soviet rule. Chapter 5 analyses Islam and

Muslim leadership among the Tatars and Bashkirs of the Volga-Urals region, and examines the ideology and politics of Tatar Bolsheviks, known as Muslim Communists, and their role in winning considerable Muslim support for the Bolshevik cause in the early Soviet period. It then proceeds to consider the impact on the Tatar and Bashkir Islamic leadership of the Stalinist atheistic assault in the 1930s. The chapter pays special attention to the theological and political credentials of the Tatar and Bashkir official and unofficial Islamic leaderships and their contribution to the making of so-called 'Soviet Islam' centred on the Sovietized muftīate in the Urals city of Ufa. Chapter 6 deals with Islam and Islamic leadership in the Soviet northern Caucasus. It examines the religious and social role of Ṣūfī sheikhs and other Islamic authorities inside and outside the regional Islamic officialdom, associated with the newly established muftīate in Buinaksk in Dagestan. It is concerned with the implications for their ethnic and Muslim identities and their Islamic authorities of the 1943/1944–57 deportations of Chechens, Ingush, Balkars and Karachais. The final section discusses the so-called 'Islamic revival' which began in the late Soviet period in the context of the region's 'reconnection' with the Islamic Middle East. It particularly focuses on the emergence of a pro-Salafī unofficial Islamic leadership and its relationship with official Muslim clergy and grassroots communities. Chapter 7 examines the official and unofficial Islamic leaderships in predominantly Shī 'ī Azerbaijan and their relationship with the Soviet political authorities. It assesses the theological credentials of *sheikh-ul-Islām* (the supreme Islamic authority) and his religious authority among the Muslims of Azerbaijan and the wider region. Chapter 8 deals with Central Asia, which was the largest Muslim-majority region in Soviet Eurasia. It begins by examining the theological position, the level of political engagement and the public influence of muftīs and other official Muslim clerics from the Spiritual Directorate of Muslims of Central Asia (abbreviated as SADUM[10] in Russian), based in Tashkent in Uzbekistan. It considers the curricula of the Islamic Institute in Tashkent and *Mir-i-Arab madrasah* (secondary Islamic school) in Bukhara and assesses their educational influence on Islamic officialdom across Muslim Eurasia. The chapter also discusses the role of unofficial traditional Islamic leaders, represented by sheikhs, *khojahs*, *ishāns*, *pīrs* and other Ṣūfī authorities. It pays special attention to the authority of the Aghā Khān in the Ismā'īlī Shī'ī community in Tajikistan. The final section analyses the factors behind the rise in popular appeal of unofficial Islamic authorities of both Islamic traditionalist and Salafī orientations in the late Soviet period.

Part III addresses the challenges facing Muslim communities and their leaderships in the context of the dissolution of the USSR and Muslim Eurasia's theological, educational and political re-engagement with the Islamic heartland. It examines the theological and political implications of the break-up of the Soviet-era centralized governance of Islam and the emergence of a plethora of competing muftīates and other official Islamic regional, ethnicity-centric and local bodies on the one hand, and the proliferation of unofficial Islamic organizations and groupings, including those of a transnational and global nature, on the other. Chapter 9 discusses the Islamic leadership in Tatar-dominated communities in independent Belarus, Ukraine and Lithuania, which in Soviet times had lacked independent Islamic structures. The chapter is included for comparative purposes as it traces the divergent trends in the development of Islamic leadership and state–Muslim relations in those parts of the former USSR which adopted

European political and confessional models compared with those which remained within the parameters of political and confessional 'Eurasianism'. It begins by outlining the historical background for the emergence of Muslim communities in these three countries and then proceeds to discuss the implications for the Muslim communities' leaders in largely Orthodox Christian Belarus and Ukraine of the countries' differing political and external orientations, including the conflicting impulses emanating from Moscow- and Kazan-based Islamic structures and Islamic organizations in Turkey and various countries of the Middle East. It pays special attention to the process of so-called 'churchification' of Islam in predominantly Catholic Lithuania and compares it to the state–Muslim relations in Spain, with which Lithuania has some historical parallels in terms of Christian–Muslim relations.

Chapter 10 examines the Islamic leadership among Russia's Tatars and Bashkirs. It addresses the ambiguity of the Tatar official Muslim clergy who have been torn between traditional 'Tatar' Islam, intertwined with Tatar ethnonationalism, and transnational Salafī Islam. It focuses on the religious and political activities of the Ufa-, Moscow- and Kazan-based muftīates and their relations with the state and the Russian Orthodox Church. It also discusses the fragmented religious authority and political ambivalence of the Crimean Tatar Muslim leadership in the aftermath of Crimea's inclusion in the Russian Federation in 2014. The chapter is particularly concerned with the role and mobilizing potential of unofficial Salafī, Islamist and jihādīst leaders, and the state and Islamic officialdom's policies responding to them. Chapter 11 focuses on the Muslim Caucasus. The first section, on the North Caucasus, examines the complex and shifting relationship between official Ṣūfī and non-Ṣūfī Muslim clergy and unofficial Salafi and jihādīst leaders and their respective policies towards the state and local communities. The chapter pays special attention to Chechnya, which witnessed an extreme degree of politicization of both Salafī and Ṣūfī Islam, as well as direct engagement with international Islamism and jihādism. The section on Azerbaijan discusses the theological and political role of the Grand Muftī of the Caucasus and his relations with the state and unofficial Shī'ī and Sunnī authorities. It considers the varying religious influences emanating from neighbouring Shī'ī Iran and Sunnī Turkey and the ensuing creeping Sunnīzation of Azerbaijan.

Chapter 12 moves to Muslim Central Asia, which has experienced a particularly intensive Islamic resurgence. In Uzbekistan, it examines the evolution of the doctrinal orientation and political engagement of the official Islamic clergy and their Salafī opponents and the state's approach towards Islam. It is also concerned with the implications of the sizeable Uzbek labour migration in Russia. The next section deals with Islamic leadership in Tajikistan. It analyses the impact of the Tajik Civil War of 1992–97 in shaping state–Muslim relations and pays special attention to the post-war involvement of Islāmīsts in Tajikistan's political structures. The following section addresses the theological and political intricacies of the newly formed Kazakhstani muftīate and its relationship with al-Azhar University and the Gülen movement. The chapter then proceeds to examine the Islamic leadership in Kyrgyzstan and pays special attention to its relations with the Tablīghī-Jamā'ah and Ḥizb al-Taḥrīr al-Islāmī, both of which operate legally in the country. The final part discusses the specifics of Islamic leadership and state–Muslim relations in Turkmenistan. It is especially concerned with the state policy of subordinating Islam to the national discourse centred on the nomadic Turkmen tribal genealogy. Chapter 13 summarizes the book's discussion by situating the Islamic leadership in post-Soviet Eurasia within the wider Islamic context. It compares the evolution of Islamic leadership and authorities and their relationship with the state in different parts of Eurasia with those in the contemporary Middle East and Western Europe. In the section on the Middle East it is particularly concerned with the relationship between Islamic reformists, Arab nationalists and Islamists and the state during the Cold War and the impact on the Islamic dynamic across Soviet Eurasia of the USSR's multifaceted cooperation with secular progressist regimes in Egypt, Iraq, Syria, Libya and South Yemen. The section on Western Europe enables the reader to compare the state–Muslims relations and the role of Islamic leadership in different parts of post-Soviet Eurasia with those in Western Europe. It addresses the specifics of Muslim communities and their leadership in Germany, France, Britain and other European countries and the models of official policy towards them. It addresses the political and cultural implications of the increased Muslim presence in Europe due to labour and refugee immigration. It is particularly concerned with the effects on state–Muslim relations and grassroots Muslim communities in Lithuania and to some extent in Ukraine and Georgia of these countries' pro-European reorientation. The section on post-Soviet Eurasia discusses the institutional and theological implications of their countries' particular post-communist political and societal trajectories for Muslim communities and Islamic leaders in the Volga-Urals, the North Caucasus, Azerbaijan and Central Asia. It concludes by assessing the future sustainability of the distinctly Eurasian type of Islamic leadership and state–Muslim relations in the face of advancing material and ideational universalization and globalized Islam.

PART I

ISLAM, ISLAMIC AUTHORITY AND LEADERSHIP BEFORE AND DURING THE RUSSIAN RULE

Chapter One

AUTHORITY AND LEADERSHIP IN ISLAM: A HISTORICAL AND COMPARATIVE PERSPECTIVE

Introduction

From the time of Prophet Muḥammad's death in 632 CE (11 HA[1]) until the present, the correlation between divine and mundane authority has dominated theological, political and cultural contention in the Muslim world. Central to it has been the notion and scope of authority in the original sources of Islam and its subsequent regional interpretations and modifications by *'ulamā'* (Islamic scholars) and *fuqahā'* (Islamic jurists) on the one side, and Muslim political and military leaders represented by *amīr*s, *sulṭān*s, *shāh*s, *khān*s and, subsequently, kings, presidents and other contemporary rulers on the other. Throughout history, deviation by various Muslim rulers from the idea of 'true' Islamic governance has been among the key drivers of the social and political mobilization towards the recreation of Prophet Muḥammad's religious and political *ummah* (Islamic community) based on the *Qur'ān* and *Sunnah* (precedents based on Muḥammad's behaviour and sayings). In a similar way, from the late eighteenth century, *jihād* (Islamized struggle) by Prophet Muḥammad and his Companions against their opponents and the quest for the revival of Islam have been invoked by leaders of anti-colonial struggles in the Middle East, West Africa, South and Southeast Asia as well as Muslim Eurasia. The most recent upsurge of Islamic revivalism and Islamized political activism was triggered by the end of the Cold War, which epitomized the global confrontation between the doctrinal anchors of secularism[2] – capitalism and communism. The removal of the socialist counterbalance to capitalism has reawakened among some Muslim thinkers and activists the caliphate ideal as the ideological alternative to the globalized capitalism spearheaded by the United States. In 1999, the idea of the caliphate was enacted in the form of the so-called Islamic State of Iraq and al-Shām (ISIS, also known by its Arabic-language acronym *Dā'ish/Daesh*) which was created on the territory of present-day Iraq and Syria, corresponding to the heartland of the caliphates of the Umayyads (*al-'Umawīyah*, 661–750 CE) and Abbasids (al-'Abbāsīyah, 750–1258). At its height Daesh territory had over eight million people, including foreign *jihādī*s (Islamized militants) who numbered between 80,000 and 200,000 from over 80 countries. Over 15,000 of them came from Muslim Eurasia, primarily from the North Caucasus and Central Asia.[3]

The renewed enthusiasm among some social strata of Muslim Eurasia (as well as in other parts of the Muslim world) for an Islamic solution (*al-ḥall al-Islāmī*) as the medium of social and political change requires a closer look at its main historical referents and protagonists. This chapter outlines the pivotal stages and events in the evolution of Islamic legal and political leadership from the time of Prophet Muḥammad till the Ottomans and Safawids. It is particularly concerned with those developments that left an enduring legacy in Muslim Eurasia, which presented the easternmost domain of early Islam. For comparative purposes the chapter pays special attention to early Islam's westernmost domain, embodied in al-Andalus.

Muḥammad, *Rāshidūn* and Umayyads

It is believed that Muḥammad was born in Mecca in c. 571 CE. He belonged to the Hāshemī clan of the powerful mercantile tribe of Quraysh which dominated most of western and northern Arabia. Genealogically, the Qurayshīs were the northern Arabs or the Adnanites, whose legendary ancestor was 'Adnān. The southern Arabs, or the Qahtanites (descendants of Qaḥṭān) derived from Yemen, were traditionally regarded as pure Arabs, and the Adnanites as Arabized.[4] Until 630 CE the Qurayshīs were polytheists and worshipped the Kaaba (*al-Ka'abah*), a cuboid granite structure situated in Mecca, which subsequently became Islamized and turned into the centre of the *ḥajj* (Islamic pilgrimage). For several centuries after Muḥammad's death the Qurayshīs retained their religious and political leadership. Thus, the *Rāshidūn* (the Rightly Guided Caliphs, 632–661 CE) and most Umayyads (661–750) and Abbasids (750–1258) were from the Quraysh tribe. It is symptomatic that the contemporary Daesh leaders, Abū Bakr al-Baghdādī (r. 2014–19) and Abū 'Ibrāhīm al-Hāshimī al-Qurayshī (r. 2019–present), claim their descent from the Qurayshīs.

According to Islamic tradition Muḥammad began to receive the Qur'ānic revelations at around 610 CE.[5] In 622 CE, faced with fierce opposition from his pagan tribesmen in Mecca, he conducted a *hijrah* (emigration) to the town of Yathrib. He was accompanied by a close group of his supporters – *al-Muhājirūn* (Emigrants). The act of Muḥammad's hijrah initiated the Islamic calendar, known as the *Hijrī* calendar, or AH. Since then Hijrī has been used for determining days for Islamic holidays, including *Ramaḍān* (the month of fasting), *'Īd al-'Aḍḥā* (Feast of the Sacrifice) and ḥajj. In Yathrib, which was later renamed Medina (*Madīnat al-Nabī*, meaning 'City of the Prophet'), Muḥammad converted to Islam members of the local tribes of Banū al-'Azd, Banū Khazrāj and Banū 'Aws, who became known as the *al-Anṣār* (The Helpers). Muhājirūn and Anṣār formed the core of the first Islamic polity, the ummah, governed by Muḥammad's Constitution – *Dustūr al-Madīnah*. According to the Dustūr, Medina became a sanctuary space – *ḥarām* – and Muḥammad its spiritual, legal, political and military leader. In 629 Muḥammad led a 10,000-strong Muslim army to Mecca and, after its conquest, converted most of its inhabitants to Islam. In the following two years Muḥammad and his Companions – the *Ṣaḥābah*[6] – spread Islam across most of the Arabian peninsula by both force and peaceful means. The Ṣaḥābah and their descendants would later participate in the Islamization of the Caucasus and Central Asia, where their graves would be turned into *mazārs* (pilgrimage sites). Among these are, as examples, the mazārs of the Kirkhlyar cemetery near Darband/Derbent in Dagestan, where 40 Ṣaḥābah are believed to be buried, the mazār of Arslanbob in Jalal-Abad region in Kyrgyzstan, and the mausoleum of Arystanbab near the ancient city of Atrar (Atyrau) in Kazakhstan.

Muḥammad's death on 8 June 632 CE (13 Rabīʿ al-Awwal 11 AH) faced the ummah with the dilemma of his succession since none of his Companions, relatives or tribesmen possessed his prophetic credentials. The succession was complicated by the absence of historical precedents, established concepts of authority or economic and political structures which could be used as points of reference. The succession crisis reignited tensions between the Meccan Qurayshīs and the Medina-based Anṣār, as well as between the Meccan traditional political and merchant elite and the Muhājirūn. Eventually, the Muhājirūn, led by Abū Bakr, 'Umar and Abū 'Ubaydah ibn al-Jarrāḥ, got the upper hand and secured the supremacy of Abū Bakr (r. 632–34), who assumed the titles of *Khalīfat Rasūl Allāh* (deputy of the Prophet of God, or caliph) and *Amīr al-Muʾminīn* (Commander of the Faithful).[7] It is important to note that the original lack of clarity regarding the meanings of both these titles subsequently led to their various interpretations. Muḥammad's immediate successors – the four Rightly Guided Caliphs Abū Bakr 'Abdullah ibn 'Uthmān (r. 632–34), 'Umar ibn al-Khaṭṭāb (r. 634–44), ʿUthmān ibn ʿAffān (r. 644–56) and ʿAlī ibn ʾAbī Ṭālib (r. 656–61) – combined religious, political and military leadership. Their authority was legitimized by means of the *bayʿah* (oath of allegiance). In 657 CE, the religious authority of Caliph ʿAlī, who was related to Prophet Muḥammad by blood, was put into question during the so-called 'First Fitnah' (Civil Strife) over the genealogical or moral qualifications of the caliph. In particular, a group of Muslim hardliners – Kharijites (*al-Khawārij*, lit. 'Those who left'), who advocated the supremacy of moral credentials over genealogy – challenged ʿAlī's agreement to arbitration with his rival and Syria's governor Muʿāwiyah ibn Abī Sufyān (Muʿāwiyah I, c. 602–680). Ever since then Kharijites have been associated with extremist Muslim sectarianism.[8]

The assassination of Caliph ʿAlī on 29 January 661 (21 Ramaḍān AH 40) by a Kharijite triggered a major split among Muslims into Sunnīs (followers of Sunnah) and Shīʿah (belonging to a Party, with 'Party' referring to the Party of ʿAlī) and further complicated the meaning of and correlation between religious, legal and political leadership among Muslims. Thus, Sunnī Muslims regarded a caliph, chosen on the basis of his qualities rather than genealogy, as their supreme religious and political authority. By comparison, Shīʿī Muslims prioritized the authority of a religious leader – imām – who had to be blood-related to Muḥammad, that is, belonging to *Ahl al-Bayt* (People of the House), and therefore understood to possess divine knowledge, moral infallibility – *ʿiṣmah* (protection) – and messianic deliverance.[9] Subsequently, *Ṣūfīs* (followers of mystical Islam), including those in Muslim Eurasia, would derive their spiritual lineages from Ahl al-Bayt. The belonging to Ahl al-Bayt would also be claimed by Eurasian *sharīfs* (noblemen) who claim their descent from Ḥasan (624–670), the elder son of ʿAlī and Muḥammad's daughter Fāṭimah (c. 605–632); *sayyīds* (masters), who regard themselves as being genealogically linked to Ḥusayn (636–680), the younger son of ʿAlī and Fāṭimah; as well as by distant offspring of Muḥammad's uncles al-ʿAbbās (c. 565–c. 653) and Abū Ṭālib (c. 535–c. 619).

After ʿAlī's death, the Sunnīs gained religious and political supremacy and established the Damascus-based Sunnī Umayyad Caliphate (661–750), whose founder was the aforementioned Muʿāwiyah I (r. 661–80), representing the Umayyad Sufyānid branch, which was named after Abū Sufyān (d. 653), a Qurayshī leader, a Companion and a first cousin of Prophet Muḥammad. The Sufyānids successively advanced into territories that were earlier controlled by their major regional rivals – Byzantium and Sasanian (Sasanid) Iran. Under the Sufyānids, most of the Ferghana valley and southern Dagestan were conquered by Muslim Arabs and Islamized. However, at that stage the Arabs' further inroads into Eurasia were halted by Turkic Khazars who dominated the northern Caucasus and other parts of central Eurasia. Muʿāwiyah I governed as an absolute theocrat who only nominally consulted the *shūrā* (tribal council). More importantly, in disregard of earlier electoral practice he nominated his son, Yazīd I (r. 680–83), as his successor, thus introducing a hereditary principle into the caliphate. The Sufyānid dynasty ended in 684 with the death of Caliph Muʿāwiyah II (r. 683–84) who succeeded Yazīd I.

The new Marwānid branch of the Umayyad dynasty was founded by Caliph Marwān I (r. 684–85). This dynasty played a particularly important role in the caliphate's north-eastern expansion, in the context of the Arabs' confrontation with Sasanian Iranians and Khazars. Under the Marwānids most of Central Asia (Bukhara, Samarqand, Khwārazm/Khoresm, Ferghana and Tashkent), as well as parts of the Caucasus were included within the Arab Caliphate, which by that time already encompassed Arabia, Syria, Palestine, North Africa, Persia and northern India.[10] The Marwānids reorganized Central Asia's Ferghana valley into the caliphal *wilāyah* (province) of Mawarannahr,[11] which however retained considerable autonomy from Damascus. The Caucasus's Darband (present-day southern Dagestan) and adjacent territories, including most of present-day Azerbaijan and eastern Georgia, formed the caliphate's wilāyah of Arrān (Caucasian Albania).[12] In 736, in the east of present-day Georgia, caliphal chieftains established the Emīrate of Tiflis which existed till 1122, when it was brought to an end by the Georgian king, David IV (r. 1089–1125). Importantly, the Marwānids finally defeated the Khazars with whom they fought two devastating wars in Eurasia. In the 730s the Arabs reached the Volga-Urals, where a notable number of Volga Bulgars (ancestors of present-day Tatars) converted to Islam.[13]

Al-Andalus

Al-Andalus is of particular interest to our discussion because alongside Sicily and Malta[14] it represented the westernmost, European, domain of early Islam. As in the case of the Caucasus and Central Asia, Islam was brought to southern Iberia by the Umayyads. In 711–18 a Berber Umayyad commander, Ṭāriq ibn Ziyād (670–720), defeated Visigothic troops and imposed Ummayad control over Visigothic Hispania (present-day southern Spain and Portugal). The conquered lands, which became known as *al-Andalus* (Andalusia), were included into the caliphal wilāyah Ifrīqīyah with its centre in al-Qayrawān in present-day Tunis.[15] Until the 740s Ifrīqīyah, including al-Andalus, were governed by Fihrīds who belonged to the Arabian clan of Banū Fihr related to the Quraysh. However, following the collapse of the caliphal authority in Damascus in

750 as a result of internal strife, the rise of the Khārijites in Iraq and an anti-Umayyad rebellion under the leadership of Abū Muslim (d. 755) in Khorāsān (in the northeast of Greater Iran), Andalusian Fihrīds became sidelined by exiled Umayyads. In 756, in Córdoba, the Umayyads established the Umayyad Amīrate (756–1031) under the leadership of a Marwānid, 'Abd al-Raḥmān I (r. 756–88).

In 929, another representative of the Umayyad Marwānid dynasty 'Abd al-Raḥmān III (r. 929–61) proclaimed himself caliph and commander of the Faithful. During his reign the Caliphate of Córdoba (*Khilāfat Qurṭuba*, 929–1031), which encompassed most of Iberia with the exception of Galicia, Catalonia and the Basque country, turned into a large Muslim polity which, like Mawarannahr and Arrān, became de facto independent from the Islamic political and legal centres in the Middle East. The Córdoba Caliphate, also like the Muslim Caucasus and Central Asia, was a multiethnic and polyconfessional empire where Jews and other non-Muslims, known as *dhimmī*, enjoyed considerable economic, legal and religious freedoms, although they were subject to higher taxation in the form of *jizyah* (a per capita yearly tax). The religious authority in al-Andalus belonged to the Córdoba caliphs and 'ulamā'. The political and military leadership was shared by the Umayyads, Islamized Berbers (self-named as Imazighen) and the *mozarabs* – local converts to Islam, while economic and financial power largely resided with the Jews. By the early eleventh century the proportion of Muslims in the Córdoba Caliphate exceeded 70 per cent with the rest of the population being Jews and Christians who spoke Spanish, Portuguese or Catalan.

From the late 1020s, the distinctively Spanish Islam and Muslim-ness received another boost under *Mulūk al-Ṭawā'if* (The Kings of the Territorial Divisions) – a succession of indigenized Arab, Berber and other North African and Middle Eastern dynasties that emerged as a result of the Córdoba Caliphate's fragmentation. Their main strongholds were in Seville, Granada (Gharnāṭah), Córdoba, Toledo, Badajoz and Zaragoza. Since Mulūk al-Ṭawā'if were not linked to the Prophet's tribe Quraysh, they claimed to be ruling in the name of the Umayyads. For the same reason they tended to bear their own regnal titles, such as 'al-Mu'taḍid of Seville', 'al-Mutawwakil of Badajoz', 'al-Muqtadir of Zaragoza' or 'Niẓām al-Dawlat', which they borrowed from titulatures of the Abbasids or Buyyīds of northern Iran.[16] From the eleventh century parts of al-Andalus came under the control of the Berber Sunnī dynasty of Almoravids (*al-Murābiṭūn*, lit. 'Those from *ribāṭ*s') who reigned over the Almoravid Empire (1040–1147) stretching from the western Maghreb to al-Andalus. In the late twelfth century parts of al-Andalus became included into another Maghrebian empire – the Almohad Caliphate (1180–1212) – with its centre in Marrakesh. It was created by the Berber Sunnī Muslim dynasty of Almohads (*Al-Muwaḥḥidūn*, lit. 'Believers in the absolute unity of Allah') which originated in the southern Maghreb. Its founder was Ibn Tūmart (c. 1078–1130), a puritanical Islamic thinker who advocated strict monotheism – *tawḥīd* – and regarded the Qur'ān and Ḥadīth as the only sources of sharī'ah. Ibn Tūmart claimed his descent from 'Alī and Fāṭimah and proclaimed himself a *mahdī* (the guided one) who was to restore true Islam that had allegedly been distorted by the Almoravids and their contemporaries. In al-Andalus, Almohads made Seville their capital. By the middle of the thirteenth century the Almohads, alongside most of the other Andalusian Muslim rulers, were defeated by the Aragon and Castile Christians. The last remaining Muslim principality was the Amīrate of Granada (1230–1492) which was governed by the Arab Muslim dynasty of Naṣrids, founded by Abū 'Abdullah Muḥammad ibn Yūsuf ibn Naṣr (d. 1273), also known as Ibn al-Aḥmar.

During its over seven hundred year-long Islamic period Spain was one of the most economically, architecturally, scientifically and intellectually developed parts of Europe. It was famous for its sophisticated irrigation system; its distinct Moorish[17] architecture which blended Islamic, Berber, Visigothic, Byzantine and Roman elements; and its centrality in the trans-Mediterranean trade in luxury goods, textiles, ceramics, glassware, metalwork and crops. In the tenth century Córdoba, with its population of half a million, was the largest city, while its 'ulamā' and fuqahā', similar to their counterparts in Darband, Bukhara and Samarqand, participated in the development of Islamic theology, philosophy and law. Al-Andalus produced some of the greatest scientists and philosophers of the time, among them, for example, Ibn Rushd (Averroes, 1126–1198), the Islamic thinker, qāḍī, polymath and encyclopaedist, who like Central Asia's al-Fārābī (Alpharabius, 872–950) or Iran's Ibn Sīnā (Avicenna, 980–1037), followed Aristotle and argued in favour of relations between philosophy and Islam and between reason and revelation.

The Abbasids and Their Challengers

In 750 CE the Syria-centred Umayyad Caliphate was superseded by the Iraq-centred caliphate (750–1258), founded by Abbasids who, unlike the meritocratic Umayyads, claimed their caliphal legitimacy on the basis of their genealogical links with Prophet Muḥammad. The Abbasids derived their name from Muḥammad's paternal uncle, al-'Abbās ibn 'Abd al-Muṭālib (d. 653 CE). The Sunnī Abbasids, in order to strengthen their social and political base, allied with Shī'ī Arabs, Muslim Persians and other non-Arab Muslims known as *mawālī* (clients of Arab tribes) residing in Iraq, Iran, Khorāsān and adjacent areas of Central Asia. It was significant that the founder of the new ruling dynasty, Abū al-'Abbās al-Saffāḥ (r. 750–54),[18] also adopted the title of mahdī, which particularly appealed to the Shī'a, and instructed his troops to fight under black flags[19] as white was associated with mourning in Persia. By contrast, the Umayyads bore white flags. The prominence of Khorāsān in the Abbasids' ascendance to power predetermined their deeper engagement with Central Asia and some other regions of Eurasia. It was under the Abbasids that Mawarannahr was effectively absorbed within the caliphate's eastern Iranian province, leading to its population's comprehensive Sunnīzation and linguistic Persianization and the region's transformation into a major regional centre of early Islamic scholarship and culture.[20]

The Abbasids also consolidated their positions in the Caucasus by dividing it into the three caliphal wilāyahs of Arrān, Arminīyyah and Azerbaijan, which were included in the caliphal tax system. In Arrān, which roughly corresponded to southern Dagestan and the northern part of the Republic of Azerbaijan, the Abbasids built a chain of fortresses, which became populated by thousands of Arab settlers from Greater Syria. Dagestan was transformed into the caliphate's northern centre of Islam and Arabic-language

Islamic scholarship. Dagestani 'ulamā' were directly involved in the codification of madhhabs and in the theological debate on the limits of *ijtihād* (independent reasoning) and its applicability after the perceived 'closure of the gate of ijtihād' in the eleventh century.[21] Of special significance was the proliferation in Dagestan (and subsequently in Chechnya and Ingushetia) of the stricter Shāfi'ī madhhab. The Abbasids were also involved in the Islamization of various peoples of the Volga region, corresponding to present-day Russia's Tatarstan. It is believed that the main trigger for this was the visit to Volga Bulgaria (the proto-Tatar polity) of Aḥmad ibn Faḍlān (d. 960), an ambassador of the Abbasid Caliph al-Mu'taḍid (r. 908–32). In 922 Volga Bulgaria became officially Muslim, thus becoming the northernmost flank of the Islamic domain.[22] Overall, the Abbasids created a huge Islamic empire encompassing most of the Middle East, North Africa and a large part of Eurasia, until their eastward expansion was stopped in 751 by Tang China (618–907).

However, from the ninth century the Abbasid political and to some extent religious supremacy was challenged by emerging Iranian, Kurdish and other non-Arab Muslim dynasties, many of which were linked to Eurasia. The period between 821 and 1063 has often been referred to as the 'Iranian intermezzo', as it was dominated by the Iranian dynasties of Ṭāhirids (821–873), Sājids (889–929), Ṣaffarids (861–1003), Sāmānids (875–999), Buyyīds (934–1062) and Sāllarids (942–979), as well as by Kurdish or Kurdicized Muslim dynasties, including the Rawwādids and the Kurdish Marwānids.[23] In the Caucasus the main Persianate dynasty were the Sharwānshāhs (Shirwan, 861–1538), descendants of the Persianized Arab Shaybānī tribe, who ruled over the lands of present-day Azerbaijan and adjacent areas. Of southern Caucasian origin were also the *Ayyūbids*, who belonged to the Kurdish clan of Rawwādīyyah. At the end of the twelfth century the Ayyūbids defeated the Shī'ī Fāṭimids and established their sulṭānate (1174–1260) on the territory of Egypt and Syria. Subsequently the Ayyūbids imposed their control also over Iraq, Hejaz, Yemen and parts of northern Africa. The dynasty's founder, Ṣalāḥ al-Dīn Yūsuf ibn Ayyūb (Saladin), immortalized himself by defeating the Crusaders at the Battle of Hattin in Palestine in 1187.

Among representatives of the 'Iranian intermezzo' in Eurasia were the Sāmānīd dynasty (819–999) in Mawarannahr and the Ghaznavid dynasty (*Ghaznawiyān*, 977–1186) in Afghanistan and adjacent areas in present-day Uzbekistan and Turkmenistan. Another Persianized dynasty, the Seljūqs (Oghuz Turks), who initially came from the area around the Aral Sea in Central Asia, created an expansive empire (1037–1194) which included Iran, Iraq, Anatolia, Syria, northern Afghanistan, parts of Central Asia and the Caucasus. It is worth noting that the Seljūqs' enduring ethnic and linguistic impact is evidenced in contemporary Azerbaijanis and Turkmen. Alongside these, the Mamlūk dynasty in Egypt, which in the thirteenth century succeeded the Ayyūbids, also had Eurasian roots. They were descendants of the Abbasids' military slaves of Cuman-Qipchaq, Oghuz Turkic, Circassian and Georgian origins. The founder of the Mamlūk dynasty was al-Mālik al-Mu'izz 'Izz al-Dīn Aybak, a Eurasian Qipchaq. In 1250 Sunnī Mamlūks established the Cairo-centred sulṭānate (1250–1517) which included Egypt, Syria, the Levant and Hejaz. Although Mamlūks claimed to rule on behalf of the Abbasids, the latter's authority was symbolic, while the real power rested first with the Mamlūk Cuman-Qipchaq Bahrī dynasty (1250–1382) and then with the Mamlūk Circassian Burjī dynasty (1382–1517).[24] It is significant that even after the Mamlūks were defeated by the Ottomans in 1517 the Burjī dynasty remained in charge of the Ottoman governance of Egypt. In the nineteenth century the Circassian presence in the Middle East would be further strengthened as a result of the influx of Circassian *muhājirs* (emigrants) from the northern Caucasus.

Islamic Debate and Division during the Golden Age

The Abbasids' doctrinal fluidity and ethnocultural pluralism were conducive to the Caliphate's cultural, economic and scientific flourishing that became known as 'The Islamic Golden Age', which persisted till the early fourteenth century. The period witnessed an intensive debate among 'ulamā' and fuqahā on the relationship between religious and political authority, the sources of sharī'ah and Islamic mysticism and the permissible limits of rationalism and ijtihād in Islam. As noted earlier, Eurasian Islamic theologians, jurists and Ṣūfī thinkers, alongside their Andalusian counterparts, were active participants in this debate. Muḥammad ibn Ismā'īl al-Bukhārī (810–869), a native of Bukhara, authored *Ṣaḥīḥ al-Bukhārī*, which would become one of the most authentic Ḥadīth collections in the Muslim world. Yusuf ibn Ḥusayn al-Lakzī (d. c. 1089), a native of Darband, was a renowned *muḥaddith* (scholar of Ḥadīth), while Abū Bakr Muḥammad al-Darbandī (c. 1058–1145), also from Darband, was a leading Ṣūfī rationalist. Abū Manṣūr al-Māturīdī (853–944), a native of Samarqand, was a leading Sunnī Islamic theologian of the *Mu'tazilī* (Islamic rationalist) school[25] who systematized the existing Islamic beliefs among the Ḥanafī theologians of Balkh and Mawarannahr. Subsequently, his teaching – *al-Māturīdīyyah* – would become dominant among Central Asians and various Turkic peoples.

Eurasian Sunnī jurists were involved in the consolidation of the four major schools or *madhhabs* – Ḥanafīsm, Mālikīsm, Shāfi'īsm and Ḥanbalīsm – named after Abū Ḥanīfa (699–767), Mālik ibn Anas (713–795), Abū al-Shāfi'ī (767–819) and Aḥmad ibn Ḥanbal (780–855), respectively. Ḥanafīs, who would prevail in Eurasia, broadly relied on the Qur'ān, Ḥadīth, *ijmā'* (consensus of Ṣaḥābah) and, most importantly, *qiyās* (deductive analogy), *istiḥsān* (juristic preference), local *'urf* ((customs), as well as ijtihād. Mālikīs, who would dominate in North and West Africa, Sudan, Kuwait, Bahrain and Dubai, were not very different from Ḥanafīs, albeit they prioritized the Qur'ān, Ḥadīth and ijmā' as the sources of sharī'ah. Shāfi'īs primarily drew on the Qur'ān and Ḥadīth and underplayed the importance of ijmā' and especially qiyās. Shāfi'īsm would become the main madhhab among the Muslims of eastern Egypt, Palestine, parts of Syria, Yemen and Hejaz. It would also be embraced by most Dagestanis, Chechens and Ingush. Ḥanbalīs were followers of the strictest madhhab which prescribed reliance exclusively on the Qur'ān and Ḥadīth; they would dominate in Arabia, Qatar, parts of Oman and Bahrain.[26] Their most influential representative would become the Syrian jurist Ibn Taymīyyah (1263–1328)[27] who formulated the Ḥanbalī notions of *bid'ah* (unlawful innovation), *takfīr* (excommunication) and *ziyārah* (religious visitation). Subsequently, Ibn Taymīyyah's thinking would influence the eighteenth-century

Wahhābīs in Arabia's Najd, as well as generations of Muslim ultraconservatives, who in the early twenty-first century would include the leaders of Al-Qaeda, *Daesh* and the *Imarat Kavkaz* (Caucasus Emirate).[28]

Among Shī'ī theologians a major contention revolved around the number of 'true imāms'. This led to the emergence of four major Shī'ī groups – Twelvers (*'Ithnā 'Asharīyah*; also known as *Imāmīyyah*), 'Alawīs/Alawites (*'Alawīyah*), Fivers and Seveners, all of whom, however, recognized 'Alī ibn Abī Tālib as the first and main imām. Twelvers believed in 12 divinely ordained imāms, who were perceived as the spiritual and political successors to the Prophet Muḥammad, their words and deeds as important as his. According to Twelvers, the last, twelfth imām would one day re-emerge as *Imām al-Mahdī*. Twelver jurists created their distinctive *fiqh* – Ja'farīsm – named after Ja'far ibn Muḥammad al-Ṣādiq (702–765), who prioritized ijtihād among other sources of the sharī'ah.[29] In the early tenth century, the Daylamites who adhered to Twelver Shī'īsm established the earlier mentioned Buyyīd state (945–1012) in northern Iran with its capital in Shiraz. Interestingly, Buyyīd shāhanshāhs, who also bore the Arab titles of *Amīr al-Umarā'* (Ruler of Rulers), *Mālik al-Mulūk* (king of kings) as well as honorific titles, such as *Mu'izz al-Dawlat* (Fortifier of the State), or *'Imād al-Dawlat* (The Basis of the State), adhered to the concept of the state rather than of the caliphate and effectively kept religious differences out of their 'cadre politics' by often appointing Sunnī Muslims and Christians to key political and economic positions.[30] Later on, in the sixteenth century, Twelver Shī'ism would be introduced by the Safawids on the territory of present-day Azerbaijan. By comparison with Twelvers, Alawites (also known as Nuṣayrīs), who were present in Greater Syria, recognized 11 imāms and regarded the 11th imam, Ḥasan al-'Askarī (d. 873), as the representative – *bāb* (gate) – of the hidden imām. The Alawites' belief system became the most doctrinally syncretic as it also contained Gnostic, Neoplatonic, Christian and pagan elements, including the concept of reincarnation.[31] Fivers, who were also known as Zaydīs, were followers of the fifth imām, Zayid ibn 'Alī, the grandson of Ḥusayn ibn 'Alī and the son of the fourth imām 'Alī ibn Ḥusayn, who in the 730s led a rebellion against the notoriously corrupt Umayyad Caliph Hishām ibn 'Abd al-Malik (r. 724–43). In the late ninth century the Zaydīs fled to Yemen where they created an imāmate which persisted, albeit intermittently, till 1962.[32]

The other major Shī'ī group was represented by the Seveners, also known as Ismā'īlīs, who followed the seventh imām Ismā'īl (d. 762), the eldest son of the sixth imām Ja'far ibn Muḥammad (d. 765). Seveners, like Twelvers, followed the Ja'farī fiqh. Doctrinally, however, they were influenced by Neoplatonism and prioritized esoteric (*bāṭin*) truth and adhered to ijtihād.[33] In the course of history Ismā'īlīs fragmented into several *ṭarīqah*s (paths), with the largest being the Nizārīs who dominated in the Fāṭimid Caliphate (909–1171)[34] centred on Egypt. They were named after imām Abū Manṣūr Nizār ibn al-Mustanṣir (1045–1095), a Fāṭimid prince who was killed by immurement. During the Fāṭimid period, which witnessed an advance in science and Islamic scholarship, Nizārīs settled in India and in the Pamir mountains where they now constitute a majority in the mountainous region of Badakhshan of Tajikistan. From the nineteenth century Nizārī imāms would bear the title of Aghā Khān. At present the Nizārīs of Tajikistan and elsewhere recognize Aghā Khān IV (b. 1936) as the 49th imām. Despite the outlined divisions Sunnī and Shī'ī theologians and jurists alike have largely agreed on the essentials of Islamic identity, known as *arkān al-Islām*, or *arkān al-dīn* (pillars of Islam), which included the profession of faith – *shahādah*, prayer – *ṣalāh*, almsgiving – *zakāh*, self-purification/fasting – *ṣawm* and pilgrimage to Mecca – *ḥajj*. Sunnī and Shī'ī jurists applied different names to some of these pillars, while various Shī'ī jurists also added to them the doctrine of the imāmate, as well as some other specific Shī'ī requirements, known as *furū' al-dīn*.

Ṣūfīsm

The Abbasid period witnessed the emergence of the mystical version of Islam – Ṣūfīsm.[35] It is believed that the first Ṣūfīs were Muḥammad's Companions who gave him their *bay'ah* (allegiance) as the expression of their devotion to Allah. Ṣūfīs opposed what they perceived as worldliness and the mundane excesses of the early Umayyads and advocated deeper, spiritual Muslim-ness on the basis of internal knowledge of the 'real' (*al-ḥaqq*, their term for Allah). By the eleventh century Ṣūfīs formed over a dozen different orders or *ṭarīqah*s (paths), which were organized along the lines of the teachings of particular grand masters or sheikhs, regarded as intermediaries between Ṣūfīs and Allah. All Ṣūfīs sought to progress in their divine knowledge from sharī'ah to *ḥaqīqah* (divine reality), then to *ma'rifah* (gnosis) and ultimately to *fanā'* (transmutation of self). However, they differed in terms of the ways of reaching these stages and the form of their *dhikr* (remembrance and recitation of the name of Allah).[36] By the twelfth century followers of particular Ṣūfī teachings and practices institutionalized into self-enclosed communities, also known as ṭarīqahs, which bore the name of their respective founding sheikhs. Initially, most Ṣūfī sheikhs claimed their origins from Muḥammad through his cousin and son-in-law 'Alī but subsequently there emerged Ṣūfī ṭarīqahs of other genealogical lineages, as well as ṭarīqahs within Shī'ī Islam. The cases in point were the Sunnī Naqshbandī ṭarīqah which traced its origins to Abū Bakr, Muḥammad's father-in-law and the first rightly guided caliph and the Ṣafawī ṭarīqah within Shī'ī Twelver Islam. Ṣūfī Islam acquired a particularly significant presence in the Caucasus, Central Asia and the Volga-Urals because of its emphasis on the transcendental and intangible side of Islam which allowed for integration within it of Persian and other pre-Islamic beliefs and customary and tribal norms – *'adat*s (customs).[37] It is significant that among trans-regional Ṣūfī authorities were, for example, a native of Darband, Abū Bakr Muḥammad al-Darbandī (c. 1058–1145), Aḥmad al-Yasawī (1093–1166) from present-day southern Kazakhstan and, later on, a native of Bukhara, Bahā' al-Dīn Naqshband Bukhārī (1318–1389) – the founder of the global ṭarīqah of Naqshbandīyyah.[38]

Muftīs

During the Abbasid period there was also formed a special class of jurists – the *muftīs* – who would be central in the Eurasian Islamic discourse from the late eighteenth century onwards. Initially muftīs were learned Muslims who were qualified to perform the *iftā'*, that is, to issue an oral or written *fatwā* (legal opinion) to individual petitioners – *mustaftīs*. Muftīs were 'ulamā' and other private learned Muslims who possessed a sound and sharp mind, who had high moral integrity and who were well versed in both the Qur'ān and Ḥadīth, as well as uṣūl al-fiqh. Some of the early muftīs were also *mujtāhids*, that is, those who were able to exercise an ijtihād. They were regarded as *muftīs muṭlaq* (absolute muftīs). Subsequently, most Sunnī muftīs tended to be *muftīs muqallid* (practitioners of *taqlīd*, or scripturalist Islam), who were restricted by Ḥanafī, Shāfi'ī, Mālikī, Ḥanbalī and other legal traditions.[39] From the eleventh century the iftā' began to assume a public function by being directed at both individual petitioners and government authorities. In view of the increasing role of iftā' as a mechanism of religious legitimization, caliphal and regional governments began to establish their control over muftīs.[40] Accordingly, muftīs and *qāḍīs* (Islamic judges) were transformed into legal state functionaries who dealt with various individual and community cases on the basis of standardized Islamic norms and fatwās.[41] By comparison, in Eurasia, from the late eighteenth century muftīs would become official intermediaries between the Christian Orthodox state and its Muslim subjects. In Shī'ī Iran, however, jurists would retain considerable autonomy from the state. This was also the case in Shī'ī Azerbaijan, including the territory of present-day Republic of Azerbaijan, until the latter was annexed to the Russian Empire in the early nineteenth century.

The Ottomans

In the middle of the thirteenth century the Islamic Golden Age was brought to an end by Mongols, who by that time presided over the largest contiguous Eurasian empire – the Mongol Empire (1206–1368), founded by Genghis Khān (c. 1155–1227) which included the Volga region, the Caucasus and Central Asia.[42] In 1258 Mongol troops under the leadership of Hulagu Khān (1215–1265), a grandson of Genghis Khān, invaded Baghdad and killed the last Abbasid Caliph al-Musta'ṣim (1213–1258). Although later on the Egyptian Mamlūks reinstated the office of Abbasid caliph in Cairo, caliphal authority became largely symbolic. However, the Mamlūks were overpowered by the Ottomans, Oghuz Turks who originated from Anatolia.[43] The main bearers of political authority among them were *emīrs* (rulers) elected among Oghuz tribal military chieftains – *beys*. Thus, Ertuğrul Bey (d. 1281), the father of the first Ottoman sulṭān, Osman I (r. 1299–1323), bore the title of emīr. From Osman I onwards the Ottoman rulers bore the title of sulṭān, reflecting the supremacy of political and military authority over religious. However, the situation began to change when in 1362 Sulṭān Murad I (r. 1362–89) conquered Adrianople, the major Byzantine city in Thrace, and made it the Ottoman capital. This military victory over the Byzantines and the Ottoman state's consequent transformation into a multi-ethnic and polyconfessional empire accounted for the strengthening of Islam as the religious legitimizer of the sulṭān's authority. The Ottomans' Islamized symbolism received another boost in 1453, when Sulṭān Mehmet II (r. 1444–46 and 1451–81) conquered Constantinople, which was turned into the new Ottoman capital under the name of Istanbul. By the middle of the sixteenth century the Ottomans had conquered most of the Middle East and parts of Eurasia and presided over a major global empire (1299–1922/23).

Following the Ottoman defeat of the Mumlūk Sulṭānate in Egypt in 1517 Sulṭān Selim I (Yavuz, r. 1512–20), who had no genealogical links to Prophet Muḥammad, for political reasons adopted the titles of caliph of all Muslims and custodian of the holy cities of Mecca and Medina (*Khādim al-Ḥaramayn al-Sharīfayn*).[44] A corollary was the increased political, administrative and legal status of the Ottoman 'ulamā' who became directly involved in the governance of the empire, albeit the sulṭans preserved their exclusive right to issue legislative decrees known as the *Kānūn*s (Laws) which took precedence over iftā', and the codification of which was completed during the reign of Sulṭān Suleyman I (Süleyman Kānūnī, r. 1520–66). Of special significance was the creation by the Ottomans in 1425 of the state office of *Muftīlik* (*Müftilik*, in Ottoman Turkish) which became subordinate to the imperial political and military leadership embodied in the High Porte (*Bāb-ı Ālī*, in Ottoman Turkish). According to Turkish historiography the first Ottoman muftī of the dominant Ḥanafī maddhab was Mollah Fenārī (d. 1431).[45] By the end of the sixteenth century the office of muftī of Istanbul, or *sheikh-ul-Islām* (*şeyḫülislām*, in Ottoman Turkish), became the highest office in the Ottoman learned hierarchy, responsible for the implementation and interpretation of the law and for education in the empire. From the middle of the sixteenth century the muftī's authority and prestige was on par with the grand vizier, the de facto prime minister. An important factor in this elevation was the friendship between Sulṭān Suleyman Kānūnī and Grand Muftī Ebussu'ud Efendi (d. 1574).[46]

By the late eighteenth century, the Ottoman Muftīlik represented a state-run Islamic bureaucracy consisting of sheikh-ul-Islām, *qāḍī-'asker*s (chief judges), *qāḍī*s (judges), *kenar muftī*s (provincial muftīs) and *mudarrises* (*müderrises*, in Ottoman Turkish, schoolteachers) who were stationed across the vast empire. Interestingly, while the Grand Muftī belonged to the class of 'ulamā', provincial muftīs who often acted as mudarrises did not necessarily have the status of 'ulamā'. Also, unlike qāḍīs, who were directly appointed and salaried by secular authorities, many provincial muftīs were not on state salaries and therefore possessed a considerable degree of autonomy from the Bāb-ı Ālī. This created a division between largely pro-secular qāḍīs and pro-sharī'ah muftīs and affected their respective relations with the political authorities.[47] Overall, the Ottomans were responsible for the creation of the state-run Islamic religious and legal administration (*maḥkamah*) and the transformation of the religious authorities from those who excelled in Islamic *'ilm* (knowledge) to those who attained a high learned office, accompanied by high salary and political influence. The Ottoman type of religious authority would subsequently influence the nature, as well as the particular titles, of Muslim clergy in the Ottoman-dominated Crimea, Batum and north-western Caucasus.[48]

The Safawids

In the Caucasus, the Ottomans were confronted by a major regional Islamic power – the Safawid Empire (1501–1736). The Safawids were Turkicized Iranians originating from Ardabil in north-western Iran.[49] Their name derived from the Ṣafawī ṭarīqah, which was influential among Muslim Kurds and some other Muslim peoples in Iranian Azerbaijan. The Ṣafawī ṭarīqah was established by the Kurdish mystic Ṣāfī al-Dīn Isḥāq Ardabīlī (1252–1334) who adhered to Sunnī Islam. In the 1440s, under the impact of rising levies from a number of Turkic tribes, the Ṣafawī ṭarīqah turned towards Shī'ī Twelver Islam which enabled it to instil a messianic vigour in its growing political and military engagement. A contributing factor was the Sunnī affiliation of the Safawids' regional rivals – the Ottomans and Central Asian Uzbeks. The Safawids' Shī'īzation campaign was conducted by the *Qizilbash* (the Red-headed),[50] Shī'ī militants from the Turkic tribal confederation.

In 1501, the Qizilbash under the leadership of Isma'īl al-Ṣafawī, a descendant of Ṣāfī al-Dīn, captured Tabriz[51] which was made the capital of the Safawid Empire, on the territory corresponding to present-day Iran. The authority and system of governance under Isma'īl al-Ṣafawī (r. 1501–24) was syncretic and drew on Iranian, Mongol, Turkic and Islamic traditions and practices. Thus, Isma'īl adopted the Sasanian title of shāh, the Turkic title of sulṭān and the Shī'ī title of *al-imām al-'ādil al-kāmil* (just and perfect imām). The Qizilbash forces, which were dominated by members of the Turkic tribes of Ustajlu and Shamlu, were headed by their commander-in-chief – amīr al-umarā'. Their mounted cavalry included representatives of the Uztajlu, Dhul-Qadr and Takkalu tribes and was led by a *qurchibashi* (tribal leader).[52] The Safawids also followed the Turkic model of territorial delimitation by dividing their rapidly expanding empire into *baylarbayliks* (provinces), headed by *baylarbays* (governors). At the same time the Safawids employed native Iranians to key administrative positions and embraced Iranian literature, music and the arts. The head of the Safawid religious administration bore the Timurid title of *sadr* which was mainly held by Tajik sayyīds.

By the early sixteenth century the Safawids controlled most of present-day Iran, thus becoming the first dynasty since the Sasanians to reinstate the political entity under the name of 'Iran' as the major regional power. From Iran the Safawids advanced to the southern and south-eastern Caucasus, where they defeated the Sharwānshāhs and other regional Sunnī Islamic and Christian rulers. In the early seventeenth century the Safawid Empire reached its territorial peak by also including Bahrain, parts of Iraq, Syria, Kuwait and Afghanistan, as well as parts of modern Turkey, Pakistan and Central Asia. Most importantly, during this period the Safawids conquered what is modern southern Azerbaijan and southern Dagestan and forcibly converted its mostly Sunnī population to Shī'īsm. For this reason modern Azerbaijanis call themselves 'sword-Muslims' (*qilinc müsəlman*, in Azerbaijani). Most inhabitants of the northern areas of Azerbaijan, for example, Sheki and Qabala, retained their adherence to Sunnīsm.[53]

Azerbaijan's official Shī'īzation was accompanied by the establishment there of Shī'ī Islamic authorities and structures. In particular, the Safawids created the office of *Sadr al-Azam* presided over by economically and politically influential Shī'ī theologians – 'ulamā', mujtāhids and sayyīds – who answered directly to the shāh.[54] In terms of the fiqh the Safawids favoured its more conservative branch – the *Akhbārī* (lit. 'Related to the News') which prioritized Ḥadīth over fatwā and, unlike the Uṣūlī (lit. 'Related to the Foundation') branch, did not practice ijtihād. Significantly, Twelver Shī'īsm has remained the dominant form of Islam in Iran, Iraq and historical Azerbaijan after the Safawids were deposed in 1734 by Nādir Shāh (Nader Shah, r. 1736–47), a Qizilbash chieftain belonging to the clan of the Afshars. In the late eighteenth century the Akhbārī branch of the Ja'farī fiqh was largely replaced by the more flexible Uṣūlī branch, which relied on ijtihād and recognized the highest religious and political authority of the *marja'-i taqlīd* (lit. 'source of emulation', supreme religious leader), occupied by the Ayatollah. During the rule of the Qajar dynasty (1789–1925) the marja'-itaqlīd became based in the Iraqi shrine city of Najaf, where in 1846 Ḥasan Najafī (d. 1850) was recognized as marja'-i taqlīd. Since then and till the late 1940s, Najaf largely remained the seat of the marja'-i taqlīd and the religious centre for the Shī'ī Azerbaijanis.[55]

Conclusion

The evolutionary and imposed changes in the nature and institutional forms of religious authority and leadership thus outlined, and their correlation with the political and military leadership in the Arab Muslim heartland and the major non-Arab Muslim empires, had lasting ramifications for various parts of Muslim Eurasia. Of particular significance was the forceful imposition of Islam by Prophet Muḥammad's Companions and their associates on various peoples of southern Dagestan, present-day northern Azerbaijan and the Ferghana valley, all of whom had been included into the Arab Caliphate. Among the implications of these developments was the prevalence among Muslims of the north-eastern Caucasus (Dagestanis, Chechens and Ingush) of the stricter Shāfi'ī madhhab, as well as the proliferation of Arabic-language culture and scholarship. On the other hand, most of the sedentary peoples of Central Asia who had a solid Persian civilizational background chose the more flexible Ḥanafī madhhab, which was adapted to the regional ethnocultural specifics by the Central Asian theologian al-Māturīdī. Central Asian merchants and missionaries played a pivotal role in spreading Ḥanafī Sunnīsm in the tenth century among the peoples of the Volga-Urals, as well as among various Turkic and Mongolian nomads of Eurasia. The Islamization of Crimean Tatars and various Circassian and Turkic peoples of the north-western Caucasus, which also occurred through peaceful means and along Sunnī Ḥanafī lines, happened much later, in the seventeenth and eighteenth centuries, due to their inclusion into the Ottoman sphere of political and cultural influence. This contrasted with the forcible conversion of Sunnī Muslims to Shī'īsm in modern Azerbaijan during the latter's domination by the Safawids between the sixteenth and eighteenth centuries.

By the time a large part of Muslim Eurasia was incorporated within the Orthodox Russian Empire, a variety of regional types of Islamic authority and leadership had formed, presenting a synthesis of Islamic Arabic, Turkic, Iranian and Mongol borrowings and local customary and tribal norms and traditions. The Russian conquest significantly modified the ensuing development of Islamic authorities and their relations with the Russian state, albeit it did not disrupt the very existence of Islam and Muslims in the Volga-Urals, the Caucasus and Central Asia – the regions which constituted the northern and easternmost domains of early Islam. Furthermore, Islam and Muslims contributed to the emergence of the distinctive multi-ethnic and polyconfessional Russian culture and state, as well as its political successors. The fate of early Islam's westernmost domain – Muslim Spain – was different. At the end of the fifteenth century al-Andalus ceased to exist as a result of Granada's annexation in 1492 to Castile in the course of the Spanish Catholic Reconquista against the Moors. Following the Castilian victory, all Muslims (as well as Jews) were ordered to convert to Catholicism or to leave what was now a militantly Christian country. Spectacular Islamic architecture, including the grand mosques of Córdoba, Seville and Zaragoza, were transformed into Catholic cathedrals and churches. Five centuries later, the divergent historical trajectories of Muslim Spain and Muslim Eurasia would be invoked in these regions' different models of state–Muslim relations and their different relationships with globalized Islam.[56]

Chapter Two

ISLAMIC LEADERSHIP AMONG TATARS AND OTHER TURKIC PEOPLES PRIOR TO AND DURING RUSSIAN RULE

Introduction

Muslim Tatars,[1] as well as their co-ethnic co-religionists, Bashkirs,[2] who historically dominated in the Volga-Urals, occupy a central place in the Eurasian Islamic discourse due to a millennium-long Tatar-Russian[3] ethnocultural and political entanglement. Long before ancestors of modern Tatars, Bashkirs and Russians converted, respectively, to Islam and Orthodox Christianity, they had interacted economically, politically and militarily because of their common Eurasian habitat lacking major water and mountain barriers. Their cultural inter-influence had also been facilitated through their participation in the north–south and east–west trans-Eurasian trade, alongside Finno-Ugric (Mari and Udmurts) and some other inhabitants of present-day western and central Russia and the Kazakh Steppe (*Desht-i-Qipchaq*). It is symptomatic that in medieval and the early modern European sources all were commonly referred to as Tartars.[4] Originally, proto-Russians who belonged to various sedentary eastern Slavic tribes dwelt along the banks of the Dniepr, Pripyat', Bug and Volkhov rivers in present-day north-western Russia and Ukraine. From the eighth century they began to settle along the Volga (*Idil'*), thus coming into even more close contact with proto-Tatars. Among their other neighbours were other Turkic peoples – Cumans (Polovets and Pechenegs) and Khazars.

Between the seventh and tenth centuries CE the Khazars presided over a large multi-ethnic empire, the Khazar Khaganate (650–969), or Khazaria, which was centred on the present-day northern Caucasus. In the early seventh century CE Khazaria served as Byzantium's proxy in its confrontation with Sasanian Iran. Following the fall of the Sasanian Empire as a result of the Arab victory over it in 637, Khazaria assumed the position of a buffer state between Byzantium, the Arab Caliphate, ancient Rus and the Eurasian nomadic confederations. Khazars played an important role in the political consolidation and religious preferences of both proto-Tatars and proto-Russians. In the middle of the eighth century, the Khazar elite, who resisted the caliphal advance in the Caucasus, adopted Judaism. By the early ninth century Khazars subjugated Turkic Biars, who at that time were politically dominant in the Volga region, and in the middle of the ninth century imposed their control on Kiev, the centre of the proto-Russian principality under the Rurik dynasty.[5] On the other hand, in the 920s, the ruling elite of the Volga Bulgars, who succeeded the Biars, turned to Sunnī Islam in response to political pressure from the Abbasid caliphs. Thus, the Islamization of Tatars goes back to the Abbasid period, as discussed in Chapter 1. In contrast, in the 980s, the Kievan ruling elite turned to Orthodox Christianity in anticipation of Byzantine backing against Judaist Khazars and Muslim Volga Bulgars.

In the middle of the thirteenth century Muslim Volga Bulgaria and various Christian Orthodox proto-Russian principalities (*kniazhestvos*) were absorbed into the Mongol Greater Horde (also known as the Golden Horde, 1241–1502), the ruling elite of which adopted Sunnī Islam a century later. Over two centuries of coexistence within the common imperial Genghizid space further strengthened the structural and cultural commonalities between proto-Tatars and proto-Russians despite their ethnic, political and religious differences. This period also witnessed the emergence of the Muscovy (Moscow)-centred Russian polity, alongside a plethora of Genghizid polities in the form of the Muslim khānates of Kazan, Astrakhan, Siberia, Nogai, Crimea and Qasimov, as well as the Kazakh khānate. Until the late fifteenth century these Genghizid khānates maintained their military, political and economic superiority over Orthodox Christian Muscovy, but in 1552 the conquest of the Kazan Khānate by Tsar Ivan IV (Ivan the Terrible, r. 1533–84) shifted the Eurasian political and religious balance of power towards Muscovy and marked its transformation into the Russian state proper. Since then Muslim Volga Tatars and, subsequently, Bashkirs, have either been under Russian rule or have been dominated by Russia. As a consequence, they developed distinctive mechanisms of religious and ethnonational survival in the Russian political and cultural environment – mechanisms that would later be adopted by other Muslim peoples of the Russian Empire. This chapter discusses the regional specifics of Islam among the Tatars and some other Muslim peoples of various Genghizid khānates in the Volga-Urals, Siberia, Crimea and the Kazakh Steppe, and is particularly concerned with the religious, social and political role of the various Islamic authorities and leaders. It then analyses the implications for 'Tatar Islam' and its leaders of the Russian conquest and pays special attention to the development of so-called 'Russian Islam', embodied in the Orenburg/Ufa-based muftīate, and the emergence among Tatars of the Islamic reformist movement – *jadīdīsm*.

Islam and Islamic Authority among Turkic Peoples of Central Eurasia

Volga Bulgaria

Unlike the various peoples of Dagestan, modern Azerbaijan and the Ferghana valley, who were forcibly converted to Islam by *ghāzis* (fighters for Islam) of the first Muslim generation, Volga Bulgars, who were largely Tengrians,[6] began voluntarily to turn to Islam under the influence of Muslim visitors, missionaries and traders from Baghdad, Bukhara and Samarqand. The ethnic origins of the Volga Bulgars, who are not related to the Danube Bulgars, is a matter of academic debate. It is most likely, however, that they originated from semi-nomadic Turkic tribes which roamed the Eurasian Steppe. From there they gradually migrated to the Middle Volga and allied with the Biars, sedentarized Turkic nomadic people, who created their polity – Biarmia – in the Volga region. At the end of the seventh century Bulgars broke away from Biarmia and formed a polyethnic and polyconfessional state – Volga Bulgaria – at the confluence of the Volga and Kama rivers.[7] Until the early thirteenth century its capital – Bulgar – was the major trade emporium navigating commercial flows between the Norse, Arabs and Caucasians.

The first conversions to Islam among the Volga Bulgars occurred in the context of the Arab confrontation with the Khazars – a semi-nomadic Turkic people who in the fifth century CE created the Khazar Khaganate[8] encompassing the Volga-Don steppes, the northern Caucasus and present-day central Russia. In the 730s, in the course of the Second Arab-Khazar War (c. 722–737) Arab troops under the command of the last Umayyad caliph Marwān II (d. 750) launched a massive attack from the Caucasus on the Khazar-controlled northern territories, including in the Volga-Urals. By the early tenth century a considerable number of Volga Bulgars had adopted Islam although many others retained their adherence to Tengrism up until the thirteenth century. On 21 May 922, the Bulgar ruler Almysh (Jafar ibn Gabdullah, d. 925), who bore the title of *baltavar* (duke), made Sunnī Islam the official religion of Volga Bulgaria. This formal conversion to Islam occurred during the visit to Volga Bulgaria of Aḥmad ibn Faḍlān (d. 960), the ambassador of the Abbasid Caliph al-Muʿtaḍid (r. 908–932) who was touring Bukhara, Khwārazm (Khoresm) and the Volga region. Interestingly, the Bulgar elite opted for the more flexible, Central Asian version of the Ḥanafī madhhab, rather than the Shāfiʿī madhhab, which was dominant in Baghdad, as advised by Ibn Faḍlān. This enabled Muslim Tatars to preserve, albeit in Islamized form, some of their pre-Islamic customs and holidays, including *Nowruz* (lit. 'New Day' in Persian),[9] *Sabantui* (Advent of Spring) and *Dzhien* (a Fair).[10]

Volga Bulgaria's official conversion to Islam enabled Khan Almysh, as well as his successors, to strengthen the religious legitimacy of their authority as they also assumed the Islamic title of *Amīr al-Muʾminīn* (Commander of the Faithful). Like Central Asian Sāmānids, the Bulgar elite pursued a policy of religious tolerance, patronized science and the arts, and advanced Islamic scholarship and education. They encouraged the building of mosques, *maktab*s (primary Islamic schools) and madrasahs across the khānate. By the end of the tenth century the capital of Volga Bulgaria – Bulgar – had become a renowned centre of Islamic learning, while its ʿulamāʾ were at the forefront of creative Islamic thinking through the medium of ijtihād, the gates of which were widely closed in Baghdad and other scholarly centres of the Muslim heartland. For example, some Bulgar 'ulamā' applied ijtihād to legalize folk elements within 'Bulgar Ḥanafī Islam', while some pro-ijtihād Bulgar fuqahā' endorsed the removal of the fifth mandatory daily prayer – '*ishā*' (*iastu*, in Tatar) – on the grounds of the particular shortness of night-time in May and June due to Volga Bulgaria's far northern location in relation to Mecca – though, this move has been contested by literalist Tatar 'ulamā' ever since.[11]

The Golden Horde and Other Muslim Genghizid Khānates

The Golden Horde

In the 1240s Volga Bulgaria, alongside most of present-day Russia and the northern Caucasus, was included into the Genghizid Golden Horde, which emerged in the process of the Mongol Empire's fragmentation following the death of Genghis Khān in 1227. Its first capital was Sarai-Batu (near the city of Astrakhan) which was founded by Khān Batu (d. 1255). During the reign of Uzbeg Khān (Öz Beg Khān, d. 1341) the capital was transferred to Sarai-Berke (near the present-day city of Volgograd). The other major Genghizid polities were the Ilkhānate (1258–1353) which encompassed parts of present-day Iran, Iraq, Afghanistan, Pakistan and Turkmenistan, as well as southern Dagestan and northern Azerbaijan; and the Chagatai Khānate (1225–1670) which corresponded to most of Central Asia, with the exception of present-day Turkmenistan. At the time of Volga Bulgaria's subjugation, the Genghizids did not belong to a single religion and professed syncretic beliefs which included elements of shamanism, Tengrism and Buddhism. In the fourteenth century most Genghizid rulers formally converted to Sunnī Islam, but continued to run their respective polities as a polyethnic and multi-confessional polity allowing for the proliferation of both Islam and Orthodox Christianity among the ancestors of modern Tatars and Russians, respectively. The main conduits of Islam among rank-and-file Mongols and various Turkic peoples under Genghizid control were Ṣūfī teachers and merchants of both Volga Bulgaria and Central Asia.[12] Importantly, at least initially, Islam was kept out of politics and in matters of authority the Genghizid tribal genealogy had precedence over Islamic genealogical credentials. It was also symptomatic that under the Golden Horde's rule the Rus Orthodox Church acquired its economic and political prominence.[13] This Islamo-Christian dualism contrasted with the largely confrontational nature of Christian–Muslim relations in contemporary Spain. On the other hand, the Genghizids' promotion in the conquered lands of their tribal customary law – the Great *Yasa*[14] – was conducive to the grassroots preservation or even strengthening of pre-Islamic and pre-Christian customary norms.[15] At the turn of the fifteenth century the Golden Horde khāns' rule weakened and the state's various principalities (*ulus*s) became de facto autonomous, albeit they continued to pay *yasak* (an annual tribute) to their Genghizid suzerain.

Kazan Khānate

Among the largest ex-Genghizid principalities was the Kazan Khānate (1438–1552) in the Middle Volga, which is believed to have been founded by a Genghizid khān Ulu Muhammad (tat. Olug Muhammat, d. 1445). Until the Russian conquest in 1552 the Kazan Khānate remained de jure under the Golden Horde's jurisdiction by paying it yasak. The Kazan elite consisted of emirs, begs, *murza*s (begs' younger sons) and landed nobility of various ethnic origins. Among the powerful landed nobility were, for example, the Crimean families of Shirin, Begadur and Chelbak lineage; the Siberian families of Rast and Kebek; the Nogai family of Zeniet; and the Kasimov family of Nur-Ali. The Khānate's smaller landowners were *tarkhan*s, while its military were represented by the privileged cavalry – *oglan*s (Genghizids of non-khān lineage) – and ordinary cavalry and Cossack infantry. The population of the khānate was multi-ethnic and consisted of Bulgars, Genghizids and various Turkic, Mongolian, Finno-Ugric and Slavic peoples. The authority of the khān was hereditary. He also relied on two representative bodies – *kurultai* (legislative assembly) and *divān* (consultative council) – the former including representatives of the Muslim clergy, headed by the Supreme Sayyīd, *karachais* (local nobles belonging to four major Bulgar clans) and oglans, while divān consisted of a selected number of karachais.[16]

During the Khānate's Golden Age its capital city of Kazan, situated on the banks of the Volga and Kazanka rivers, turned into a major Eurasian commercial and cultural hub and the regional Islamic centre. The Kazan Muslim clergy who included sayyīds, muftī, sheikhs, *akhuns* (chief imāms), imāms, mullahs, *dervishs*, *khojahs*, *hajjees*, *ḥāfizes* (*abyzes*) professional readers of the Qur'ān), *danishmends* (Islamic teachers) and *sheikh-zadehs* and *mullah-zadehs* (sons and pupils of sheikhs and mullahs) acquired significant political and economic influence. For example, the Supreme Sayyīd who was elected from 'ulamā' of the sayyīd lineage was the second most important person after the khān and acted as head of state during succession crises, as well as the khān's senior diplomatic representative abroad. Muslim clergy were responsible for the provision of Islamic education through the network of madrasahs and maktabs. The Muftī was an akhun who also acted as the intermediary between the khān's authorities and believers. Akhuns oversaw such local Muslim clergy's activities as interpreting the sharī'ah, the resolving of property-related disputes and the correct performance of Islamic rites.[17] An important proselytizing and educational role belonged to the Ṣūfīs of Yasawī and Naqshbandī ṭarīqahs, which originated in Central Asia. Overall, Muslim clergy possessed considerable wealth and landed property in the form of *waqf* (endowment). Among contemporary reminders of their importance are such area names as Seitovo (from 'sayyīd'), Kul'seitovo (from 'kul sayyīd'), Khadiashevo (from 'khoja'), Shikhzada and Aryshikhazada (from 'sheikh-zadeh') and Derbyshki and Alderbysh (from 'dervish') in modern Tatarstan.[18]

A special note should be made of the resettlement in the fourteenth century of some Volga Tatars to the then-powerful Grand Duchy of Lithuania (GDL), the territory of which corresponded to most of modern Lithuania, Poland and Belarus. The resettlement occurred in the context of the active involvement of the then-pagan Lithuanian Grand Dukes[19] in an inter-Genghizid power struggle. On several occasions Lithuanian rulers offered refuge to failed contenders and their followers. These Tatar migrants formed the historical core of mosque-based Muslim communities known as *jamiats* (*jamā'ahs*) in modern Lithuania, Poland and Belarus. By 1591 the GDL had around 100,000 Muslim Tatar inhabitants and 400 mosques. Jamiats were headed by mullahs who were chosen on the basis of their public credentials rather than their knowledge of sharī'ah and Arabic. The region lacked any institutionalized Islamic structures and formalized Islamic education. It is symptomatic that the first translation of the Qur'an into Polish was done only in 1858.[20]

Astrakhan Khānate

Another important Muslim Tatar principality was the Astrakhan Khānate (tat. Hājītarkhān, 1466–1556) which is believed to have been founded on the right bank of the Volga River by the Genghizid khān Maḥmūd (tat. Məxmüt, d. c. 1472). Astrakhan Khānate was populated by Tatars, Nogais and various other peoples of Turkic, Iranian and Caucasian ethnic origins.[21] Although it was one of the smallest Genghizid polities in terms of its territory, due to its strategic location in the Lower Volga, it played a key role in the lucrative trade along the Volga River between Iran, Khwarāzm, Bukhara, the Caucasus and Kazan. It also controlled the pilgrimage of various Eurasian Muslims to Mecca and Medina; and Astrakhan rulers often forged alliances with militarily more powerful Crimean and Nogai khāns.

Like other Genghizids, Astrakhan khāns possessed supreme authority which was secured genealogically, while Muslim clergy ('ulamā', and Ṣūfī sheikhs, *ishāns*, imāms and others) oversaw Islamic education, the spreading of Islam among Kazakhs and other pagan nomads of Dasht-i-Qipchaq and the pilgrimages (*ziyārats*) to Ṣūfī shrines across the region. At times, however, Muslim clerics, particularly Ṣūfī sheikhs of the Naqshbandī and Kubrawī ṭarīqahs, accompanied khāns during their military raids on Kabarda and other principalities in the Caucasus. At the top of the Muslim clergy were the sheikh al-Islām and muftī, who adhered to the Ḥanafī madhhab, although some of the khānate's Muslim clerics and ordinary Muslims followed Shāfi'ī or Mālikī madhhabs. In the early sixteenth century, under the influence of neighbouring Safawids, some of the khānate's Nogais converted to Shī'īsm. Like other Genghizid jurists, Astrakhan fuqahā' routinely exercised ijtihād by adjusting sharī'ah rulings to the local conditions. Among them were, for example, al-Kardarī (d. 1424) and Yazydzhioglu (d. 1449) who authored compendia of fatwās – 'Al-Fatāwa al-Kardarīyyah' and 'Muḥammadīyyah'.[22]

Nogai Horde

Astrakhan's powerful neighbour was the Nogai Horde, also known as Mangyt Yurt (nog. *Manğıt Yurtu*).[23] Its name derived from the Genghizid khān Nogai (d. c. 1299) who formed an army on the basis of the Qipchaq-Mongol tribe of Mangyt. In c. 1440 a Mangyt emir Yedigei (1352–1419) broke away from the Golden Horde and founded a separate nomadic state – the Nogai Horde (c. 1440–1634) – consisting of 18 Qipchaq and Mongol tribes. Nogais controlled a large territory encompassing the Pontic-Caspian steppe, western Siberia and north-western and southern parts of modern Kazakhstan. In the 1550s, as a result of internal conflicts and a devastating plague which killed nearly 80 per cent of Nogais, the Nogai Horde split into the Greater Nogai Horde (the large steppe area along the Volga River), the Smaller Nogai Horde (steppe areas around the Azov Sea and Kuban River) and the Alty Uly Nogai Horde (the steppe zone between the rivers of Yaik, Emba and Syr Darya). In 1557, the Greater Horde recognized Muscovy's suzerainty, while the other two hordes retained independence until the early seventeenth century when they were defeated by Mongolic-speaking Kalmyks (Oirats). During the seventeenth century the remnants of the Nogais migrated to the northern Caucasus or were absorbed into the Kazakh Kichi Horde. The Nogais' Islamic beliefs and practices were of a syncretic nature and contained strong shamanist and pagan components. This, in turn, accounted for the prevalence among the Nogais of the genealogical tribal leadership over the Islamic one.

Crimean Khānate

The Crimean Khānate (tat. *Qırım Hanlığı*, 1441–1783) differed from other Genghizid khānates due to its fascinating pre-Genghizid history, its longer period of resistance to Russian rule and its particularly close relations with Russia's major geopolitical rival – the Ottoman.[24] Prior to the khānate's era, the Crimean Peninsula endured successive Greek, Roman, Scythian, Turkic, Byzantine, Khazar and Genoese dominations, which became reflected in its extremely multi-ethnic and polyconfessional population which included Christian Orthodox Greeks, Christian Apostolic (Gregorian) Armenians, Catholic Armenians, Catholic Italians, Jews (Krymchaks and Karaites), Turks and Tatars. The Khānate was founded by Haji I Giray (d. 1466), a descendant of Khān Juchi, Genghiz Khān's eldest son, in the northern part of the Crimean Peninsula, while the Crimea's southern part remained the domain of the Genoese who controlled the city of Kaffa (Theodosia), which for centuries had been the emporium of the Asian-European trade. In order to succeed in politically and economically complex conditions Khān Haji I Giray, who ruled between the 1440s and 1460s, adhered to a multidimensional foreign policy. He fought Russians and steppe warlords, while allying with the Ottomans, Lithuanians as well as some Circassian and Turkic rulers of the north-western Caucasus.[25] In 1453, the Ottoman Turks took Constantinople, which they renamed Istanbul, and in 1454 they raided Kaffa. In 1475, they seized the Crimea's Genoese colonies and transformed them into the Kaffa *eyalet* (province) of the Ottoman Empire, which was administratively allocated to the Anatolia region of the empire.[26] In 1478, the Ottomans made the Crimean Khān Mengli Giray (d. 1515) a vassal of the Ottoman Empire. From then until 1774 the Khānate was closely allied with Istanbul in its confrontation with St. Petersburg, while the Black Sea was transformed into a de facto 'Turkish lake'.[27] The multifaceted Ottoman presence in the Crimea channelled the development of Islamic authority and structures there along Ottoman Turkish lines.[28]

Qasimov Khānate

Unlike the Crimean Khānate, the Qasimov Khānate (tat. *Qasim Hanlığı*, 1452–1681) was the first to accept Russian suzerainty and contribute to Russia's conquest of other Genghizid khānates. It was founded by Qāsim Khān (d. 1469), a son of the first Kazan khān Ulu Muḥammad, on the territory of the present-day Russian region of Ryazan situated in the middle course of the Oka River. This land, which was originally populated by Mishar Tatars,[29] as well as Meshchera, Muroma, Mordva and other Finno-Ugric peoples, was gifted to Qāsim Khān by *Kniaz* (Grand Duke) Vasily II (d. 1462) of Muscovy to ensure Qāsim's loyalty. Subsequently, the Qasimov Khānate, which was ruled by khāns from the Kazan, Crimean, Golden Horde, Kazakh and Siberian Genghizid dynasties, was settled by Kazan Tatars, who became known as Qasim Tatars, as well as Russians, while the Meshchera were largely assimilated into Muslim Mishar Tatars. Qasim khāns took part in all Russian raids on Kazan. On the other hand, they acted as an agency of persistent Genghizid and Islamic influence on the Russian state and culture.[30] Following the Russian conquest of Kazan in 1552 the Qasimov Khānate was put under the governance of Russian *voevoda*s (military commanders). In 1681, the Khānate was dissolved and its territory absorbed by the Russian state. The in-between position of the Kasimov Khānate predetermined the gradual decline of its Islamic leadership represented by Kazan sayyīds, imāms, mullahs and ḥāfiẓes, some of whom were subjected to partial Christianization.

The Khānate of Sibir (Siberia)

The Sibir Khānate[31] was founded in western Siberia in 1468 by the descendants of Hajjee Muḥammad (d. 1427), the nomadic ruler of the Tiumen khānate (1359–1563), which was formed on the basis of the Golden Horde's Sibir ulus. Ḥajjee Muḥammad belonged to the Genghizid lineage via Shaybān, the fifth son of Juchi (d. 1227), the eldest son of Genghis Khān. The Khānate encompassed steppe expanses between the Siberian rivers of Irtysh, Ob' and Tobol and bordered the Nogai Horde and the Kazakh Khānate. Modern Kazakhs and Uzbeks are also of Shaybānid descent. Initially the centre of the Khānate was Chingi-Tura (present-day Tiumen); later on it moved to Qashlyk (near present-day Tobol'sk on the Irtysh River). It was populated by Turkic, Mongolian and Finno-Ugric peoples (Khanti, Mansi and Nenets). As in the case of Nogais, the Islamic authorities among the Sibir Khānate's members were affected by their nomadism and continuing adherence to shamanism. In 1582, the Sibir Khānate was conquered by Cossack troops under the leadership of ataman Yermak (1532–1585) and subsequently absorbed into the Russian state.

Kazakh Khānate

As noted above, other Eurasian descendants of Shaybān lineage are present-day Kazakhs in Central Asia. In 1465, their representative, Kerei Khān (d. 1473), split from the Uzbek tribal confederation under the Shaybānid ruler, Abulkhair (d. 1468), and established the Kazakh Khānate (kaz. *Qazaq Handyğy*, 1465–1848), characterized by a loose tribal structure. Nomadic Kazakhs dominated a large part of Dasht-i-Qipchaq, which roughly corresponded to the territory of modern Kazakhstan. In the early seventeenth century the Kazakh Khānate split into three tribal confederations – hordes, or *juz*es: the *Ulu Juz* (the Great Horde), the *Orta Juz* (the Middle Horde) and the *Kichi Juz* (the Small Horde). The largest was the Orta Juz (around 40 per cent of Kazakhs) which corresponded to present-day central Kazakhstan. By comparison, the Ulu Juz (around 35 per cent of Kazakhs) dominated southern Kazakhstan and the Kichi Juz (25 per cent of Kazakhs) prevailed in western Kazakhstan). By the middle of the eighteenth century, Kazakhs of the Small and Middle Hordes, exhausted by their lengthy conflict with nomadic Mongolian-speaking Jungars (Oirats), had recognized Russian tutelage and agreed to pay yasak to the Russian tsar. A century later all three hordes were disbanded and its territories absorbed into the Russian Empire. As in the case of other nomads, the Kazakhs' Islamic practices and beliefs were syncretic and strongly influenced by Tengrism and shamanism. A crucial regulator of the Kazakh social order was the code of Khān Tauke (d. 1718), known as the *Jeti Jarghy* (Seven Verdicts), which, among other practices, legitimized blood revenge and the right of collective assistance in case of loss of livestock and seasonal works. Importantly it endorsed the supremacy of *biy*s (tribal chieftains) and other tribal authorities over qāzīs/qāḍīs in legal matters. The main bearers of Islamic authorities among Kazakhs were iterant *khojah*s (Ṣūfī elders) of Yasawī and Naqshbandī ṭarīqahs. At the same time mosque mullahs were held in low esteem and their presence in a Kazakh *yurt* (nomadic tent) was associated with bad luck.[32]

Russian Policy on Islam and Islamic Leadership

Between the Sixteenth and the Late Eighteenth Centuries

Muscovy's defeat of its Genghizid Muslim suzerain had major lasting implications for Eurasian Muslims and their Islamic authorities and leadership. In order to overcome Muscovy's intrinsic political and cultural 'Genghizidness' its rulers began to emphasize the newly formed Russian state's Byzantinism, its capital city of Moscow's perceived role as the 'Third Rome' and its alleged divine mission as the gatherer of the former Golden Horde's territories. A corollary was Moscow's initial ruthless stance towards the Genghizid political and religious elite. Kazan, which had been the centre of anti-Russian resistance, was subjected to Russification and demonstrative Christianization. The large part of its Muslim residents who refused baptism was expelled from the city into surrounding rural areas. The Kazan Cathedral mosque[33] was demolished and in its place the Orthodox Church of the Annunciation was erected. Many representatives of the Genghizid nobility and senior Muslim clergy were killed, and their land redistributed among members of the Russian ruling elite and the Orthodox monasteries. By the early seventeenth century most Genghizid khānates, with the exception of the Crimea and Kazakh khānates, were conquered by Russians and transformed into Russia's provinces, ruled by *voevoda*s (military governors). Some Genghizid dignitaries were forced to convert to Orthodox Christianity, thus safeguarding their social status and property, and some were subsequently admitted to the Russian state service and integrated into the Russian nobility. Those who refused baptism were stripped of their nobility and property and forced into commerce. Yet others fled to Muslim Central Asia, the Caucasus, Hejaz, as well as the GDL and other parts of non-Russian Eurasia.

A leading ideologist of Moscow's anti-Islamic policy was the Orthodox Metropolitan Macarius (rus. Makarii, d. 1563), a confidant of Tsar Ivan the Terrible. Macarius masterminded a campaign of coercive Christianization of Muslim Tatars, as well as various Finno-Ugric peoples, who were predominantly pagan. He was behind the mass destruction of mosques, madrasahs, maktabs; the confiscation of waqf land and property; and the persecution of sayyīds, 'ulamā', akhuns and other Muslim clergy. In 1555, Kazan acquired a special archbishop's department which was tasked with the conversion of Tatars and other Muslims to Orthodox Christianity.[34] A century later, another major wave of coercive Christianization was orchestrated by the Russian Patriarch Nikon

(1605–1681). Those Tatars and other Muslims who were forcibly baptized during this period and earlier became known as *starokreshchennye* (old converts), while those Tatars who were Christianized in the middle of the eighteenth century were referred to as *novokreshennye* (new converts).

Overall, until the middle of the eighteenth century the official Russian policy towards Islam was not consistent, alternating between ruthless suppression and moderate toleration. The 'suppression' approach generated resistance, culminating in a series of anti-Moscow Muslim uprisings (e.g. the Kazan Tatars' revolts in 1570–72 and 1581–84), a movement of *otpadenie* (secret return to Islam) among baptized Tatars, and Muslim appeals to Ottoman sulṭāns and Crimean khāns for religious protection.[35] The Russian assault on Muslim clergy led to the de facto destruction of Tatar 'ulamā' and the Islamic scholarship associated with them, and the reduction of Islam to its popular rural form, characterized by static ritualism and strong intermingling with 'adats and other pre-Islamic beliefs and practices. Under these circumstances, Islamic leadership among the Tatars shifted to akhuns and abyzes. Akhuns played the role of unofficial intermediaries between the authorities and believers, oversaw Islamic rites and provided sharī'ah-based guidance in cases of family and property disputes. Abyzes, who were predominately Ṣūfīs, were custodians of Islamic traditions within *dzhien*s (local assemblies), which became governed by councils of *aksakal*s (elders). They also acted as secretaries and translators for religious figures.[36] Among Tatar and other Muslim women, the main Islamic authorities were *abystai*s (*bibi-otun*s). In contrast, tolerance towards Islam witnessed the restoration of ownership rights to some surviving Genghizid dignitaries and their co-optation within the Russian hereditary nobility. At the grassroots level, the 'toleration' approach facilitated productive economic interrelationships and cultural and linguistic mutual borrowings between Russians and Muslims (as well as representatives of other confessions and belief systems) which were made possible by their common sociopolitical, economic and cultural Eurasian-ness and their common Genghizid past, in particular.[37]

Catherine the Great and the Making of 'Russian Islam'

In the early eighteenth century Tsar Peter the Great (Peter I, r. 1682–1725), a representative of the new Romanov dynasty (1613–1917) and a determined Europhile, initiated Russia's political and cultural reorientation from 'Asiatic' Eurasian-ness towards 'civilized' European-ness. A symbol of this radical geopolitical turn was the transfer of Russia's capital from Moscow, located in the polyconfessional heart of central Russia, to the newly founded St. Petersburg, situated on Russia's north-western frontier with Europe. In order to make his country acceptable to the club of great European powers, Peter the Great imposed on Russia and its inhabitants 'European' political and administrative structures, etiquette, dress and personal looks. Hence, at political and administrative levels, Russian tsardom, which had been modelled on Byzantium and the Golden Horde, was replaced by the Russian Empire, resembling the British and other major European empires. At the manufacturing level, Petrine reforms enabled Russia to acquire modern arms, iron and other essential industries. At the military level, Russia was transformed from a predominantly infantry- and cavalry-based state into a maritime empire. At the international level,

Russia turned from its primary involvement with its other post-Genghizid counterparts and, subsequently, with the Ottomans and Safawids, towards both adversarial and collaborative engagement with Sweden, Prussia, the Netherlands, Austria and other European states. At a personal level, beards, longer coats and loose pants among men, which had been similarly worn by Russians and Muslims, were banned and replaced by 'European' facial shaving, jackets and tight trousers.

Nevertheless, Russia's Europeanization was superficial and did not significantly interfere with the existing Eurasian power structures, centre–periphery relations, economy or its ethnic and confessional pluralism. The Russian manufacturing boom was fuelled by further intensification of serfdom, while its commerce, local government, judiciary and civic society remained hugely underdeveloped. Among the ideational implications of Peter the Great's European thrust was the embrace by St. Petersburg's elite of European philosophy and science, German and French as court languages, as well as some superiority attitudes towards Tatars, Bashkirs and others of Russia's Muslims. Subsequently, during Russia's advance into the Muslim Caucasus, the Kazakh-dominated Dasht-i-Qipchaq and Central Asia, a Europeanized civilizational discourse became a factor in Russian policy towards Islam and Muslims.

The first major territorial expansion of imperial Russia into Muslim Eurasia occurred under Empress Catherine the Great (Catherine II, r. 1762–96), who inaugurated the policy of 'enlightened despotism' which combined serfdom-based absolutism and ruthless suppression of any form of dissent with the granting of liberties to the Russian nobility and deference towards Voltaire and other leading representatives of the European Enlightenment. She began her reign by brutally crushing a mass popular revolt under the leadership of Yemelian Pugachev (c. 1742–1775). The Pugachev rebellion (1773–75) was preceded by an Islamized revolt (1754–55) under the leadership of Bashkir imām Batyrsha Galiyev (1717–1762) who mobilized the Urals' Muslims against the official renewal of baptizing and other discriminatory policies towards Muslims. By comparison, the Pugachev rebellion included Christian Orthodox Yaik Cossacks, Russian peasants, Old Believers,[38] predominantly pagan Mordva, Mari, Udmurts, Buddhist Kalmyks and Muslim Bashkirs, Kazakhs and Tatars, all of whom united against St. Petersburg's intensified serfdom, poll tax and military conscription, religious persecution and enforced Christianization. It was the involvement in this rebellion of a large number of Muslims which prompted Catherine the Great to develop a new approach towards Muslims, with the aim of their partial economic and cultural integration into the Russian state and society. At the ideological level, Catherine the Great's policy towards the empire's Muslims marked a radical departure from earlier discriminatory state policies on Islam associated with Metropolitan Macarius and Patriarch Nikon.

At the core of Catherine the Great's new approach towards the empire's Muslims was their legal institutionalization and ethnocultural and religious integration into the fabric of Russian society. It was implemented through the granting of economic and trade preferences to Muslim Tatars and Bashkirs, the introduction of legislative restrictions on the Russian Orthodox Church's proselytism among Muslims and members of other non-Orthodox confessions and, most importantly, the legalization and 'étatization' of Islam with the granting of limited privileges to Muslim clergy. In 1763, Tatar merchants were permitted to create in Kazan their Chamber of Commerce, which practised Islamic finance, and were given rights to trade all over the Russian Empire, as well as to found their trade settlements in the Kazakh Steppe. By the early nineteenth century, due to acquired preferences, Tatars controlled 148 textile, leather, soap-boiling and other factories and companies across the Volga-Urals.[39]

Catherine the Great's Law on Religious Tolerance of 1773 limited the Russian Orthodox Church's interference in the life of various Muslim communities, which were enabled to make their own decisions regarding mosques, madrasahs, sharī'ah courts, waqfs and *caravan-sarais* (merchant stations). Catherine the Great's decree of 1783 legalized the right of Tatars and other Muslim Turkic peoples to elect their akhuns. By the imperial decrees of 1784 and 1786, Muslim Tatars and Bashkirs, who for over two centuries had barely had any access to structured Islamic education, were officially permitted to study at the *Mir-i Arab* madrasah and other distinguished centres of Islamic learning in Bukhara, Samarqand and Kabul. They were also granted rights to open maktabs, madrasahs and Islamic publishing houses in the Volga-Urals and in the Desht-i-Qipchaq along the route of the ancient Silk Road. As a result, by the end of the eighteenth century, madrasahs functioned in Kazan, Ufa, Orenburg, Astrakhan and Tobol'sk, as well as in the Tatar villages of Izhbodia, Menger, Qashgar, Qursa, Saba, Satysh, Sterlibash and Tunter. In 1800, Kazan witnessed the opening of the first Islamic publishing house, printing hundreds of Islamic books per year. However, it was the creation in 1788 of the Orenburg Mohammedan Spiritual Assembly (OMDS, muftīate)[40] which paved the way for the emergence of apolitical 'Russian Islam' and the Russian official Islamic leadership.

OMDS was headed by a muftī who was appointed by the state. It also included five or six qāẓīs, a *muhtasibat* (audit office) consisting of several *muhtasib*s (auditors), and a *mutavalliiat* (a body of local mullahs and *mu'azzins* – callers for prayer). Senior Muslim clergy were exempt from corporal punishment and the death penalty, though mosque mullahs became subject to military conscription and taxation according to their social estate, primarily as peasants.[41] The first Russian muftī was Muhamedzhan Khusainov (tat. Muḥammejān ibn al-Ḥusain, in office 1788–1824). The level of authority and functions of muftī Khusainov and his successors differed significantly from those expected of their counterparts in the Muslim Middle East. As discussed in Chapter 1, in the Middle East and some other Muslim-majority countries muftīs, though controlled by political rulers, relied on their own authority as experts of sharī'ah. They also had to be either from the 'ulamā' or at least to have had a good Islamic education. Russia's muftīs, in contrast, were in the first place government officials pursuing state interests among the Muslims of Russia and only in the second place fatwā-givers and spiritual leaders.[42] The muftīs' religious functions included the selection of politically reliable local qāzīs and mullahs; overall control of Muslim communities in Kazan province, which corresponded to most of the Volga-Urals region; the legal adjustment (via the mechanism of iftā') of Muslim life within the Russian Empire; and the Islamization, or re-Islamization, of Kazakhs and other 'unruly' nomads along the lines of mosque-based 'Russian Islam'.

The OMDS' muftīs became involved in St. Petersburg's religious and foreign policies and were often decorated for their service to the Russian crown. Among the latter were, for example, muftī Gabdessaliam Gabdrakhimov (in office 1825–40), who carried out espionage assignments in the Kazakh Kichi Juz, as well as muftīs Salimgirei Tevkelev (in office 1865–85) and Muhamadiar Sultanov (in office 1886–1915).[43] It is noteworthy that among the muftīate's clergy there were also some independent minded and charismatic Islamic authorities, for example, Naqshbandī ishān Zainulla Rasulev (al-Rasūlī, 1833–1917) who had many thousands of followers in the Volga-Urals and the Kazakh Steppe.[44] On the other hand, some influential Muslim clergy refused to join the muftīate and either conducted hijrah to Central Asia or Ottoman Turkey, or minimized their links with the OMDS, or attempted to create alternative religious organizations. Among the leading representatives of the first group was Sāliḥ Salīmī Kazanī; of the second group 'Abdarrahim ibn 'Uthmān al-Bulgarī (Utyz-Imyanī, 1754–1834) and Shihabuddīn Marjanī; and of the third group Habiballah ibn al-Khusain al-Arūwa and Bahā' al-Dīn (Vaisov). By the second half of the nineteenth century the muftīate began also to play the role of a national centre for Tatars and other Turkic Muslims of the Volga-Urals region.[45]

Parallel to this accommodating policy Catherine the Great embarked on the military conquest of largely Muslim Crimea, as well as the northern Caucasus and the Kazakh Steppe.[46] In 1783 Russia annexed the Crimea/Taurida[47] and put an end to the pro-Ottoman Genghizid Giray dynasty. In 1794 Catherine issued a decree on the creation of the Taurida muftīate – the Taurian Mohammedan Spiritual Directorate, consisting of the state-appointed and salaried muftī, who also bore the Ottoman title of qāẓī-asker, and five qāẓīs. However, the actual establishment of the Taurida muftīate in the town of Bakhchysarai occurred only in 1832 during the reign of Nicholas I (r. 1826–55). Taurida's first muftī was qāẓī-asker Seyit-Mehmet effendī. Under the Taurida muftīate's control were the Muslims of the Crimea, Lithuania, Poland and the western provinces of the Russian Empire. Unlike the Volga Tatars, who by the nineteenth century were largely integrated within the Russian political and cultural space, the majority of Crimean, Lithuanian and Polish Tatars retained a stronger attachment to Ottoman Turkey and were less politically and culturally Russified. Following the Russian conquest many Crimean Tatars emigrated to Turkey.[48]

Jadīdism

Russia's defeat in the Crimean War (1853–56) triggered its belated modernization. In 1861 Tsar Alexander II (r. 1856–81) finally abolished serfdom and embarked on 'Great Reforms' of Russia's anachronistic military, economic, political and educational system. These reforms, despite its top-down character and considerable superficiality, accelerated Russia's bourgeois development and stimulated the ethnonational awareness of various peoples of the multi-ethnic Russian Empire. The Tatars' history and their lengthy period within the Russian domain determined their leading role in the national awakening among Russia's Muslims. From the 1860s, a number of Tatar intellectuals began campaigning for the modernization of the existing rigid and scholastic confessional education, dominated by rote memorizing of Islamic texts in Arabic. One of them, Khusain Faizkhanov (1823–1866), proposed the creation of a network of secularized Tatar secondary schools modelled on Russian gymnasia, which would also teach Tatar language and Tatar history. However, due to the overwhelming predominance of madrasah education among the Tatars this project fell on deaf ears. Two decades later, a comprehensive reform began within Islamic confessional education itself. It became known as *al-uṣūl al-jadīd*, or a new method of madrasah teaching which was pioneered in 1884 by Ismaīl Gaspiralī (Gasprinski, 1851–1914), a European-educated Crimean Tatar. Al-uṣūl al-jadīd involved a phonetization of reading instead of memorization from Arabic, a switch from Bukharan textbooks written mainly in Arabic, Persian or Chagatai to those in Ottoman Turkish, or new Tatar textbooks in Arabic or modified Ottoman Turkish, as well as the introduction into the curricula of arithmetic, geography, history and Russian language, as well as painting, singing and theatre arts.[49] It is important to note that until the Russian bourgeois-democratic revolution of 1905–7 the number of jadīd madrasahs remained relatively small and the majority of schools continued to teach along *qadīmīst* (traditional) lines. The qadīmīst approach was defined by *taqlīd* (tradition) going back to the Prophet's Companions and the unquestioning acceptance of the established madhhabs.[50] A special case was the madrasah Rasulīyyah (est. 1884), founded by the aforementioned Bashkir sheikh Zainulla Rasulev in the town of Troisk in the southern Urals, which combined jadīdīst and qadīmīst teaching methods.

Al-uṣūl al-jadīd transcended the educational sphere and turned into a wider Islamic reformist and national phenomenon – a jadīdīsm which reflected the needs and aspirations of the growing Tatar bourgeoisie who sought wider business opportunities and markets in the Muslim-populated parts of the Russian Empire and beyond its frontiers. At the theological level, jadīdīsm was informed by thinking of Jamāl al-Dīn al-Afghānī (1838–1897), Muḥammad 'Abduh (1849–1905), Syed Aḥmad Khān (1817–1898) and other leading Islamic reformers who were reacting to the ambivalent impacts on Muslim societies of modernity emanating from outside. Jadīdīsm's other important sources included works by Tatar intellectuals such as Abū Naṣr al-Qursawī (1776–1812), the aforementioned Khusain Faizkhanov, Shihabuddīn Marjanī (1818–1889) and Abdul Qayum al-Naṣirī (1825–1902) who aspired to Muslim Tatars' comprehensive involvement in the all-Russia modernization process rather than distancing themselves from it. Consequently, Tatar pro-jadīd Islamic scholars[51] rejected Islamic scholasticism and appealed to ijtihād in order to remove dogmatic constraints on the Tatars' ability to fully participate in Russia's economic and political life. In particular, they opposed the Sunnī–Shī'ī division as well as madhhab divisions within Sunnī Islam, and advocated the adjustment of *namāz* (prayer), zakāt and other basics of Muslim-ness to Russia's geographic, cultural and political realities.

Of particular significance was the political dimension of jadīdīsm, which provided an ideological framework for the formation of a modern Muslim Tataro-Turkic nation, or *millet*, on the basis of common language, action and thought (*dilde, iste, fikirde birlik*). Ismaīl Gaspiralī even opposed the ethnonym 'Tatar' and advocated its replacement with 'Turk'. Through his newspaper, *Tercuman* (Translator),[52] he promoted Turkī – a simplified version of Ottoman Turkish – as the single language for Tatars and other Turkic-speaking peoples of Eurasia. It is significant that the majority of Tatar and others of Russia's Turkists differed from their counterparts in Turkey in advocating Turkic union within the boundaries of the Russian state rather than of Ottoman Turkey.[53] The Jadīds' emphasis on ethnonational rather than Islamic unity put them on a collision course with Islamic traditionalists or qadīmīsts, who associated Tatar-ness with rigid and ritualistic Tatar Islamic traditionalism. The ensuing jadīd–qadīmist opposition had major implications for Islam and the nature and authority of Islamic leadership among Tatars, Bashkirs and some other Turkic peoples. This debate would reignite yet again during the post-communist 'Islamic revival'.

Conclusion

Muslim Tatars played a defining role in the evolution of Islamic authority and leadership, as well as in the shaping of state–Muslim relations, across Eurasia. This was largely due to their lengthy historical engagement with Russians going back to their pagan past. Subsequently, over two centuries of Tatar and Russian coexistence within the Islamized Golden Horde enhanced their economic, political and cultural entanglement despite official adherence, from the tenth century, to different religions – Islam and Orthodox Christianity. Following the Russian conquest of Kazan in 1552, the Russian Orthodox state unleashed a massive assault on the Tatar Muslim clergy and Genghizid ruling elite which resulted in the near destruction of Tatar Islamic scholarship and the ruralization and ritualization of Islam among Tatars and Bashkirs. In the late eighteenth century, the legalization of Islam by Catherine the Great laid foundations for the emergence of so-called 'Russian Islam' embodied in the state-controlled muftīate headed by

Figure 2.1 Suyumbike Tower (Khān mosque), Kazan, Tatarstan.

Tatar muftīs. Unlike Bulgar and Kazan 'ulamā', the majority of these muftīs and other muftīate's clergy lacked structured Islamic education and proficiency in Islamic scholarship. Their key role was to ensure the political loyalty to St. Petersburg of its Muslim subjects. Until the middle of the nineteenth century Tatar Muslim clergy were involved in the re-Islamization, along the lines of 'Russian Islam', of 'unruly' Kazakhs and other steppe nomads. At the theological level, many of them adhered to scholastic Islamic traditionalism and rejected Tatar Islamic reformism – jadīdīsm. Meanwhile, the muftīs' dependence on the Russian state was a factor in strengthening the authority among Tatars of jadīds, on the one hand, and unofficial Tatar Islamic leaders represented by Ṣūfī sheikhs, folk mullahs and abystais, on the other. Subsequently, under Soviet rule, Tatar-dominated 'Russian Islam' would evolve into 'Soviet Islam', associated with four regional pro-government muftīates. It is not for nothing that 30 years after the end of the USSR the muftīate model continues to define state–Muslim relations across most of post-Soviet Eurasia.

Chapter Three

ISLAM AND ISLAMIC LEADERSHIP IN THE CAUCASUS

Introduction

Historically, the evolution of Islam in the Caucasus has been shaped by the region's mountainous landscape, its strategic location between Europe and Asia and its extreme ethnolinguistic and confessional diversity.[1] The magnificent Greater Caucasus mountains divided the region's multi-ethnic inhabitants into the plain dwellers and highlanders with their distinctive ways of life and social and political organizations. The Caucasus' frontier position accounted for its cultural diversity and its numerous polities' varying and conflicting external orientations. The region experienced either a complete or partial domination by major Middle Eastern and Eurasian empires, including the Sasanian Empire, the Khazar Khaganate, Byzantium, the Arab Caliphate, the Seljūq Empire, the Genghizid Empire, the Ottoman Empire, the Safawid Empire and the Russian Empire. On the whole, external political and cultural influences were more powerful on the plains, which hosted a succession of externally dominated khānates, emīrates, kingdoms and other principalities. By comparison, in the mountains various tribal, neighbourhood and religious communities managed to retain a substantial detachment from both external and regional political centres and largely preserved their social order based on *'adats* (customary norms).

The Caucasus's strategic location was also a factor in its early encounter with Islam, which was brought to the region by Prophet Muḥammad's Companions – Ṣaḥābah – and their followers. Unlike the Volga-Urals, the Caucasus was included in both the Umayyad and Abbasid Caliphates and experienced an influx of Arab and Arabized Muslims from Greater Syria, which contributed to a considerable Arabization of the north-eastern Caucasus, the prevalence there of Shāfi'ī madhhab and the persistence of Arabic-language proficiency among the region's 'ulamā' and other Muslim clergy. This part of the Caucasus also witnessed the proliferation of Ṣūfism, as well as the development of sharī'ah-'adat legal pluralism. On the other hand, parts of the southern Caucasus, corresponding to modern Georgia and Armenia, withstood the Islamizing pressure and remained within the tenets of Christianity.

We begin with a brief historical account of the Caucasus' Islamization and an examination of the implications for Islamic authority and leadership of the region's initial partial inclusion in the Umayyad and Abbasid Caliphates. We pay special attention to the role of Ṣūfism in shaping Islamic authority in the northern Caucasus. The chapter then discusses the impact of the Seljūqs, Genghizids, Ottomans, Crimeans and Safawids on shaping the Islamic discourse in the north-western and southern Caucasus. The next section examines the correlation of ʻadat and sharīʻah legal norms and its impact on the Islamic leadership in the northern Caucasus. The final section addresses the evolution of the Caucasus War (1817–64) into a *ghazawāt* (holy war) of Dagestanis, Chechens and other Muslims against the advance in the region of Orthodox Christian Russia. It pays special attention to the role of the Naqshbandī ṭarīqah in this war and the establishment on the territory of present-day mountainous Dagestan and Chechnya of a sharīʻah-based imāmate.

Geography, Stages and Forms of Islamization

The Caucasus within the Arab Caliphate

As we saw in Chapter 1, Islam was brought to the Caucasus in the seventh century CE by Muslim Arabs in the context of their confrontation with Sasanian Iran, Byzantium and the Khazar Khaganate, or their proxies. In 636 CE the Arabs defeated the Sasanians in battle at Al-Qādisīyah (in present-day Iraq) and continued their advance northwards. In 643/44 CE Arab troops under the command of Salmān ibn Rabīʻah al-Bāhilī and Ḥabīb ibn Muslim took Darband (Derbent) in southern Dagestan, and then, in 645 CE, Bardhʻa/Partaw (in present-day Azerbaijan) and Tiflis/Tbilisi (in present-day Georgia). By 651, the Arabs had conquered most of the territory of the present-day Republic of Azerbaijan.[2] In parallel, they expanded into Central Asia where they conquered Khorāsān in 644 and Merv in 655.[3] The Arabs named Darband *Bāb al-Abwāb* (Gate of all Gates), referring to its position as the gateway to their northern territories. Bardhʻa became the Arabs' base of military operations against the Khazars.[4] In 685/86 the Umayyads turned Bāb al-Abwāb and adjacent areas into the Caliphate's *wilāyah* (province) under the rule of Mughīrah ibn Shuʻbah al-Thaqafī, Prophet Muḥammad's Companion.[5] In 705, the Arabs together with some Arabized Muslims finally defeated Caucasian Albania, which was turned into a caliphal province of Arrān. In 733, in Darband, they opened the first large mosque. In 736, Umayyad caliphal emissaries established the Emīrate of Tiflis (736–1122) in the east of present-day Georgia (Jurzān, in Arabic sources).[6] At that stage the Arab conquerors were primarily concerned with the imposing of their political control over the Caucasus and the obtaining of taxes from its population rather than with the latter's full-fledged Islamization. Therefore the conversion to Islam, which occurred both by force and peacefully, did not bear a comprehensive character. The region's first Muslims were predominantly merchants, craftsmen and other urbanites. In southern Azerbaijan new converts to Islam were granted the inferior status of *mawālī* (clients) while those who retained their Zoroastrian, Christian and Judaist beliefs were permitted to do so on condition of paying an individual tax.[7]

The Abbasids consolidated their positions in the Caucasus by dividing it into the three caliphal wilāyahs of Arrān, Armінīyyah and Azerbaijan, the borders of which were unstable. Arrān roughly corresponded to southern Dagestan and the northern part of the Republic of Azerbaijan, Arminīyyah to the present-day Republic of Armenia and parts of eastern Turkey, and Azerbaijan[8] to the present-day homonymous province in north-western Iran.[9] In southern Dagestan the Arab and Arabized Muslim commanders built a chain of fortresses, from which they conducted raids on nearby lands and imposed Islam on the local population. They also promoted Arab settlements and forged alliances with some local dignitaries and chieftains. According to Balādhurī (d. 892),[10] during the Abbasid period over 24,000 Arabs from Greater Syria settled in southern Dagestan. This resulted in the area's substantial ethnic, linguistic and cultural Arabization. Arrān was subjected to the caliphal tax system consisting of *'ushr* (tithe) and *zakāh* (alms) for its Muslim population, and *jizyah* (individual tax) and *kharāj* (land tax) for non-Muslims.[11] This system was retained in southern Dagestan under local Arabized Muslim dynasties which from the late ninth century became de facto independent from Baghdad.

Of special significance was the introduction in Dagestan (and subsequently in Chechnya and Ingushetia) of the stricter Shāfi'ī madhhab dominant in eastern Egypt, Jordan and Palestine, as well as Dagestan's transformation into the Caliphate's northern centre of Islam and Arabic-language Islamic scholarship. As shown in Chapter 1, Dagestani 'ulamā' were directly involved in the codification of madhhabs and in the theological debate on the limits of ijtihād and its applicability after the perceived 'closure of the gate of ijtihād' in the eleventh century. Among renowned *muḥaddiths* (scholars of Ḥadīth) was Yūsuf ibn Ḥusain al-Lakzī (d. c. 1089),[12] a native of Darband. Dagestan's 'ulamā' were particularly influenced by the Ḥadīth collections 'Maṣābīh al-Sunnah' and 'Al-Arba'īn al-Nawawīyah' by the Middle Eastern Islamic scholars of Shāfi'ī madhhab al-Baghawī (1041–1122) and al-Nawawī (1234–1277), respectively. Alongside Darband, such Dagestani towns and localities as Akhty, Tsakhur, Kumukh, Akusha, Sogratl', Hunzakh, Enderi, Yarag and Bashly remained recognized sites of Islamic learning until the sixteenth century, while Arabic was a main language of literature and education, as well as a lingua franca up till the nineteenth century. A wide network of madrasahs offered a structured Islamic education in the Qur'ān, *kalām* (Islamic theology) and *fiqh* (Islamic jurisprudence), while mosque maktabs ensured some Islamized literacy at the grassroots level.[13] Dagestan's Arabized Islamic legacy has retained its pertinence throughout history: in the nineteenth century, it manifested itself in the establishment of the sharī'ah-based imāmate, partially modelled on Arab caliphates; in the late twentieth century, it contributed to Dagestan's centrality in the post-Soviet 'Islamic revival', while in the early 2000s it accounted for the comparatively higher proportion of Dagestanis among the region's Salafīs, as well as jihādīs, including those who joined Daesh.

By contrast, historical Azerbaijan, including the southern part of the present-day Republic of Azerbaijan, became the centre of the anti-Abbasid rebellion of *Khorram-Dinan* (lit. 'Those of Joyous Religion') under the leadership of Bābak Khoramdīn (c. 795–838), who advocated the restoration of Iran's political and religious supremacy in the region. The ideology of the Khoramdīn rebellion, which waged in western and central Iran for over 20 years, presented a bizarre mixture of Zoroastrianism with elements of Shī'īsm. In particular, Khorram-Dinan combined their respect for dogs, drinking wine and promiscuity with a belief in the return to earth of prophets and their imāms and in *taqīyyah* (lit. 'prudence', concealing of Islamic faith under persecution), the principle which would ensure the persistence of Shī'ī Islam in Azerbaijan under Soviet atheism. The defeat in 838 of Khorram-Dinan by the Abbasid troops was accompanied by the enforced Islamization of Azerbaijanis along the lines of Sunnī Islam. However, some local dynasties (e.g. Sāllarids) retained their adherence to Shī'īsm till the middle of the tenth century, while a small number of Khorram-Dinan existed till the sixteenth century when they became assimilated into the Shī'ī-Zoroastrian group of *Ahl al-Ḥaqq* (People of the Truth).[14] In the middle of the ninth century Sunnī Islam became the official religion of the Persianate Muslim dynasty of Sharwānshāhs (Shirwan, 861–1538), which ruled over most of Azerbaijan either as a vassal of the Abbasids or other regional powers, or independently. Sharwānshāhs were descendants of the Persianized Arab Shaybāni tribe who deviated from the caliphal structures and governance in favour of the Sasanian model. At the end of the tenth century Sharwānshāhs adopted the Sasanian names Anūshirwān and Qubāth.[15]

Stages of Islamization

The process of Islamization of the various peoples of the Caucasus lasted about nine centuries.[16] It had different agencies and trajectories in the north-eastern, north-western and southern Caucasus – differences that had implications for Islamic authority and leadership across the region. As noted above, the first Muslims were inhabitants and Arab settlers of the caliphal provinces of Arrān and Azerbaijan. Among the early indigenous converts to Islam were many Lezgins, Tabasarans, Rutuls, Tsakhurs and Caucasian Albanians of southern Dagestan and present-day Azerbaijan. From Arrān Islam spread slowly in northern and western directions. The proliferation of Islam was aggravated by the region's difficult mountainous terrain, the territorial, political and ethnolinguistic fragmentation of its various peoples and the resilience among them of pagan, Zoroastrian, Judaist and Eastern Christian beliefs. In the northern Caucasus a major obstacle to comprehensive Islamization presented itself in the form of 'adats. Nevertheless, the Islamic domain gradually expanded under the influence of Muslim missionaries, merchants and Ṣūfīs. By the twelfth century, many Dagestani Laks (Kazi-Kumukhs) and Aguls had converted to Sunnī Islam of Shāfi'ī madhhab. In the course of the following three centuries Shāfi'ī Sunnīsm became the religion of various peoples of central Dagestan, including the Avars, Archis, Kubachis, Kaitags and Dargins. By the sixteenth century, most of Dagestan's Akhvahs, Bagulals, Bedzhits, Botlikhs, Ginuz, Godobers, Gunzibs, Didoy, Karatins, Tindals, Khvarsh and Chamals had embraced Sunnī Islam of Shāfi'ī madhhab.[17] Finally, between the eighteenth and the end of the nineteenth centuries the Vainakhs (the Chechens and Ingush), some of whom had adopted Sunnī Islam in the second half of the sixteenth century, became fully Islamized along Shāfi'ī lines, a catalyst for their mass conversion being their participation in the anti-Russian ghazawāt.[18]

By comparison, in the north-western Caucasus and some parts of the southern Caucasus Islamization occurred along Sunnī Ḥanafī lines under the influence of Turkic and Turco-Mongol invaders. Thus, Ḥanafī Seljūqs, who controlled part of the Caucasus in the eleventh and twelfth centuries, enhanced the proliferation of Sunnī Islam of Ḥanafī madhhab among various local Turkic peoples. This process received another boost in the thirteenth century when most of the northern Caucasus was included in the Genghizid Golden Horde, which became Islamized from the fourteenth century onwards. During this period most Turkic Nogais and Kumyks adopted Sunnī Islam of the Ḥanafī madhhab. From the sixteenth century, as a result of Ottoman missionary activities and raids by Crimean Tatar ghazīs, the Sunnī Islam of Ḥanafī madhhab spread among both Adyghe (Circassian[19]) and Turkic peoples of the north-western Caucasus. It is worth noting that despite the Adyghe's formal conversion to Islam they retained considerable adherence to paganism. By the early nineteenth century most Karachai-Balkars (a Turkic people) embraced Ḥanafī Islam.[20] The Sunnī orientation of the Muslim Caucasus received a setback in 1538 when Shī'ī Safawid Shāh Tahmasp I (1524–1574) defeated the Sharwānshāhs and imposed Shī'ī Islam of the Twelver school on the majority of their subjects. The forcible Shī'īzation of Azerbaijanis was accompanied by the promotion among them of the Ṣafawī ṭarīqah, the Twelver's fiqh and the establishment of Shī'ī Islamic authorities and structures. At the same time, the Black Sea Batum region (present-day Adjara) came under the control of the Ottomans, who ensured the preservation of Ḥanafī Sunnīsm and channelled the theological, educational and organizational development of the Batumi Muslim clergy along Ottoman lines.[21]

Ṣūfīsm and Ṣūfī Authorities in the Caucasus

Islamization of the north-eastern Caucasus, corresponding to modern Dagestan, Chechnya and Ingushetia, had a strong Ṣūfī dimension. The first Ṣufīs appeared in southern Dagestan between the tenth and eleventh centuries. Darband, in particular, hosted such influential Ṣufī thinkers as Abū al-Ḥasan al-Jurzāni (d. c. 1098) and Abū Bakr Muḥammad al-Darbandī (c. 1058–1145), who followed in the steps of the leading Ṣūfī rationalists, Abū al-Qāsim al-Junayd al-Baghdādī (830–910) and Abū al-Qāsim al-Qushayrī (986–1074). Abū Bakr Muḥammad al-Darbandī authored *Raiḥān al-Ḥaqāiq* (Garden of Truths), a comprehensive encyclopaedia of Ṣūfī terms and ethical principles.[22] In it he outlined the factors behind the Ṣūfī form of Islamization in the Caucasus. Al-Darbandī was acquainted with the greatest Islamic minds, including Abū Ḥamid al-Ghazālī (1058–1111), the author of the magnum opus *Iḥyā' 'ulūm al-dīn* (*The Revival of the Religious Sciences*) which highlighted the ideological dimension of Ṣūfīsm in the Islamic faith. Alongside Ṣūfī scholarship Dagestan and some other parts of the Caucasus witnessed the proliferation of so-called popular Ṣufīsm which defined the Muslim-ness of its adherents. Its spread increased during the region's domination by the Seljūqs and Genghizids who favoured Ṣufī Islam. During this period Ṣūfī ṭarīqahs and *wirds* (ṭarīqah's branches) began to form in the Dagestani highlands. Some of them were linked to relevant ṭarīqahs outside the Caucasus and thus inadvertently acted as agencies of external Islamic and political influence. Until the fifteenth century the most influential among them was the Suhrawardī ṭarīqah, which was backed by the rulers of Iran; from the sixteenth century, the Suhrawardīyyah was superseded by the Naqshbandīyyah,[23] which was backed by the Ottomans.

In Dagestan and Chechnya, the Mujaddidī-Khālidī branch[24] of the Naqshbandīyyah gained particular prominence. It was named after the Ottoman Naqshbandī sheikh, Diyā' al-Dīn Khālid al-Kurdamirī (1779–1827), who deviated from the Ṣūfī triad of sharīʻah-ṭarīqah-haqīqah, which was upheld by his spiritual predecessor, sheikh Aḥmad Sirḥindī al-Farūqī (1564–1624). Instead, Diyā' al-Dīn Khālid prioritized sharīʻah, which he perceived as the Muslims' sole defence against rule by foreign *kāfirs* (infidels). He regarded the Ottoman sulṭān as the guarantor of the ummah's vitality.[25] The reduction of the Naqshbandīyyah-Khālidīyyah to its sharīʻah base, as well as its political engagement with the Sublime Porte, paved the way for the ṭarīqah's further politicization and militarization during the invasion of the Muslim Caucasus by Russia in the late eighteenth century. Among other implications of this process was the transformation of the originally inward-looking Naqshbandīs into militant ghāzīs under the leadership of Ṣūfī sheikhs and murīds, some of whom acted as exclusively religious leaders, while others combined the functions of Islamic, political and military leadership. The former included, for example, Muḥammad-efendī al-Yarāghī (d. 1838), 'Abd al-Raḥmān al-Sughūrī (d. 1882) and Il'as Tsudakharī (d. 1908).[26] Among the latter were the leaders of the anti-Russian ghazawāt Ghāzī Muḥammad (1793–1832), Gamzat-bek (1801–1834) and Shamīl (1797–1871). Still, there was no full agreement among Naqshbandī sheikhs on the permissibility of military jihād against the Russians. For example, sheikhs Jamāl al-Dīn al-Ghumūqī (d. 1866) and Maḥmūd al-Almānī (d. 1877) refused to endorse it on religious grounds.[27] The ghazawāt also split the Vainakhs. While most Chechens, as well as some Ingush *taips* (tribes, in Vainakh languages) supported it, the majority of Ingush taips sided with Russia. The same dynamic would occur a century later, when most Ingush would refuse to join in the 'Chechen jihād' against Russia.[28]

Following St. Petersburg's eventual crushing of the ghazawāt, a large number of Chechen and Dagestani Naqshbandīs conducted hijrah to the Ottoman Empire. The remaining Naqshbandīs either went underground or switched their allegiance to the Qādirī ṭarīqah,[29] the leaders of which, unlike the Naqshbandīyyah-Khālidīyyah, opposed an armed struggle against the Russians and favoured peaceful coexistence with them within the Russian state.[30] The Qādirī wird of sheikh Kunta-hajjee Kishiev (d. 1867) acquired a particular prominence among Chechens and Ingush, his followers becoming known as *dhikrists* (those who conduct dhikr). In the early twentieth century, Dagestan also acquired the Shādhilī ṭarīqah, which was founded by an influential Moroccan Ṣūfī sheikh Abū al-Ḥasan al-Shādhilī (1196–1258). Shādhilīyyah was close to the Naqshbandīyyah in terms of its teaching and practices; in fact, some Dagestani sheikhs taught along both Naqshbandī and Shādhilī lines.[31] Overall, the century-long ghazawāt strengthened the popular, ritualistic dimension of regional Ṣūfīsm when it largely became a person's hereditary characteristic and was reduced to the performance of a particular dhikr and other Ṣufī ritualistic practices. In the northern Caucasus popular Ṣufīsm coexisted with other non-Ṣufī forms of popular Muslim-ness, defined by the Sunnī Islam of Shāfiʻī and Ḥanafī madhhabs. By comparison, theological Ṣūfīsm, which required a lengthy and sophisticated period of initiation, remained the domain of a relatively small number of Dagestani 'ulamā'.[32]

In Azerbaijan, there was some Ṣūfī presence in the Shirwan and Nakhchivan areas. Among the Sunnī Muslims of notable prominence was the Yasawī ṭarīqah,[33] which was established during the Seljūq domination of the region. It was followed by the tarīqahs of Khalwatīyyah and Bairāmīyyah, which were close to the Yasawīyyah in terms of their teaching and dhikr. In the sixteenth century there appeared in northern Azerbaijan the Naqshbandīs and Qādirīs, while in the south, among the Shī'a, Kubrawīs.[34] However, the Sunni–Shī'ī divide there was often ambiguous due to the aforementioned Shī'ī practice of *taqīyyah*. By contrast, Ṣūfī Islam did not take root among various Adyghe (Circassian) peoples of the north-western Caucasus whose Islamized belief system retained a strong pagan component.

Social, Political and Legal Role of 'Adats

Among the reasons for the particular prominence of popular Ṣūfism in the north-eastern Caucasus was the strength there of 'adats, which had long predated the arrival of Islam in the region. Unlike 'normative' Islam, Ṣūfism's greater doctrinal and practical elasticity and fluidity allowed for the coexistence or even merger of Islamic and 'adat norms and practices resulting in the emergence of a distinctive 'regional Islam'. 'Adats represented people's key survival mechanisms in the region's precarious mountainous conditions. They ensured order, peace and social justice in the absence, or at least weakness, of state-endorsed legal norms and institutions. 'Adats acted as social and moral regulators and were compulsory for all community members irrespective of their religion. At the same time they were specific to different ethno-territorial communities and thus accounted for the considerable fragmentation and syncretism of social and legal norms in the region. To live according to 'adats meant to be part of the community and to live by a shared understanding of justice. Historically, 'adats developed out of agreements between peoples, clans and neighbourhoods which with the passing of time turned into codified precedents of 'proper' behaviour in peace and wartime, modes of reconciliation and mediation, and prohibitions and punishments. 'Adats were not static and continued to evolve in response to the changing religious, political and socio-economic environment. Unlike more generic sharī'ah norms, 'adat norms were restricted to a particular community and were invalid outside of it. Initially 'adats were transmitted verbally, and every community member had to know them by heart. In the eleventh century some Dagestani communities began to record their 'adats; and by the sixteenth century most mountainous communities had their 'adats recorded.

'Adats cemented a person's indivisibility from his or her particular community. In Dagestan, the dominant form of communal organization was the patrilineal *tukhum* ('seed', in Turkic languages). Several tukhums made a larger neighbourhood community – a *jamā'ah* ('community', in Arabic), or a so-called 'free society', which functioned as a semi-autonomous economic and sociopolitical entity.[35] Among Chechens, the basic community unit was the taip, which was formed either along kinship or neighbourhood lines. Several taips united into large territorial communities – tukhums.[36] From medieval times such communities coexisted with socially stratified polities, such as the Avar Nutsiyat, the Kaitag Usmiyat, the Tarki Shamkhalat in Dagestan, or Alania, Kabarda and Digoria in the north-western Caucasus. In these polities 'adat norms were socially differentiated. Jamā'ahs and neighbourhood communities were headed by democratically elected foremen aided by several assistants; smaller communities had one foreman, while larger ones might have had over 10. Legal authority in communities resided with 'adat courts consisting of elders, and, in cases of arbitration, of elders and a judge.[37] Women were not involved in the court decision-making, although they had the right to propose a court case.[38] From the eighteenth century in Kabarda and some other polities there were separate 'adat courts for the nobility and ordinary people.[39]

Following the region's Islamization some 'adats became Islamized, while some sharī'ah prescriptions turned into 'adats.[40] The correlation between 'adat and sharī'ah norms varied substantially in different historical periods and between different communities. 'Adats often prevailed in dealings with various forms of violence, especially blood revenge (*kanly*), 'blood price' (*diiat*, or *alym*), military raids and responses to them, as well as ownership rights, and inter-family and inter-communal relations. On the other hand, sharī'ah tended to regulate life-cycle practices such as marriage, circumcision and burial, as well as inheritance matters. However, there were no fixed boundaries between the spheres of 'adats and sharī'ah, and in some cases they were used interchangeably or simultaneously. There also emerged 'adats which recognized the supreme military authority of the qāḍī during a time of war and enforced the observance of some Islamic norms and practices, such as Islamic prayer, fasting during the holy month of Ramaḍān and payment of zakāh.[41]

During the Genghizid rule, some local 'adats, especially among the region's various Turkic peoples, were significantly affected by Genghizid customary law – the Great *Yasa* – which was prevalent across the Dasht-i-Qipchaq. The introduction of the Genghizid Yasa also enhanced the distinctive northern Caucasian Golden Horde ethnopolitical entity, whose members shared a wider Eurasian 'state' affinity and mentality.[42] Following the official Islamization of the Golden Horde in the early fourteenth century those norms of the Great Yasa which were related to crime were largely superseded by sharī'ah. On balance, the strength of 'adats defined the level of legal sharī'atization among the region's various communities and polities. Thus, 'adats were historically stronger among the mountain Dagestanis, Vainakhs, Alans (Ossetians) and other highlanders, as well as the descendants of highlanders – for example, the Kabardians, Cherkess, and Karachai-Balkars – who in the eighteenth and nineteenth centuries had been forcibly resettled on the plains.[43] During the eighteenth and nineteenth centuries, positions of the sharī'ah strengthened among Dagestani and Chechen participants of the ghazawāt.

Islamic and Political Leadership during the Ghazawāt

As noted above, during the anti-Russian ghazawāt, the relationship between 'adats and sharī'ah acquired a political dimension. Among the ghazawāt's charismatic leaders were the Chechen sheikh Manṣūr (1760–1794) and aforementioned Dagestani imāms Ghazī Muḥammad, Gamzat-bek, and Shamīl. Under their guidance, the Naqshbandīyyah morphed into *murīdism* (lit. 'related to Ṣūfī disciples'), a militant Ṣūfīsm-related movement where the function of the *murshid* (Ṣūfī master) was transformed into that of the *nāib* (lit. 'deputy', a military commander). In 1828, murīdism culminated in the establishment of an Islamic state, an imāmate (1828–59), on the territory of present-day Dagestan and Chechnya. The organization and functioning of the imāmate followed Ṣūfī, Salafī, as well as non-Islamic ideational and political models. For example, imām Shamīl employed the traditional Ṣufī practice of dispatching his deputies into various communities in order to bring the remote areas of Dagestan and Chechnya under his control. These deputies were charged with recruiting new ghāzīs into the imām's army on the one hand, and enforcing the legal supremacy of sharī'ah within the imāmate's borders on the other. In parallel, imām Shamīl, who aspired to both religious and political leadership, drew on the centralizing policies of the Ottoman and Russian rulers. At the head of the Islamic state was the imām, who combined religious, political and military authority and who executed his political authority through an elaborate system of nāibs who governed the imāmate's provinces – wilāyahs. Although many nāibs were from the traditional ruling houses they owed their appointment to their loyalty to the imām and to their personal merits rather than to their noble origin. Their power therefore ceased to be interpreted in traditional terms and derived from their association with the imām. The legal authority in wilāyahs rested nominally with a muftī who relied on locally elected qāḍīs. However, a muftī's actual power was limited as he had to report to the imām.[44]

The imāmate's economic system was modelled on the Medina-based caliphate. The main part of the treasury's income derived from one-fifth of the booty (*khums*) while four-fifths were divided among the raiders. In accordance with sharī'ah Shamīl established 'pensions' for Dagestani sayyīds and set up special funds for supporting orphans, the disabled and the poor, for rewarding outstanding bravery, and for construction and repair of roads, bridges and fortifications. Shamīl also introduced the traditional Muslim taxes – kharāj and zakāh. In order to top up the treasury's coffers he introduced a new system of fines for stealing, avoidance of conscription and other offences. The fertile plains of low land Chechnya were turned into the imāmate's property, cultivated by a newly formed class of state peasants. The imāmate's army consisted of the imām's privileged cavalry guards – *murtaziqah* (mercenaries) – ordinary cavalry, infantry and artillery regiments. Murtaziqah, who were recruited by Shamīl and his nāibs from among the best horsemen, received a fixed income from the treasury; the rest of the troops had to be armed and maintained by their families.[45]

The ideological underpinnings of imām Shamīl's state-building project were the imāmate's sharī'atization and Arabization, which involved an attack on community elders and some independent local Ṣūfīs who he suspected of potential disloyalty and who he regarded as a major obstacle to centralized resistance to the Russians. In 1834, inspired by the thinking of the late seventeenth century Dagestani puritanist 'ālim Muḥammad ibn Musa al-Kudukī, Shamīl introduced sharī'ah as the single legal foundation of the imāmate and unleashed a campaign against 'adats, which were deemed to be *shirk* (polytheism). Arabic was made the official language of the imāmate.[46] At the centre of the anti-'adat campaign were imām Shamīl's special edicts – *niẓām*s – which were declared to be the sole civil, criminal and religious rulings. Niẓāms especially targeted such 'adat-based customs as kanly and *kalym* (the bride price) and obliged local qāḍīs and mullahs to rely exclusively upon sharī'ah in ownership-related and other disputes. A particular group of niẓāms was aimed at promoting what was perceived to be the true Muslim way of life. The imāmate's residents were obliged to observe Ramaḍān, women were forced to cover their heads and faces and to dress modestly, while music and dancing were prohibited. In some areas, however, Shamīl had to accept the power of ʻadats. In particular, he employed the ʻadat-endorsed practice of burning villages and seizing the horses and cattle of his opponents whom he framed as kāfirs.[47] He also did not enforce the amputation of limbs for repeated thefts, as prescribed by the sharīʻah.[48] But in 1859 imām Shamīl surrendered to the Russians, the imāmate was dissolved and its territory, as well as adjacent areas in the northern Caucasus, was annexed to the Russian Empire. These were put under the mixed Russian-local administration – the 'military-popular governance' (*voenno-narodnoe upravlenie*) – which drew on traditions of ʻadat-sharīʻah legal pluralism. However, in some other areas of the northern Caucasus the Tsarist authorities promoted Orthodox Christianity in order to strengthen their control over the locals. This policy brought some results in Ossetia where a significant part of the population adopted Christianity.[49]

Conclusion

The Caucasus' geographical and ethnocultural characteristics defined the specifics of its Islamization and the nature and forms of Islamic authority and leadership in the region. The Islamization of Bāb al-Abwāb (southern Dagestan and northern Azerbaijan) by the Prophet Muḥammad's Companions or their immediate successors in the seventh and eighth centuries CE, and these regions' inclusion within the Arab caliphates, accounted for their strong Arabo-Muslim scholarly tradition, the proliferation there of a stricter Shāfiʻī madhhab of Sunnī Islam, and the partial ethnic Arabization of its indigenous population. A corollary was the direct participation of local ʻulamā' in the compilation of ḥadīths, the formulation of *ʻaqīdah* (Islamic creed), fiqh and kalām. Meanwhile, the Islamization of the highlands of central Dagestan and some other mountainous areas, which were similarly populated by various indigenous Caucasian peoples, was influenced by the prevalence there of semi-autonomous tribe- and neighbourhood-based communities (jamāʻahs and tukhums) regulated by local ʻadats. The lengthy interaction between Islam and ʻadats in the region accounted for the emergence of a distinctly Caucasian legal, religious and political dualism. Among its key features were the high authority of communal elders, who were either on a par with or even superior to imāms and other representatives of the Muslim clergy. In the case of the Tarki Shamkhalat, the Sharwānshāhs and other polities, which emerged in the plains, the ultimate authority rested with shāhs, shamkhals and other temporal rulers while Islamic authorities were restricted to the legal and religious spheres.

From the eleventh century, the Caucasus's invasion and domination by a sequence of Turkic and Turco-Mongol empires contributed to the Turkicization of its plains and, subsequently, the proliferation in the region of Sunnī Ḥanafī Islam and popular Ṣūfīsm. Between the sixteenth and eighteenth centuries the Islamic dynamic in the Caucasus was affected by its contestation by the Ottoman Empire (together with the Crimean Khānate) and Safawid Iran. A corollary was the influx in the north-western Caucasus of the Ottoman Islamic proselytizers and merchants and the development there of the Ottoman Muslim infrastructure. On the other hand, the establishment of Safawid rule over the present-day Republic of Azerbaijan led to the Shīʿīzation of a large part of its population, the formation of Shīʿī Islamic authorities and the wide spread of taqīyyah as the Shīʿa's survival mechanism in a politically and religiously hostile environment.

From the late eighteenth century, the advance of Orthodox Christian Russia into the Muslim Caucasus provoked different reactions among its established polities and semi-autonomous tribal and neighbourhood communities. While the former largely accepted Russian suzerainty without much fighting, the latter united in fierce resistance leading to the devastating century-long Caucasus War. In the north-western Caucasus, the Russian expansion caused an exodus of between a half million and a million Circassians to the Ottoman Empire. They became known as *muhājirs* (emigrants).[50] Their ancestral lands became populated by Cossacks.[51] In the north-eastern Caucasus, the war evolved into an anti-Russian Islamized ghazawāt and enhanced the proliferation of Islam among the Chechens, Ingush and some Adyghe and Turkic peoples of the Caucasus. It also played an important role in the politicization of Naqshbandī Ṣūfīsm and its mutation into militant murīdism, leading to the establishment of the sharīʿah-based imāmate on the territory of Dagestan and Chechnya. In the late nineteenth century, Russia's defeat of the ghazawāt pushed many of surviving ghāzīs to the Ottoman Empire. Over a century later some of their descendants would return to the Caucasus to fight a new jihād against Russia in the course of the successive Russo-Chechen wars of 1994–96 and 1999–2009. On the other hand, the incorporation of the northern Caucasus into the Russian state was accompanied by the convergence of the region's sharīʿah-ʿadat dualism with Russian civic and criminal legal norms embodied in 'military-popular governance'. The outcome of this development was the emergence of the distinctive regional legal, political and religious order which has de facto preserved some of its main features until the present.

Chapter Four

ISLAM, ISLAMIC AUTHORITY AND LEADERSHIP IN CENTRAL ASIA

Introduction

The specifics of Islam and Islamic authority and leadership in Central Asia have been shaped by the region's ancient civilizational core, the early arrival of Islam to the Ferghana valley (Transoxiana) situated between the Amu Darya (Oxus) and Syr Darya (Jaxartes) Rivers, and its sedentary-nomadic dualism. Long before the birth of Islam, the wider Central Asian region, centred on the Ferghana valley and historical Khorāsān – the territory of which encompassed today's north-eastern Iran and Afghanistan – harboured a developed Iranian sedentary civilization dating from the third millennium BCE. The bulk of its Persian-speaking urban and agrarian inhabitants were either direct descendants of or borrowers from materially, culturally and spiritually sophisticated Persian empires, including the Achaemenid Empire (550 BCE–330 BCE), the Parthian Empire (247 BCE–224 CE) and the Sasanian Empire (224 CE–651 CE). In the seventh century their main civilizational successors were Sogdia (Sogdiana) and Khwārazm (Khoresm), which territorially corresponded to most of present-day Uzbekistan, Tajikistan and Turkmenistan. For many centuries they played a central role in the lucrative Silk Road trade between China, Iran, India, the Hellenized Middle East and Europe. Among the enduring reminders of the region's Iranian cultural matrix are, for example, its Iranian-speaking Tajiks and Badakhshanis, as well as the widespread celebration of the ancient Iranian spring holiday of Nowruz.

As in southern Dagestan and northern Azerbaijan, Islam was introduced to Ferghana valley by Prophet Muḥammad's Companions in the middle of the seventh century. As discussed in Chapter 1, Arabs successively included the Ferghana valley, which they referred to as Mawarannahr, into the Umayyad and Abbasid Caliphates. Throughout history, the introduction of Islam in the region by members of the first Muslim generation has been of great importance to Central Asia's official and popular Islamic leadership and authorities, especially to the Ṣūfī sheikhs who have continued to claim their legitimacy from their perceived descent from the Prophet, his Companions (Ṣaḥābah) or Four Righteous Caliphs (Rāshidūn). However, despite the Arabo-Islamic lineage of some Central Asian Muslim 'ulamā' and Ṣūfī sheikhs the region's Islamization occurred along Persian-Islamic, rather than Arabo-Islamic lines. In this respect, the situation was different from southern Dagestan where initial Islamization followed Arabo-Islamic patterns. Among the initial promoters of Persianized Islamic legal and cultural influences were eastern Iranian-speaking Sogdians and western Iranian-speaking Sāmānids.[1]

Subsequently, the influx into the region of Turkic and Turco-Mongol nomads, who originally adhered to shamanist and other non-monotheistic beliefs and customary norms, channelled their Islamization along syncretic lines with a strong Ṣūfī component. Importantly, it accounted for the persistent supremacy of tribal political leadership over Islamic authorities across Central Asia.

The conquest of Central Asia by the Orthodox Christian Russian Empire, which occurred at the end of the nineteenth century, triggered significant changes in the position and role of Islam and Islamic authorities/leadership in the region. These changes were more pertinent in the areas under St. Petersburg's direct control – that is, in the Kazakh Steppe and parts of present-day Uzbekistan. By comparison, in Bukhara Emīrate and Khiva Khānate, which retained their statehood albeit under the Russian protectorate, the religious, social and political role of Islam was barely affected. Nevertheless, Russian rule contributed to the limited proliferation among the Central Asian elite of Russian-language European education, on the one hand, and Islamic modernism – *jadīdīsm* – on the other. A corollary was the further divisions and modifications within the Islamic authorities and leadership relating to their differing attitudes to the new non-Islamic suzerain.

The chapter begins with a brief account of the arrival in the region of Islam and its regional and local characteristics. It examines the relationship between Islam and power in the Sāmānid, Qarākhānid, Genghizid and Timūrid periods and pays special attention to the role of Ṣūfī authorities. It then examines the social, political and ideological role of Islam in the Bukhara Emīrate, Khiva Khānate and Kokand Khānate. It proceeds to analyse the specifics of Islamic beliefs and practices among the Kazakhs and other nomads. It is particularly concerned with the relationship between the established Muslim clergy and unofficial *khojah*s (Ṣūfī masters) and tribal elders. The concluding section discusses the implications of Russian rule for the religious and political leadership in Russian Turkestan and the Russian protectorates – the Bukhara Emīrate and Khiva Khānate.

Arrival of Islam and the Specifics of Islamization

Central Asia within the Arab Caliphate

The Muslim Arab advance in the region was part of the broader confrontation between the Islamic Arab Caliphate and largely Zoroastrian Sasanian Iran. In 651, Muslim Arabs conquered Merv (in present-day Turkmenistan), which administratively belonged to the Sasanian province of Khorāsān,[2] and advanced towards the Ferghana valley. However, it took them several decades to overcome the resistance of Khwārazmians and Sogdians and to establish their control over the valley. In the early eighth century a 50,000-strong Arab army under the leadership of Qutaybah ibn Muslim (d. 715) crossed the Amu Darya and conquered Sogdia, including its main cities of Bukhara and Samarqand; Khwārazm, with its capital city of Khiva; as well as the Uyghur-populated part of Xinjiang and the oasis city of Kashgar (Kashi). The conquered areas were made into the Mawarannahr province of the Umayyad Caliphate. However, unlike the Bāb al-Abwāb in the Caucasus, which became effectively the Umayyad Caliphate's province, the wilāyah of Mawarannahr initially preserved its semi-independence from Damascus.

It was only in the aftermath of the Battle of Talas,[3] which took place in 751 between the Abbasids and Tang China on the territory of modern Kyrgyzstan, that caliphal rule was fully recognized by the Central Asian rulers. Sogdia was politically and culturally absorbed within the Abbasid Caliphate's eastern Iranian province; consequently Sogdians and most of the other eastern Iranian speakers converted to Sunnī Islam and underwent linguistic Persianization – that is, switching to Farsi (a western Iranian language and the official language in modern Iran). The period witnessed the emergence of a distinctive Central Asian Ṣūfīsm, an early representative of which was sheikh Abū Khoshīm Qūfī (d. 767).[4] Among Pamiris who inhabited the present-day Badakhshan region of Tajikistan the eastern Iranian language was preserved. It should also be noted that the Pamiris' Islamization occurred several centuries later and along the lines of Shī'ī Isma'īlīsm emanating from the Fāṭimid Caliphate. A major role in the introduction of Isma'īlism among the Pamiris is attributed to Nāṣir Khusraw Qubādiyānī Balkhī (1004–1088),[5] a native of the village of Qabodiyon in present-day Tajikistan and the author of the legendary *Safarnāma* (*A Book of Travel*).

The Sāmānids

In the ninth century in Mawarannahr the new Sunnī ruling dynasty of Sāmānids (819–999) emerged, succeeding the Persianate Sogdians who dominated the region between 1000 BCE and the ninth century CE. The founder of the dynasty was Salman Khuda, a Persian noble of Sasanian lineage. The Sāmānids, although formally under Abbasid suzerainty, soon acquired considerable autonomy from Baghdad and became one of the main polities of the Islamic Golden Age. At the peak of their territorial expansion the Sāmānids controlled most of contemporary Central Asia and northern Afghanistan. The Sāmānids, like their Sogdian ancestors, played a central role in the trans-Eurasian Silk Road trade and similarly prioritized political expediency and cultural syncretism over the personal, dynastic or doctrinal affiliation of members of their entourage, and encouraged the development of the sciences, arts and architecture. Their capital cities of Bukhara and Samarqand epitomized cultural and religious diversity and evolved into renowned centres of Islamic scholarship. During their rule Bukhara and Samarqand and other parts of Central Asia hosted al-Rūdhakī (858–941), Abū Naṣr al-Fārābī (872–950), Ferdowsī (940–1020), al-Bīrūnī (973–1048), Ibn Sīnā (Avicenna, 980–1037) and other luminaries, who greatly contributed to the advance of learning in geography, astronomy, mathematics, physics, medicine, history and literature.

In terms of 'aqīdah, fiqh and kalām the Sāmānid period was associated with Muḥammad ibn Ismā'īl al-Bukhārī (810–869), Abū 'Īsā al-Tirmidhī (824–892) and Abū Manṣūr al-Māturīdī (al-Samarqandī) (853–944). Al-Bukhārī and al-Tirmidhī authored two of the most authentic Ḥadīth collections in Sunnī Islam – *Ṣaḥīḥ al-Bukhārī* and *Jamī' al-Ṣaḥīḥ*, respectively. Al-Māturīidī produced the Arabic-language *Kitāb al-tawḥīd* (*Book of Monotheism*) in which he outlined the doctrinal framework for the flexible Sunni theological school which was subsequently named after him as al-Māturīdīyyah and which became one of the principal theological schools within Sunnī Islam. At its core was the integration of the teaching of Abū Ḥanīfa with some aspects of Mu'tazilism, old Persian dualistic religions and local 'adats. Particularly significant was al-Māturīdī's emphasis on philosophical reasoning rather than fatalism in Islam, and his argument against the eternal nature of the Qur'ān. Subsequently, al-Māturīdīyyah paved the way for the development of Central Asian Persianized Islamic scholarship and culture, characterized by the domination of Ṣūfīsm, scientific advances and a sophisticated musical tradition. Linguistically, the Sāmānids' imprint can be observed in modern Tajiks[6] who, like modern Iranians, speak the western Iranian language. It is symptomatic that the political and intellectual leadership of independent Tajikistan would choose the Sāmānids as the forebears of the Tajik nation.

The Qarākhānids and Qarā Khitais

From the late tenth century the evolution of Islamic authority in Central Asia began to exhibit significant deviations from that in the Arab Caliphate. The key factor for this was a succession of Turco-Mongol nomadic invasions in the region. Among the first of these were Uyghur-speaking Qarākhānids (*Qarākhāniyān*) who defeated the Sāmānīds and proceeded to include former Sāmānid and Khwārazmian lands into the Qarākhānid Khaganate (940–1040) with its centre in Kashgar. In the middle of the eleventh century the Qarākhānid Khaganate split into the Samarqand-centred western Qarakhanid Khaganate and the Taraz-centred eastern Qarākhānids Khaganate whose respective rulers, who were originally Tengrians, converted to Sunnī Islam and largely absorbed the dominant Persianized Islamic culture. Some leading representatives of the post-independence Kazakh political and intellectual elite would regard the adoption of Islam by the Qarākhānids in the tenth century as the starting point of Kazakh Islamization.[7] Like the Sāmānīds, the Qarākhānids patronized the arts, sciences and Islamic scholarship and were known for their confessional tolerance. Under their rule, 'ulamā' enjoyed a high social status and generous endowments were made on madrasahs and hospitals. At the same time, the Qarākhānids strengthened the Turco-Mongol ethnolinguistic and religious elements in Central Asian Islam. Among the implications of this process was the proliferation of vernacular Ṣūfism which was associated with both Persian- and Turkic-speaking sheikhs. Especially influential was the Ṣūfī sheikh and poet Aḥmad Yasawī (1093–1166), a resident of the town of Yasi (present-day Turkistan in southern Kazakhstan), who initiated an oral, rather than book-based, version of Ṣūfīsm, infused with elements of Turco-Mongol shamanism and musical traditions. Yasawī was also the first Ṣūfi sheikh who used Turkī (a local Turkic language) rather than Farsi in his teaching and poetry. It is believed that Aḥmad Yasawī received his *ijāzah* (Ṣūfī permission) from sheikh 'Abd al-Khāliq Gijduvanī (d. 1179) from Bukhara, who followed the teaching of sheikh Yūsuf Ḥamadanī (1062–1141), a native of Merv in present-day Turkmenistan. For many centuries Aḥmad Yasawī has been one of the most venerated Eurasian Ṣūfīs bearing the honorific title of 'khwājah' ('master').[8]

In the twelfth century most of the present-day Kyrgyzstan and adjacent areas were included in the proto-Mongol Qarā Khitai Empire (1124–1218) which originated from northern China.[9] The founder of the dynasty of Qarā Khitais (Black Khitans, also known as the Western Liao) was Yelü Dashi (r. 1124–43). As their capital Qarā Khitais chose the ancient Silk Road city of Balasagun, situated in present-day Kyrgyzstan. It is interesting that the Mongolian- and Sintic-speaking Qarā Khitais were not Muslims as they followed a mixture of Buddhism and their tribal religions, which included sacrifice cults. Also, unlike other Islamized Central Asian rulers who bore the titles of khagan, sulṭān, mālik or shāh the Qarā Khitais employed Chinese imperial titles. At the same time, because of the Qarā Khitais' non-interference in the legal and ritual practices of Central Asian Muslims, the region as a whole remained part of *Dār al-Islām* (Abode of Islam).[10]

Ghaznavids

Another major dynasty which left a significant imprint on the evolution of Central Asia's Islam and especially its Islamic and political leadership was the Ghaznivids (*Ghaznawiyān*) who rose out of the remains of the Abbasid Caliphate. The founder of the dynasty was Sebuktigin (r. 977–97), a Turkic *mamlūk* (military slave).[11] The Ghaznavids reached their peak under sulṭān Maḥmūd (r. 998–1030) when they presided over the vast Ghaznavid Empire (977–1186) which included most of wider Eurasia, encompassing present-day Afghanistan, Pakistan, northern India and what are now Uzbekistan and Turkmenistan. Its capital was the city of Ghazna (Ghazni) in eastern Afghanistan. The Ghaznavids, like the Sāmānīds, were Persianate and similarly encouraged the development of the sciences, astronomy, the arts, literature, as well as Islamic scholarship. Thus, during their rule Ghazna developed into a great regional scientific and literary centre hosting such luminaries of historical narration as Abū al-Qāsim Ferdowsī (c. 935–c. 1019), the creator of the famous epic *Shāh-Nāmeh* (*Book of Kings*) and Abū al-Faḍl Bayhaqī (995–1077), the author of *Tarīkh-e Beyhaqī* (*Bayhaqi's History*). Of special significance was the adoption by the Ghaznavid rulers of the title of sulṭān (lit. 'authority') as a symbol of their political independence from the Abbasid caliph, while delegating Islamic authority to Ṣūfī sheikhs, 'ulamā', qāḍīs and imāms.

The Seljūqs

In 1037 the Ghaznavids were defeated by Oghuz Turks – the Seljūqs (*Āl-e Saljūq*) – who originated from the area around the Aral Sea in Central Asia. The Seljūqs, who were Sunnī Muslims, oversaw an expansive Seljūq Empire (1037–1194) stretching from the Hindu Kush to eastern Anatolia and the Persian Gulf and, at its peak, included Iran, Iraq, Anatolia, Syria, northern Afghanistan, parts of the Caucasus and Central Asia.[12] Like the Ghaznavids, Seljūq rulers embraced Islamo-Persian patterns of government and administration and overall culture. In a similar way, they bore the titles of sulṭān or shāh; from 1055 they also employed the title of mālik (king).[13] The Seljūqs patronized the sciences, arts and Islamic scholarship. Their rule accommodated such luminaries as the mathematician, philosopher and poet Omar Khayyam (1048–1131) and the philosopher and Sūfī thinker Abū Ḥāmid al-Ghazālī (1058–1111), both of whom left a powerful cultural and religious legacy in Central Asia. A special mention should be made of the educational and political role of the Seljūq vizier Niẓām al-Mulk (in office 1064–92), who established a network of Sunnī Islamic schools – *Niẓāmīyyah*s – and in his famous political treatise – *Siyāsat-Nāmah* (*Book of Government*) – outlined the fundamentals of effective government in Muslim society. Under the Seljūqs, New Persian[14] became the language of historical records, while the centre of Arabic-language Islamic scholarship and culture moved from Baghdad to Cairo. Importantly, the Seljūqs heralded the transfer of political domination in the Muslim Middle East from the Arabs and Iranians to the Turks. In parts of Central Asia their reign enhanced the supremacy of Turkic tribal rulers over Islamic authorities and contributed to the linguistic Turkicization along Oghuz lines of modern Turkmen, alongside the Caucasus' Azerbaijanis.

The Role of Genghizids, Timūrids and Shaybānids

The Genghizids

In the thirteenth century Central Asia, along with most of Eurasia, was conquered by the Mongols under the leadership of Genghis Khān (r. 1206–27) who created the largest continental empire (1206–1368), which also included western China, parts of present-day Turkey, Iran, Iraq, western Afghanistan and south-western Pakistan. The empire's military elite consisted of Genghizids – Mongolic-speaking nomadic chieftains, who originated from northern Mongolia, albeit its armies were dominated by Turkic nomads while its government included Persian, Tatar and other urbanites. The Genghizid rulers bore the title of khān. An important principle of Genghizid governance was non-interference in the religious creeds and practices of their ethnically and confessionally diverse subjects. It is significant that the Genghizids who originally adhered to a syncretic belief system safeguarded the privileged positions of religious leaders of different persuasions and exempted them from taxation and public service.

In the early fourteenth century the Genghizid elite converted to Sunnī Islam. Meanwhile, they continued to run their empire as a loose polyethnic and polyconfessional confederation and relied strongly on local elites and functionaries of Iranian, Turkic or Chinese origin. Over time, the Genghizids merged with Central Asia's Iranian and Turkic dignitaries and tribal chieftains and absorbed their Persianized and Turkicized Islamic culture. They tended to keep religion out of politics while recognizing the supremacy of Genghizid genealogical authority over the authority of 'ulamā' and other Muslim clergy. Geopolitically, however, the Genghizids played the crucial role in the demise of the Abbasids and the end of the Islamic Golden Age. As discussed in Chapter 2, following Genghis Khān's death the empire split into four large parts: the Golden Horde (the Greater Horde, 1241–1502), the Ilkhānate (1256–1353), the Chagatai Khānate (1225–1670) and the Yan Khānate (1271–1368). Most of present-day Russia and the North Caucasus were included within the Golden Horde; most of Central Asia in the Chagatai Khānate; and most of the South Caucasus, together with today's Turkmenistan, in the Ilkhānate.

The Timūrids

In the middle of the fourteenth century Genghizid authority in Eurasia began to crumble due to internal squabbles among the elites and external threats in the form of Muscovy in the west and Qipchaqs in the east. Nevertheless, the Genghizid might was revived by Timūr (Tamerlane, 1336–1405), a Chagatai chieftain who succeeded in integrating much of the former Genghizid domain within the Samarqand-centred Timūrid Empire (1370–1507). Samarqand then was transformed into a jewel of Islamic architecture and a world centre for the sciences and arts.[15] Unlike the Genghizids, however, the Timūrids failed to subjugate the Muscovy principality. It is worth noting that Timūr, who lacked a direct blood link to Genghiz Khān and therefore could not bear the title of 'khān', assumed the caliphal title of *Amīr al-Mu'minīn* in order to legitimize his authority.[16] For the same reason, Timūr, who was a follower of the Qubrawī ṭarīqah, brought into his entourage a number of highly respected 'ulamā' and Ṣūfī sheikhs. Like the Sāmānīds, the Timūrids combined their Islamic devotion with a polyconfessional meritocracy and the quest for scientific excellence. They treated religion on a par with natural sciences and philosophy. Thus, amīr Timūr was personally engaged in a debate with Ibn Khaldūn (1332–1406), a prominent North African 'ālim, a follower of the Ash'arī rationalist school and a forebear of modern sociology and political economy.[17] The Timūrid sulṭān Ulugh Beg (1394–1449) was a brilliant mathematician and astronomer and built the famous Samarqand observatory, which continues to fascinate its visitors by its architectural splendour and scientific genius.

During Timūr's reign the ancient city of Bukhara became the birthplace of the Naqshbandīyyah, which would evolve into the global Ṣufī ṭarīqah named after khwājah Bahā' al-Dīn Muḥammad Naqshband al-Bukhārī (1318–1389), a resident of Bukhara, who, like Aḥmad al-Yasawī, belonged to the Ṣūfī line of khwājah Yūsuf Ḥamadanī. Bahā' al-Dīn further developed his teacher's path by drawing on the Central Asian Islamic tradition of flexibility and syncretism, while his Ṣūfī practices were based on dhikr-i khāfi. These principles and practices enabled his murīds to retain their faith in their hearts while participating fully in economic and political life. Under Timūr's successors, the Naqshbandīyyah turned into an influential political and economic force, an important role in this process belonging to khwājah 'Ubaydallah Ahrār (1404–1490), who was close to sulṭāns Abū Sa'id (d. 1469) and Aḥmad (d. 1494).[18] Significantly, the leaders of post-independence Uzbekistan would choose Timūr as their main forefather and leadership role model for Uzbeks.

The Shaybānids

From the late fifteenth century the Timūrids went into decline and could not withstand invasions by various Turkic, Kalmyk and other nomads who brought their empire to the end. Some Timūrids moved to India where they founded the Mughal Empire, while others succumbed to the rule of Qipchaq and other nomadic suzerains. The most powerful among these was Abulkhair (1412–1468), a Genghizid chieftain of the Uzbek[19] tribal confederation which was initially established in the southern Urals and Siberia. Abulkhair claimed his descent from Shaybān, the fifth son of Juchi (1181–1227), the khān of the Golden Horde; in 1426, adopting the Genghizid title of khān, he established his domination over the Ferghana valley. However, in 1456 Abulkhair was defeated by the Mongolian-speaking Kalmyks originating in western Mongolia. This prompted several

Uzbek tribes to abandon him in favour of his Genghizid rivals, Girei Khān (d. 1473) and Janibeg Khān (d. 1480), who controlled most of present-day Kazakhstan. These Uzbek defectors became known as Kazakhs; in post-independence Kazakhstan khāns Girei and Janibeg are regarded as the forefathers of the Kazakh nation.

In the early sixteenth century the Uzbeks under the leadership of Muḥammad Shaybānī, Abulkhayr's grandson, re-established their control over most of the Ferghana valley and eastern Khorāsān where they created the Shaybānid Khānate (later referred to as Bukhara Khānate, 1500–1599) with its capital first in Samarqand and later on in Bukhara. The Shaybānids reached the peak of their territorial expansion during the reign of Abdullah Khān (r. 1583–98) when their state also included Khwārazm, Balkh and the Khānate of Sibir. In terms of the patterns of governance and religious policy the Shaybānids, who adhered to Sunnī Islam of Ḥanafī madhhab, to a considerable extent followed Timūrid patterns, including their patronizing of the arts and poetry in the Turkic language. The Shaybānids encouraged an intra-Islamic theological debate and sponsored Islamic scholarship and education. During their reign Bukhara acquired its famous Mir-i Arab madrasah,[20] which has ever since been a major centre of professional Islamic training in Central Asia and wider Eurasia. However, contrary to the Timūrids, who bore the caliphal title of 'amīr', the Shaybānids reasserted the supremacy of genealogical tribal authority of the khān over that of an Islamic leader, while they relegated 'ulamā' and other Islamic authorities to the domain of Islamic scholarship.

Naqshbandī Dynasties and Mazārs

Under the Shaybānids, the Naqshbandīyyah underwent further institutionalization and politicization. The ruling elite favoured Ahrāris, followers of the aforementioned khwājah 'Ubaydallah Ahrār whose *ziyārat*[21] near Samarqand turned into the Naqshbandīyyah's official centre. As a result, the Ahrāris evolved into a dynasty of politically influential sheikhs, wealthy landowners, merchants and *mutawallīs* (waqf trustees). They were also granted hereditary rights to the title of sheikh-ul-Islam (supreme sheikh) of Samarqand. Among other emerging politically and economically influential Naqshbandī dynasties were those related to khwājah Aḥmad Kasanī (d. 1542) and khwājah Sad (d. 1589), who was a son of the Shaybānid ruler Muḥammad Sulṭān Juybarī (d. 1563). Khwājah Kasanī, who became known as *Makhdūm-i A'zam* (The Great Master),[22] acquired a particularly large following among Uzbeks, Tajiks and Chagataids in Kashgar, while his grave near Samarqand developed into a major ziyārat. Khwājah Sad's followers, who became known as Juybarīs, secured their hereditary control over the position of sheikh-ul-Islam of Bukhara, which they retained till the end of the nineteenth century.[23] Khwājah Sad's tomb in the village of Sumitan on the western outskirts of Bukhara became the Juybarīs' spiritual centre, known as Char Bakr. A special mention should be made of *Aga-i Buzurg* (Great Lady) who became a major Ṣūfī female authority.

Of particular importance was the institutionalization and 'Qipchaqization' of the Naqshbandī ṭarīqah which occurred during that period. Central to this process were the ziyārats related to Ṣūfī sheikhs, ancestors and natural sacralized objects. The main bearers of the regional Ṣūfi Islam were *khojahs* (khwājahs) who embodied vernacular – compared to scripture-based – Islam intertwined with shamanism, ʻadats and tribal norms and customs. It was khojahs, rather than imāms and mosque mullahs, who acted as the principal Islamic authorities and promoters of Islam among the nomads. Khojahs were widely viewed as Prophet Muḥammad's spiritual successors, possessing a special relationship with Allah. It was also believed that their perceived supranatural qualities allowed them to conduct *barakah* (blessing) and to perform miracles and assist those who asked for their help. These beliefs were accompanied by shamanistic rituals which appealed to the feelings and which therefore had a greater impact on people's psyches than the sermons of mosque mullahs. Furthermore, these practices provided believers with a personal esoteric and mystical detachment from a harsh physical and social reality.[24]

The Khānate/Emīrate of Bukhara and the Khānates of Kokand and Khiva

At the end of the sixteenth century the Shaybānid state disintegrated due to internal strife and changing regional and global conditions, such as the rise of Shīʻī Safawids who were succeeded by Afshārids (1736–96),[25] and the discovery of new trade routes between China and Europe which dealt a fatal blow to the Silk Road trade, mediated by Central Asians. Consequently, three major sedentary-nomadic polities became dominant in the region – the khanate/emīrate of Bukhara, and the khānates of Kokand and Khiva, all three of which were ruled by Uzbek dynasties related to the Shaybānids. The closeness of Shīʻī Iran strengthened the Sunnī adherence of Bukharan, Kokandi and Khivan rulers. At the same time the existence in the region of a privileged Muslim group – *awlāt*, *khojah*s, *sayyīd*s, *tura*s, *ishān*s and other perceived descendants of the Righteous Caliph ʻĀlī – ensured the continuing indirect religious influence there of Iran.[26]

Bukhara Khānate/Emīrate

In 1599, Baqī Muḥammad (1579–1605), a chieftain from the Uzbek clan of Janīd (Astrakhan), deposed the last Shaybānid khān, Pir Muḥammad II (r. 1598–99), and asserted himself as the first khān of the new Bukharan dynasty of Janīds (1599–1747). It was the Janīds who in 1602 defeated the Safawid troops in northern Afghanistan and thus prevented the Safawid conquest and Shīʻīzation of Central Asia. Under the Janīds the Bukhara Khānate turned into the largest Central Asian polity, which included territories in modern Tajikistan, most of Uzbekistan, with the cities of Bukhara and Samarqand, and parts of Turkmenistan. It was populated by Farsi- and Uzbek-speaking urban dwellers and peasants, who were referred to as Sarts by nomads, and various Qipchaq-speaking nomads. Among the Janīds' subjects were also some Oghuz-speaking Turkmen and Farsi-speaking Bukharan Jews. From the 1740s the Janīds were significantly weakened as a result of Nādir Shāh's invasion in 1740 of Bukhara. They were superseded by non-Genghizid Manghits, members of the Mangit clan via *ataliq* (the prime minister) Muḥammad Raḥīm (1713–1758). In 1785, the Manghits established a new ruling dynasty which stayed in power till 1920. Manghits, like the Timūrids, compensated for their lack of Genghizid legitimacy by strengthening their Islamic credentials. They similarly adopted the Arabic title of emīr (amīr) and their state became known as the Bukhara Emīrate. They sidelined Genghizid dignitaries and began to rely primarily on Farsi-speaking administrators, military and, in particular, the sheikh-ul-Islam, 'ulamā' and other Muslim clergy. Under their influence the Manghits introduced an Islamic land-ownership and tax system. The Emīrate's land was divided into *amlāk* (state-owned), *mul'k* (private) and waqf, while its Muslim subjects were subjected to *zakāt* and *kharāj*, and non-Muslims to *jizyah*.[27]

The Khānate of Kokand

The Kokand Khānate (1709–1876) was established by the Uzbek dynasty of Ming[28] in the southern part of the Ferghana valley. It was centred on the ancient city of Kokand in the eastern part of modern Uzbekistan. The khānate reached its peak in the early nineteenth century when it encompassed some areas in present-day Uzbekistan, Tajikistan, southern Kazakhstan and Kyrgyzstan, as well as Xinjiang. Under Kokand's control were the cities of Tashkent, Margilan, Namangan, Chimkent and Khujand. The Kokandī ruling elite, who adhered to Ḥanafī Sunnī Islam, was characterized by religious piety and patronized the 'ulamā' and Islamic education. Because many of them were Ṣūfīs the political role of khwājahs was significant. However, from the early nineteenth century the Mings' authority was challenged by Kyrgyz (Qipchaq) nomads who invaded the khānate from the Tian Shan mountains. The influx of Kyrgyz was accompanied by the strengthening of tribal and 'adat-based mechanisms of political legitimization and the weakening of the political role of the 'ulamā' and Muslim clergy. Ultimately, it led to the breakdown of the existing political and military alignments and Kokand's vulnerability to external invasions. In the 1870s the Russian army defeated the Kokandī troops and most of the khānate's territory became absorbed within the newly established Governorate General of Turkestan with its centre in Tashkent.[29]

The Khānate of Khiva (Khwārazm)

The Khānate of Khiva (1511–1920), centred on the city of Khiva, covered the territory of much of present-day Turkmenistan, south-western Kazakhstan and western Uzbekistan. Initially it was ruled by the Uzbek dynasty of Yadigarids, who were sponsored by the Genghizid tribe of Kongrat. In the early nineteenth century, the real power shifted to non-Genghizid Inakids, who originated from Mehmet Emīn, *inak* (prime minister) of Khān Temīr Ghāzī (d. 1763). From 1804 the Inakids had been the de facto rulers until the khānate's dissolution by the Bolsheviks in 1920. The Inakids, similar to Bukhara's Manghits, strongly relied on Farsi- and Turkic-speaking dignitaries and bureaucrats, as well as the 'ulamā' and other Muslim clergy.[30] They appealed to Islam for legitimization purposes and patronized the building of mosques and madrasahs; they also encouraged the construction of irrigation facilities that contributed to the further sedentarization of the Uzbeks.

At the grassroots level, Bukharan, Kokandī and Khivan societies were centred on neighbourhood or kinship communities – *mahallah*s in urban areas and *qishlaq*s in rural parts. The difference between urban and rural settlements was rather blurred since they shared many common characteristics, including border walls, a mosque, a common meeting place and, in some cases, a bazaar. They also enjoyed considerable autonomy from central authorities which were primarily concerned with taxes and military recruitment in times of war. Both urban and rural local communities were headed by an elected leader – *aqsaqal/oqsoqol/arbob* – who was advised by a council of elders and an imām. A community leader was the ultimate authority while an imam led daily prayers and oversaw the residents' major life-cycle events such as circumcisions, marriages and funerals. Imāms also acted as teachers in *maktab*s which were attached to the mosque. They taught the fundamentals of *adab* (rules of a Muslim's behaviour), Arabic and the Qur'ān. The most popular maktab textbooks were the *Chahar Kitāb* (*Four Books*) and the *Haftiak* (*Excerpts from the Qur'ān*), which was used in memorizing basic Islamic expressions in Arabic. Girls received their elementary Islamic education at home from *halfa*s/*otin*s (female mullahs). Particularly large urban communities had their own madrasahs and *qāzī*s (*qāḍī*s) who were bearers of the sharī'ah. The correlation between 'adats and sharī'ah norms in legal procedures varied considerably from one community to another. Generally, albeit not everywhere, customary norms had priority over sharī'ah rulings and such sharī'ah-based punishments as the stoning of adulterers or the chopping off of the hands of thieves were relatively rare. *Khojah*s, *ishān*s, *tura*s, *pīr*s and other Ṣūfī authorities usually possessed higher social and religious status than mosque imāms.[31] However, Bukhara, Khiva and the other main ancient cities of the region hosted numerous 'ulamā', and the Mir-i Arab madrasah was the leading Eurasian centre of Islamic scholarship and education.

Islam and Authority among Nomadic Kazakhs, Kyrgyz and Turkmen

The political, social and economic development of Bukhara, Kokand and Khiva was affected by their relations with nomads. These relations were both symbiotic and conflictual in nature. Of particular influence in the region were the Mongolian-speaking Jungars (Oirats), the Qipchaq-speaking Kazakhs and Kyrgyz, and the Oghuz-speaking Turkmen. The Jungars, who originated from Jungaria in northern Xinjiang, were nominally Buddhists, while the Kazakhs, Kyrgyz and Turkmen formally adhered to Sunnī Islam of the Ḥanafī maddhab. For over a century the Jungars clashed with the Kazakhs over the control of vast territorial expanses stretching from southern Siberia to present-day southern Kazakhstan. This exhausting confrontation was an important factor in the rapprochement of some Kazakh rulers with the Russians.

As discussed in Chapter 2 the Kazakhs were divided into three juzes: the Ulu Juz, the Orta Juz and the Kichi Juz. The Kazakh elite, represented by khāns and *biy*s (tribal chieftains), converted to Sunnī Islam of Ḥanafī madhhab in the fourteenth century, while the Islamization of the rest of the Kazakhs continued till the eighteenth century.[32] However, as noted earlier, the relations of Kazakhs and other nomads with established religions and with Islam in particular were ambivalent as they continued to prioritize genealogical solidarity over the Islamic one. In particular, they embraced vernacular, rather than book-based Ṣūfī Islam of the Naqshbandī and Yasawī ṭarīqahs, which allowed them to integrate in it their tribal and customary beliefs and practices. Consequently, the supreme authority among Kazakhs rested with a khān or biy, while Ṣūfī iterant khojahs (khwājahs) often commanded higher respect than a mosque mullah.

The Kyrgyz were ethnically and linguistically close to the Kazakhs. The southern Kyrgyz, who historically were included in various polities in the Ferghana valley, were more Islamized and adhered to mazār-centred Ṣūfī Islam. However, the northern Kyrgyz, who never succumbed to the Timūrid or Kokandī rule, had greater reliance on shamanism, Zoroastrianism and animism, as well as 'adats. In the case of the nomadic Turkmen, some of whom adopted Islam as early as the seventh century, the Ṣūfī Islamization produced several sacralized tribal formations, or *awlāt,* including the *Ata* (Forefather), the *Mujavur* (Neighbours), the *Magtym* (Master) and the *Pakyr Shikh* (named after Pakyr Shikh). As with other Central Asian nomads, Turkmen opted for the vernacular Ṣūfīsm of Naqshbandī and Yasawī orientation.[33] Nevertheless, the supreme authority was widely retained by tribal leaders of 'normal' Turkmen tribal confederations, the largest of which were the Tekke, Yomud, Ersary, Saryq, Qara Yusuf and Kanjyghaly. Historically, the most powerful were the Tekke and the Yomud: the former dominated the Ahal-Tekke and Merv oasis and the latter prevailed in the areas along the border between modern Iran and Turkmenistan. The Ersary controlled the border region between modern Turkmenistan and Afghanistan; the Saryq, the southernmost part of modern Turkmenistan; the Qara Yusuf, the Caspian Sea zone; and the Kanjyghaly, the areas adjacent to the present-day Kazakh-Turkmen border.

Islam and Islamic Authority under Russian Rule

Muslim Kazakhs and the Russian Empire

Russia's inroads into the traditional habitat of Muslim Kazakhs were preceded by its steady eastwards expansion following Muscovy's defeat of the Muslim Kazan Khānate in 1552. The main drivers of Russia's expansion were the insecurity of its eastern borders due to the absence of any physical geographical barrier between the Russian state and the Kazakh Steppe, and the lengthy history of Turco-Mongol invasions into it from the east. In the course of the sixteenth and seventeenth centuries the Russian state absorbed the Urals and Siberia and began to encroach on the Kazakh Steppe, commonly referred to as the Kirghiz Steppe.[34] In the face of the threat from the Jungars some Kazakh chieftains began to seek Russia's protection. Consequently, in the first part of the eighteenth century the khāns of the Kichi Juz and the Orta Juz accepted the Russian protectorate in exchange for military assistance against the Jungars. At the beginning of the nineteenth century St. Petersburg abolished their khān titles and incorporated the territory of the Kichi Juz[35] and the Orta Juz into the Ural'sk, Turgai and Akmolinsk *oblasts* (regions) of the Russian Empire. In contrast, the Ulu Juz's leaders initially opted for the Chinese protectorate but in the middle of the nineteenth century were forced into accepting Russian suzerainty and the territory of the Ulu Juz became part of the Semipalatinsk oblast' of the Russian Empire. Governors of these Kazakh-dominated regions were answerable to the Russian Ministry of Interior, and Kazakhs were subjected to the all-Russia land, administrative and criminal system which paralleled the existing customary and sharī'ah courts.[36] Of special relevance was Catherine the Great's policy of re-Islamization of 'unruly' Kazakhs along the lines of mosque-based Islam. The main agents of this policy were Volga Tatar imāms and mullahs who were encouraged to proselytize and to settle among nomadic Kazakhs. The Tatars' Islamic proselytism among the Kazakhs was facilitated by their common Qipchaq ethnolinguistic heritage. Consequently, Tatars and, later on, Uzbeks acquired dominance in the Muslim establishment among the Kazakhs. Nevertheless, until the end of the Soviet period it was unofficial khojahs and tribal elders, rather than mosque mullahs and other representatives of the Muslim clergy, who commanded higher authority among most Kazakhs.

Russian Turkestan

In the middle of the nineteenth century St. Petersburg increased its political and military pressure on Kokand, Khiva and Bukhara.[37] Throughout the 1860s Russian troops steadily advanced into the Kokand-controlled territory in present-day northern Kyrgyzstan and imposed their control over the towns of Tokmak and Pishkek (Bishkek). From there they expanded towards the Ulu Juz's zone in present-day southern Kazakhstan and seized the towns of Chimkent (Shymkent) and Aulie (Taraz). In 1865 the Russians gained control over Tashkent which they made the centre of the newly established Turkestani province of the Russian Empire. In 1867 Russian Turkestan was transformed into the Governorate General of Turkestan under the rule of Governor General Konstantin von Kaufman (in office 1867–82). In the following three decades the Russian Governorates of Turkestan, Orenburg, Western Siberia and the Steppe Governorates underwent a series of politico-administrative reorganizations which, among other consequences, created new divisions within previously homogeneous ethno-territorial communities. In 1876 the Kokand Khānate, which since 1868 had been under Russia's suzerainty, was abolished. In the early 1880s the Russians finally overcame the fierce resistance of Tekke and other Turkmen tribes and annexed their territory, thus completing the Russian conquest of Central Asia. The external western borders of Russia's Central Asia were finalized in 1907 when the British accepted Russia's supremacy in present-day Central Asia in exchange for their recognition of Britain's domination in present-day Afghanistan and Kashmir. This geopolitical arrangement put an end to the active phase of the British–Russian rivalry for the control of Asia known as the Great Game.[38]

The incorporation of the Kazakh Steppe, the Kokand Khānate and Turkmen-dominated areas into the Russian Empire inevitably had implications for their inhabitants. The traditional nomadic lifestyle of some Kazakhs was affected by the Russian policy of their sedentarization and the agrarian settlement of Cossacks, Russians and Ukrainians on Kazakh lands. Tashkent and other urban areas witnessed an influx of Russians, Ukrainians and Balts who began to dominate the civil service, transportation, communications and industry. Russian rule was accompanied by the introduction of some colonial practices and civilizational attitudes. Still, in most rural and steppe areas the impact of Russian rule on the daily life of locals was rather marginal and considerably weaker than in Russia's Volga-Urals and southern Caucasus. Importantly, St. Petersburg did not introduce there the muftīate-based system of state–Muslim relations; sharī'ah courts were maintained; the hajj and other Islam-related activities were safeguarded; the Russian Orthodox Church was proscribed from proselytizing in the region; and Central Asian Muslim men were exempted from Russian military service. This meant that the nature of the Islamic authorities and their infrastructure remained largely intact.

Khiva (Khwārazm) and Bukhara under the Russian Protectorate

In 1868 the Russians annexed Samarqand from the Bukhara Emirate and included it within the Turkestan Governorate. However, unlike the Kokand Khānate, St. Petersburg preserved the Bukhara Emīrate and Khiva Khānate on protectorate terms. In 1868 Russian suzerainty was recognized by the Bukhara Emīr Muzaffar al-Dīn (r. 1860–85) and in 1873 by the Khiva Khān Muḥammad Rahīm II (r. 1864–1910). Although the protectorate status imposed constraints on the foreign and military affairs of the Bukharan and Khivan rulers, its effects on the social order and Islamic practices of their subjects were negligible. The majority of the sedentary population continued to live in territorially or kinship-defined communities – mahallahs – which were headed by an elected and highly respected elderly leader – aqsaqal – who was advised by a council of elders and an imām. The aqsaqal and the community council continued to oversee the organization of communal works and events and to solve internal disputes by drawing on local 'adats, '*urf* (tribal customs) and sharī'ah.

Conclusion

Russia's conquest of Central Asia affected both Russia and Central Asia. On the one side, Russia's governance of Central Asia was largely in line with the priorities and practices of the earlier Eurasian empires. Among these were a focus on military and security matters and a minimal interference in the social order, culture and religion of St. Petersburg's Central Asian subjects. For this reason many Central Asian 'ulamā' continued to regard the region as Dār al-Islām. Russia's absorption of over 18 million Central Asian Muslims transformed it into the major Orthodox Christian–Muslim empire, comparable with the Islamized Genghizid empire which for more than two centuries united Orthodox Christian Muscovy, the Muslim Volga-Urals, the Muslim Caucasus and Muslim Central Asia. The imposition of Russian rule was accompanied by the region's partial economic, technological and educational modernization. Consequently, some representatives of Central Asian elites acquired either a pro-jadīd or secular Russian education and initiated the first regional periodicals in the Kazakh, Turkī and Farsi languages as well as the bilingual Russian-native periodicals, such as *Turkestan Wilayatining Gazeti* (Newspaper of Turkestan Province, 1870–1917) and *Dala Wilayatining Gazeti* (Newspaper of the Steppe Province, 1888–1902). The region also witnessed a limited proliferation of jadīdīsm as a wider Islamic reformist sociocultural and political movement. It is significant that while many Kazakh jadīds, including Abubakir Kerderi (1858–1903), Shakarim Kudaiberdi Uli (1858–1931), Aqmolla Muhammadiar Uli (1839–1895) and Mashur Jusup Kopei

(1857–1931), like their Tatar counterparts, perceived the Islamic reform within the wider context of the social and political modernization of the Russian state, Ahmad Makhtum Qalla (Donish, 1826–1897), Mahmud Khoja Behbudi (1874–1919), Munawwar Qari (1878–1931), Abdurauf Fitrat (1886–1938) and other leading Uzbek and Tajik jadīds were more in tune with the Islamic reformist movement in the Middle East and South Asia.

The Russian conquest introduced a physical and ideational barrier between various Muslim peoples of Central Asia and their co-ethnics and co-religionists in Xinjiang, Afghanistan, Iran and Turkey. As a result, the participation of Central Asian 'ulamā' and other representatives of Islamic authority and leadership in the wider Islamic debate became stifled. Russian rule was accompanied by colonization by agrarian settlers, the nomads' sedentarization, the promotion of cotton monoculture and other colonial practices. Of particular significance were the architectural and ethnolinguistic Russification of Tashkent and some other urban centres and the introduction of Russian Orthodox civilizational attitudes towards local Muslims.[39] These attitudes contributed to the emergence among some Central Asian Muslims of pro-Ottoman aspirations and the rise of Islamized anti-Russian resistance, culminating in revolt under the leadership of Naqshbandī sheikh Muhammad Ali Madali (Dukchi Ishān, 1856–1898) in Andijan in May 1898[40] and, later on, the protracted *basmachi*[41] revolt of 1916–34.

Overall, unlike in the Volga-Urals, Russian rule did not significantly alter the existing social order defined by Sūfī-dominated Central Asian Islamic traditionalism, 'adats and the political supremacy of khāns, beys and emīrs over the religious authority of muftīs, qāḍīs and imāms. In this respect, the conquest of Muslim Central Asia by the Christian Orthodox Russian Empire contrasted with the conquest of Muslim Andalusia by Catholic Christian Spanish rulers that led to a complete destruction of Islamic religion and culture in the Iberian Peninsula. In the twentieth century, however, the nature and influence of both the political and religious leadership in Central Asia, and the wider Soviet Eurasia, would undergo a radical transformation in the course of comprehensive Sovietization, which nevertheless would not disrupt Islamic tradition and culture in the region. Part II explores the implications of Soviet rule for religious and national leadership across Muslim Eurasia.

PART II

ISLAMIC AUTHORITY AND LEADERSHIP IN THE USSR

Chapter Five

THE VOLGA-URALS

Introduction

In October 1917, in the course of the October Revolution,[1] the Bolsheviks under the leadership of Vladimir I. Lenin (Ulyanov, 1870–1924) seized power in Petrograd (formerly St. Petersburg) and dissolved the Russian Empire. After five years of the ensuing and devastating Civil War and external intervention they established their control over most of the former imperial lands.[2] The Bolshevik takeover was accompanied by a country-wide structural, political and societal transformation which included state–Muslim relations. Among the key factors which enabled the Bolsheviks to consolidate their power and to create a radically new polity – the USSR (1922–91) – were the Russian Empire's internal political turmoil, aggravated by major human and economic losses during the First World War, and the Bolsheviks' revolutionary socio-economic and national programme. Of particular appeal to an impoverished multi-ethnic population was the Bolsheviks' promise of land, bread, peace and equality, as well as the right to self-determination for Muslim and other non-Russian peoples.

The 1917 October Revolution had been preceded by two bourgeois-democratic revolutions, in 1905–7 and in February 1917, which unleashed mass political activism, including in Muslim-majority parts of the empire. The 1905 October Manifesto issued by Emperor Nicolas II (r. 1894–1917) granted Russia's Muslims the right to participate in the parliamentary process, to form their own political parties and to publish periodicals and books in Arabic, Tatar and other languages of Russia's Muslims. Consequently, in August 1905, Russia's Muslim politicians, businessmen and intellectuals convened the First All-Russia Muslim Congress; and at the Second All-Russia Muslim Congress, which took place in January 1906, the first Islamic political party – *Ittifāq al-Muslimīn* (Union of Muslims, 1906–17) – was established. Ittifāq's members, many of whom were Tatars, formed their faction in the Russian parliament with a sociopolitical programme close to that of the party of Russian liberals, the *Kadet* Party (Constitutional Democratic Party, 1905–17). And during the Third All-Russia Muslim Congress, which convened in August 1906, Azeri and Kazakh political activists established their National Parties – *Musavat* (Equality) and *Alash*, respectively.

For historical reasons Tatars, and to a lesser extent Bashkirs, dominated Muslim politics prior to the October Revolution and for nearly three decades after it. In this chapter we discuss the impact of the 1917 Bolshevik Revolution on both the Tatar and Bashkir intellectual and religious elites and on ordinary people, and their responses to it. It pays special attention to the agendas and politics of Tatar Muslim Communists and Bashkir nationalists. It then proceeds to analyse the implications of the harsh anti-Islamic

Stalinist policies for the Tatar and Bashkir national leadership and Islamic authorities of both jadīdist and qadīmist orientation. The final section examines state–Muslim relations and the role of Soviet muftīs and other 'official' Tatar and Bashkir Muslim clergy in the forging of 'Soviet Islam'.

Tatar and Bashkir Leadership during the Revolutionary Period

The 1905–7 Russian Bourgeois-Democratic Revolution and the First World War

The Russian bourgeois-democratic revolution of 1905–7 prompted religious and national activism by pro-jadīd Tatar and Bashkir leaders who hoped that the revolution would lead to the Russian Empire being reorganized into a constitutional democratic multi-ethnic state. Among them was Musa Bigi (Bigiev, 1875–1949),[3] a Tatar theologian and an Ittifāq member, who was an ardent supporter of the constitutional monarchy, based on proportional representation for all nationalities, and legal, political and social equality for all of Russia's people irrespective of their ethnicity and religion. Ittifāq's other prominent member and a Duma Deputy, Sadri Maksudi Arsal (Maksudov, 1878–1957), who took the floor in the second and third Duma more than a hundred times, promoted the idea of cultural autonomy for all of Russia's Muslims within a democratized and modernized Russian state. Sadri Maksudi's proposals included the right of Muslims to elect themselves their own muftī, rather than him being appointed by the Russian Minister of the Interior; the reinstitution of waqf property; the right of *shakirds* (madrasah students) to defer their military service until graduation; the exemption of mullahs from military service and taxes and their elevation to nobility after 20 years of service; and the recognition of Friday as the official holiday for Muslim civil servants and workers. In 1916, during the deepening crisis related to Russia's defeats at the fronts of the First World War, some left-wing Tatar politicians left the Muslim faction and joined the Duma faction of *trudoviks* (lit. 'labourers'), which campaigned for the free distribution of land and the abolition of all forms of discrimination on national and religious grounds. However, a minority of Tatar leaders saw the Tatars' future outside Russia. For example, Yusuf Akchura (1876–1935), an Ittifāq member, called for the Tatars' political withdrawal from Russia and their participation, alongside the Ottoman Turks and other Turkic peoples, in a pan-Turkist political project.

Outside the Duma, the Tatar leftists were affiliated to the parties of *Iṣlāḥ* (Reform), *Brek* (Union), *Tangchi* (Dawn) and the Party of Young Tatars, all of which were active during the revolution of 1905–7. Members of the Brek and Tangchi were politically close to the Socialist Revolutionary Party (the SR); the Iṣlāḥ united radical shakirds from the Kazan-based madrasah of Muḥamadīyyah, who fought on the revolutionary barricades alongside students from Kazan University. A group of radical Iṣlāḥists under the leadership of Huseyn Yamashev (1882–1912) fully embraced the Bolshevik programme and joined the Russian Social Democratic Labour Party (RSDRP, est. 1898). In Crimea, Abdureshid Mehdi formed the Party of Young Tatars, which campaigned for the abolition of the monarchy, the equal distribution of land among peasants and equal political and social rights for all of Russia's Muslims, as well as a comprehensive switch to al-uṣūl al-jadīd education in Muslim confessional schools. A special mention should be made of Tatar politicians Hanafi Muzaffar and MirsaidSultan-Galiev, who argued in favour of the compatibility of Islam and socialism and provided a socialist interpretation of pan-Islamic solidarity – *Islāmīyyah.*

Among the new generation of Tatar and Bashkir leadership were also educators, publishers and journalists. The 1905–7 revolution gave a boost to the advance of uṣūl al-jadīd in confessional education and to pro-jadīd publishing. Alongside Gaspiralī's *Tercuman*, there emerged *Idil'* (Volga), *Iktisad* (Economics), *Kazan Mukhbire* (Kazan Messenger), *Magarif* (Knowledge), *Millet* (Nation), *Shuro* (Council), *Vatan Khadimi* (Servant of the Motherland), *Yulduz* (Star) among other Tatar and Bashkir periodicals. Among specifically Islamic periodicals were *Bayān al-Ḥaqq* (Exposition of Truth), *Dīn va Adab* (Religion and Ethics) and *Dīn va Maghishat* (Religion and Life). In terms of political orientation the vast majority of these periodicals did not question Muslims' loyalty to the tsar and Russia. It is significant that at the outbreak of the First World War, in which Russia confronted Muslim Turkey, most of them unambiguously supported St. Petersburg. At the same time the bulk of village mullahs and ordinary Tatar and Bashkir Muslims remained politically indifferent during the war, despite attempts by some nationalist and Islamist agitators to instigate popular disturbances in support of Turkey.[4]

The 1917 Russian Bourgeois-Democratic Revolution and Its Implications

In February 1917, Russia experienced the second bourgeois-democratic revolution which resulted in the overthrow of the Russian monarchy and the establishment of the Provisional Government tasked with Russia's political restructuring into a parliamentary democracy. The February Revolution caused new divisions among the Tatar and Bashkir political and religious leadership. Some of Ittifāq's members and other political moderates feared that the abolition of the monarchy would destabilize the Russian multi-ethnic and polyconfessional state. On the other side, most pro-jadīd Muslim liberals welcomed the Provisional Government and formed the Moscow-based Provisional Central Bureau of Muslims and the Kazan-based Islamic Committee, both of which allied themselves with the Provisional Government. At the First All-Russia Muslim Congress, which was held in May 1917 in Moscow, Sadri Maksudi, most other Volga Tatar delegates, as well as some Azeri delegates rallied round the unitarist project – that is, the preservation of a unitary state and the establishment of national cultural autonomy for Turco-Tatars of the Volga-Urals and Siberia. They opposed Russia's federalization along ethnonational lines as they feared this would be detrimental to the Russian ummah. However, the majority of delegates from the northern Caucasus, the Kazakh Steppe and Turkestan, as well as a minority of Tatar and Bashkir delegates (e.g. Hadi Maksudi and Zeki Velidi Togan) favoured the federalist project – that is, the Russian state's reorganization into a democratic federation of national republics. In contrast, a number of Crimean Tatar politicians under the leadership of Noman Çelebicihan (Chelebeev, 1885–1918) and Jafer Seydahmet (Kirimer, 1889–1960) pursued a separatist agenda and formed a national party, *Millī Firqāh* (National Party), for its implementation. Meanwhile, a group of Tatar and Bashkir social radicals under the leadership of Mullanur Vahitov (1885–1918) allied with the Bolsheviks; in April 1917 they formed the Muslim Socialist Committee which subsequently turned into the centre of Bolshevism in the Volga-Urals.

At the Second All-Russia Muslim Congress, which was convened in July 1917 in Kazan, the Tatar unitarists prevailed and formed the major bodies of the projected Turco-Tatar autonomy – the *Millī Idare* (National Administration) under the leadership of Sadri Maksudi, the *Millī Mejlis* (National Assembly) and the *Harbī Shuro* (Military Council). Of particular significance was the creation within the Millī Idare of the Ministry of Religion – *Dinya Nazaraty* (1917–20) – which replaced the Ufa-based muftīate. The Dinya Nazaraty was headed by democratically elected muftī Galimjan Barudi (Galeev, 1857–1921), a highly respected Tatar 'ālim of jadīdist orientation. In November 1917, Bashkir Muslim clergy who resented the Tatar domination in the Dinya Nazaraty and other Turco-Tatar governing bodies established a separate muftīate of Bashkurdistan (1917–20) under the leadership of ishān Muhammed-Gabdulkhay Kurbangaliev (1889–1972).

Between the Bolshevik Revolution and the Second World War

The Anti-Bolshevik Turco-Tatar Leadership

Unlike the earlier bourgeois-democratic revolutions, the 1917 October Revolution created an anxiety, even an overt hostility, among the majority of the Tatar and Bashkir political, business, intellectual and religious elite. Muslim conservatives and liberals alike were alarmed by the Bolsheviks' rejection of private property, their social and gender egalitarianism, their radical national programme and, above all, their atheism. Most Tatar and Bashkir qadīmists did not recognize the legitimacy of the Bolshevik authority and advocated the restoration of the Romanov monarchy as a perceived guarantor of the stability and territorial integrity of the Russian multi-ethnic and multi-confessional state. In a similar way, the majority of pro-jadīd Tatar and Bashkir liberals, who dominated Muslim politics during the inter-revolutionary period, opposed the Bolsheviks' radicalism. Some of them withdrew from politics, some emigrated to Turkey or other countries, while some joined the opposition White movement. For example, muftī Galimjan Barudi organized special Muslim regiments to join the Whites in their fight against the Bolsheviks.

Overall, in the aftermath of the October Revolution the leadership among the Tatars, Bashkirs and Kazakhs shifted from the Islamic authorities towards those who embraced a national agenda. In Ufa, in November 1917, Bashkir politicians under the leadership of Zeki Velidi Togan (1890–1970) formed the Millī Mejlīs, which, in June 1918, created the Bashkir bourgeois-nationalist government which claimed to control most of the Ufa *guberniia* (province). For a short period, Bashkir nationalists strengthened their positions by allying with Kazakh nationalists from the party of *Alash Orda* (Kazakh Horde, 1917–20) under the leadership of Ahmet Baitursynuly (Baitursynov, 1872–1937),[5] the Cossacks under the command of General Alexander Dutov and the White Army of Admiral Alexander Kolchak. However, in February 1919 Zeki Velidi (as well as

Ahmet Baitursynuly), having fallen out with the Whites and Cossacks, was forced to side with the Bolsheviks. For a year Zeki Velidi Togan was in charge of *Bashrevkom* (Bashkir Military Revolutionary Committee); then, following the Bashrevkom's dissolution by the Bolshevik leadership, Zeki Velidi Togan moved once again to opposition. Meanwhile in March 1918, in Kazan, Tatar politicians under the leadership of Sadri Maksudi and Ayaz Ishaki (1878–1954) proclaimed the Idel-Ural state which claimed to unite Tatars, Bashkirs, Volga Germans and the Chuvash. Maksudi assumed the presidency and Ishaki became Minister of Foreign Affairs; however, the Idel-Ural lasted only four weeks before being disbanded by the Bolshevik forces.[6]

In the Crimea, Bolsheviks faced opposition from members of the Millī Firqāh, Kadets, Socialist Revolutionaries, Mensheviks and German and other foreign interventionists. In December 1917, Millī Firqāh's leaders Noman Çelebicihan and Jafer Seydahmet established a coalition government which first appealed to the German Kaiser Wilhelm II (r. 1888–1918) to provide it with military assistance. With Germany's backing the Millī Firqāh's leaders and activists established the Crimean Parliament – the *Qurultai*. Noman Çelebicihan also assumed the role of the muftī of the Crimea, Lithuania, Poland and Belorussia. In November 1918, following the departure of the German troops from the Crimea, the Qurultai leadership attempted a short-term alliance with British and French interventionist armies and the White Russians. A year later, a group of Millī Firqāh members under the leadership of Veli Ibraim (Ibraimov, 1888–1928) agreed to collaborate with the Bolsheviks. They created a separate pro-Bolshevik Crimean Muslim Bureau which operated in parallel to the Qurultai. In November 1920, foreign troops were forced to leave the Crimea, and the Red Army under the leadership of Mikhail Frunze (1885–1925) asserted full control of the Crimean Peninsula.[7] In October 1923, the Crimea was transformed into the Crimean Soviet Autonomous Republic under the leadership of Veli Ibraimov (in office 1924–28).

It is important to note that some of the politically defeated Turco-Tatar national leaders continued to fight the Soviet government from emigration. Ayaz Ishaki founded the Tatar-Bashkir Committee of *Idel-Ural* in exile and played a leading role in the Warsaw-based international anti-Soviet Turkic League, *Prometheus*, among members of which were also Jafer Seydahmet and Mustafa Chokay (Shokay, 1890–1941), a leader of the anti-Bolshevik Turkestan Autonomy[8] (see Chapter 7). In the 1920s and 1930s Ayaz Ishaki, alongside other influential Tatar émigrés, disseminated their national agenda on the pages of the Paris-based journal *Prométhée*, which served as a wider anti-Soviet forum for émigrés from the Volga-Urals, Crimea, Caucasus, Turkestan and Ukraine. In 1928, Ishaki founded an emigrant journal *Milli Yol* (The Way of the Nation, 1928–39),[9] which was specifically concerned with Tatars and other Turkic peoples of the former Russian Empire. And in 1933, in Paris, Ishaki published a book *Idel-Ural* which outlined the ideology of Turco-Tatar separatism.

Muslim Communists

As noted earlier, a number of Tatar and Bashkir pro-jadīdist national leaders embraced Bolshevist Marxism. It was they who formed the core of the Turco-Tatar Bolshevik political, economic and military leadership. Alongside their pro-Bolshevik Jewish, Ukrainian, Armenian, Georgian and Polish counterparts, they welcomed the Bolsheviks' decision to withdraw Russia from the devastating world war, as well as their radical redistribution of land and wealth and their recognition of the national equality of all peoples of Russia and their right to self-determination. Of particular benefit to the Bolshevik regime were Mullanur Vahitov, Mirsaid Sultan-Galiev (1876–1935) and other Turco-Tatar revolutionaries who adjusted the Bolshevik programme to the needs of the Muslim majority through the ideology of Muslim Communism. Both became key figures in the Muslim Committee (*MusCom*) within the Nationalities Ministry (*Narkomnats*), headed by Joseph Stalin (Dzhugashvili, 1878–1953). They were directly involved in the formulation of the pivotal Bolshevik documents on national and Muslim issues – 'The Declaration of Rights of Peoples of Russia' of 2 November 1917 and 'The Address to All Muslim Toilers of Russia and the East' of 20 November 1917. In November 1918, Sultan-Galiev initiated the creation of the Central Bureau of Muslim Communists within the Russian Communist Party of Bolsheviks (RCPb), which dealt specifically with the Sovietization of the Muslim-majority parts of Russia.

Ideationally, Muslim Communism presented a fusion of Bolshevism and left-wing jadīdism. Muslim Communists subscribed to the Bolshevik socio-economic programme, though they opposed atheism and believed in the productive compatibility of Islam and socialism on the basis of such allegedly common characteristics as social justice, communalism, the priority of group over individual interests, concern for the poor and denunciation of slavery and usury (*ribā'*), which was likened to capitalist profit. Politically, Muslim Communists were in favour of a separate Muslim Communist Party of Russia and the establishment of an Islamic Court (*Al-Maḥkamah al-Islamīyyah*) in charge of special Muslim local administrations, courts and jadīd schools. Ethnically, Muslim Communists were mainly Tatars who claimed Islamic leadership across Bolshevik Russia and regarded Kazan as the Islamic capital of Russia and the centre for the export of Communism into the Muslim East. The Tataro-centricity of Muslim Communism alienated from it some non-Tatar left-wing Muslim politicians. This became apparent at the First Congress of the Peoples of the East, which was held in Baku in 1920. Nevertheless, Muslim Communists played an important role in advancing the Bolshevik message among the Muslim population and preventing a country-wide, Islamized anti-Bolshevik revolt and its merger with other anti-Bolshevik domestic and international forces. Consequently, the bulk of Russia's Muslims maintained neutrality during the critical period of the Russian Civil War and foreign intervention in Russia in 1918–21, albeit sporadic and enclave outbreaks of anti-Bolshevik resistance persisted throughout the 1920s.

Vahitov, Sultan-Galiev and their likes moderated the early Bolshevik policy towards Islam and Muslims compared to the blatant atheistic assault on the Russian Orthodox Church which for the Bolsheviks was associated with the Russian monarchy. During this period Joseph Stalin, Sergei Kirov (1886–1934)[10] and other Bolshevik leaders spoke favourably about Islam and promised to preserve the office of muftī, as well as sharī'ah courts in Muslim-majority regions of the Soviet state. Muslim Communists were also behind the Bolsheviks' decision to return to Muslims of Central Asia the venerated Qur'ān of Caliph 'Uthmān which was confiscated by the Russians in 1868 and placed in

St. Petersburg's museum. Among other tactical moves by the Bolsheviks was the return to Muslim communities of the Qaravan-Sarai Mosque in Orenburg and the Suumbike Mosque in Kazan. These Bolshevik policies gained the support of some 'ulamā' and other Muslim clergy who became known as 'Red Sharī'atists'. Among them was, for example, Gabdrahman Rasulev (1889–1950), a son of the influential Bashkir Naqshbandī sheikh and educator Zainulla Rasulev. Red Sharī'atists took part in the propagandist campaign 'For the Soviet Rule means for the Sharī'ah'.

Muslim Communists were also actively involved in Bolshevik foreign policy by promoting solidarity between Bolshevik Russia and oppressed Muslims in British, French and other Western colonies. The main Bolshevik external platform was the Eastern Bureau of the Communist International (the *Comintern*, 1919–43), which attracted left-wing Muslim revolutionaries from Western colonies and semi-colonies. They regarded Russia's Muslims as the vanguard of the forthcoming pan-Islamic revolution against Western colonialism, and Moscow as the new Mecca which would facilitate the liberation of the *Dār al-Islām* from the Western *Dār al-Ḥarb*. In November 1922, at the Comintern Fourth Congress Tan Malaka (1871–1949), an Indonesian revolutionary, called for a strategic alliance between communists and Islamists. Moscow became the training centre for Muslim left-wing leaders across the world. The main providers of free Marxist education were the Communist University of Toilers of the East (KUTV), the Institute of Red Professorship (IKP), the Agrarian Institute (MAI) and the Oriental Institute.

Muftīate

Initially, the Bolsheviks did not interfere with the institution of muftīate, which retained its three-tier structure. At the top were the muftī and six qāzīs; the middle level was represented by *muhtasibats* headed by *muhtasibs* and two deputies; and the lower level – the *mutavalliiat* – included mullahs, *mu'azzins* (*mu'athins*) and secretaries. In 1920, at the First All-Russia Muslim Congress, which was held in Bolshevik-controlled Kazan, the Dinya Nazaraty was transformed into the Central Spiritual Directorate of Muslims of Inner Russia (TsDUM). The first Soviet muftī was a Kazan Tatar 'ālim Galimjan Barudi (in office 1920–21), the former head of the Dinya Nazaraty and ex-editor of *Al-Dīn va al-Adab* (Religion and Ethics). The Second All-Russia Muslim Congress, which took place in 1923 in Ufa, elected the next Soviet muftī, a Bashkir 'ālim and philosopher Riḍā al-Dīn ibn Fakhr al-Dīn (Riza Fahretdinov, in office 1923–36). The Congress re-established the *Goliamlar Shurasy* (Council of 'Ulamā'), among whose members were such highly respected 'ulamā' as Djihangir Abzgil'din (d. 1938) and Hadi Atlasi (d. 1938).

In spite of muftī Fahretdinov's collaboration with the Bolshevik state he managed to retain considerable autonomy from it and to defend the religious rights of Muslim believers. In his sermons and on the pages of the muftīate's journal *Islam Majallasy* (*Journal of Islam*), he referred to Abū Ḥanīfa's teaching about respect for political authority and propagated the compatibility of sharī'ah and Bolshevik rule. At the same time he gained significant concessions from Moscow. For example, in 1923 he succeeded in legalizing the teaching of Islam to Muslim children and in declaring the Kurban-Bayram an official holiday for Russia's Muslims. As a result, by 1925 in the Volga-Urals alone there were over a hundred functioning madrasahs attended by around 30 per cent of Tatar and Bashkir children. Muftī Fahretdinov was also able to maintain limited contacts with Islamic authorities abroad. In 1926 he headed a group of Russia's Muslim hajjees to Mecca where he participated in the All-Muslim Congress. It is significant that muftī Fahretdinov backed the idea of convening the All-Muslim Congress in Mecca rather than in Cairo on the grounds that he regarded the congress in Cairo as part of the British plans to strengthen their control over Muslim lands by means of promoting Egypt's King Fu'ād I (r. 1922–36) as a possible new caliph.[11]

The Stalinist Assault on the Turco-Tatar National and Islamic Leadership

By the end of 1923 the Bolsheviks had consolidated their power in the Volga-Urals, Crimea and most Muslim-majority parts of the former Russian Empire and had turned their attention to Sovietization. The new approach included a major politico-administrative reorganization of Muslim-majority territories, increased restrictions on Muslim institutions and practices and an encroachment on Turco-Tatar national and religious leadership. Due to the Muslim Tatars' and Bashkirs' historically leading religious and political role among Russia's Muslims they suffered particularly badly from the toughened Stalinist stance on Islam. When the Soviet Union was established in December 1922, both the Tatars and Bashkirs, despite their large populations, were denied the superior status of union republic. (Union status was subsequently granted to numerically much less populous Armenia, Kyrgyzstan and Turkmenistan.) Instead, the Bolsheviks created two separate Tatar and Bashkir Autonomous Soviet Socialist Republics within the union republic of Russia – the Russian Socialist Federative Soviet Republic (RSFSR). This territorial delimitation was meant to prevent Tataro-Bashkir political consolidation along the lines of the Idel-Ural project and to leave a considerable number of ethnic Tatars and Bashkirs outside their ethnic autonomies. Thus, the Tatar republic included only 1.5 million out of a total of 4.2 million Tatars living in Soviet Russia. In the Bashkir republic, ethnic Bashkirs became a minority outnumbered by Tatars and Russians. In the Autonomous Soviet Socialist Republic of Crimea, which also became part of the RSFSR, Crimean Tatars made up just a quarter of the total population, dominated by ethnic Russians and Ukrainians.[12]

Following Lenin's death in January 1924, the Stalin leadership unleashed repressions against national and religious leaders across the USSR. Among its first targets were Muslim Communists and other Communist Party activists of Muslim heritage who were arbitrarily accused of petit bourgeois nationalism, excluded from the Party and, subsequently, either executed or imprisoned. Sultan-Galiev and Veli Ibraimov were executed and their names were pejoratively used for a country-wide purging campaign against *Sultan-Galievshchina* and *Veli-Ibraimovshchina* – blanket terms for any perceived nationalist or Islamist deviations from the Party's line. In the course of the Stalinist purges, thousands of Tatar and Bashkir Bolsheviks perished or were sent to the Gulag. The purges affected Tatar and Bashkir 'ulamā', established Muslim clergy and Ṣufīs. In comparative terms the scale and implications of anti-Islamic purges in the Volga-Urals were greater than in the Muslim Caucasus and the Ferghana valley. By the early 1930s, the number of Muslim clergy was reduced ten times and Ṣūfī transmission in the region was terminated.[13] It is important to bear in mind that Tatar and Bashkir leaders constituted only a fraction of the victims of the Stalinist terror, which was aimed at any intellectually and politically independent individuals, irrespective of their ethnic and confessional affiliation.

In 1925, the Kremlin established the League of Militant Godless, the motto of which was 'A war against religion is a war for socialism'. The League, which was headed by Yemelyan Yaroslavsky (Minei Gubel'man, 1878–1943), included thousands of militant functionaries who were tasked with the elimination of any religious beliefs and activities on the territory of the USSR. In the course of the sustained anti-Islamic efforts of the League's militants the vast majority of mosques (10,000 out of 12,000) and madrasahs in the region were either destroyed or closed, or converted into mundane premises. Sharī'ah courts were banned, waqf property was sequestered and the publication of most Islamic literature and periodicals discontinued. Following the death of muftī Fahretdinov in 1936, the activity of the muftīate under the new muftī Gabdrahman Rasuli (Rasulev, in office 1936–50) was paralysed. At the grassroots level, unofficial Muslim authorities were similarly undermined in the course of country-wide collectivization (1928–37). The Stalinist purges also targeted communists and left-wing revolutionaries in the Middle East and other Muslim countries,[14] the attack on them occurring against the background of the changed strategy of the Comintern. The previous line, for a united anti-imperialist front, which was endorsed by the Comintern's Second and Fourth Congresses in 1920 and 1922, was modified towards exclusively proletarian solidarity. The change had a devastating effect on the communist movement across the Middle East and other parts of the Muslim world as communists became isolated from national-liberation struggles in their respective countries.

Muslim Leadership between 1941 and 1991

Islam and Muslim Leadership during the Second World War

The Second World War (1939–45), which turned into the Great Patriotic War of various peoples of the USSR against Nazi aggression (1941–45),[15] presented a serious test for the Muslim leadership and ordinary Muslims in the Volga-Urals, as well as other Muslim-majority parts of the Soviet Union. Nazi Germany launched a massive propaganda campaign aiming at stirring the national and religious feelings of Muslims so as to solicit their collaboration against Moscow. In return for collaboration Russia's Muslims were promised political independence and the recognition of the Idel-Ural state. The Stalinist leadership reacted to the German propaganda by appealing to supranational Soviet patriotism and by suspending anti-Islamic policies. Some Muslim clerics, as well as representatives of the Russian Orthodox Church and other confessions, were rehabilitated and encouraged to participate in the country's war mobilization. In early 1942 the Kremlin lifted the ban on Islam-related activities and disbanded the League of the Militant Godless. In May 1942, in Ufa, Russia's Muslim clergy were allowed to hold a Muslim Congress, at which muftī Rasulev, who held several personal meetings with Stalin, called upon Muslims to fight against the German aggression, citing Prophet Muḥammad's saying: *Ḥubb al-vaṭan min al-imān* (Love for the motherland derives from the true faith). In March 1943, a leading Soviet newspaper *Izvestia* (News) published muftī Rasulev's 'An Address to Russia's Muslims', in which he urged the faithful to participate in all possible war-related efforts, which he equated to jihād. The muftī also volunteered to organize a collection of funds for the Red Army and he himself donated 50,000 rubles for the fund designated for the formation of a tank column.[16]

In October 1943 the Stalinist leadership reinstituted the Ufa muftīate in the form of the Spiritual Directorate of Muslims of the European Part of the USSR and Siberia (DUMES, 1943–92)[17] and endorsed the establishment of three other muftīates – in Tashkent, Buinaksk and Baku. In May 1944 the Kremlin created, within the Soviet government, the Council for the Affairs of Religious Cults (CARC), which in 1965 was superseded by the Council of Religious Affairs (CRA).[18] The establishment of DUMES and the three other muftīates signified the institutionalization of Soviet Islam and the official Islamic leadership. Overall, during the war, the Stalinist leadership largely succeeded in securing the loyalty to Moscow of the Tatar and Bashkir Muslim clergy and the bulk of ordinary Tatars and Bashkirs, many thousands of Tatars and Bashkirs fighting side by side with their non-Muslim compatriots against the Nazi invasion. A Tatar poet Musa Jalil (Zalilov, 1906–1944), who chose death over collaboration with the Germans, became a symbol of a new phenomenon, Soviet Muslim patriotism. Still, German propaganda yielded some limited success in the Crimea and the Caucasus. Jafer Seydahmet and some other former activists of Millī Firqah formed the Central Muslim Committee which organized eight battalions of Crimean Tatars to fight on the side of Nazi Germany, which occupied the Crimean Peninsula in October 1941. Following the Soviet liberation of the Crimea from the German occupation in 1944 all Crimean Tatars were deported to Central Asia.

The Tatar and Bashkir Muslim Leadership within Official Soviet Islam

In the mid-1950s, the Kremlin's relative religious liberalism was yet again replaced by the tightening of its control over the Islamic sphere. The post-Stalin Soviet leadership was concerned that the Islamic resurgence which occurred during the war period might get out of control and pose a threat to state atheism. In order to suppress the revival of Islam, as well as Orthodoxy and other religions, the Communist Party's Central Committee (CC CPSU) issued a series of resolutions aimed at the full eradication of religiosity among the Soviet people and the 'emancipation of various national cultures from religion'. Islam-related activities became closely monitored by both the CPSU and the security services. The opening of new mosques and madrasahs was prohibited and the national cultures of various Muslim peoples were to be cleansed of Islamic components. Because of the new official restrictions mosque functions shifted to underground prayer houses which were disguised as clubs and other non-religious public places where they had a disguised *qiblah* (the orientation towards Mecca) and a *miḥrāb* (a prayer niche in the qiblah wall). Most Tatar, Bashkir and other Soviet Muslims could not observe the five pillars of Islam, with only *shahādah* (the testimony of belief in Allah) being conducted universally. Still, many Tatar and Bashkir families continued secretly to follow Islamic norms with regard to weddings, name-giving, circumcision, divorces and especially funerals. These Islamic rituals and practices were administered by unofficial Islamic authorities represented by undisclosed and itinerant mullahs and *abystai*s (female Islamic authorities) who lacked structured Islamic education and often knew only the basics of the traditional (regional) form of Islam. They acquired their fragmented Islamic knowledge either from their grandparents or through self-teaching. Despite these limitations, they often commanded a higher moral authority than the representatives of official Islam.[19]

The embodiment of Soviet official Islam was the Ufa-based DUMES.[20] Compared to the Russian imperial period its powers were further curtailed, as it did not control Islamic education, did not administer any waqf and had no right to create new muhtasibats. Its domestic functions were limited to fatwā – issuing and overseeing a small number of registered mosques, including nominating their mullahs. Nevertheless, the muftī and other DUMES senior clergy became actively involved in the Soviet state's international politics by representing Soviet Muslims abroad.[21] Particularly influential among the latter was Ahmedzian Mustafin (1902–1986), imām-khatyb of the Moscow Mosque and a proponent of jadīdism.[22] From the late 1960s, the religious and political supremacy of DUMES was challenged by the Tashkent-based Spiritual Directorate of Muslims of Central Asia and Kazakhstan (SADUM)[23] and, from the 1980s, also by the Baku-based Spiritual Directorate of Muslims of Transcaucasia (DUMZ).[24] SADUM, in particular, as the only provider of structured Islamic education through the Mir-i Arab madrasah in Bukhara and the Islamic Institute of imām Bukhārī in Tashkent (est. 1971), trained imām-khatybs for DUMES. It was also granted sole authority to send a limited number of Muslim students for further training to al-Azhar and some other leading Islamic universities in the Muslim East. In the 1960s, the DUMES was inadvertently affected by SADUM's pro-Salafī leaning. This was evidenced, for example, in the fatwās by DUMES muftī Shakir Khiyaletdinov (in office 1951–74) who denounced the existing practices of pilgrimage to mazārs, prayers at burials and women's attendance at burials in cemeteries.

Gorbachevian Perestroika and 'Young Imāms'

The ascendance of Mikhail Gorbachev (b. 1931) as the pro-reform Communist Party leader had significant implications for Islam and the Muslim leadership of the USSR. The Gorbachev leadership's drive towards political and economic liberalization and increased engagement with the West was accompanied by an escalation in anti-Islamic campaigning, aimed at fighting the alleged Islamic influences germinating both within society and emanating from abroad. An aggravating factor was the Soviet invasion of Muslim Afghanistan in 1979–89 which provoked ambivalent feelings in some sectors of the Muslim population of the USSR. Another significant factor was a new wave of purges among Communist Party and Komsomol members of Muslim Tatar and Bashkir origins.

Against the background of the perestroika-driven political democratization there emerged a movement of religious Muslim activists, known as the 'young imāms', the bulk of whom were graduates of Mir-i Arab madrasah, while some had also studied in Islamic universities abroad. The 'young imāms', who were at the forefront of the so-called 'Islamic revival',[25] demanded the restoration of the Islamic infrastructure (mosques, madrasahs, waqfs) on the pre-revolutionary scale and the wider involvement of Soviet Muslims in social and political life. Under their pressure the authorities conceded in reprinting the 1963 Russian translation of the Qur'ān, in opening several new mosques, in relaxing travel restrictions for Soviet Muslims and in allowing into the country a limited number of foreign Muslim missionaries, educators and publishers. The 'young imāms' were critical of the so-called 'old imāms' who dominated Soviet Islamic officialdom on the grounds of their alleged passivity, conformism and anti-democratic practices. In the Volga-Urals, they rose against the perceived authoritarian leadership of DUMES[26] muftī Talgat Safa Tadzhuddinov (b. 1948, in office 1980),[27] who by the end of the Soviet period controlled 773 registered Muslim communities. (These coexisted with 347 unregistered Muslim communities.)[28] Subsequently, the anti-Tadzhuddinov revolt among the registered Muslim clergy led to the establishment of dozens of Turco-Tatar muftīates across European Russia and Siberia.

In December 1991 the Gorbachevian perestroika culminated in the collapse of the Soviet system and the disintegration of the USSR. The country's fragmentation led to the organizational break-up of the Soviet Islamic establishment and the creation of new ethnonational and regional muftīates under the leadership of 'young imāms' who claimed their independence from the four Soviet-era muftīates. In Tatarstan and Bashkortostan national Tatar and Bashkir muftīates were formed which were unaffiliated to DUMES, their muftīs joining forces with the opposition Tatar and Bashkir ethnonational leadership. New muftīates also appeared in regions with substantial Muslim (largely Tatar) populations and in the cities of Moscow and Leningrad (St. Petersburg), while the Crimea acquired its own qāḍiyāt.

Conclusion

By the end of the Soviet period, most Tatar and Bashkir Muslims, alongside other Muslim peoples of the USSR, had acquired a distinctive identity as 'Soviet Muslims'. They continued to identify themselves as Muslims, but they tended to treat Islam as part of their national culture. As such, Islam remained an important regulator of their family, communal and social life, while becoming compatible with general Soviet patterns of behaviour and socialization which were enhanced through the state-imposed young people's membership of *Octobrist*, *Young Pioneers* and *Komsomol* organizations.[29] In other words, they largely reconciled their Muslim-ness with life in the atheistic Soviet state. Consequently, they became culturally different from their ethnic brethren and co-religionists abroad while developing sociocultural commonalities with other Soviet peoples of both Islamic and non-Islamic religious backgrounds. Within the Soviet atheistic and internationalist context the political and social role of various representatives of the Islamic leadership drastically declined, although at a family level, and especially in rural areas, some folk male and female mullahs continued to command notable authority.

At a formal level, Tatar and Bashkir Muslims were administered by the Ufa-based muftīate-DUMES, which consisted of a muftī and other senior Muslim clergy who acted as official intermediaries between the Soviet state and grassroots Muslim communities. DUMES was closely monitored by CARC and the security services. In practice, the relationship between muftīs, as well as that between other official Muslim clergy and both unofficial Muslim authorities and the Soviet state, was complex. In the case of the former, it involved common theological points of reference, mutual respect, collaboration and even family connections. In the case of the latter, it included elements of subordination and collaboration, but also some distancing. Thus, DUMES acted as the medium for state control and management of Tatar and Bashkir Muslim communities and as an agency for state foreign policy in the Middle East and other parts of the Muslim world. In response to state demands DUMES muftis utilized concepts of ijtihād and *idtikrār* (a compelling duty) as adjustment mechanisms within the conditions of official atheism. Accordingly, in their fatwās socialist work was equated with Islamic virtue, while a time-related and dietary flexibility was permitted during Uraza-Bayram and Qurban-Bayram. At the same time, the DUMES leadership, alongside their counterparts in Tashkent, Baku and Buinaksk/Makhachkala,[30] retained links, albeit limited, with 'ulamā' abroad, who never accused them of *shirk* (polytheism), or *kufr* (non-belief in Islam). Following the demise of the USSR, Tatar and Bashkir muftīs were recognized by various Muslim states as official representatives of the Tatar and Bashkir Muslims.

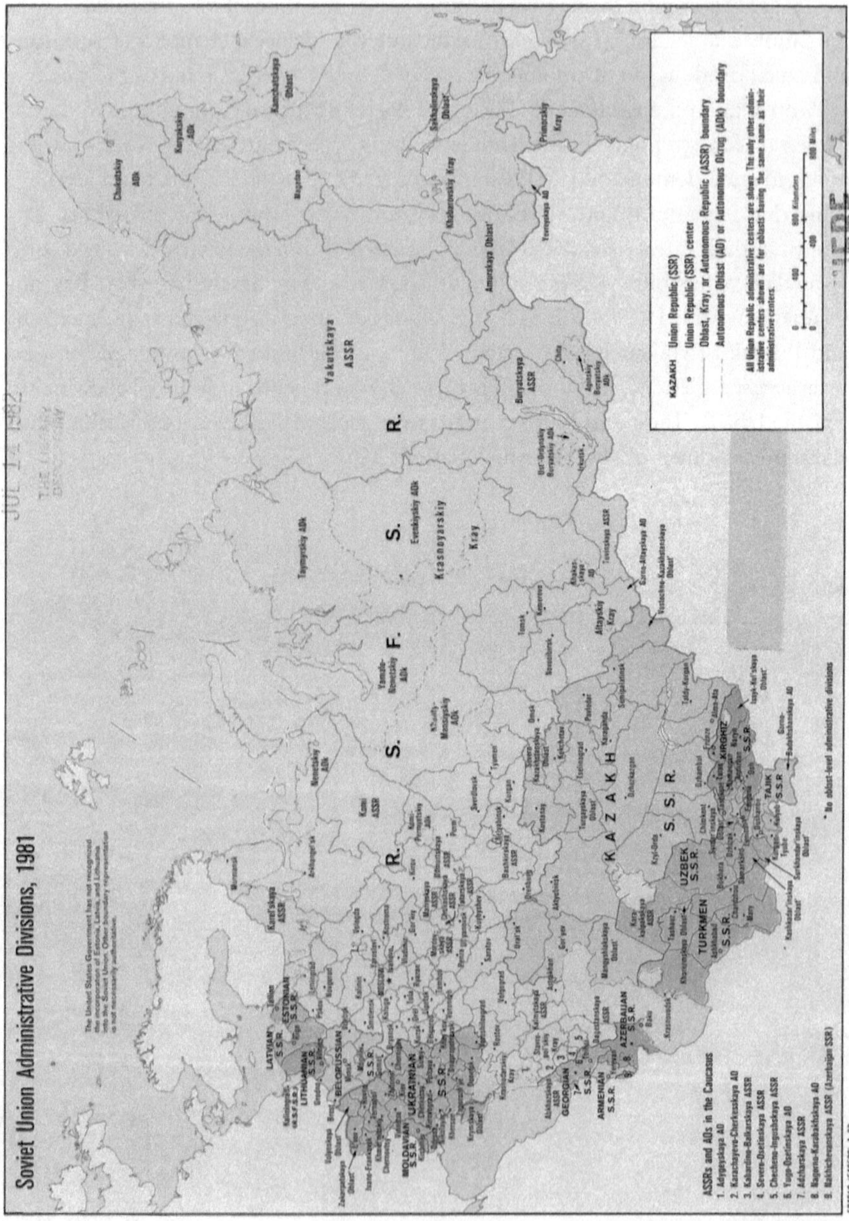

Figure 5.1 Map of the USSR.

Chapter Six

THE NORTH CAUCASUS

Introduction

Unlike Tatar and Bashkir Muslims who had been within the Russian state since the middle of the sixteenth centuries the various Muslim peoples of the North Caucasus, with the exception of several Kabardian families,[1] came under Russian rule only at the end of the nineteenth century. The protracted and brutal Caucasus War (1817–64) and the ensuing establishment of Russian rule over the Muslim Caucasus forced many surviving Muslim leaders and their followers to conduct hijrah to Turkey to seek the protection of Ottoman sulṭāns who since 1517 had claimed caliphal authority. As a result, Ottoman Turkey acquired a sizeable Cherkess diaspora, while the muhājirs' ancestral land was subjected to an influx of Cossack, Russian and other non-Muslim settlers. These factors affected the attitudes and the religious and political positioning of the North Caucasian Muslim leaders and ordinary Muslims during the Russian bourgeois-democratic and Bolshevik Revolutions. Following the establishment of Bolshevik rule in the north-eastern Caucasus, the region's Sovietization was hampered because of its difficult mountainous terrain and the extreme polyethnicity of its population. At the same time, the high mountains and wild forests served as a safe haven for the remaining 'ulamā' and Ṣūfī sheikhs, thus allowing for the continuation in the north-eastern Caucasus of the Arabic-based Islamic learned tradition and of Naqshbandī, Shādhilī and Qādirī Ṣūfī ṭarīqahs.

It took the Bolsheviks over two decades to incorporate the North Caucasus into the Soviet politico-administrative and economic system. Moreover, the Stalin leadership still remained suspicious of Chechens, Ingush, Karachais, Balkars and some other Muslims of the region, who in 1943–44 were deported en masse to Central Asia where they came to constitute the majority among the deportees. A life in deportation (1943/44–1957) affected the Muslims' world view, Islamic beliefs and practices while children born during that period would make up a pool of potential national and religious leaders in the post-Soviet period. One of them would be General Dzhokhar Dudayev (1944–96), who in 1994 mobilized Chechens for an Islamized national-liberation struggle against Moscow. In the north-western Caucasus, the religious and national dynamic was also affected by the continuing political, economic and cultural imbalance between the privileged Circassians and the disadvantaged Turkic Karachai-Balkars. Among the implications of this phenomenon was the greater role among Karachaevo-Balkars, compared to Circassians, of popular Muslim authorities. However, the absence of a Karachai-Balkar diaspora, comparable to the Chechen diaspora in Turkey and the Middle East, accounted for the lower scale of Islamization and jihādization of the Karachai and Balkar national movements in the late Soviet and early post-Soviet periods.

The chapter begins by outlining the main ethnocultural and doctrinal differences between Muslims in the eastern and western parts of the North Caucasus. It is especially concerned with the impact of these differences on the religious and political authorities across the region. It then examines the political and religious stance of regional leaders during the turbulent period of the Russian bourgeois-democratic and Bolshevik Revolutions. It proceeds to examine the variety of responses of regional leaders towards the Bolshevik project, as well as their relations with Turkey. The chapter then discusses the implications of Sovietization for Islam and the Islamic leadership in particular. It pays special attention to the impact of the deportations on the ethnonational and religious development of Chechens, Ingush, Balkars and Karachais. The next section addresses the regional specifics of 'Soviet Islam' in the North Caucasus and examines the relationship between the Buinaksk-based muftīate and Ṣūfī sheikhs and other popular Islamic authorities. The concluding section deals with the 'Islamic revival' and its leaders at the end of the Soviet era.

Islamic Leadership: Ethnocultural and Political Contexts

Throughout history the nature of Islamic authority and the status of Islamic leadership have differed significantly between the north-eastern and north-western Caucasus. This is because although there are no obvious physical barriers within the North Caucasus its eastern and western parts exhibited considerable differences in their ethnocultural, religious and political outlook even though both parts possessed many characteristics common to the North Caucasus and the Caucasus as a whole. In the eastern part these differences were largely due to its extreme polyethnicity, its strong Arabic-based Islamic tradition and the prevalence of popular Ṣūfism. In the western part they related to its adjacency to the Black Sea and, consequently, to the greater influence of Ottoman Turkey and the Crimea on its Islamization, which occurred much later than in the east.

The north-eastern Caucasus is the historical habitat of Vainakhs (Chechens and Ingush, both of the Caucasian ethnolinguistic family) and Dagestanis,[2] consisting of over a hundred different peoples belonging to the Caucasian, Turkic and Indo-European ethnolinguistic families. Among Dagestan's Caucasian peoples are the Avars, Andis, Dargins, Laks, Lezgins (Lezgis), Tabasarans, Rutuls, Tsakhurs and Chechens, who speak mutually incomprehensible languages belonging to the Nak'kh and Nak'kh-Dagestani branch of the Caucasian language family. Dagestan's Turkic peoples include Kumyks (Kumuks), Nogais and Azeris. Among Dagestan's Indo-European inhabitants are Persians, Alans, Kurds, Tats and Mountain Jews who speak various languages of the Iranian branch of the Indo-European language family. From the seventeenth century, and especially during the nineteenth, Dagestan and Chechnya were populated by Cossacks, Russians and other Slavs. The population of the north-western Caucasus has consisted of Circassians/Adyghe (Kabardians, Adyghe, Abaza, Shapsughs (Shapseghs), Abadzekhs and Ubykhs), Karachai-Balkars and Nogais (all Turkic peoples), as well as Christian Armenians, Cossacks, Russians and other Slavs. Given the plethora of languages, grassroots political and economic interaction throughout the Caucasus was enabled by a variety of *linguae francae* – Arabic, Farsi, Kumyk, Nogai, Azeri and Russian.[3]

In religious terms, Islam of the Shāfiʿī madhhab was much stronger in the north-eastern Caucasus, especially among Dagestan's Avars, Andis, Dargins and Kumyks of northern and north-western Dagestan. In the course of the Caucasus War Shāfiʿī Islam also strengthened its positions among the Chechens and Ingush. Of lasting impact was the establishment by imām Shamīl of the sharīʿah-based imāmate (1828–59).[4] The region was home to many influential ʿulamāʾ of both qadīmist and revivalist orientation, as well as venerated Ṣūfī sheikhs who enjoyed great authority among local Muslims. By comparison, most Muslims in the north-western Caucasus followed the Ḥanafī maddhab. It is significant that although by the sixteenth century most Circassians had converted to Islam their belief system remained syncretic, retaining Christian, Judaist and especially pagan components. In the seventeenth and eighteenth centuries, under the influence of Ottoman and Crimean missionaries and traders, the majority of Karachai-Balkars embraced Ḥanafī Islam. Subsequently, Islam among the Karachais, Balkars and Nogais became stronger than among their Circassians neighbours.[5] Nevertheless, across the whole region sharīʿah norms coexisted with ʿadats, which in some cases even took precedence.

At the turn of the twentieth century the North Caucasus was divided between several *guberniias* and *oblasts* of the Russian Empire. Unlike the provinces in central Russia, which were governed on the basis of Russian imperial civil law, most of the North Caucasus was under so-called military-popular governance (*voenno-narodnoe upravlenie*) which combined Russian military and traditional neighbourhood- or kinship-based administration in the form of elected councils of elders who adhered to ʿadats and sharīʿah law. The Russian military authorities favoured ʿadat-defined legal proceedings, which were executed by respected elders, over sharīʿah-based rulings, conducted by qāḍīs, largely because ʿadats were perceived as being more flexible and adaptable to Russian civil law. In the South Caucasus, however, St. Petersburg relied on established Muslim clergy and, from the 1840s, appointed muftīs. In 1862 the Russian imperial authorities endorsed the establishment in Tiflis (Tbilisi) of the offices of the Sunnī muftī and Shīʿī sheikh-ul-Islām.[6]

Muslim Leaders between the Russian Revolutions of 1905–7 and 1917

As discussed in Chapter 5, in the first decade of the twentieth century Russia's Muslim theological and political discourse was dominated by Tatar Islamic reformists – jadīds. As a result, the majority of ʿulamāʾ, Ṣūfī sheikhs and Muslim intellectuals in the North Caucasus, and especially in Dagestan, remained aloof from it. The reform-minded minority included Magomed-Mirza Mavraev (1878–1964), Abū Sufyān Akaev (1872–1932), Mustafa-qāḍī Ismailov (1879–1929), Muḥammad-qāḍī Dibirov (al-Qarākhī, 1875–1929) and ʿAlī Kaiaev (al-Ghumūqī, 1878–1934), all from Dagestan. In general, pro-reform ideas were more widespread in the urban centres and in the Kumyk-dominated plains, while Islamic traditionalism prevailed among the Avar- and Dargin-dominated mountains. In 1903, in Temir-Khan-Shura (from 1922, Buinaksk), Mavraev and Akaev established the first Arabic script publishing house – *al-Maṭbaʿat al-Islāmīyyah* – which began to publish Islamic literature of a reformist and general nature in the Avar, Kymyk, Lak and Dargin languages. In 1913, also in Temir-Khan-Shura, Kaiaev founded the first Arabic script–based Dagestani newspaper – *Jarīdat Dāghistān* (1913–18) which was critical of local ʿadat and Ṣūfī practices which it regarded as being incompatible with true Islam.[7] Compared to the Volga-Urals and Central Asia the number of jadīd schools in the region did not exceed a dozen.[8] It is also significant that unlike Tatar jadīds, who emphasized pan-Turkic Muslim solidarity, Dagestani Muslim reformers were primarily concerned with Islamic solidarity among polyethnic Dagestanis. Furthermore, their interpretation of Islamic reform was informed by the concept of *iṣlāḥ* (lit. 'restoration', meaning 'restoration of the Golden Age of Islam – GY), which was characteristic of Muḥammad ʿAbduh and many other Egyptian and Middle Eastern Muslim reformers. They also did not use the term 'jadīds' to describe proponents of Islamic educational reform.[9] Akaev and Ismailov represented the political Muslim scholars (*ahl al-siyāsah min al-ʿulamāʾ*), as they combined their publishing with political activism, and in the aftermath of the 1917 bourgeois-democratic revolution they became involved in the Islamic Committee – *Jamʿīyyat al-Islāmīyyah* – dominated by Kumyks. The Islamic Committee's political programme was based on four principles: sharīʿah, freedom, justice and equality. In September 1917, Jamʿīyyat al-Islāmīyyah morphed into an Islamo-national organization – *Millī Komitet* (National Committee) – headed by Daniyal Apashev (1870–1920). Among the Milli Komitet's priorities were the Arabization of education and the sharīʿatization of all legal proceedings in the North Caucasus.

Only a small fraction of the region's Muslim leaders were engaged in all-Russian politics. Among those were, for example, Magomed Dalgat (Dalgat Khalikov, 1849–1922) and Jelāl al-Dīn Korkmasov (Korkmas, 1877–1937), both from Dagestan. Dalgat was a Duma deputy from the Party of Progress[10] and Korkmasov represented the Dagestani Peasant Centre. In the Duma Dalgat advocated wider religious, cultural and political rights for northern Caucasians, including their right to establish a regional muftīate, while Korkmasov was mainly concerned with granting voting rights to the region's Muslims within a broader agenda of universal suffrage. A handful of northern Caucasian Muslims joined the Russian Social Democratic Labour Party (RSDRP). These included Magomed-ʿAlī Dahadaev (Makhach, 1882–1918),[11] Ibrahim-Bek Gaydarov (1879–1949), Ullu-Biy Buinaksky (1890–1919) and aforementioned Jelāl al-Dīn Korkmasov, all from Dagestan. Unlike the majority of Tatar and Azeri social-democrats, who adhered to the unitarist principle of the future Soviet state, most Muslim left-wingers from the North Caucasus favoured the federalist model and emphasized the principle of national self-determination. However, Akhmet-bey Tsalikov (1882–1928), a Menshevik of Ossetian ethnic origin, sided with the Muslim federalists. These divisions became apparent during the First and Second All-Russia Muslim Congresses which took place in May and July 1917.[12]

On the outbreak of the First World War, in which the Russian Empire confronted Ottoman Turkey, some of the region's Muslim leaders and dignitaries attempted to establish links with Ottoman Muslim clergy and politicians in the hope of the Ottoman Sulṭān and caliph's backing for the North Caucasus' secession from Russia. In May 1917, in Vladikavkaz, the First Congress of Peoples of the North Caucasus and Dagestan proclaimed the creation on the territory of Dagestan and Terek region of the Union of Mountainous Peoples of the North Caucasus and Dagestan (*Gorskaia Respublika*), which existed till early March of 1918. The Union was headed by 'Abdul Mejīd Chermoev (Tapa, 1882–1937), a Russian noble of Chechen origin. In August 1917, the Second Congress of Peoples of the North Caucasus and Dagestan elected the Avar 'ālim and advocate for the restoration of Shamīl's imāmate, Najmuddīn Gotsinsky (1859–1925), as muftī of the North Caucasus. Gotsinsky, together with the Union's military commander and the Avar Ṣūfī sheikh Uzun-hajjee al-Saltī (Saltinsky, 1848–1919), appealed to the Muslims of the North Caucasus to submit only to the authority of 'ulamā' and to defend their freedom and sharī'ah by arms. In August 1917, at the Second Congress of Peoples of the North Caucasus and Dagestan, which took place in the village of Andi, where in 1847 imām Shamīl and his *nā'ib*s (deputies) laid out the organizational principles of the imāmate, Gotsinsky and Uzun-ḥajjee attempted, albeit unsuccessfully, to proclaim an imāmate under the leadership of 'imām' Gotsinsky and to wage a renewed ghazawāt against the Russians. Among close allies of Gotsinsky and Uzun-ḥajjee were members of the Qādirī Bamat Girei-hajjee *wird* under the leadership of sheikh Ali Mitaev (1881–1925) and Sayid-bey (1901–1981), a grandson of imām Shamīl. At the same time some influential Ṣūfī sheikhs, such as the Dagestani Naqshbandī sheikh 'Alī-ḥajjee Akushinsky (al-Aqūshī, 1847–1931) and the Chechen Naqshbandī sheikh Deni Arsanov (1871–1917), rejected the imāmate of Najmuddīn. Deni Arsanov, for example, advocated non-violent forms of struggle and called for the Muslims' alliance with Terek Cossacks. The validity of the imāmate was also questioned by Abū Sufyān Akaev, 'Alī Kaiaev and some other Dagestani Muslim reformers.

From the Bolshevik Revolution to the Great Patriotic War

Bolsheviks and the Islamic Leadership

The 1917 October Revolution and the Bolsheviks' negation of religion, in particular, were met with hostility by the majority of the region's Muslim leaders and ordinary Muslims who reacted to it by military and political resistance, or through emigration, or by going underground. The legitimacy of Bolshevik rule was rejected by Uzun-ḥajjee al-Salty and Naqshbandī sheikh Magomed Balakhansky (d. 1925) from the Avar village of Balakhani. At the same time, Naqshbandī sheikh 'Alī-ḥajjee Akushinsky from the Dargin village of Akusha and Naqshbandī and Shādhilī sheikh Ḥasan Ḥilmī al-Qaḥī (Kakhibsky, 1852–1937)[13] from the Avar village of Kakhib welcomed the arrival of the Bolsheviks,[14] while Jelāl al-Dīn Korkmasov, as well as Magomed-'Alī Dahadaev and Ullu-Biy Buinaksky directly participated in the establishment of Soviet rule in the region. 'Alī-ḥajjee Akushinsky, for example, believed that the Naqshbandīs' alliance with the Bolsheviks would secure the autonomous status of Dagestan as a sharī'ah-based polity within Soviet Russia.[15] Other high-profile Caucasians, who joined the regional branch of the RSDRP, which was dominated by ethnic Russians and other outsiders, were Alibek Takho-Godi (1892–1937), a Dargin, and Tashtemir Eldarkhanov (1870–1934), a Chechen.[16]

It took the Bolsheviks over a decade to ensure their full control over the North Caucasus due to the fierce combined opposition of ghāzīs, ethnonational separatists, Terek, Kuban and Don Cossacks, White Russians, Turkish and other foreign interventionists. In March 1918 the Bolsheviks established their power in Petrovsk-Port (from 1921, Makhachkala) and some other main cities, albeit the rest of the region remained under the control of their various adversaries. In April 1918 a group of regional dignitaries and Muslim leaders formed the Union of Mountainous Peoples of the North Caucasus and Dagestan, or the second Mountainous Republic (*Gorskaia Respublika*, 1918–19) under the leadership of the aforementioned 'Abdul Mejīd Chermoev. The Mountainous Republic comprised seven confederative states: Dagestan, Ingushetia, Chechnya, Ossetia, Karachai-Balkaria, Kabarda-Cherkessia and Adygea, as well as the Nogai Steppe. Other key figures in the Republic's government were Pshemakho Kotsev (1884–1962), a Kabardian noble; Rashitkhan Kaplanov (1883–1937), a Kumyk noble; Gaidar Bammat (Bammatov, 1889–1965), a Kumyk noble; Nukh-Bek Tarkovsky (1878–1951), a Kumyk prince; and Vassan-Girei Jabagiev (1882–1961), an Ingush intellectual. The Republic's headquarters were in Temir-Khan-Shura, albeit it subsequently moved to Tiflis. It allied with Cossacks under the command of General Lazar Bicherakhov (1882–1952) and received financial and military backing from Turkey, Germany and, later on, from Britain. In April 1919, following the advance on Temir-Khan-Shura of White Russians under the command of General Anton Denikin (1872–1947),[17] the Republic's government relocated to the Azerbaijan Democratic Republic (ADR, 1918–20)[18] and, soon after, was disbanded.

In September 1919, the Bolshevik positions were challenged by the North Caucasian Emīrate, which was proclaimed by Uzun-ḥajjee and Najmuddīn Gotsinsky on the territory of Chechnya and western Dagestan. The Emīrate was centred on the Chechen village of Vedeno. Uzun-ḥajjee adopted the official title of imām, while Gotsinsky assumed the role of military commander. The Emīrate's leaders secured the protection of the Ottoman Sulṭān Mehmet VI (r. 1918–22) and forged close links with the Democratic Republic of Georgia (DRG, 1918–21) and some Kabardian and Ossetian dignitaries. The Emīrate's fate, however, was sealed as a result of the advance into its territory of White Russians who sought the reintegration of the North Caucasus into the resurrected Great Russian Orthodox state. Consequently, Uzun-ḥajjee, unlike Gotsinsky, was forced to submit to the Bolsheviks.[19] In March 1920, following Uzun-ḥajjee's death, the Emīrate's territories became incorporated into the newly established Mountain Autonomous Soviet Socialist Republic (1921–24)[20] and the Autonomous Soviet Socialist Republic of Dagestan (1921–91). An important factor in the consolidation of the Bolsheviks' power in Dagestan was their collaboration with Naqshbandī sheikhs 'Alī-ḥajjee Akushinsky[21] and Ḥasan Ḥilmī Kakhibsky. Nevertheless, until the end of the 1920s the Bolsheviks' power in Dagestan, especially among Avars in the mountain areas, remained fragile due to the sporadic Islamized insurgencies of followers of Najmuddīn Gotsinsky who yet again claimed the title of imām. In September 1925 Gotsinsky was captured by the Reds and executed by an OGPU (secret police)[22] squad in Rostov-on-Don.[23] Still, the last outbreak of their ghazawāt took place as late as in 1940.

Specifics of Sovietization

Sovietization of the North Caucasus followed country-wide patterns, albeit with some regional nuances. As in other Muslim-majority parts of Soviet Russia/the USSR, initially, for tactical reasons, the Bolshevik leadership pursued a relatively liberal Islamic policy in the region. In November 1920 at the Congress of Peoples of Dagestan in Temir-Khan-Shura Joseph Stalin proclaimed the establishment of the Soviet Autonomy of Dagestan and assured Dagestanis of the Soviet state's legitimization of sharīʿah and ʿadats.[24] The Kremlin promoted the alliance between Soviet and Islamic authorities and emphasized its respect for Ṣūfī sheikhs and other Islamic authorities and promised its non-interference in sharīʿah courts.[25] Sheikh ʿAlī-ḥajjee was made Head of the Sharīʿah Court of Dagestan and district and local sharīʿah courts continued to function on the basis of both sharīʿah and ʿadats. They consisted of a *dibir* (mosque imām), a head of the district/village council of elders and an *ʿāmil* (secretary); courts of large districts also included a few qāḍīs.[26] Until the mid-1920s, the regional Bolshevik authorities involved the leading traditionalist and reform-minded ʿulamāʾ in the decision-making through the convening of regular meetings with them. The Bolsheviks also succeeded in co-opting Muḥammad-qāḍī Dibirov, Abū Sufyān Akaev, ʿAlī Kaiaev and some other influential pro-Salafī Muslim intellectuals into the Soviet system, primarily in the areas of education and publishing. Thus, Dibirov was made a member of the Executive Committee of Dagestan and the editor of the Avar-language newspaper *Krasnye Gory* (Red Mountains) and the Kumyk-language newspaper *Sovetskii Dagestan* (Soviet Dagestan), while Akaev began to publish the Arabic-language journal *Bayān al-Ḥaqāʾiq* (Exposure of the Truth). Those and other newly established periodicals[27] debated such vital theological and political issues as the understanding and scope of *ijtihād* (reasoning) and *taqlīd* (tradition), *bidʿah* (unlawful innovation), *tashayykh* (Ṣūfī practices), *al-ʿadālah* (sharīʿ ah justice), *musāwah* (equality), *ḥurrīyyah* (freedom) and the compatibility of the imāmate with the Soviet system. However at the end of the 1920s the Stalinist leadership, having strengthened its grip on the region, turned against Muslim reformers whose views regarding the role of religion and Arabic in the educational system increasingly diverged from the Kremlin's atheism and the centrality of the Russian language. Many Muslim reformers and socialists were accused of membership of the allegedly anti-Soviet *Dīnī Komitī* (Religious Committee) and persecuted.[28]

At the politico-administrative level, the North Caucasus underwent multiple rearrangements, albeit that, unlike the South Caucasus – which was divided into the three union republics of Azerbaijan, Georgia and Armenia – it was kept within the union republic of the Russian Federation. By the mid-1930s, the region was divided into Russia's autonomous republics of Dagestan, Kabardino-Balkaria, Checheno-Ingushetia and North Ossetia and the autonomous oblasts of Karachaevo-Cherkessia and Adygea, which were parts of Russia's Stavropol' and Krasnodar *krais* (provinces), respectively. Meanwhile, the region's Muslim Nogais, Abazas and Shapsughs were denied any form of autonomy. In the interests of the Soviet planned economy and in order to prevent the national consolidation of Turkic and Circassian peoples, the ethnically close Karachais and Balkars were separated and joined up with the similarly divided Cherkess and Kabardians, while the Adygeis[29] became a minority within the Russian/Cossack-dominated Adygei autonomous oblast. Under the Stalinist nationality policy,[30] the Kremlin opted for *korenizatsiia* (nativization) of the regional Bolshevik leadership, which was originally dominated by ethnic Russians and other non-Muslims. In doing so, it followed the imperial Russian practice of favouring the representatives of some ethnic groups over others. For example, in Dagestan, it privileged the Avars; in Kabardino-Balkaria, the Kabardians; and in Karachaevo-Cherkessia, the Cherkess. However, in Checheno-Ingushetia, the korenizatsiia was partial, as the Kremlin kept ethnic Chechens or Ingush away from the republic's leading Communist Party positions up until the late 1980s.

During the 1930s, the North Caucasus, like the rest of the USSR, underwent a radical economic and sociopolitical transformation in the process of industrialization, agrarian collectivization and the introduction of free comprehensive and standardized education and health care. Soviet education and young Caucasian Muslims' socialization via state-sponsored *Oktobrist*, Young Pioneers and Komsomol membership,[31] as well as army conscription were aimed at forging a new social entity – a Soviet people free of religious and national affiliations. The replacement of the Arabic script first with the Latin (*Yanalif*) in 1927–31 and then with the Cyrillic in 1937–39 dealt a severe blow to Islamic scholarship and broke the intergenerational transmission of the Islamic heritage. During the anti-religious campaign spearheaded by the League of the Militant Godless, sharī'ah courts were banned, the bulk of mosques and madrasahs were shut down or converted into mundane premises, most Islamic books were destroyed, waqfs were abolished and thousands of 'ulamā', Ṣūfī sheikhs, imāms and other Islamic authorities were executed or sent to the Gulag. In Dagestan alone, over 1,200 Muslim clerics were executed, exiled or imprisoned, while many remaining imāms and qāḍīs refused to conduct their religious duties out of fear of Bolshevik repression.[32] Nevertheless, some Ṣūfī authorities – for example, the earlier mentioned Naqshbandī sheikh Ḥasan Ḥilmī Kakhibsky – were co-opted within the ruling Soviet structures. Some others managed to survive by hiding in barely accessible mountainous villages, where, under conditions of extreme secrecy, they kept alive some of the Arabic-based Islamic scholarly traditions, as well as Naqshbandī and Shādhilī ṭarīqahs.[33]

On the whole, however, the Great Terror and the anti-religious campaign were most detrimental to the Sufis, especially the Qādirīs. There were no living Qādirī sheikhs left and next generations of Chechens and Ingush had to follow the teaching of the deceased sheikhs Kunta-hajjee, Bamat-Girei and others. Under these circumstances public dhikr and other external manifestations of Ṣūfī affiliation gained precedence over spiritual attributes. Furthermore, from the late 1920s, a growing number of Naqshbandīs began to accept the Soviet order and to return to public life, albeit in a non-religious capacity. A number of undisclosed Naqshbandīs even infiltrated the Communist Party and Soviet administration of Dagestan and Checheno-Ingushetia. Among them was, for example, Bagautdin Arsanov, a Chechen Naqshbandī, who reached the rank of colonel of the Soviet secret services – the NKVD (later KGB)[34] – and who used his insider position to save the lives of many local Naqshbandīs. At the same time, and inevitably under the conditions of Soviet atheism, the 'quality' of Ṣūfīsm deteriorated leading to its morphing into *ṭarīqatism* (lit. 'belonging to a ṭarīqah'). The latter differed significantly from classical Ṣūfism due to its ancestral rather than spiritual essence and its integration into local clan- and jamāʻah-based structures. Among the implications of this phenomenon was the increased distancing of the region's Ṣūfī sheikhs and other Ṣūfīs from their foreign counterparts outside the USSR, some of whom they began to regard as *mutasheikhs* (false sheikhs).[35]

Deportations

As discussed in Chapter 5, the Second World War posed a loyalty test to the Muslims of the USSR. This was especially the case in the North Caucasus which in August 1942 came under German occupation and was subjected to particularly aggressive Nazi propaganda promising freedom from Soviet atheism. Some local leaders responded to the German propaganda and agreed to collaborate. In February 1940, in anticipation of Nazi Germany's invasion, Hasan Israilov (c. 1903–1944), a Chechen and a former correspondent of the *Krestianskaia Gazeta* (Peasants' Newspaper), headed an anti-Soviet uprising in Checheno-Ingushetia. For a short period, rebels under the leadership of Israilov were able to control Galanchozh, Saiasan, Chaberloi and parts of Shatoi district, where they established the Povisional Popular-Revolutionary Government of Checheno-Ingushetia. In early 1942, Mairbek Sheripov (1905–1942), a Chechen ex-lawyer, organized another anti-Soviet revolt in Shatoi and Itumkal and joined forces with Hasan Israilov. It is important to note that most Chechen Muslim clergy did not support the rebels despite the fact that during the occupation, which lasted till February 1943, a number of mosques were reopened. The north-western Caucasus also witnessed the formation of several collaborationist cells, including the Karachai National Committee, the Representation of the Interests of Kabardino-Balkaria and the *Dikaia Diviziia* (Wild Division) of Adygea. According to some estimates, Germany's supporters numbered around 28,000 people.[36] The vast majority of the region's Muslim men, however, fought courageously alongside other Soviet men on the fronts of the Great Patriotic War against the German invaders.[37]

But the relatively few cases of political disloyalty provoked a disproportionately severe reaction from the Stalin leadership. In 1943–44, entire national groups of Chechens, Ingush, Karachais and Balkars were deported to Kazakhstan and other parts of Central Asia. Among nearly a million deportees,[38] the Chechens constituted 408,000, the Ingush 92,000, the Karachais 73,000 and the Balkars 43,000.[39] Deportations were executed in the most brutal fashion with many deportees not surviving the journey or dying of hunger and disease upon arrival as they were not provided with any accommodation or subsistence. The forceful resettlement of the Chechens, Ingush, Balkars and Karachais was accompanied by the redrawing of the region's politico-administrative borders. The Checheno-Ingush Autonomous Republic was liquidated, the Kabardino-Balkar Autonomous Republic was transformed into the Kabardian Autonomous Republic, while the Karachaevo-Cherkess Oblast' was disbanded and absorbed within the Stavropol' krai.

The forceful uprooting of whole national groups and the enormous hardships experienced by the deportees had a powerful impact on their national consciousness. In 1957, following the formal rehabilitation and the return of many Chechens, Ingush,

Balkars and Karachais to the Caucasus, they remained politically, economically and educationally disadvantaged. In the late Soviet period, Chechen grievances related to their deportation would become a major theme in their national mobilization under the leadership of General Dudayev. Similarly, the Balkars and Karachais would rise against Circassian domination and would demand the establishment of autonomous republics of their own.[40] Deportations also strengthened the Ṣūfī identity of Chechens and Ingush, who persisted with dhikr and other Ṣūfī practices related to the Qādirī wirds of Kunta-ḥajjee, Batal-ḥajjee and Golnar-ḥajjee, as well as to the newly formed and more flexible wird of Vis-ḥajjee Zagiev, which allowed its adepts to work in such non-Islamic industries as wine production.[41]

Muslim Authorities and Leadership after the Great Patriotic War

The Muftīate of the North Caucasus

During the Great Patriotic War the North Caucasus acquired its own muftīate, the Spiritual Directorate of Muslims of the North Caucasus (DUM SK, in Russian), based in Buinaksk (formerly Temir-Khan-Shura), one of the main historical centres of Islamic scholarship in Dagestan. The DUM SK had all the trappings of the Ufa-based DUMES and was similarly closely monitored by the Communist Party and security services. At the same time, its creation presented an important step towards the legalization and normalization of Islam and Muslim authority in the region. For historical and theological reasons the DUM SK was dominated by Dagestani 'ulamā'. Until 1975 all its muftīs were from Dagestan: Hizri Gebekov, a Kumyk (in office 1944–50), Magomed Kurbanov, an Avar (in office 1950–75), and Abdulhafiz Omarov, an Avar (in office 1975–78). Only the last Soviet muftī, Mahmud Gekkiev (in office 1978–89), was an ethnic Balkar. Officially, the DUM SK administered around 50 Muslim communities, situated in Dagestan, Kabarda and in other Muslim-dominated administrative units of the North Caucasus and Krasnodar and Stavropol' krais.[42] Within the DUM SK's jurisdiction were also matters related to the issuing of fatwās related to the duration of fasting during Ramaḍān, the slaughter of animals and the payment of *zakāt al-fiṭr* (a payment during Ramaḍān).[43] From the 1950s, the DUM SK leadership, alongside their counterparts from the DUMES, SADUM and DUMZ (the muftīate of Transcaucasia), became involved in the promotion of Soviet foreign policy in the Middle East and other parts of the Muslim world which was then witnessing the rise of national-liberation movements against the British, French and other imperial powers.

Unofficial Islamic Leaders

The creation of the DUM SK introduced the dichotomy of official and unofficial Islam which had previously existed among the Turco-Tatar Muslims of the Volga-Urals. However, due to the survival of Ṣūfī networks in the north-eastern Caucasus, the muftīate's leaders, including its first three muftīs, were secret *murīds* (disciples) or sympathizers with local living Naqshbandī and Shādhilī sheikhs, or of Qādirī Kunta-hajjee and other deceased *ustādh*s (masters). This meant that the relationship between Islamic officialdom and unofficial Islamic authorities was particularly complex, as undisclosed Ṣūfī sheikhs often commanded higher authority than muftīs. Some sheikhs had an ijāzah to teach along both Naqshbandī and Shādhilī ṭarīqahs and had thousands of followers. By the late Soviet period, among Dagestan's most influential sheikhs, who altogether had around 20,000 murīds, were Tabasaran sheikh Abdulla Kurikhsky (d. 1987) from Derbent; Avar sheikh Muhammad Meseiasul (d. 1987) from the village of Nechaevka in Kyzyliurtovskii *raion* (district); Dargin sheikh Magomed-Amin Gadzhiev (d. 1999) from the village of Paraul in the Karabudakhenskii raion; and Avar sheikh Tadzhuddin Ramazanov (d. 2001) from Khasaviurt. Their followers were organized in underground groups which were characterized by structural rigidity, closeness, strict discipline and unconditional submission to particular sheikhs in both the religious and mundane spheres. An important part of the Ṣūfīs' existence were their secret *ziyārat*s (visitations) to the graves of such venerated sheikhs as Muḥammad al-Yaragī, 'Abdurahman al-Sughurī, 'Ali-hajjee Akushinsky, Arsanuka (Amay) and some others. In terms of ethnic make-up the Naqshbandīs included Avars, Dargins, Kumyks, Lezgins, Laks, Tabasarans, Rutuls, Aguls, Chechens, Ingush and Azeris. Shādhilīs were mainly Avars, as well as some Dargins and Kumyks, while Qādirīs were dominated by Chechens, Ingush and Andis.[44] By comparison, in the north-western Caucasus, unofficial Muslim authorities were represented by unregistered mullahs of traditionalist Ḥanafī orientation, as well as by village and community elders who continued to play a central regulatory role while often enjoying a higher moral authority than the registered Muslim clergy. Unofficial Islamic authorities also included several pro-Salafī 'ulamā, who were not affiliated to the DUM SK. Among these was, for example, an 'ālim, Muhammad-Rasul Mugumayev, who in 1957 authored 'An Appeal to Muslims of the Free World on the Conditions of Muslims in the Soviet Union' in which he was critical of the muftīate's subservience to the atheistic state, and because of which he ended up in jail.[45]

The 'Islamic Revival'

From the mid-1980s, in the context of the Gorbachevian political and economic liberalization, the North Caucasus, alongside the Ferghana valley, turned into the epicentre of the 'Islamic revival', which had three major implications for its official and unofficial Islamic leaders. The first related to the temporary breakdown of state–Muslim relations and the radical cadre shake-up within the state-controlled muftīate. The second was the emergence of the new generation of Muslim political activists of Salafī orientation. The third related to the influx in the region, in conditions of political liberalization and the relaxation of external border controls, of foreign Islamic proselytizers, educators and activists who treated local Islamic beliefs and practices as bid'ah. In May 1989, the DUM SK muftī Mahmud Gekkiev (1935–2007) was forced to resign in response to the pressure from representatives of the younger generation of Muslim clergy – the 'young imāms'[46] – who accused him of corruption and collaboration with the KGB. The resignation of Gekkiev and some other 'old imāms' triggered the DUM SK's disintegration along ethnonational and politico-administrative lines and the emergence in 1990 of several new muftīates, headed by 'young imāms'. Of significance was the now undisguised prevalence in the muftīates of Dagestan and Checheno-Ingushetia of ṭarīqatists. In Dagestan, the first muftī was the young Naqshbandī sheikh Muhammad Mukhtar Babatov, an ethnic Kumyk (1954–2015), while in Checheno-Ingushetia it was Shahid Gazabayev, a Chechen (in office 1990–91). Following the separation between Chechnya and Ingushetia in June 1991,[47] Chechnya acquired the first muftī of its own – muftī Magomed-Bashir Arsanukaev (1913–1998) – a highly respected 'ālim and Naqshbandī ustādh, who was a grandson of the aforementioned Deni Arsanov. The newly established muftīate of Ingushetia was headed by Sulambek Evloyev (1937–2008); and the first muftīs of Kabardino-Balkaria and Karachaevo-Cherkessia were 'young imāms' Shafig Pshikachev, a Kabardian (b. 1962),[48] and Ismail-hajjee Berdiyev, a Karachai (b. 1954),[49] respectively.

Unlike the 'young imāms', who included representatives of both the traditionalist and Salafī orientation, Islamic political activists were predominantly Salafīs.[50] Their first organization, the all-USSR Islamic Renaissance Party (IRP) was established in June 1990 in the city of Astrakhan. Among the IRP's leaders were Dagestanis Akhmad-qāḍī Akhtayev (1942–1998) and Bagauddin Kebedov (Bagauddin Dagestani, b. 1945), both ethnic Avars. Akhmad-qāḍī was a professional medical doctor and a self-taught Islamic reformist scholar, while Bagauddin Kebedov studied at Islamic institutes in Syria and Saudi Arabia.[51] Following the IRP's break-up in autumn 1991, its Dagestani branch (alongside the Tajikistani branch) turned into a full-fledged Islamist party – the Islamic Renaissance Party of Dagestan (IRPD). IRPD's members were critical of the ṭarīqatists' ziyārats as being allegedly incompatible with tawḥīd (a belief in the one-ness of God). They advocated the re-Islamization of Dagestani society through Islamic education and the promotion of Islamic family ethics. It is significant that Akhtayev and Kebedov differed in their interpretations of the concepts of jihād and *takfīr* (excommunication). The former considered jihād in moral terms and opposed the use of takfīr to non-Salafī Muslims, while the latter viewed jihād as the Muslims' duty to spread Islam across the world by both peaceful means and by force, and endorsed the employment of takfīr to 'non-proper' Muslims. Bagauddin Dagestani called for the liberation of the North Caucasus from Russian rule by armed jihād and the creation there of an Islamic state. He propagated his ideas among his followers who formed the first Salafī jamā'ah in the town of Kyzyliurt. The jamā'ah also had its own madrasah and publishing house *Satlanda*, which subsequently relocated to Moscow where it was renamed the *Badr* Publishers.[52]

In Dagestan and Chechnya, alongside the IRP and Bagauddin's jamā'ah, there emerged several other, albeit less influential, Islamo-nationalist parties and organizations. Among them were, for example, the organization 'Islamic Path' under the leadership of Bislan Gantemirov (b. 1963) in Chechnya and the Islamic Democratic Party under the leadership of Abdurashid Saidov in Dagestan. Both Gantemirov and Saidov who had an atheistic background perceived ṭarīqatist Islam as a national symbol of Chechens and Dagestanis. Gantemirov was a former policeman, and Saidov a medical doctor.

The proliferation of Salafism in the region was enhanced by the rising presence there, as well as in other Muslim-populated regions of the USSR, of various government and non-government Islamic funds and organizations based in Saudi Arabia, the UAE, Kuwait, Egypt, Libya, Syria, Pakistan, Turkey, Malaysia and other Muslim countries. Most active were the Saudi-based Muslim World League and the Islamic Foundation of *Al-Ḥaramain* and *Ibrahīm al-Ibrahīm*.[53] They generously invested in Islamic construction and publishing and in Saudi and other foreign Islamic proselytizers, educators and Islamists. In the conditions of state paralysis and the drastic personnel changes in Islamic officialdom these foreign Islamic foundations managed to exert considerable influence on the new muftīates' cadre and educational policies. Newly opened madrasahs and Islamic institutes became partially staffed by foreign Islamic teachers and hundreds of the region's young Muslims received scholarships to study at Islamic universities and colleges abroad. Accompanying this was a growing division between some old and some young Muslims who began to perceive the regional version of Soviet Islam as bid'ah.

Conclusion

By the end of the Soviet period, the North Caucasus had become largely integrated within the muftīate-centred system of state–Muslim relations which between 1788 and 1917 had been restricted to the Tatars, Bashkirs and other Muslims of central Russia. In the course of the USSR-wide Sovietization the region's Muslims, especially in urban areas, were transformed into 'Soviet Muslims' and their Islamic beliefs and practices largely became part of their cultural heritage and national identity. Consequently, the Turkish Islamic influence, especially in the north-western Caucasus, drastically diminished, compared to the pre-1917 period. On the other hand, the historically stronger positions of Islam in the region, especially in Dagestan, accounted for significant differences in the region's Islamic dynamic and the evolution of Islamic authority and leadership in particular. These regional Islamic specifics included, for example, the continuing dominance among most Dagestanis, Chechens and Ingush of the stricter Shāfi'ī madhhab of Sunnī Islam and the persistence of the social function of Islam in many local rural communities in spite of their collectivization. The reason for this was the region's inaccessible mountain landscape and its enclave industrialization resulting in some preservation of social and legal practices informed by sharī'ah and 'adats. Another distinctive feature was the retention, albeit much reduced, of the Islamo-Arabist scholarship of both the traditionalist and revivalist orientations and the persistence, at least in the north-east, of Naqshbandī, Shādhilī and Qādirī ṭarīqahs. Among important repositories and transmitters of the region's Islamic legal and Ṣūfī traditions were the region's Institutes of History, Literature, Archaeology and Ethnography,[54] some members of which came from respected 'ulamā' dynasties and outshone official Muslim clergy and underground sheikhs in their knowledge of Arabic, the Qur'ān, Ḥadīth and fiqh. They continued to secretly fulfil many functions of 'ulamā' and remained aware of contemporary Islamic debate. At the end of the Soviet era, these regional Islamic specifics were translated into the particularly intensive 'Islamic revival' and the merger of Islam with politics. They also accounted for the predominantly Ṣūfī orientation of Dagestani, Chechen and Ingush 'young imāms', compared to their Tatar counterparts. Later on, in the late 1990s, they contributed to the transformation of the Chechen national movement into the Chechen front of global jihādism, and in the 2010s to the comparatively high proportion of Chechens and Dagestanis among Eurasian fighters for Daesh.

Chapter Seven

THE SOUTH CAUCASUS

Introduction

Unlike the Muslim-majority North Caucasus, which since the 1920s has been part of the Russian Federation, the Soviet South Caucasus, or Transcaucasia, was divided into three union republics of historically Muslim Azerbaijan and Christian Armenia and Georgia. Among the decisive factors for the politico-administrative inequality between the Caucasus' northern and southern parts may have been Transcaucasia's mostly peaceful history of incorporation into the Russian Empire and the comparatively greater number of ethnic Georgians, Armenians and Azerbaijanis among the Bolshevik leadership. In terms of population size Transcaucasia was on par with the North Caucasus; by the end of the 1930s the largest republic was Georgia (3.5 million), followed by Azerbaijan (3.2 million) and Armenia (1.3 million).[1] A major difference between the Muslim North Caucasus and Muslim Azerbaijan relates to the prevalence among Azerbaijanis (Azeris)[2] of Shīʿī Twelver Islam, which has affected the nature of their Islamic leadership and its relationship with the state. Significant also was the existence in Azerbaijan of a sizeable Sunnī minority (Lezgins, Avars, Kurds and some others) and of the Christian Armenian population in the Nagorno-Karabakh Autonomous Oblast' (NKAO). Christian Georgia has had significant Muslim minorities, represented by Meskhetian Turks (Ahiska Turks) and Adjarians, both of Sunnī Ḥanafī orientation.

Due to Azerbaijan's oil riches its level of industrialization in the late imperial Russian and Soviet periods was significantly higher than in other Muslim-majority parts of Eurasia (with the possible exception of the Volga region). Consequently, the degree of societal secularization there was greater, while Azerbaijanis' Turkism-based national consciousness began to compete with, or even to supersede, their Shīʿī Islamic identity. The decline in the Azerbaijanis' religiosity was accompanied by the significantly reduced influence of both the official and unofficial Islamic authorities. The Transcaucasian muftīate (DUMZ, in Russian) which, unlike in the imperial Russian period, was established in Baku became de facto co-opted within the Azerbaijani Soviet political establishment.

The chapter focuses on the Islamic and Islamo-national leadership in Soviet Azerbaijan. First, it offers a brief account of the region's Islamic and Islamo-national dynamic prior to the 1917 Bolshevik Revolution. It then examines the political standing of Azerbaijani Muslim and national leaders during the Russian Civil War and during the time of the Azerbaijan Democratic Republic (ADR, 1918–20), in particular. It proceeds to discuss the implications for both Shīʿī and Sunnī clergy of Azerbaijan's Bolshevization. After this we address the impact of the Second World War on Islam and its leadership in the region. The chapter then examines the DUMZ's Shīʿī and Sunnī leadership and their relations with the state and grassroots Muslim communities. The final section discusses the 'Islamic revival' and the impact on it of the 1978 Islamic Revolution in Iran and the Armenia–Azerbaijan conflict over Nagorno-Karabakh which erupted in 1988.

Islamic and National Leadership in the Late Nineteenth and the Early Twentieth Centuries

Incorporation within the Russian Empire

The South Caucasus became part of the Russian Empire in the nineteenth century in the course of a series of Russo-Ottoman and Russo-Iranian wars. Unlike the North Caucasus, which was conquered by Russia through the brutal Caucasus War, the South Caucasus was incorporated relatively peacefully as a result of political treaties between St. Petersburg and the region's Georgian and Muslim rulers. In 1801 Georgia's largest polity of Kartli-Kakheti accepted St. Petersburg's suzerainty and its capital city of Tiflis (Tbilisi) was made the centre of Russian Transcaucasia, where the Russian governor general resided.[3] In the following decades St. Petersburg subjugated Georgia's other polities, as well as the Muslim khānates of Shirwan, Kuba, Sheki (Shaki), Karabakh, Irevan (Yerevan), Ganja and Nakhchivan (Nakhichevan) which previously had different degrees of dependency on neighbouring Iran. In ethno-confessional terms these khānates were dominated by Turkic Azeris who were largely Shī'a, although some adhered to Sunnī Islam either of Shāfi'ī or Ḥanafī madhhabs. Among the khānates' other residents were Kurds, Armenians, Jews and representatives of other ethnic groups who professed Zoroastrianism, Gregorian Christianity and Judaism, respectively. Transcaucasia's Azeris were kin to the more numerous Azeris in northern Iran. The Shī'ī Azeri community became divided as a result of the 1813 Gulistan and the 1828 Turkmanchay treaties between Russia and Iran, according to which the Azeris living to the north of the Aras River came under Russian rule while those to the south of the river remained in Iran. In the 1850s St. Petersburg instrumentalized the Azeris' Shī'īsm by mobilizing them against the Sunnī ghazawāt of imām Shamīl, and in its confrontation with the Sunnī Ottoman Turks. By the early twentieth century Russian Transcaucasia, which unlike the North Caucasus was governed by a civil administration, was divided into the guberniias of Tiflis, Baku, Elizabethpol and Irevan, as well as Batum oblast'. In 1878, by the San-Stefano Treaty, signed in the aftermath of the Russo-Ottoman war of 1877–78, the Russian Empire annexed the Black Sea Batum region populated by Sunnī Adjarians.

The Transcaucasian Muftīate

An important aspect of the Russian governance of Transcaucasia was St. Petersburg's control over its Muslim population, especially in the context of the unfolding ghazawāt in the North Caucasus. Following the Russian annexation in 1804 of the Khānate of Ganja, which was renamed Elizabethpol, St. Petersburg took steps towards establishing good relations with the local Muslim authorities. In 1805 Tsar Alexander I (r. 1801–1825), issued a 'Legal Act on Institutionalization of Islamic Clergy in Transcaucasia' and in 1823 he endorsed the establishment of an official post of Shīʿī sheikh-ul-Islām. In 1832, the office of sheikh-ul-Islām was supplemented by that of a muftī who was to administer Sunnī Muslims. Sheikh-ul-Islām and the muftī were appointed by the Tsar, on the basis of a proposal from the governor general. Candidates for both posts were chosen from loyalist 'ulamā' and *mujtahids* (Shīʿī jurists) who received generous rewards from the state. The first sheikh-ul-Islām was *akhund* ('Islamic cleric', in Persian) Muhammad Ali Guseinov, while the first muftī was Tadjuddin Mustafin. Both were tasked with appointing 'suitable' mullahs and qāḍīs in local Muslim communities.[4]

In 1872 Tsar Alexander II (r. 1855–81) authorized the creation in Tiflis of the Transcaucasian muftīate – the Directorate of Shīʿī and Sunnī Muslims who resided in the Baku, Elizabethpol, Tiflis and Irevan *guberniias* (provinces). The muftīate was headed by Shīʿī sheikh-ul-Islām, akhund Ahmed Guseinzadeh and Sunnī muftī, hajjee Gamid-efendi Mustafa-efendi-zadeh. Within the muftīate's competence were the nomination of local qāzīs (qāḍīs), mosque imāms (mollahs)[5] and mudarrises, the formulation of the madrasah curriculum, the management of waqf properties and the handling of Muslims' complaints against the civil authorities. At the provincial level, the muftīate was represented by *majlises* (councils), which consisted of three senior Muslim clergy and which acted as intermediaries between sheikh-ul-Islām and the muftī, on the one side, and local Muslim communities, on the other.[6] From 1881, candidates for the posts of sheikh-ul-Islām and muftī were to be chosen by the Russian Minister of the Interior. They were put on the state payroll with an annual salary of 1,600 rubles each, which was equivalent to the salary of an army colonel. Sheikh-ul-Islām, the muftī and other registered Muslim clergy were exempt from any other state duties and entitled to a state pension and extra expenses and subsistence during their travel. Children of muftīate officials who worked for 20 years or more were granted the same rights as children of the Russian nobility.[7] The establishment of the Transcaucasian muftīate marked the inclusion of the Shīʿī and Sunnī Muslims of Transcaucasia into the imperial Russian system of state–Muslim relations, which earlier had been exclusively centred on the Orenburg muftīate. A corollary was the emergence of a stratum of pro-government official Muslim clergy who had ambivalent relations with both Islamo-national leaders and unofficial Islamic authorities.

Islamo-national Leadership

From the 1860s the Muslim part of Transcaucasia witnessed the rise of an Islamo-national reformist movement, *maarifchilik* (enlightenment), which developed against the backdrop of the Baku-centred oil-related economic boom and accompanying partial social modernization. Like jadīdism among the Tatars, maarifchilik was initially mainly concerned with the language and curriculum of Islamic education. Among its leading figures were Mirza Fatali Akundzadeh (Akhundov, 1812–1878), a renowned Azeri Muslim philosopher and playwright, Seyid Azim Shirvani (1835–1888), an Azeri poet and liberal politician, as well as Azeri intellectuals and publicists

Hasan-bey Malikov-Zardabi (1837–1907), Ahmet Agaoglu (Agayev, 1869–1939) and Jalil Mammadguluzadeh (1866–1932). Akundzadeh was the first to raise the issue of replacing the Arabic-based Azeri alphabet by the Latin-based one as a medium for enlightenment of the region's Muslims. On the other hand, Shirvani, who similarly denounced the existing system of confessional education controlled by Muslim clergy who he accused of stifling the Azeris' modern development, favoured a switch to the Russian language which he regarded as the means for the Azeris' intellectual and cultural modernization. In 1869, in the town of Shemakhi, he founded the first Russo-Azeri school, the curriculum of which included the Russian language and various humanities and science subjects.

By comparison, Malikov-Zardabi, who associated Arabic- and Persian-based Islamic education with backwardness, adhered to linguistic and cultural Turkism. Like Ismaīl Gaspiralī in the Crimea Malikov-Zardabi founded the first Azeri-language periodical, the newspaper *Ekinchi* (Ploughman, 1875–77) which advocated the creation of a unified Turkic language as the way for the cultural unity of Russia's Muslims and for the Azeris' distancing of themselves from Persian-based Shīʿī Islamic traditionalism. On the other hand, Ahmet Agaoglu and Jalil Mammadguluzadeh focused on the religious dimension of their critique of local mollahs who they accused of corruption and distortion of the Qur'ān's teaching, and called for the lessening of their influence on the Muslims of Transcaucasia. Mammadguluzadeh circulated his ideas on the pages of the journal *Mollah Nasreddin* (1906–20), which he founded in Tiflis. By the late nineteenth century, maarifchilik evolved into a wider sociopolitical movement which included proponents of liberalism, Turkism and Islamism.[8] Azeri liberals, who were mainly merchants and industrialists, viewed themselves as part of the Russian and the wider European liberal movement. Azeri Turkists, on the other hand, stressed the Turkic element in the Azeris' national identity and saw their future lying in close links with the Ottoman Turks. Meanwhile, Azeri Islamists continued to prioritize the Islamic component in the Azeri identity. The essence of the Azeri national debate was summarized by the Azeri intellectual Ali-bey Husein-zadeh (1864–1941) as *Turklashmak, Islamlashmak, Avropalashmak* (Turkify, Islamize, Europeanize).[9]

Socialist-Democratic Leadership

In the early twentieth century industrial Baku became one of the main revolutionary centres of the Russian Empire. In 1904, in Tiflis was established the first Muslim social-democratic organization in the region, the *Gummet* Party (The Party of Energy, 1904–20), which united over a hundred Azeri left-wing politicians.[10] It began to publish its own newspaper *Gummet* in the Azeri language. Gummet's Marxist orientation was strengthened when it was joined in 1905 by Meshari Azizbekov (1876–1918) and Nariman Narimanov (1870–1922), members of the Russian Social Democratic Party (RSDRP). During the Russian bourgeois revolutions of 1905–7 and 1917, Gummet's members, alongside Armenian left-wingers, were involved in the organization of protests by oil industry workers.

Between the Russian Civil War and the Second World War

The 1917 Bolshevik Revolution intensified political activism across the region and led to the establishment in April 1918 of Soviet power in the form of the Baku Commune and the Tiflis-centred Transcaucasian Democratic Federation (ZDFR, in Russian), which included Georgia, Armenia and Azerbaijan. Among the Baku Commune's leaders were Gummet members and other Bolsheviks and leftist Socialist Revolutionaries (SR), while the leadership of ZDFR consisted of Georgian, Armenian and Azeri Mensheviks, liberals and nationalists. The Baku Commune lasted till the end of July 1918. ZDFR was replaced in May 1918 by the three independent national states of Georgia (DRG, 1918–21), Armenia (The First Republic of Armenia, 1918–20) and the ADR under the leadership of Mammad Emin Rasulzadeh, the chairman of the Azeri National Party *Musavat* (Equality).[11] The establishment of the ADR symbolized the victory, albeit short-lived, of the secular Azeri liberal national leadership. In 1918, the ADR's *Milli Mejlis* (National Council) endorsed the separation of religion from the state as well as universal suffrage, thereby making Azerbaijan the first Muslim country that enfranchised women.[12] At the same time, the Rasulzade leadership retained the Tsarist institution of the muftīate as the medium of state control over Muslims. In 1918 the office of the muftīate was moved from Tbilisi to Baku.[13] In 1920–21, the ADR, together with Armenia and Georgia, ceased to exist and their territories were incorporated into the Soviet state. Initially, the Bolsheviks united Georgia, Armenia and Azerbaijan within the Transcaucasian Soviet Federative Socialist Republic (ZSFSR, 1922–36). Subsequently, the ZSFSR was divided into three union republics – the Azerbaijani Soviet Socialist Republic (AzSSR,1936–91), the Armenian Soviet Socialist Republic (Ar.SSR, 1936–91) and the Georgian Soviet Socialist Republic (GSSR, 1936–91).

The Sovietization of Azerbaijan was entrusted to the Revolutionary Committee (RevCom) under the leadership of Nariman Narimanov who oversaw the implementation of Lenin's decrees on the nationalization of land as well as of oil and other heavy industries – measures largely supported by the impoverished Muslim majority. The siding of most Muslim clergy with khāns and beks, who previously owned most of the land, undermined the authority and mobilizing potential of the former. Meanwhile, as elsewhere, the Bolsheviks' approach towards Islam was relatively liberal, compared to their ruthless stance on Orthodox Christianity. In July 1922, Friday was made the official day off and the traditional Azerbaijani holidays of *Ashura Gunu* (The Day of 'Āshūrā'), *Gurban-Bayrami* (The Feast of Sacrifice), *Ramazan-Bayrami* (The Holiday of Fasting) and *Mawlīd* (Birth of the Prophet Muḥammad) were declared public holidays, with local mosques being provided with food supplies on these days. Still, some Azerbaijani Muslim clergy, especially among the Sunnīs, were able to incite a series of anti-Soviet revolts in Gubatly, Zakatala, Sheki, Shemakhi and Quba. The Bolsheviks responded by applying the divide-and-rule tactic, by privileging the Shī'ī clergy, some of whom formed the movement of Red Mollahs who subscribed to the slogan 'The Soviet power is compatible with Islam'. By 1925 the RevCom succeeded in securing the backing of the majority of Azerbaijani Muslims and the neutrality of most Muslim clergy, whose theological credentials were further undermined as a result of the replacement in 1924 of the Arabic-based Azerbaijani alphabet by the Latin one and, a decade later, by Latin's replacement by Cyrillic. They were also weakened by the loss of their external patron – Ottoman Turkey – due to the dissolution of the Caliphate by the nationalist leadership under Kemal Atatürk (1881–1938).[14]

From the mid-1920s, the Bolsheviks' relative tolerance of Islam and the Muslim clergy was succeeded by their indiscriminate assault on Islam. As was the case across the whole of USSR, a key agency of the anti-religious campaign was the Azerbaijani branch of the League of the Militant Godless, which became engaged in the persecution of akhunds, mujtahids and mollahs; in the mass closures of mosques, madrasahs and sharīʿah courts; in the administrative and propaganda campaign against the Shīʿī procession of *taṭbīr* (self-flagellation during ʿĀshūrā'), known as *Shakhsei-Vakhsei*,[15] and other public Islamic gatherings; and in enforcement of *hujūm* – the forcible de-veiling of Azerbaijani women. Between 1925 and 1936 several thousand Azerbaijani Muslim clergy were either killed or sent to the Gulag, while the number of mosques was reduced from around 3,000 to 206, many of them being converted into leisure clubs. Among the mosques destroyed was the Bibi Heybet mosque,[16] which was one of the holiest Islamic sites in the region.[17] The hujūm was symbolically launched in 1927 on 8 March – international women's day. It involved organized meetings and other public gatherings during which Muslim women were encouraged to throw away their *paranjas* (body veils). Within the hujūm campaign Muslim women were subjected to enforced socializing through their enrolment in school and college education and employment. The women's de-veiling was achieved in record time; in 1929 the number of de-veiled women did not exceed 2,300, but by the early 1930s the majority of younger women did not wear paranjas.[18] In 1929, Shakhsei-Vakhsei processions were officially banned on the grounds of health and safety concerns. Overall, the combination of Sovietized secularism and a direct atheistic assault on Muslim clergy dealt a severe blow to Islam and Muslim leadership in Azerbaijan. Still, the Shīʿī principle of taqīyyah enabled some Azerbaijani imāms, Ṣūfīs and other Muslim authorities, as well as ordinary people, to retain their Islamic beliefs. An important role in the perpetuation of Islamic tradition belonged to mazārs – *pīrs* which became disguised as historical and cultural objects.

Islamic Leadership and Authority during and after the Second World War

The Transcaucasian Muftīate

As we saw in Chapter 5, the invasion of the USSR by Nazi Germany on 22 June 1941 introduced major changes in the Kremlin's policy towards Islam and its leadership. The situation in the Caucasus was particularly grave as the Germans were advancing towards northern Iran and Azerbaijan. In August 1941 the USSR, alongside Great Britain, invaded neighbouring Iran in order to prevent Germany from seizing the Iranian oilfields.[19] Domestically, the Kremlin moved from a policy of suppression towards collaboration with the region's Muslim leadership. Azerbaijan's Muslims and their leaders were spared deportation.[20] In April 1944 the Stalin leadership decided to establish in Baku the Transcaucasian muftīate – the Spiritual Directorate of Muslims of Transcaucasus (DUMZ, in Russian) – as the official representative body of Muslims of the region. Like its Tiflis-based predecessor, the DUMZ was headed by Shī'ī sheikh-ul-Islām, who had overall authority, and a Sunnī muftī. The first Soviet sheikh-ul-Islām was akhund Aga Alizadeh (in office 1944–54), while the first muftī was Ibrahim Efendi-zadeh. Like Ufa muftī Rasulev and Tashkent muftī Babakhan, Aga Alizadeh was a son of a highly respected Islamic scholar. He studied in Iran and returned to Baku in 1898 to serve as imām in Baku's Taza-Pīr mosque.[21] Compared to the imperial Russian period, both sheikh-ul-Islām and the muftī were elected by Muslim clerics, rather than being appointed by the Interior Minister but they were still closely monitored by the Council for the Affairs of Religious Cults (CARC). Another difference related to the fact that sheikh-ul-Islām, the muftī and DUMZ's other members were not put on the state payroll and were left to fend for themselves. Among the main sources of their income were zakāt and *ṣadaqah* (voluntary payment for various Muslim rituals), which were substantial during the holidays of 'Āshūrā', Ramazan-Bayrami and Gurban-Bayrami.[22] In other respects, DUMZ's functions were not dissimilar to those of its pre-revolutionary predecessor. It acted as the only official Muslim governing body, which registered and administered the Muslim communities of Transcaucasia, including Sunnī Adjarians in Georgia, and, alongside SADUM, DUMES and DUM SK, represented Soviet Muslims abroad. It was also responsible for the organization of hajj of a small number of carefully screened Muslims to Mecca, Medina, as well as to the Shī'ī holy sites in Karbala, Najaf and Meshed.[23] DUMZ was also actively involved in the Soviet state's external politics, especially during the short existence in 1945–46 of the pro-Kremlin Azerbaijani People's Government in northern Iran.

By 1947, in Azerbaijan, DUMZ oversaw 22 mosques which employed around 70 mollahs and other Muslim clergy. In the mid-1950s, in the context of another anti-religious wave, the number of functioning mosques was reduced to 16, with only two mosques in Baku.[24] Like other Soviet muftīs both sheikh-ul-Islām and the muftī issued Qur'ān-, or Ḥadīth-based rulings for various aspects of Muslims' life under atheistic Soviet rule. Muftīs in their fatwās eulogized the Soviet way of life and made non-obligatory the observance of Uraza, Gurban-Bayrami, Ramazan-Bayrami and the payment of zakāt. The latter was justified by the disappearance of the poor under socialism.[25] Among the DUMZ's special features, in comparison to the other three Soviet muftīates, was its association with the Azerbaijani Communist Party and the Azerbaijani Soviet authorities. These informal ties enabled the DUMZ to safeguard itself from the closure of over 40 disguised pīrs.[26] In the 1980s, relations between the Azerbaijani Communist Party and the muftīate received a further boost due to the close personal relations between Heydar Aliyev (1923–2003), Azerbaijan's charismatic Communist Party leader and a member of the Soviet Politburo, and sheikh-ul-Islām Allashukur Hummat Pashazadeh (in office 1980–). During this period DUMZ excelled SADUM in representing the USSR's Muslims abroad.

Unofficial Muslim Authorities

As in other parts of Soviet Muslim Eurasia, Muslim clerics, affiliated to the muftīate, coexisted with more numerous underground folk mollahs, itinerant mollahs, sayyīds, Ṣūfīs, as well as *marthiakhans* (religious singers).[27] Unofficial Muslim authorities secretly used empty unregistered mosque buildings as assembly points, as well as for prayer services and for the provision of basic Islamic education. They also looked after pīrs and other Ṣūfī sites, ran over 40 *mollah-khanas* (prayer houses) and administered, alongside registered Muslim clergy, rites of passage, especially those related to Muslim burial. According to CARC's statistics, in the late 1950s there were 65 functioning pirs, out of a total of 305 that existed in the pre-Soviet period.[28] Over 20 of the most active pirs, which attracted thousands of pilgrims in the month of Muharram, were situated in Nakhichevan ASSR. During pilgrimage believers would chant marthiahs and flog themselves. In some parts of Azerbaijan small groups of Bahā'is' were also active.[29]

In Karabakh's Jebrayil district, considerable influence was exerted by the so-called *Chelebis*, who followed the Ṣūfī teaching of *Maqām-i Chelebi* (Head of the Order), a direct descendant of Mawlānā Rūmī (1207–1273),[30] the founder of the Mevlevī ṭarīqah. In the 1960s, Chelebis de facto controlled the villages of Khavusly and Sirik where they introduced compulsory zakāt and fiṭr payment on each family.[31] In Sunnī-dominated northern Azerbaijan, Naqshbandī Ṣūfīs had some religious and political influence. Arguably, unofficial Muslim authorities played a pivotal role in the transmission, albeit on a low scale, of Islamic traditions and ensured the perpetuation of various aspects of Islamic religiosity among some sectors of Azerbaijani society. Overall, in comparative terms, throughout the Soviet period the level of such disguised religiosity was higher in Shī'a-dominated southern Azerbaijan, especially in Nakhichevan Autonomous Republic and the districts of Masally, Bilesuar, Jalilabad and Lankaran. For example, during *Muharramlik* ('Āshūrā' festival) many male and female inhabitants of the rural areas of southern Azerbaijan abstained from work.[32]

Meskhetian Turks and Adjarians

Outside Azerbaijan, the largest Muslim communities were those of Meskhetian Turks (Ahiska Turks) and Adjarians, both of whom were Ḥanafī Sunnīs. The fate of the former was tragic: during the Second World War they, alongside Chechens, Ingush, Balkars, Karachais and Kalmyks from the North Caucasus, were 'preventively' deported from Georgia's Meskheti, Javakheti and Adjara regions to Central Asia's Fergana valley, to the Tashkent and Samarqand oblasts of Uzbekistan, to Chui and Osh oblasts of Kyrgyzstan and to southern Kazakhstan. The total number of deportees from Georgia was over 120,000 persons including, apart from the Meskhetian Turks, Hemshins, Batumi Kurds and Terekeme. In 1957, with the post-Stalin thaw, when most deportees from the northern Caucasus were allowed to return to their homeland, the Meskhetian Turks along with the Volga Germans and Crimean Tatars were denied such a right. Throughout the 1960s around 25,000 Meskhetian Turks, whose passport nationality was registered as 'Azerbaijanis', managed to resettle in Azerbaijan while hoping for a return to Georgia.

In 1969 the Kremlin reinstated the Meskhetian Turks' civic rights, albeit it did not legitimize their return to Georgia. In June 1989, against the background of a land dispute, over a hundred Meskhetian Turks were killed during ethnic pogroms in the Ferghana province of Uzbekistan. Subsequently, over 70,000 of them fled Uzbekistan and settled in Azerbaijan, Russia and Ukraine, as well as Kazakhstan and Kyrgyzstan.[33] Even now, during the rest of the Soviet era and after the end of the USSR, the Meskhetian Turks have been unable to return to their homeland in Georgia. The Meskhetian Turks' ensuing inferior socio-economic and legal status turned them into ethno-confessional outcasts. This, in turn, strengthened the ethnonational, rather than religious, markers of their identity, thus accounting for the prevalence among them of national rather than Islamic authorities.[34]

As discussed in Chapter 3, the Islamic leadership of Batumi Muslims, who until 1878 had been under the direct protection of the Ottoman Caliphate, was structurally and doctrinally influenced by their Ottoman counterparts, albeit formally they were within the jurisdiction of the Transcaucasian muftīate. Before the Bolshevik takeover the Batum oblast' had over a hundred mosques, several dozen madrasahs and maktabs, as well as functioning sharī'ah courts. However, in the course of the Stalinist anti-Islamic campaign, which was particularly brutal in Georgia, almost all Islamic infrastructure was destroyed, while most Muslim clergy perished. In the 1950s, just one mosque – the Batumi Central Mosque – was reopened during the Khrushchevian 'thaw'. As a result, Muslim beliefs and rituals were perpetuated, albeit on a low scale, by underground folk mullahs. These mullahs secretly oversaw celebrations of *mawlīd* (Prophet's Birthday) and administered funerals and other major events of the life cycle. In mountain areas, their authority was higher as they had some functions of qāẓī during the mediation of land, property- and family-related disputes.[35]

The 'Islamic Revival'

The Impact of the Islamic Revolution in Iran

The 1978 Islamic Revolution in demonstratively Westernized Iran sent shock waves through neighbouring Azerbaijan. These events posed an existential challenge to some ethnic and, especially practising, Azerbaijani Shī'a who became exposed to Khomeini's radio propaganda coming in the Azerbaijani language from Tabriz. A group of young Shī'ī Azerbaijanis established an underground Islamist organization, *Khomeinichiliar Tashkilaty* (Organisation of Khomeini's Followers), in the village of Nardaran, 35 kilometres north of Baku. In the early 1980s, it evolved into the *Azerbaijan Islam Partiiasy* (Azerbaijan Islamic Party, AIP) under the leadership of Alikram Aliyev and Hajjee-Vaqif. AIP united several dozen local Islamic activists who were involved in distributing leaflets and other Islamic publications which spread knowledge about Shī'ī Islam and which advocated closer links with Iran's Shī'a and the establishment in Azerbaijan of an Islamic state headed by an imām. The Azerbaijani authorities responded by tightening control over the information flow from Iran and by emphasizing Azerbaijan's ethnonational, rather that Islamo-national, unity. It is significant that both DUMZ's sheikh-ul-Islām and its muftī sided with official Baku's message of national unity. In the same year they also openly supported the Soviet military invasion of Afghanistan, compared with the reserved reaction to it from the leaders of the DUMES, DUM SK and SADUM. Subsequently, the leadership-independent Azerbaijan as well as its Islamic officialdom have remained wary of the Islamic Republic of Iran and opted for much closer links with secular Turkey, the majority population of which were Ḥanafī Sunnīs.[36]

The Nagorno-Karabakh Conflict

A decade later, the Islamic component of Azerbaijani national identity was evoked in the course of its conflict (1988–94) with historically Christian Armenia over the 'ownership' of Armenian-dominated NKAO in Azerbaijan.[37] The conflict started as a secessionist movement of Karabakh Armenians who took advantage of political and ideological chaos and the crumbling Communist Party and Soviet structures. It soon evolved into a wider ethno-territorial confrontation which, externally, was perceived along the lines of the 'clash of civilizations'. An important factor in this framing was the ideational and actual involvement in the conflict of representatives of the large Armenian diaspora, who treated it as part of an 'eternal' Turkish-Armenian and, implicitly, as an Islamo-Christian conflict, which in 1915 led to the deaths of over a million Christian Armenians at the hands of Muslim Turks. The conflict provoked international Islamic solidarity with Azerbaijanis on the part of the Organisation of Islamic Cooperation (OIC), Saudi Arabia, Pakistan, Iran and other Muslim states. Inside Azerbaijan, however, the conflict acted as a powerful factor in the national consolidation of secular and practising Shī'ī and Sunnī Azerbaijanis, including their official and unofficial Islamic authorities.[38] At the official level, at least initially, the Azerbaijani political and religious elite primarily relied on the Communist Party and Soviet mechanisms for the conflict's de-escalation and perceived Moscow as its only viable broker.[39]

Perestroika and the Islamic Leadership

The Islamic Revolution in Iran and the Nagorno-Karabakh conflict significantly affected the pace and nature of the 'Islamic revival' in Azerbaijan. Unlike the USSR's other Muslim-dominated regions, which during Gorbachevian perestroika experienced an Islamic building and publishing boom and an influx of foreign Islamic foundations and proselytizers, Azerbaijan's 'Islamic revival' was subdued as it was over-shadowed by its Karabakh-related national, rather than religious, mobilization. Another factor was official Baku's nervousness regarding the potential spread of Khomeini's Islamist ideology within Azerbaijan and therefore its continuing tight immigration control, especially on the Azerbaijani-Iranian border. For these reasons Azerbaijan's opening up to the Islamic world was measured and state-controlled, with sheikh-ul-Islām Allahshukur Pashazadeh acting as its main mediator in channelling its increased international activity in the Islamic world. In 1986 Baku hosted the OIC-sponsored international Islamic conference 'Muslims in the Struggle for Peace', which was attended by over 600 delegates from 60

Muslim countries. In 1987 Pashazadeh was elected as the head and co-chairman of the International Forum 'For a Nuclear-Free World, for the Salvation of Mankind', held in Moscow, and in 1991 he became a member of one of the OIC committees.

At the same time Azerbaijan witnessed the emergence of a number of small Islamic political, educational and ethical organizations, which operated either within the pro-democracy national movement or USSR-wide ethical and ecological networks. Among the former was, for example, the abovementioned AIP under the leadership of Alikram Aliyev (1940–2011) who advocated Azerbaijanis' re-Islamization through education. In 1988 Aliyev became a member of the *Azad Dindarlar Shurasy* (Council of Free Believers), a special structure within the anti-establishment Popular Front of Azerbaijan (PFA) which campaigned for Azerbaijan's greater economic and political autonomy from Moscow. In contrast, the *Tovba* (Repentance) Society, headed by hajjee Abdul Abdulov (b. 1940),[40] promoted Islamic ethics as part of the Gorbachevian anti-alcohol campaign. Abdulov's pro-government position enabled him to expand the *Tovba*'s structures across Azerbaijan; in 1989 the government of Ayaz Mutallibov (b. 1938) permitted the *Tovba* to take hold of the historical Ashumov mosque, which had not been registered with the DUMZ. The mosque was then renamed after Imām Ḥuseyn. Other low-key and short-lived Islamic organizations included the *Azerbaijan Taraqqi Islam Partiyasy* (The Azerbaijan Islamic Party of Progress), the organization of *Azad Ruhanilar* (Free Muslim Clergy) and the organization of *Qardashlyk* (Brotherhood).[41]

Conclusion

By the end of the 1980s, for historical and socio-economic reasons the level of Sovietized secularization of Azerbaijani and other Transcaucasian Muslims was considerably higher than in the North Caucasus and Central Asia, comparable in many respects to that in the Volga-Urals. The Transcaucasian muftīate – the DUMZ – had become de facto co-opted within the Soviet establishment and the bulk of the region's Muslims had turned into so-called 'ethnic Muslims',[42] who recognized their Islamic heritage but ceased to observe daily prayer or comply with Islamic requirements and the traditional Muslim dress code. Only around 10 per cent of the Muslim population continued to practise Islam in one form or the other. *Jum'ah-Namāz* (Friday Prayer) was observed among some elderly men in rural areas during the winter period, when agricultural work was suspended. Even then the number of mosque attendees barely exceeded several dozen,[43] though their number was considerably higher during the Gurban-Bayrami and Uraza-Bayrami holidays. The same could be said about Muharramlik in Nakhchivan and other areas along the Iranian border, and about the celebration of Mawlīd in Zakataly and Balaken districts in north-western Azerbaijan. As for the rich Islamic scholarly heritage of the South Caucasus, especially related to the period of Sharwānshāhs, it was severely undermined by decades of state-sponsored atheism. Still, as in other Muslim-majority parts of the USSR, its fragmented perpetuation was safeguarded by orientalists working in the Azerbaijani branch of the Soviet Academy of Sciences (est. 1935) and the Institute of the Peoples of the Near and Middle East (est. 1958).

The Azerbaijanis' Muslim-ness was however maintained through the morphing of their Islamic beliefs and practices into national traditions, as well as their absorption into various Soviet practices and rituals. Thus, the widely celebrated ancient Iranian holiday of *Nowruz* (the vernal equinox) acquired an Islamo-national dimension, while Bibi-Heybet, Rahim-Hanim and other venerated Islamic pīrs were transformed into Azerbaijani national cultural objects which continued to attract mass pilgrimages. In rural parts of Azerbaijan, civil marriage was often reinforced by a *kebin* (an Islamic marriage), conducted by an unofficial mullah; in some cases, an Islamic marriage even took priority and was not accompanied by its state registration. Similarly, Islamic marriages were dissolved by folk mollahs in accordance with the sharī'ah principle of *ṭalāq*.[44] The only universally and secretly observed Islamic practices were male circumcision (*sunnet*), Islamic burial (*janazah*) and post-burial wakes, all of which also involved a mollah. It is significant that these practices were followed even by some Azerbaijani Communist Party and Soviet leaders and functionaries despite their official adherence to atheism. So, on balance, the authority of these unofficial mollahs was probably greater than that of the DUMZ-affiliated Muslim clergy.

Chapter Eight

CENTRAL ASIA AND KAZAKHSTAN

Introduction

The Sovietization of Central Asia and Kazakhstan[1] posed the biggest challenge to the Bolshevik leadership because of the size of both the region and its Muslim population[2] and the particularly strong position there of Islam. Unlike Muslims of the Volga-Urals and Transcaucasia, who, prior to the Bolshevik takeover, were included in the imperial Russian system of state–Muslim relations based on the state-controlled muftīate, most Muslims of Central Asia, alongside the North Caucasus, remained outside it. St. Petersburg's focus on military control over the region also meant that Russian social and cultural interference in the region, with the exception of Tashkent and a handful of other areas in Russian Turkestan, was negligible, and the social and legal order, as well as the ethics of the bulk of the sedentary population, was defined by Islam. Consequently, 'ulamā', imāms, Ṣūfī sheikhs and other traditional Muslim authorities maintained high religious and moral authority, especially in the Ferghana valley. In the case of Kazakhs and other Muslim nomads, some of whom had been subjected to direct imperial Russian governance, their lifestyle and value system were shaped by a combination of nomadism, Genghizid genealogical tribalism, shamanism and Islam. Among them, authority rested with tribal biys and itinerant Ṣūfī sheikhs – *khojahs*. From the late nineteenth century the region witnessed the limited proliferation of Islamic reformism – jadīdism – which, however, differed significantly from Russia-centred jadīdism among the Tatars, many of whom were involved in the all-Russia political and cultural debate. The thinking of Central Asian jadīds, on the other hand, was shaped by the Islamic reformist movement in the Middle East and South Asia which developed in reactive opposition to the modernity emanating from outside.

It took the Bolsheviks over five years to assert their control over most of Central Asia and the Kazakh Steppe. Subsequently, because of the greater role of Islam in the region, the Bolsheviks allowed for the considerably longer preservation there of sharī'ah courts and Islamic infrastructure compared to other Muslim-majority regions of the USSR. It was only towards the end of the 1920s that the Stalin leadership changed policy and ushered in an indiscriminate attack on Islam and the Muslim authorities of Central Asia. At the core of this policy were the hujūm campaign[3] for de-veiling Muslim women, who were perceived as a 'surrogate proletariat', and the persecution of the Central Asian national and religious leadership. By the late 1930s most Central Asian women were de-veiled, and the 'ulamā' and other Muslim clergy had been comprehensively purged. The Bolsheviks' assault on Islam and the Muslim authorities occurred alongside their equally brutal campaign of sedentarization and collectivization of the Kazakhs and other nomads. In the early 1940s, during the Great Patriotic War of 1941–45 against Nazi Germany, the Kremlin finally included the Muslims of Central Asia and Kazakhstan into its governance through the medium of the Spiritual Directorate of Muslims of Central Asia and Kazakhstan – SADUM, which was established in 1943 in Tashkent. By the end of the 1980s, in the course of the region's full-fledged Sovietization, Central Asian Muslims had become 'Soviet Muslims'. Still, for historical and cultural reasons, Islam and its Muslim official clerics, informal imāms and Ṣūfī sheikhs retained significant authority, while SADUM continued to act as the only provider of structured Islamic education for the whole of USSR. In the late 1970s, in the context of the Soviet invasion of Afghanistan, the Ferghana valley was the first Soviet region to germinate the green shoots of the 'Islamic revival' which occurred along both traditionalist and Salafī lines.

The chapter begins by analysing the views and political orientation of the region's Muslim and political elite prior to the 1917 Bolshevik Revolution. It proceeds to discuss a variety of Muslim responses to the revolution and pays special attention to the Islamized basmachi movement. It then examines hujūm and other regionally specific Stalinist policies towards Islam, and their implications for Central Asia's Muslim authorities and leadership. The next section deals with the Central Asian muftīate – the SADUM – and is particularly concerned with the theological views of SADUM's muftīs and their relations with the Soviet state, on the one hand, and unregistered underground 'ulamā' and Ṣūfī authorities – on the other. The chapter also touches upon the role of the Aghā Khān in the Shī'ī Ismā'īlī community in Tajikistan. The final section is concerned with the 'Islamic revival' of the late Soviet period, addressing the factors behind the rise in popular appeal of the unofficial Islamic authorities of both traditionalist and Salafī orientation.

Islamo-national Leadership between the Russian Revolutions of 1905–7 and 1917

Due to the earlier outlined specifics of imperial Russian rule over the Kazakh Steppe and most of Central Asia the ramifications there of the Russian bourgeois-democratic revolution of 1905–7 were weaker than in the Volga-Urals or Azerbaijan. Still, the revolution prompted some publishing and political activism among a small number of Kazakh and Uzbek Islamo-national intellectuals and Islamic reformist thinkers. It witnessed the emergence among the Kazakhs of such periodicals as *Ishim Dalasi* (Ishim Steppe), *Ay Qap* (Come On, Kazakhs), *Kazakhstan* and *Kazakh*; while in Turkestan there appeared the journal *Al-Iṣlāḥ* (Reform) and the newspapers *Tudjor* (Merchants) and *Khurshid* (Sun). These publications were dominated by Islam-related topics and general news but abstained from discussing pan-Turkism, pan-Islamism and other politically sensitive issues, while at the same time advocating Muslims' loyalty to the tsar, referred to as *Aq Padishāh* (White Sovereign). Special note should be made of the pro-jadīd newspaper *Bukhoro-yi Sharif* (Noble Bukhara) edited by Mirkhaidar Mirbadalev (1860–1938), a Bukharan interpreter who acted as the intermediary between the Emir of Bukhara and St. Petersburg. Only a few Kazakh and Turkestani Muslims were represented in the Duma's Muslim faction, which was dominated by Tatar and, to a lesser extent, Caucasian Muslims. Among these were, for example, were Alikhan Bukeikhanov (1866–1937) and Mustafa Chokay (Shokay, 1890–1941), both ethnic Kazakhs, who broadly adhered to the Kadets' programme with the emphasis on the provision of greater autonomy for the empire's Muslims in religious, educational and cultural matters.

In contrast, the First World War (1914–18) prompted notable political activism in the Kazakh Steppe and Central Asia for two main reasons. Firstly, in this war the Russian Empire confronted the Ottoman Empire, the sulṭān of which was regarded by some Central Asian Muslim authorities and ordinary Muslims as their caliph. Secondly, in June 1916 Petrograd[4] introduced conscription for Kazakhs and Turkestani Muslims, who previously had been exempted. This decree, which left no choice to Kazakh and Turkestani Muslims but to fight against their co-religionist Turks, had a catalytic and divisive effect in the region. A small pro-jadīd minority welcomed it, while the majority, including some ʻulamā' and imāms, opposed it on the grounds that it presented unacceptable interference by the Christian Russian government into their life defined by sharīʻah, tribal and customary norms. In July 1916, in Khujand, the widespread resentment against the conscription triggered an anti-Tsarist rebellion, which soon escalated into a mass *gazāt* (*ghazawāt*) – a precursor of the Islamized basmachi movement – that engulfed a large area between the Syr Darya River and the Urals. The rebels were particularly active in Semirech'e *oblast'*, where they targeted Russian agrarian settlements, military garrisons, administrative and police buildings and railway stations. Only in January 1917 did Russian troops crush the uprising, leaving many thousands dead. However, the brutal suppression of the gazāt undermined the authority of Aq Padishāh and contributed to the Central Asians' increased receptiveness to pan-Islamist and anti-monarchist propaganda, emanating from Istanbul and Petrograd, respectively.

The 1917 February bourgeois-democratic revolution, which resulted in the abolition of the monarchy, introduced further divisions among the Muslim and national leaders in the Kazakh Steppe and Central Asia. In July 1917, the victory of proponents of the unitary Russian state at the All-Russia Muslim Congress in Kazan alienated those Kazakh and Turkestani politicians and intellectuals who adhered to federalism. Among them was Alikhan Bubeikhanov who founded in Orenburg a Kazakh national party *Alash Orda* (Kazakh Horde, 1917–20) which sought the establishment of Kazakh administrative autonomy within the future federal democratic Russian state. In Bukhara and Khiva there appeared organizations of 'Young Bukharans' and 'Young Khivans' modelled on the 'Young Turks' in Ottoman Turkey. Both organizations were dominated by reform-minded Muslim leaders, including Abdurauf Fitrat, Mahmud Khoja Behbudi and Munawwar Qari,[5] alongside such political radicals as Faizulla Khojaev (1896–1938), Abdul Qadir Mukhitdinov (1892–1934) and Akmal Ikramov (Ikromov, 1898–1938). They called for the removal from power of both the emīr and khān, constitutional reform and for wide political and cultural autonomy for Bukhara and Khiva. By contrast, the majority of the region's traditionalist ʻulamā' and other representatives of Muslim authority met the 1917 February Revolution with dismay as they feared that it might unleash uncontrolled political and social turmoil with dire consequences for the region.

The 1917 Bolshevik Revolution and the Central Asian Elite

The Bolsheviks faced a grave difficulty in establishing their power in the Kazakh Steppe and Central Asia because of the very small number of Marxist and other left-wing politicians among ethnic Kazakhs and other Central Asians and the near absence of an industrial working class in the region. For this reason the Bolsheviks chose Tashkent, which had a considerable Russian working class, as their stronghold. In late October 1917 they seized power from the Tashkent-based Provisional Government's Turkestan Committee and created a revolutionary authority – the Soviet (Council) of Soldiers' and Workers' Deputies under the leadership of Fedor Kolesov (1891–1940), an ethnic Russian. In April 1918 the Bolsheviks proclaimed the establishment on the territory of the former Turkestan Governorship of the Turkestan Autonomous Soviet Socialist Republic (TurASSR, 1918–24), which became part of the RSFSR. TurASSR's leadership was dominated by Russians and other non-Muslims, albeit it included a small number of revolutionaries of Central Asian Muslim background. Among these were, for example, Turar Ryskululy (Ryskulov, 1894–1938), an ethnic Kazakh, who in 1919 became the leader of the Muslim Bureau of the Turkestan Communist Party and in 1922–24 headed the Turkestani government.

Outside Tashkent, the Bolsheviks encountered fierce opposition from a variety of pro-jadīd, nationalist, White Russian, foreign interventionist and Islamist forces. Thus, in Kokand, in November 1917 a group of pro-jadīd politicians under the leadership of Mustafa Chokay (Shokay), a Kazakh; Muhamejan Tynyshpaev (1879–1937), an ethnic Kazakh; and Shah-Islam Shagiahmetov (1886–1922), an ethnic Tatar, proclaimed a Kokand Autonomy[6] encompassing most of Russian Turkestan. The Kokand Autonomy was envisaged as a secular republic headed by a president and functioning on the basis of five official languages – Uzbek, Kazakh, Kyrgyz, Tajik and Russian. But at the end of February 1918 the Bolsheviks liquidated the Kokand Autonomy and included its territory within the Turkestan Soviet Republic. Mustafa Chokay managed to flee first to Turkey and subsequently to France where he became involved in anti-Bolshevik publishing and journalistic activities.[7] Meanwhile, in Orenburg, in December 1917, Alikhan Bubeikhanov and other leaders of the Kazakh Alash Orda created the Alash Orda Autonomy (1917–20), which first allied with the Orenburg Cossacks and then with the White Russians. Alongside the Alash Orda the Bolsheviks were also confronted by the British military intervention in Transcaucasia and present-day Turkmenistan. In April 1919, the Red Army forced the British troops to withdraw and return to their bases in the Punjab and Meshed; and in March 1920, the Bolsheviks finally defeated the Alash Orda and established Soviet power on its territory.

However, it was the basmachis who turned out to be the most difficult opponents to Bolsheviks in the region. By the middle of 1918 the basmachi resistance engulfed a large part of the Ferghana valley. It was reinforced by troops loyal to the Bukhara Emīr Alim-Khān (1880–1944) and Turkmen tribes under the leadership of Junaid-Khān (1857–1938). In the autumn of 1921, the 16,000-strong basmachi movement received a further impetus when it was joined by Enver Pasha (1881–1923), the former Ottoman Minister of War, who channelled it along both pan-Islamic and pan-Turkic lines.[8] In the spring of 1925, the basmachis under the leadership of Uzbek *kurbashi* (chieftain) Ibrahim-Bek (Chokaboyev, 1889–1931) defeated Red Army units. But in June 1926 the basmachis were finally overpowered by the Red Army and were forced to flee to Afghanistan, from where they continued to conduct sporadic raids into eastern Bukharia (present-day Tajikistan). Only in June 1931, in Mazar-i-Sharif, were their remnants destroyed by the Bolshevik military intelligence (OGPU) and the border between Soviet Central Asia and Afghanistan effectively sealed.[9]

The Creation of the Central Asian Republics and Their Leadership

The region's particularly large territory and its ethno-religious complexities determined the staged process of its incorporation into the Bolshevik state. Central to this was Moscow's relations with the region's various Muslim and national leaderships. In April 1920, in the midst of the confrontation with the basmachis and other opposition forces and alongside the newly established TurASSR, the Bolsheviks opted for the creation on the territory of the former Khiva Khānate of the People's Soviet Republic of Khorezm (Khwarāzm, 1920–24) and, in October 1920, of the People's Soviet Republic of Bukhara (1920–24) within the former borders of the Bukhara Emīrate. The political leadership in both republics was initially dominated by pro-jadīd Young Khivans and Young Bukharans. The Khorezmian Soviet Republic was headed by Palvan-Hajjee Yusupov, chairman of the Young Khivan central committee, while among the Bukharan Soviet Republic's leaders were the Young Bukharan Abdul Qadir Mukhitdin(ov), Faizulla Khojayev and Abdurauf Fitrat. In both republics *mahkama-i sharī'ah*s (sharī'ah courts) and madrasah education were preserved, albeit placed under the control of pro-reform Muslim clergy, such as Domla Ikram and Sharifjan Makhdum. At the same time, qadīmist 'ulamā' were sidelined, while some were even executed. Some qadīmists joined the basmachis, while others went into exile in Afghanistan.[10] Gradually, the first leaders of the Bukharan and Khoresmian republics, with the exception of Faizulla Khojayev, were made the Bolsheviks' appointees.[11]

In 1924/25 the Bukhara and Khorezm People's Soviet Republics were amalgamated into the Uzbekistan Soviet Socialist Republic (UzSSR) under the leadership of Faizulla Khojayev, who was succeeded by Akmal Ikramov. Initially, UzSSR included the autonomous Soviet socialist republics of Tajikistan and Turkmenistan which, later on, were upgraded to union republics. The Bolsheviks' territorial delimitation of the Kazakh Steppe and other steppe and desert areas, populated by nomads who did not recognize fixed borders, was even more problematic and was contingent on the nomads' sedentarization. In 1920, the Kazakh-dominated Ural'sk, Turgai and Semipalatinsk oblasts, together with parts of the Caspian and Orenburg oblasts, were organized into the Kyrgyz Autonomous Soviet Socialist Republic (KyrASSR), which, in 1925, was renamed the Kazakh Autonomous Soviet Socialist Republic (KazASSR)[12] within the Russian Soviet Federative Socialist Republic (RSFSR). Only by 1936 did Moscow finalize the borders of Central Asia's newly created five union republics of Uzbekistan, Tajikistan, Kazakhstan, Kyrgyzstan and Turkmenistan. Until the middle of the 1930s, most Communist Party leaders of Uzbekistan and Tajikistan were ethnic Uzbeks and

Tajiks of Young Bukharan and pro-jadīd background. Following the Stalinist purges of 1936–38 they were replaced by new and more easily controllable Uzbek and Tajik apparatchiks. In Soviet Kazakhstan and Kyrgyzstan, the Communist Party leadership was dominated by ethnic Russians and other non-Muslims till the end of the 1920s and in Soviet Turkmenistan till the late 1940s.

The Stalinist Assault on Islam and the Muslim Leadership

By the late 1920s the Stalinist leadership felt confident about embarking on a full-scale attack on Islam and the Muslim clergy in Central Asia. As elsewhere, the main agencies of the anti-Islamic campaign were regional communist parties, the League of the Militant Godless, which set up its first branch in Tashkent in 1928, and *Zhenotdel*s (women's departments). A stark embodiment of the anti-Islamic campaign was the hujūm which was aimed at de-veiling Uzbek and Tajik women who wore *paranja*s (body veils) and *chachvon*s (face veils) and were secluded at home. The Bolsheviks equated the veiling with the perceived backwardness of arranged marriages, child marriages, *kalym* (bride price), polygamy and *purdah* (seclusion). Zhenotdels, which primarily consisted of non-Muslim women, organized public rallies and mosque gatherings in support of de-veiling and broader women's emancipation. The hujūm split Muslim clergy into two camps. One included a limited number of pro-reform Muslim clerics who supported the campaign on the grounds that veil-wearing was not prescribed by the Qur'ān. The other and more numerous camp consisted of qadīmist clergy who compared de-veiled women with prostitutes and fiercely opposed the hujūm. They played a major role in the widespread anti-hujūm resistance which persisted throughout the 1930s and cost many thousands of female and male lives. However, by the late 1930s the Bolsheviks' goal was achieved and the bulk of the region's women ceased to wear paranjas and chachvons, child marriages were drastically reduced and some Muslim women got involved in public and professional activities, while some even joined the Communist Party.

Apart from hujūm, Akmal Ikramov and other regional Communist Party leaders spearheaded the campaign against qadīmist 'ulamā', Muslim clergy and Ṣūfī sheikhs. The Muslim authorities' economic independence was irreversibly undermined as a result of the confiscation of waqf land and the shutting down of hundreds of mosques, mahkama-i sharī'ahs and qadīmist madrasahs. Teaching in the famous Mir-i Arab madrasah was suspended. Most remaining mosques and pro-jadīd madrasahs became subordinated to the Ufa-based muftīate. As in other Muslim regions of the USSR the Bolsheviks especially targeted Ṣūfīs due to the clandestine nature of the sheikh-murīd relationship which was practically impossible to control. This was particularly pertinent for Kazakhs and other nomads whose main Islamic authorities were Ṣūfī khojahs. Persian- and Arabic-based Central Asian Islamic scholarship was disrupted in the course of the mass physical destruction of Islamic books and the dual alphabet change from Arabic to Latin and then from Latin to Cyrillic. The scope and value of madrasah education, which had previously been only available to boys, was greatly diminished as it was superseded by the USSR-wide free co-educational secular primary education. It should be noted that the Bolshevik promotion in Central Asia of compulsory school education was a major undertaking in the context of a literacy level that varied between 2.3 and 6 per cent of the total population. It was achieved through the dispatching to the region of thousands of teachers from European Russia and the establishment there of dozens of teacher training colleges for local students. Sovietized secular education was conducted in newly opened schools in Uzbek, Tajik, Kazakh, Kyrgyz, Turkmen and the region's other languages, literary versions of which were developed by Soviet linguists on the basis of existing vernaculars. In parallel, the Bolsheviks increased the school teaching of Russian and designated Russian as the country's lingua franca. It is significant that Soviet schoolteachers acquired notable authority and were respectfully addressed by Uzbeks and Tajik Muslims as *domullos* (imāms).[13]

The peak of the Stalinist attack on Central Asia's Islamic leadership occurred during the Great Terror of 1936–38 when hundreds of its various representatives were executed or exiled to the Gulag. Alongside Muslim leaders, the purges were also directed against Central Asian Bolshevik leaders, writers and educators of both Muslim and non-Muslim heritage. Thus, among its high-profile victims accused of bourgeois-nationalist leaning were Faizulla Khojayev, Akmal Ikramov and Turar Ryskulov, as well as Rahim Inogamov (1902–1938) and Ubaidulla Ruzybayev (1900–1938). Among the Kazakhs, the Stalinists particularly targeted Bolsheviks from the Orta and Kichi Juzes that in the past were better accommodated to Russian rule than the Ulu Juz. As a result, in the course of *korenizatsiia* (nativization) representatives of the Ulu Juz acquired political supremacy which they have retained until the present. Political repressions were preceded by, or occurred in parallel with, anti-*kulak* (the prosecution of well-off peasants) and collectivization campaigns during which a large number of Kazakhs died. The Kazakh population, who strongly opposed collectivization, was reduced by over 40 per cent because of *asharshylyk* (famine, 1930–33), caused by the slaughtering of their livestock, and their mass migration to China, Mongolia, Afghanistan and Iran.[14]

Muslim Leadership during and after the Great Patriotic War

The Sociocultural Implications of the War

The Great Patriotic War (1941–45) had major implications for Central Asia and its Muslim leadership in particular. The war greatly accelerated the region's industrialization and modernization due to the relocation there of major Soviet military and other industries from the western regions of the USSR which were occupied by the Germans. As a result there was a sharp increase in the involvement of Central Asian men and women in industrial production, alongside workers and professionals coming from European parts of the USSR. The war also enhanced the Central Asians' social and cultural mingling with other peoples of the USSR, both Muslims and non-Muslims. Unlike in the imperial Russian period, Central Asian men were subjected to conscription and fought side by side with servicemen from other parts of the Soviet Union. Furthermore, the region's ethnic and confessional make-up was affected by the arrival there of over a million civilian evacuees from other Soviet regions, as well as of over a million deportees from the Caucasus, the Volga region, the Baltics and the Far East. In Kazakhstan alone deportees made up one-fifth of the republic's population, and Kazakhs turned into an ethnic minority.

The war, which demanded a USSR-wide anti-Nazi mobilization, prompted the Stalin leadership to moderate its anti-religious stance. In July 1941, the activities of the infamous League of the Militant Godless were suspended.[15] In July 1943 Stalin summoned Eshon Bobokhon (1858–1957), an influential Tashkent 'ālim, to Moscow and tasked him with convening a *kurultai* (congress) of Central Asian 'ulamā' with the purpose of creating a unified Muslim administration which would coordinate the Central Asian Muslims' war efforts. In October 1943, such a kurultai, which gathered 160 Muslim clerics from Uzbekistan, Tajikistan, Kazakhstan, Kyrgyzstan and Turkmenistan, was held in Tashkent. An important role in its organization belonged to the Soviet Uzbekistan leader, Yuldosh Akhunboboyev (in office 1938–43). The kurultai endorsed the creation of the Central Asian muftīate – the SADUM[16] – and elected Eshon Bobokhon as its muftī (in office 1943–57). From the first days of its existence SADUM was engaged in the collection of funds, food, livestock and clothes for the army and provided material assistance to families of those soldiers who were killed or wounded at war.

Spiritual Directorate of Muslims of Central Asia and Kazakhstan

The SADUM which in 1943 administered the USSR's largest, 16 million-strong Muslim community, soon turned into the leading Soviet muftīate. It presided over a multilayered Islamic governance consisting of Tajikistani, Kazakhstani, Kyrgyzstani and Turkmenistani *qāziyats*, which in turn oversaw *oblast'* and *raion* Muslim clergy represented by mosque imāms, mullahs and *mu'azzins* (callers for prayer). Additionally, at the grassroots level, registered mosques were put under the control of *dvadtsatka* (20 people), the executive organ and the inspection committee, consisting of local elders.[17] In 1948, the SADUM administered 183 mosques (79 in Uzbekistan, 36 in Kyrgyzstan, 28 in Kazakhstan, 23 in Tajikistan and 17 in Turkmenistan).[18] From 1943 and until its dissolution in 1989, SADUM was headed by 'ulamā' from the Bobokhon family who, in spite of their collaboration with the Soviet state, were respected among both unofficial Muslim authorities and ordinary Muslims. In 1945 muftī Eshon Bobokhon, together with several other Central Asian Muslim clerics, conducted hajj to Mecca and Medina. In 1946 he presided over the reopening of the Mir-i Arab madrasah which assumed the role of the only official provider of Islamic structured education in the USSR.[19] In 1947 the Mir-i Arab madrasah employed three mudarrises and had only 26 students. Later on, among its high-profile graduates were Talgat Tadjuddin, Allashukur Pashazadeh and Akhmad Kadyrov. From the 1960s, SADUM was the only Soviet muftīate that had the right to send a small number of vetted students to study at Islamic universities and colleges in Egypt, Syria, Jordan, Algeria and Libya. In 1968, SADUM acquired its own publishing house, which began to issue its own journal *Musul'mane Sovetskogo Vostoka* (Muslims of the Soviet East),[20] promoting a positive image of Soviet Muslims in the Muslim world. In 1971, also in Tashkent, SADUM, under muftī Ziyouddinkhon Bobokhon (in office 1957–82), succeeded in opening the Islamic Institute of al-Bukhārī, where the total number of students, however, never exceeded 30.[21] During this period, the SADUM muftī and other senior Muslim clergy became actively involved in the Kremlin's foreign policy by promoting a favourable image of Soviet Muslims in the Muslim abroad.

The SADUM, like the other three Soviet muftīates, was closely monitored by the CARS and aligned its activities and religious messages to the needs of the Soviet state. Its muftīs similarly, like their Ufa-, Buinaksk- and Baku-based counterparts, utilized the principle of *ijtihād* (an independent judgement) and issued fatwās aimed at reconciling Soviet and Islamic realities. In these fatwās honest labour for the benefit of the Soviet state was equated with Islamic virtue; the slaughter of sheep during *Kurban-Ait* (*'Īd al-Aḍhā*, Feast of Sacrifice) was discouraged; fasting for physical workers during Ramazan (Ramaḍān) was deemed unnecessary; the wearing by women of paranjas and chachvons was denounced and the payment of zakāt for the needy was abolished. At the same time, SADUM muftīs retained greater autonomy from the state, compared, for example, with those from DUMZ, and wielded respect among foreign 'ulamā', who never accused them of *shirk* (polytheism), *kufr* (disbelief) or *bid'ah* (unlawful innovation).

The doctrinal position of SADUM's muftīs and their entourage was ambiguous, however. The first muftī, Eshon Bobokhon, belonged to the Naqshbandī tarīqah and adhered to Maturīdīyyah-based Islamic traditionalism. However, both his son and grandson, that is, muftīs Ziyouddinkhon and Shamsuddinkhon (in office 1982–89), leaned towards Salafī Islam. It appears that both of them were influenced by the pro-Salafī teaching of the Lebanese 'ālim Shami Domullo al-Tarablusi (d. 1932) who came to Central Asia in 1919 via eastern Turkestan.[22]

For example, they treated as bid'ah such manifestations of the Central Asian Islamic tradition as *ziyārats* (visitations) to graves of local Ṣūfī sheikhs and other Muslim saints and other sacred sites (in the case of Kazakh, Kyrgyz and Turkmen Muslims); remembrance wakes on the third and seventh days after the death of a Muslim and loud weeping by women at funerals; conspicuous celebrations of circumcision and other major events of the life circle; and kalym practices and the recognition of the religious authority of *otins* and *khalfas* (female mullahs). SADUM's pro-Salafī orientation was also evidenced in the curricula of the Mir-i Arab madrasah in Bukhara and the Islamic Institute in Tashkent, both of which provided the professional Islamic cadre for the other three Soviet muftīates. In both cases the teaching was focused on Arabic, the *tajwīd* (proficiency in reading the Qur'ān), the *tafsīr* (exegesis of the Qur'ān) and the Ḥadīth, based on Arabic primary sources rather than Persian- or Chagatai-based medieval commentaries on fiqh, as well as Ṣūfī literature.

Unofficial Muslim Authorities

The institutionalization of the Islamic leadership, represented by SADUM muftī and other registered Muslim clergy, created the phenomenon of unofficial Islamic authorities who were more numerous and diverse than their official counterparts. They included underground 'ulamā', self-proclaimed teachers of Islam, folk mullahs and otins, guardians of *mazārs* (sacred places), khojahs and other influential Ṣūfīs. Some unofficial 'ulamā' were able to teach a very small number of followers in underground groups – *hujrahs*.

Among such pro-Salafī teachers was, for example, Shami Domullo al-Tarablusi. In the bazaars of Uzbekistan and other parts of Central Asia, self-made Islamic educators disseminated primitively photo-copied or *samizdat* (hand-copied) versions of the Qur'ān and other Islamic texts, cassette recordings of prayers and chain-letters. Among the latter were the so-called 'testaments of Aḥmad Yasawī' which were widely circulated in the late 1940s across underground networks in Uzbekistan. These testaments denounced the sins of contemporaries who did not observe Ramazan and the five daily prayers and did not pay zakāt. However, Yasawī's forgiveness was promised to those who passed these testaments on to nine other people. It is also known that Islamic chain-letters were distributed in the 1970s among schoolchildren in Turkmenistan.[23]

Folk mullahs, who were based in unregistered mosques or in private houses which functioned as mosques, conducted basic Muslim rituals related to the life cycle. Some of them also ran clandestine maktabs for boys where they taught Arabic, the Qur'ān and sharī'ah. Otins and khalfas, who were, in some cases, mullahs' wives, taught the fundamentals of Islam to girls at home. The regional abundance of mazārs, which despite their formal ban continued to attract pilgrims, especially among women, accounted for the preservation of a special stratum of unofficial Muslim clergy – mazār custodians who were commonly called sheikhs or khojahs. In the late 1940s in Uzbekistan there were 275 active mazārs, while in Tajikistan's Leninabad oblast' alone their number exceeded 150.[24] During some religious festivals they attracted between 60,000 and 100,000 pilgrims. Mazār custodians, some of whom claimed their descent from holy men, conducted prayers and exercised their supposedly supernatural powers in respect to pilgrims' requests backed by donations. Mazār sheikhs were attributed with the ability to heal disease, to cure infertility and to fulfil a pilgrim's wishes. In Turkmenistan each clan had a special saint, whose tomb was attended by a sheikh, the saint's perceived descendant. Sometimes a whole tribe had a forefather saint.[25] It is also important to note that despite considerable disruption by the Bolsheviks of Ṣūfī networks in the region, a few Naqshbandī, Kubrawī and Yasawī groups remained active. They were centred on particular sheikhs or teachers who were known as *ishāns*,[26] *pīrs* (elders), *ustathes* (teachers), *murshids* (guides) or khojahs. In some rural areas ishāns had hundreds of undisclosed murīds who also penetrated district, village and kolkhoz governing structures.[27]

Ismā'īlī Muslims and Their Authorities

As discussed in Chapter 4, since the eleventh century the Gorno-Badakhshan region of present-day Tajikistan has harboured a sizeable Ismā'īlī Shī'ī community who, unlike the numerically dominant Tajiks, belonged to the eastern Iranian ethnolinguistic group. In the late 1940s, the Ismā'īlīs, who numbered around 40,000, made up around 75 per cent of the region's total population. Ismā'īlīs were divided into several groups, each administered by a pīr. Their Islamic rites were conducted by local *khalifas*, or elders. Ismā'īlīs were formally subordinated to the authority of the Aghā Khān III (1877–1957)[28] in Bombay; however, from the late 1950s they became largely integrated within the SADUM-based system of state–Muslim relations and their khalifas stopped visiting the

Aghā Khān. In addition to Ismā'īlīs, in Bukhara and Samarqand there continued to exist small groups of Twelver Shī'a.[29]

The 'Islamic Revival' and the New Islamic Leadership

In the 1980s, for historical and demographic reasons, Central Asia harboured a particularly intensive 'Islamic revival', which affected the Muslim-populated regions of the USSR. A specifically regional catalyst for the rise of Islam was the Soviet invasion of neighbouring Afghanistan (1979–89), which enhanced the Central Asian conscripts' interaction with their co-ethnics and co-religionists across the border. Since 1985 the Gorbachevian perestroika had created favourable conditions for the re-engagement of Central Asian Muslim clergy and thinkers with their counterparts in other parts of the Muslim world. Among the leading participants of this debate were Ḥajjee Domla Hindustoniy (d. 1989), Muhammad Sodiq Yusuf, Rahmatulla 'Alloma-Qori, 'Abduvali-Qori Mirzoyev and Hakimjan-Qori of Margilan who were critical of SADUM's conformist clergy and called for their replacement by new Islamic leaders who would be prepared to work towards gradual societal re-Islamization, the reinstating of waqf and the development of comprehensive Islamic education. They differed, however, in terms of their doctrinal orientation and attitudes towards Muslim political activism. Thus, Ḥajjee Domla's views presented a synthesis of Islamic traditionalism and reformism with a particular emphasis on quietism and *sabr* (patience). Others leaned towards Salafīsm and endorsed Muslim political engagement.[30]

In the Ferghana valley, young Muslims who had studied in underground pro-Salafī *ḥujrahs* (cells) became particularly politically assertive. Despite their relatively small number, they had a considerable influence on Muslim youth due to their educational capacity, their engaging and socially and politically relevant sermons, and their substantial material and financial resources emanating from their entrepreneurial activities and from various official and non-government Islamic funds and organizations, based in Saudi Arabia, the Gulf and some other Muslim states. These Islamic activists were especially critical of both registered and folk imāms for their allegedly poor knowledge of 'true Islam' and their condoning of 'non-Islamic' funeral and wake practices, as well as mazār-related activities. Some of them self-organized into Islamic and Islamo-national political parties and organizations, including the organizations *Islam Lashkarlari* (Warriors of Islam) and *Adolat* (Justice) under the leadership of Tohir Yoldoshev (Yoldosh, 1967–2009) and Juma Khodjiyev (Namangani, 1969–2001) who, in the 1990s, would head the armed Islamic opposition in Uzbekistan.[31]

Conclusion

By the end of the Soviet period Central Asian Muslims were largely integrated into the nationwide system of state–Muslim relations based on the institution of the state-controlled muftīate, initiated by Catherine the Great in 1788. From 1943 they had been administered by the SADUM under the leadership of muftīs belonging to the Bobokhon 'ulamā' dynasty. In compliance with the state's demands official muftīs exercised ijtihād in order to reconcile the Muslims' religious beliefs with Sovietized secularism. Subsequently, most Central Asians acquired the generic characteristics of Soviet Muslims, developing considerable social, cultural and linguistic affinities with other Soviet peoples of both Islamic and non-Islamic background, and they began to perceive Islam as part of their particular Uzbek, Tajik, Kazakh, Kyrgyz and Turkmen national traditions.

At the same time, because of the region's comparatively lower level of industrialization and, consequently, its higher retention of communal traditionalism, especially in rural areas, Islam, albeit implicitly, preserved its important regulatory function in people's family, communal and social life. The intergenerational transmission of some Islamic norms and ethics was insured by numerous folk imāms, otins, ishāns and custodians of mazārs, while the Islamic theological tradition, although in a restricted form, was maintained through the network of underground hujrahs. For this reason, the Gorbachevian relaxation of state control over the religious sphere turned Central Asia and the northern Caucasus into epicentres of the Eurasian Islamic resurgence. Central to this process was the emergence of new Muslim leaders who challenged the existing system of state–Muslim relations and sought Central Asia's reintegration within the wider Muslim world.

PART III

ISLAMIC AUTHORITY AND LEADERSHIP IN POST-SOVIET LANDS

Chapter Nine

BELARUS, UKRAINE AND LITHUANIA

Introduction

The dissolution of the Soviet Union in 1991 was accompanied by the demise of the system of state–Muslim relations which had persisted, albeit with modifications, since 1788. The four state-controlled regional muftīates were superseded by a plethora of new muftīates, which were created along ethnonational and regional lines. New muftīates were headed by so-called 'young imāms' who politically distanced themselves from their Soviet-era predecessors and competed for the right to represent particular Muslim communities at regional, national and international levels. In the western part of the ex-USSR, where Muslims historically constituted a minority that used to be within the domain of the Ufa-based Spiritual Directorate of Muslims of the European Part of the USSR and Siberia (DUMES), there appeared independent muftīates which lacked historical precedence and which were headed by muftīs recruited both internally and from abroad. At the same time, there emerged various alternative Muslim organizations that negated the muftīate model and affiliated themselves with pan-European, or trans-national Islamic structures or movements. In terms of doctrinal orientation, they largely opposed national Islamic traditions and adhered to Salafī Islam. The Islamic dynamic in ex-Soviet Belarus, Ukraine and Lithuania,[1] all three of which have sizeable Tatar-dominated Muslim minorities, has also been affected by these countries' frontier location between Russia-centred political and cultural Eurasianism and European Union (EU)-driven Europeanism. A particular case in point has been independent Lithuania which, alongside neighbouring Latvia and Estonia, joined the implicitly anti-Russian EU and the North Atlantic Treaty Organization (NATO).

This chapter examines how the differing political models and external engagements of Belarus, Ukraine and Lithuania have affected state–Muslim relations and Muslims themselves, and the doctrinal orientation and politics of Muslim leadership in these post-Soviet states, which had previously lacked independent Islamic structures. It begins by providing a brief historical background for these countries which were not specifically discussed in Parts I and II. It pays special attention to the implications of the Second World War for the Belorussian, Lithuanian and Ukrainian societies and Muslims, and their leaders in particular. It then proceeds to examine how Muslim communities and their leaders in largely Orthodox Christian post-Soviet Belarus and Ukraine have negotiated conflicting powerful impulses coming from Moscow- and Kazan-based muftīates, on the one hand, and European, Turkish and Middle Eastern Islamic organizations and 'ulamā', on the other. The final section discusses the Islamic trajectories and Muslim leadership in predominantly Catholic Lithuania which since 2004 has been part of the EU.

Historical Background

Compared to the Volga-Urals, the Caucasus and Central Asia, where ethnic Muslims make up the bulk of the population, in the three discussed countries they constitute minorities.[2] However, in terms of their origins and ensuing development they share considerable similarities with their co-religionists in the rest of post-Soviet Eurasia. Thus, unlike Western Europe where, with the exceptions of Spain and Sicily, Muslim communities emerged relatively recently in the context of labour and refugee migrations, most Muslims in Belarus, Ukraine and Lithuania are part of these countries' autochthonous populations. The majority of them are Tatars whose Genghizid descendants began to settle there in the fourteenth century.[3] During this period the territories of these three countries, as well as some of modern Poland, were part of the Grand Duchy of Lithuania (GDL). Between 1569 and 1795 they were included in the joint Polish-Lithuanian Commonwealth (PLC, Rzeczpospolita), the official religion of which was Roman Catholicism. According to various sources, by the end of the sixteenth century there were around 200,000 Tatars and 400 mosques on the territory of the PLC. Although PLC rulers pursued relatively tolerant policies towards their Muslim subjects and most Lithuanian Tatars (known as Lipka Tatars) were able to preserve their faith, they nevertheless were subjected to linguistic and cultural assimilation, which was reflected, for example, in the change of their surnames in accordance with either Lithuanian or Polish language conventions. Those Tatars who resisted assimilation fled to Ottoman Turkey or the Crimean Khānate. Following the tripartite divisions of Poland[4] between Prussia, the Habsburg monarchy and the Russian Empire in 1772, 1791 and 1795, present-day Belarus, Lithuania and most of Ukraine (except for Galicia which had been transferred to Habsburg Austria), as well as eastern Poland, were included within the Russian Empire. It is descendants of these Lipka Tatars who now constitute the indigenous Muslim population in post-Soviet Belarus, Ukraine and Lithuania.

From the late eighteenth century and until the 1917 Bolshevik Revolution Muslims of present-day Belarus, Lithuania and most of Ukraine were included in the Russian system of state–Muslim relations introduced by Catherine the Great in 1788. Unlike the vast majority of Russia's Tatars who became administered by the Ufa-based muftīate, Lithuanian and other Tatars of the western regions were assigned to the Bakhchysarai-based muftīate of Taurida (Spiritual Directorate of Muslims of Taurida/Crimea). Due to the stronger influence of Turkish Islam among Crimean Muslims and the greater spatial distance between the Taurida muftīate and Russia's western provinces St. Petersburg's control over western Muslim communities was weak and the latter were de facto governed by local Muslim authorities. In 1851 the Russian government acceded to local Muslims' request to elect mullahs from among themselves, albeit they still needed formal certification by the Taurida muftīate. It should be noted that the Russian authorities repeatedly rejected requests by local 'ulamā' to establish their own regional muftīates.[5]

In the aftermath of the 1917 October Revolution Soviet Russia lost most of the western provinces of the Russian Empire, including the territories in the western part of modern Belarus, western Ukraine and Lithuania. The Vilnius region and adjacent areas of present-day western Belarus were included into the Polish Republic (1918–39).

In 1925, in Vilnius, the Polish authorities established a muftīate under the leadership of muftī Jakub Szynkiewicz (1884–1966), a Berlin university graduate in Islamic Studies and a critic of Tatar Islamic traditionalism. Between 1925 and 1939 the Vilnius muftīate acted as the main spiritual and administrative centre for over two dozen Muslim communities (*jamā'ats*) which existed in the region. The administrative centre for the remaining Tatars moved to Kaunas, which served as the temporary capital of Lithuania.[6] In 1939, at the beginning of the Second World War, western regions of Belarus were included in the Soviet Socialist Republic of Belorussia. In 1940, and yet again in 1944, most of modern Lithuania and western Ukraine came under Soviet control and became part of the Lithuanian and Ukrainian Soviet Socialist Republics, respectively. Consequently, local Muslim communities were withdrawn from the jurisdiction of the Vilnius muftīate, the seat of which moved to Warsaw, and included into the Soviet system of state–Muslim relations that persisted until 1990.

The Second World War was particularly devastating for the region, as between 1941 and 1944 most of Belorussia and Ukraine were occupied by Nazi Germany and became the war's major battlegrounds. Under occupation, the multi-ethnic population of Belorussia and Ukraine was subjected to genocide conducted in the framework of the Nazi programme of 'Ost' ('East'). Belorussia's capital city of Minsk and other cities, towns and villages were fully destroyed in the course of intensive bombings. The Nazis created a network of concentration camps (260 on the territory of Belorussia and 180 on the territory of Ukraine), where hundreds of thousands of Slavs, Jews, Roma and Soviet prisoners of war (POWs) were exterminated. In Ukraine alone, over 1.3 million POWs were executed. The Nazis particularly targeted members of the Communist Party and Komsomol. In Belorussia, as a result of the Nazi Holocaust and other mass killings over 1.5 million people of different ethnic and religious backgrounds, including local Muslim Tatars, lost their lives and the country's total population of eight million was reduced by 22.4 per cent. In Ukraine, the Nazis killed over 1.3 million people out of the total population of 31 million. Additionally, over two million Belorussians and Ukrainians lost their lives fighting Nazi aggressors on the war fronts.[7]

The occupation was fiercely resisted by the bulk of the population of Belorussia and Ukraine. In Belorussia there operated a mass partisan movement which was coordinated with the anti-Nazi Polish Krajowa Army that was active in Poland and Lithuania. Nevertheless, in western parts of Belorussia and Ukraine, as well as in Lithuania, there were pockets of pro-Nazi supporters. Among these were, for example, Ukrainian nationalists from the Organization of Ukrainian Nationalists (OUN) and the Ukrainian Insurgent Army (UPA), as well as members of the pro-Nazi Lithuanian police battalion 'Kaunas' who were involved in punitive massacres against local partisans and civilians. Of particular relevance for our discussion was the pro-Nazi position of muftī Szynkiewicz and his supporters. In the early 1940s, the Third Reich appointed muftī Szynkiewicz, who was nominally subordinated to the pro-Nazi Grand Muftī of Jerusalem, Muḥammad Amīn al-Ḥusaynī (1895–1974), as 'Muftī of Ostland' with the job of administering the Muslim population of the projected German governorates of Lithuania, Latvia, Estonia and Belarus. Szynkiewicz was also tasked by Joseph Goebbels (1897–1945), the Minister of Propaganda of the Third Reich, to incite local Muslims to enrol in the Third Reich's 'Muslim battalions'. However, muftī Szynkiewicz's pro-Nazi activism had very limited success and most Muslims refused to collaborate with the Third Reich.[8] Meanwhile, in the occupied Crimea there were incidents of collaboration among the Crimean Tatars. By the end of the war, which resulted in the reintegration of Belorussian, Ukrainian and Lithuanian territories within the USSR, the region's Muslim population was significantly reduced, while most mosques and other Islamic infrastructure were destroyed. Not a single madrasah was left. In the light of the pro-Nazi stance of muftī Szynkiewicz, who fled to Germany,[9] the Stalinist leadership dismissed the hopes of the region's Muslims of acquiring their own regional muftīate, and instead formally affiliated them to the Ufa-based DUMES.[10] In Lithuania, Muslim Tatars reverted to self-governing on the basis of grassroots Muslim communities – *jamāʿat*s – while in Belorussia and Ukraine Muslims lost any local organizational structures.[11]

The Muslim Community and Its Leadership in Belarus

In the late 1980s in Belorussia there were around 11,000 Muslims who constituted under 0.2 per cent of the total population of 10.2 million.[12] Two-thirds of them were Tatars and the rest included Azerbaijanis and other Muslims originating from other parts of the USSR. The Muslims' relatively small number accounted for the much weaker 'Islamic revival' among them compared to other Muslim-majority parts of the USSR. This trend persisted after Belorussia's transformation in 1991 into an independent state – Belarus – which has remained under the leadership of the Soviet apparatchik, Alexander Lukashenko (b. 1954), who, unlike his counterparts in neighbouring Russia, Ukraine and Lithuania, has preserved most of Soviet economic and administrative structures.[13] Meanwhile, Belarus' legislative and political sovereignization was conducive to the institutionalization of Islam and the emergence of a number of Muslim organizations and societies. The legal basis for this process was the 1994 Constitution which guaranteed freedom to all religions existing in Belarus. The same year, Belarus for the first time in its history acquired its own muftīate – the Muslim Religious Association (MRS[14]) – which began to publish its own Russian-language newspaper *Zhizn'* (Life). MRS was headed by muftī Ismail Aleksandrovich (b. 1929), a local Tatar who had only a limited knowledge of the fundamentals of Islam and no Arabic. At first MRS controlled 11 Muslim communities and one mosque; by 1998 it was administering 24 Muslim communities and four mosques. In 2016 MRS also acquired the newly built Cathedral mosque in Minsk. In 2001 Aleksandrovich was succeeded by muftī Abu Bekir Shabanovich (b. 1939), who similarly lacked a structured Islamic education and strongly relied on Turkish theological guidance and educational assistance.[15]

From 1997, following the establishment of political unity between Russia and Belarus in the form of the Russo-Belarusian Union State, state–Muslim relations in Belarus have largely been aligned with those in Russia. Thus, in 2002, the initially constitutionally proclaimed religious equality was similarly 'corrected' by the Law on Freedom of Religions and Religious Organizations, which recognized the leading role of the Orthodox Church in the historical development of Belarus while acknowledging contributions to this development of other so-called 'traditional religions', such as Catholicism, Lutheranism, Judaism and Islam. The Law prohibited any religious activity by unregistered groups, limited the activity of religious communities to the area of their official registration, restricted foreign proselytizing and imposed state control over the printing, import and distribution of religious material.[16] In the case of Islam, the Law legitimized MRS-affiliated 'traditional' Muslim communities of Lipka Tatar heritage and criminalized all others, dubbed as 'untraditional' communities or organizations.

At the same time, because of the near absence in Belarus of educated Muslim clergy and Islamic scholarly expertise there has been confusion and ambiguity in the definition of 'traditional Islam', which allowed doctrinally different Muslim organizations to claim 'traditional' status and get state registration. The 'traditional' MRS welcomed the financial and educational assistance emanating from Islamic organizations and charities based in Saudi Arabia, Turkey and other foreign Muslim countries, which in Russia, the Caucasus and Central Asia were officially regarded as promoters of allegedly destabilizing 'untraditional' Salafī Islam. In 2002, the MRS's doctrinal duplicity led to the formation of another muftīate – the Spiritual Directorate of Muslims of Belarus (DUMB) – which controlled only five Muslim communities. The DUMB was headed by muftī Ismail Voronovich (d. 2012), who had previously worked as muftī Aleksandrovich's deputy. Muftī Voronovich criticized the MRS leadership for their alleged embrace of Salafīsm and other forms of 'untraditional' Islam and advocated the need for future imāms to be trained along the lines of the Lipka Tatars' 'traditional' Ḥanafī Islam. Muftī Voronovich therefore promoted future imāms' studies in Islamic universities situated in Moscow, Kazan and Bulgar (Tatarstan), but this did not prevent his successor, muftī Ali Voronovich (in office 2012–), from establishing in 2012 collaborative links with the pro-Salafī Spiritual Directorate of Muslims of Ukraine-'Ummah' (DUMU-Ummah). Also, the leaderships of both the MRS and DUMB have claimed their adherence to *al-Wasaṭīyyah* (Centrist Islam) which tends to be associated with Salafīsm.[17] The Muftīates' day-to-day activities, related to the administering of ritual practices, the maintenance of Muslim cemeteries and the running of weekly classes on the fundamentals of the Qur'ān, 'aqīdah and fiqh, have also been not dissimilar. At a structural level, both the MRS and DUMB have functioned as umbrella organizations for Tatar Islamo-national organizations and groups that regard Islam as part of the Tatars' national identity. Among such MRS affiliates has been, for example, *Dhikr al-Kitāb* (est. 1991), headed by muftī Shabanovich (b. 1939), while DUMB has supervised *Chimsha* (est. 1998), which is a member of the Kazan Tatar-centred World Congress of the Tatars (WCT),[18] as well as *Homyel* (est. 2002).

Overall, the role of the MRS and DUMB among local Muslims has been problematic as only just over one-third of Belarusian Muslims recognized their religious authority. One reason for this is the relatively high level of local Muslims' secularization and their cultural and linguistic Belarusification. Thus, the majority of local Tatars consider themselves as 'secular believers' and although they identify themselves as Muslims they do not follow Islamic rituals and do not seek Islamic leadership and guidance.[19] Another reason is the Tatar-centricity of both the MRS and DUMB which alienates the more religious recent Muslim immigrants from Chechnya, Turkmenistan, Azerbaijan, Turkey and some Arab countries, who have accordingly been seeking religious guidance outside Belarus.

Islamic Organizations and Their Leaders in Ukraine

Ethnocultural and Political Specifics of Islam and Muslims

Ukraine's Muslim community is considerably larger and more diverse than in Belarus. At the end of the Soviet era, it numbered around 87,000 people who made up around 0.2 per cent of the total population of 51.4 million,[20] the vast majority of them Volga Tatars who resided in Donetsk and Luhansk regions in the east of the country. Since 1991 Ukraine's Muslim demographics have undergone significant changes. In the early 2010s, there were already over 450,000 Muslims who constituted around 0.8 per cent of the total population of around 45 million. They were dominated by Crimean Tatars (350,000), followed by Volga Tatars (27,500), Azerbaijanis (19,200) and Muslim immigrants from other parts of post-Soviet Eurasia as well as the Middle East.[21] The major factor behind the sharp rise in the Crimean Tatar population was their mass repatriation from Siberia and Central Asia, where they were deported in 1944 on the accusation of alleged collaboration with the occupying Nazis. At the time of their deportation the Crimea was part of Russia, albeit in 1954 it was arbitrarily assigned by the Khrushchev government to Ukraine. Therefore, after the break-up of the USSR in 1991, returning Crimean Tatars found themselves on the territory of newly independent Ukraine. Following the Crimea's transfer to Russian jurisdiction in 2014, between 20,000 and 35,000 Crimean Tatars relocated to the central and western regions of Ukraine.[22] The remaining majority accepted Russia's suzerainty, and the Crimean muftīate (DUMK in Russian)[23] under the leadership of Emirali Ablayev (b. 1962, in office 1999–)[24] was integrated within the pan-Russian Muslim structures, Muftī Ablayev joining the Moscow-based Council of Muftīs of Russia (SMR) under the leadership of muftī Ravil Gaynutdin.[25]

The Islamic dynamic in independent Ukraine has differed considerably from that in neighbouring Belarus due to the country's continuing political instability on the one hand, and its more liberal religious legislature on the other. (Unlike in Russia and Belarus, the 1996 Ukrainian Constitution and successive religious laws retained religious freedom for all confessions, without dividing them into 'traditional' and 'untraditional', and continued to guarantee religious tolerance.) Since 1991 Ukraine has had six presidents, each of them negating the policies of his predecessor. The country underwent two regime changes in the form of the so-called Orange Revolution of 2004–5 and Euromaidan of 2014. Since 2014 eastern Ukraine has been engulfed in Civil War, its political upheavals and ongoing armed conflict accounting for persistent socio-economic hardships and the significant permanent and seasonal labour emigration from Ukraine to Russia, Poland, Germany and some other countries of the EU. Among the implications of this process has been the steady decline in Ukraine's overall population, including its Tatar segment. On the other hand, the country's liberal immigration and religious legislatures have attracted Muslim immigration to Ukraine from conflict-ridden zones in the Caucasus, Central Asia and the Middle East, particularly from Palestine, as well as from Jordan.

Ukraine's Muftīates

The ethnic and cultural diversity of Ukraine's Muslims and their different political histories have been reflected in their particular organizational and doctrinal diversity. Following the inclusion of the Crimean muftīate in 2014 within the Russian system of state–Muslim relations, 14 Muslim communities of Crimean Tatars, who resettled in central and western areas of Ukraine, established an alternative muftīate of Crimean Tatars which bore the same name. This muftīate formed an alternative Council of 'Ulamā' which consisted of both traditionalist and Salafī imāms.[26] Like its pre-2014 predecessor, the alternative muftīate has been closely linked to the Turkey-backed Mejlīs of Crimean Tatars which was founded in 1991 by a Crimean Tatar activist Mustafa Jamil(ev). The Mejlīs has acted as a surrogate parliament of the Crimean Tatars, and its representatives were included in the muftīate's board.[27] After 2014, the Mejlīs, which since 2013 has been headed by Refat Chubarov, has been recognized as the representative body of the Crimean Tatars in Ukraine, while in the Crimea it has been banned on the grounds of its alleged extremism. Significantly, the Islamo-national politicization of the Ukraine-based Crimean Tatar muftīate has contributed to its low authority among the country's non-Tatar Muslims.

Since 2014 Ukraine's most prominent muftīate has been the Spiritual Directorate of Muslims of Ukraine (DUMU in Ukrainian), which was founded in September 1992 in Kiev (Kyiv). It claims to control over 1,200 Muslim communities, including representatives of different ethnic groups.[28] The DUMU has been actively involved in inter-confessional dialogue and has been a member of the All-Ukrainian Council of Churches and Religious Organizations. It administers the Islamic University, the Centre of Islamic Studies and Translations, as well as the madrasah Al-Irshād (Guidance), all based in Kiev. The DUMU also has its own website, www.islam.ua, a radio channel *MPlus* and publishes a newspaper *Minaret*.[29] From its establishment, the DUMU has been headed by sheikh Aḥmad Tamīm (b. 1956), a Lebanese 'ālim belonging to Al-Aḥbāsh Ṣūfī reformist movement (also known as the Association of Islamic Charitable Projects, AICP), which was founded by an Ethiopian Islamic scholar 'Abdullah al-Hararī (1910–2008). Sheikh Tatīm has officially promoted Ṣūfīsm, including such practices as *'awliyā'* (the cult of saints) and *du'ā'* (the possibility of supplication to the Prophet) and denounces *Ḥizb al-Taḥrīr al-Islāmī* (HT, Party of Islamic Liberation), the Muslim Brotherhood and other pro-Salafī organizations operating in Ukraine. In 2010, Aḥmad Tamīm, who adopted the title of 'muftī of Ukraine', spearheaded the creation in Kiev of the Spiritual Centre for the Crimean Muslims (DTsMK) under the leadership of Ridvan Veliev in an attempt to undermine the authority of the Crimean muftīate among Crimean Tatar Muslims.

Another muftīate which aspires to an all-Ukrainian status has been the DUMU-Ummah, which was founded in 2008. The muftīate, which has been headed by muftī Saeed Ismagilov (b. 1978), a graduate of the Moscow Islamic University, claims to control 14 Muslim communities, situated in Kiev and across eastern Ukraine. It has its own Council of 'Ulamā', consisting of seven imāms, including the muftī, has its own website, www.umma.in.ua, and publishes a newspaper *Ummah*. In terms of dogmatic orientation

DUMU-Ummah is closer to Salafīsm and is critical of DUMU's pro-Aḥbāsh leaning. Since the first days it has collaborated with the Arab diaspora-centred social Islamic organization *Al-Rāid* (Forward). It is symptomatic that the main training destinations for DUMU-Ummah's candidates have been Islamic universities in Lebanon and Jordan.

Among Ukraine's regional muftīates, particularly prominent has been the Spiritual Centre of Ukrainian Muslims (DTsUM), referred to as the Donetsk muftīate, established in 1994 in Donetsk under the leadership of muftī Ruslan Abdikeev (b. 1976), a graduate of al-Azhar. It unites over 20 Muslim communities in eastern Ukraine (Donetsk, Vinnytsia, Kharkiv and Luhansk regions). The vast majority of its members have been Volga Tatars who settled in the region in the nineteenth century. Donetsk muftīate positions itself as a muftīate of the new, inclusive type, thus distancing itself from the Ṣūfī-oriented DUMU, the Salafī-oriented DUMU-Ummah and the Crimean Tatar-centred Crimean muftīate and Crimean Spiritual Centre while developing links with Islamic institutions outside Ukraine.[30] Since 2014, in the context of the inter-Ukrainian armed conflict in Donbass, there has been an influx of several hundred Muslim Tatars from the Volga region who have been fighting on the side of the self-proclaimed Donetsk People's Republic (DNR) and Luhansk People's Republic (LNR), as well as of Muslim fighters from the North Caucasus who have joined the pro-Kiev forces.[31]

In 2007, members of the Tatar diaspora in Kiev established the Religious Directorate of Muslim Communities of Ukraine which became known as the 'Kievan muftīate', headed since then by sheikh Kanafiya Khusnutdinov. The 'Kievan muftīate' claims to control several Muslim communities in Kiev, Kharkiv, Lviv and some other cities, runs the Kiev Islamic University and publishes the magazine *Ukraine and the Islamic World*. Until 2014, the Crimean muftīate, the DUMU-Ummah and the 'Kievan muftīate' contemplated some sort of unification against the dominant DUMU. In particular, in 2009, they attempted to create a Council of Spiritual Directorates and Centres of Ukraine under the leadership of muftī Ablayev. In 2011, the Council, which mainly dealt with ḥajj-related issues, ceased to exist. Since 2014, the 'Kievan muftīate' has prioritized its links with muftīates in Belarus and the Moscow-based Council of Muftīs of Russia (SMR).[32] Muftī Khusnutdinov, alongside muftī Ablayev of the Crimean muftīate, has been an ardent campaigner for the establishment of the Council of Muftīs of the Commonwealth of Independent States (CIS).

Al-Rāid, Fethullah Gülen's Movement and Other Islamic Organizations

Alongside several muftīates Ukraine has also hosted a number of Islamic organizations and parties of a transnational nature. The most influential among them has been *Al-Rāid* (Forward) which positions itself as a social rather than religious organization. Al-Rāid was established in Kiev in 1997 by Arab immigrants under the leadership of Mu'az Abū Obeida (in office 1997–99).[33] By 2020, Al-Rāid had created over 20 branches in Kiev, Odessa, Kharkiv, Vinnytsia, Zaporizhia and Sumy. It has generously sponsored charitable educational and health-related projects aimed at young people and women. In particular, it has run free classes in Islam and Arabic. Al-Rāid has its own website, www.arraid.org, and a publishing house which prints books on Islam, fiqh and the Qur'ān for children and adults, most of them authored by 'ulamā' from al-Azhar and other major Islamic centres in the Middle East. As noted earlier, Al-Rāid has developed close collaborative links with the DUMU-Ummah and the Islamic Studies academic community.[34] Al-Rāid's impressive financial resources suggest external funding emanating from the Middle East. Doctrinally, it has promoted Salafī Islam and has been critical of popular Tatar Islam; its activities have been conducive to re-Islamization, or first-hand Islamization, of young Ukrainians along Salafī lines.

A special mention should be made of the activities in Ukraine of the transnational Islamic movement *Hizmet* (Service)[35] which was founded by Fethullah Gülen (b. 1941), a Turkish preacher. It was particularly influential among the Crimean Tatars until 2014. The movement positioned itself as being moderate and inclusive and claimed to pursue a purely altruistic and educational agenda. It funded and staffed a network of schools and colleges across the Crimea and supplied pro-Gülen Islamic literature. De facto, however, it acted as a medium of Turkey's soft power penetration in Muslim communities in the Crimea and other Turkic-speaking Muslim regions, as well as in other parts of the world. Initially, Gülenists acted in alliance with the Turkish government. However, following the break-up between Fethullah Gülen and Turkey's President Recep Erdoğan (in office 2014–) in 2013, Gülen fled to the United States and began to pursue his proselytizing projects independently from official Ankara. Since then the Erdoğan government has pressurized the authorities in Ukraine and other parts of post-Soviet Eurasia to shut down or to restructure the Gülenist schools and other educational facilities which operated there.[36] The main official channel of Turkey's Islamic influence has been the Government Directorate of Religious Affairs (*Diyanet*), which has supplied Turkish imāms to the Crimean mosques and provided scholarships for Crimean Tatars seeking higher Islamic education at Turkish Islamic colleges and institutions. It is noteworthy that since the late 2010s Turkish Islamic soft power in Muslim Eurasia has been a part of Ankara's quest for the establishment of a Turkey-led Union of Islamic States, with Arabic as its lingua franca.

Another noticeable transnational Islamic organization has been the previously mentioned Ḥizb al-Taḥrīr al-Islāmī, which was founded in 1953 by a Palestinian, 'ālim Muḥammad Taqī al-Dīn al-Nabhānī (1914–1977). HT pursues an Islamist agenda, seeking the worldwide intellectual, cultural, as well as political and economic liberation of Muslims from Western domination.[37] In Ukraine, HT has been operating since the 1990s, and since the early 2000s its presence in the country has grown due to the arrival of Taḥrīris from across most of Muslim Eurasia, where their activity has been criminalized. Additionally, Ukraine and Kiev, in particular, has hosted a plethora of smaller Islamic Salafī organizations, including the radical international Islamist organization *Al-Takfīr wa al-Hijrah* (Excommunication and Exile),[38] the Salafī organization of Crimean Tatars, as well as some Shī'ī and Sūfī groups.[39] Overall, however, despite the large number of Muslim organizations in Ukraine, their actual authority among the country's Muslims has been rather weak. As in the case of Belarus, the main reason for this has been the high level of secularization of local Muslims and their cultural and linguistic Ukrainization or Russification (in the Donbass region). Consequently, over 80 per cent of Ukraine's Tatar population do not associate themselves with any particular muftīate and do not practise Islam, even while regarding it as part of their ethnocultural identity. In contrast, the level of Islamic religiosity, especially of Salafī orientation, has been more intense among Ukraine's Muslim immigrants originating from the Middle East, the Caucasus and Central Asia, as well as among local converts. They have sought their Islamic guidance from Al-Rāid and other pro-Salafī Islamic organizations, as well as from abroad and especially online.

Islam and Muslim Leadership in Lithuania

Muslims' Ethnocultural Composition and Legal Status

In 1991 Muslims in Lithuania numbered around 11,000, which constituted under 0.3 per cent of the country's total population of 3.7 million.[40] Among them the Lithuanian Tatars proper (the descendants of the Lipka Tatars) made up just over 2,000, while the rest were represented by Muslims who came to Lithuania from the Volga-Urals, the Caucasus and Central Asia after the Second World War. Unlike Ukraine, Lithuania has lacked Middle Eastern Muslim immigrants of the student-turned-resident type. As for the Soviet-era Muslim settlers, many of them were repatriated back to their countries of origin during Lithuania's post-Soviet ethnonational sovereignization. As a result, the size of Lithuania's Muslim community dramatically contracted. According to the 2011 census, there were only 2,727 Muslims within the total population of three million. Just over half of them were Tatars, and the rest were represented by Lithuanian converts, Azerbaijanis, Chechens and Central Asians. Despite the Muslims' small number the 1995 Law on Religious Community recognized Sunnī Islam as one of the country's nine traditional religions.[41] The Law facilitated the formation of a unitary Sunnī Muslim community, headed by an umbrella organization – the muftīate.[42] Importantly, contrary to the situation in Belarus, Russia and most of post-Soviet Eurasia, where the state has effectively maintained the Soviet system of state–Muslim relations, the Lithuanian state has fully departed from this system and ceased to interfere into the muftīate's domain.[43]

Muftīates of Lithuania

The first Lithuanian muftīate, which bears the official name of the Spiritual Centre of Lithuanian Sunnī Muslims, was established in Vilnius in 1998 by Lithuanian Tatars from Vilnius and Kaunas. Since then it has been headed by muftīs from a Lithuanian Tatar background. The first muftī Romualdas Krinickis (b. 1973, in office 1998–2008) was a native of Vilnius; the second muftī Romas Jakubauskas (b. 1974, in office 2008–)[44] was a native of Kaunas. The Muftīate controls six town- and village-based Muslim Tatar communities, one relatively big mosque in Kaunas and three small village mosques,[45] which only function during 'Īd al-Fiṭr, 'Īd al-Aḍha and other major Islamic festivities. There is not a single madrasah and future imāms go for training abroad. Its infrastructure is pretty basic: only in 2013, in Vilnius, did the muftīate acquire its own premises consisting of a muftī's office, a *musallah* (prayer room) and several classrooms. The muftīate's functions have been limited to the administering of Islamic funeral and other rituals and the organization of summer camps for Lithuanian Tatar youth with the aim of enlightening them about their Islamic roots. As in the case of the Crimean Tatars, who (at least till 2014) had a dual – muftīate and majlīs – official leadership, the muftīate's authority over Lithuanian Tatars has been contested by the two Tatar regional organizations based in Vilnius and Kaunas. These organizations have competed for scarce resources and for official representation of Lithuanian Tatars. To some degree the Vilnius–Kaunas juxtaposition has been a continuation of the inter-war mutual mistrust between the 'Polish' and 'Lithuanian' Tatars.[46] Additionally, from 2015, the muftīate's authority has been contested by a rival Islamic organization – The Council of Lithuanian Muslim Religious Communities – a Muftīate which has been headed by muftī Ramadan Yaqoob (b. 1981),[47] who came from the province.

Both muftīates have been regarded as legitimate Muslim organizations entitled to receive state funding, albeit this is very modest. They also have the prerogative to decide which Muslim communities could be qualified as 'traditional' and therefore to be registered. However, the muftīates' criteria for 'traditional' status have been ambiguous. For example, muftī Romas Jakubauskas endorsed the establishment in 2007 of the Klaipeda City Muslim Community Al-Tawhīd and in 2009 of the Klaipeda Region Muslim Community Imān, both in the seaport of Klaipeda, where there have never been any Tatars, that is, 'traditional Muslims'. These organizations mainly consisted of recent migrants and converts of 'non-traditional', and predominantly Salafī, orientation. Overall, the authority of the official Muslim clergy has been marginal due to the accelerated pace of Lithuanian Muslims' assimilation within a Catholicism-dominated society. Muslim self-identification among Lithuanian Tatars has been falling and in the 2010s only around 10 per cent of them observed Islamic duties and rituals.[48] On the other hand, since independence Lithuania has acquired some new Muslims – recent converts to Islam and immigrants from Muslim Eurasia and the Middle East, who are not however affiliated to official Muslim bodies. They are mostly observant Muslims of Salafī orientation who seek their religious guidance either outside Lithuania or online and among themselves.[49]

Conclusion

Since the disintegration of the USSR, the state of Islam and Islamic leadership as well as state–Muslim relations in Belarus, Ukraine and Lithuania have displayed significant differences due to these countries' differing political trajectories and external orientations. Thus, in Belarus, which has exhibited considerable continuity with the Soviet political and socio-economic model and has retained close links with Russia, the Islamic dynamic has been broadly congruent to that in wider post-Soviet Eurasia. There have been two state-controlled muftīates which followed the organizational patterns of their imperial Russian and Soviet predecessors. They have been closely monitored by the governmental religious departments reminiscent of the Soviet Council for Affairs of Religious Cults (CARC) and have acted, at least rhetorically, as the bearers of 'traditional', that is, Tatar,

Islam. Accordingly, various 'untraditional' Islamic leaders and communities have been de-legitimized or even criminalized on the grounds of their alleged extremism.

By comparison, in Ukraine, which since the 2000s has steadily deviated from the Soviet-era Eurasian political legacy and from 2014 minimized its links with neighbouring Russia while greatly increasing political and economic engagement with the EU and the United States, the Islamic dynamic and state–Muslim relations have been hybrid in nature. Significant cultural differences between the western and eastern parts of Ukraine, as well as the ongoing conflict in Donbass, have accounted for the coexistence there of 'European' and 'Eurasian' models of state–Muslim relations. Thus, the official Islamic domain has included a plethora of muftīates and a new type of Muslim organization of both folk Islamic and Salafī orientation. Significantly, Al-Rāid and other pro-Salafī organizations have been much more active among young Muslim urbanites than the major muftīate – DUMU.

In Lithuania, which, along with neighbouring Estonia and Latvia, radically broke away from the Eurasian political model and became externally reoriented towards the EU and the United States, the Islamic dynamic and state–Muslim relations have undergone the most drastic transformation. Under the impact of the nationalistically driven policies of successive Lithuanian governments a significant number of Lithuanian Muslims have emigrated. The remaining Tatars have experienced further assimilation by the Catholic majority, while the role among them of the newly established muftīates has been symbolic. At the same time, an increasing number of religious Muslim immigrants and converts have relied on Islamic leadership and guidance from outside Lithuania. Overall, the political and cultural 'Europeanization' of Lithuania (alongside other post-communist countries of eastern and central Europe) has altered the traditional outlook and functions of its Islamic governing bodies and has led to both top-down and bottom-up 'churchification'.[50]

Chapter Ten

EUROPEAN RUSSIA

Introduction

As we've already seen, the dissolution of the Soviet state in December 1991 led to the break-up of the system of state–Muslim relations centred on the four muftīates situated in Ufa, Makhachkala, Baku and Tashkent. The Soviet muftīates were either disbanded or fragmented, and replaced by a plethora of new muftīates, some of which were formed on the basis of the Soviet ones or their regional branches – *muhtasibat*s and *qāḍīyāt*s – while others were established from scratch by 'young imāms' in various Muslim-populated regions of the former Soviet Union. The multiplication of muftīates was especially intensive in the Volga-Ural and Siberian regions, which are home to over eight million autochthonous Muslims of Tatar, Bashkir and other ethnic origin. There emerged over two dozen new muftīates which declared their independence from the Ufa-based Spiritual Directorate of Muslims of the European Part of the USSR and Siberia (DUMES/TsDUM)[1] under muftī Talgat Safa Tadzhuddinov (Tadzhuddin/Tazeev, b. 1948, in office 1980–).[2] Since the mid-1990s, the main challenge to Tadzhuddin's supreme Islamic leadership has come from Ravil Gaynutdin (Gaynutdinov, b. 1959),[3] who engineered the creation in Moscow of the Spiritual Directorate of Muslims of the Central European region of Russia (DUMTsER/DUM RF),[4] and the Council of Muftīs of Russia (SMR), both of which he headed. Through the 1990s among the DUMES/TsDUM's other powerful opponents were the Kazan-based Spiritual Directorate of Muslims of Republic of Tatarstan (DUM RT) under the leadership of Gabdulla Galiulla (Galiullin, b. 1954)[5] and Gusman Iskhakov (b. 1957);[6] the Tobol'sk-based Spiritual Directorate of Muslims of the Asian Part of Russia (DUM AChR)[7] under the leadership of Nafigulla Ashirov (b. 1954);[8] and the Saratov-based Spiritual Directorate of Muslims of Saratov oblast' (DUMSO) under Mukaddas Bibarsov (b. 1960).[9] By 2000, in central Russia, alongside the three largest muftīates – SMR, TsDUM and DUM RT – there were over 20 regional muftīates headed by 'young imāms', many of whom were educated at Islamic institutions in the Middle East and implicitly adhered to Salafī Islam. In Tatarstan, official Islamic discourse became influenced by the Tatar version of Euro-Islam,[10] which was anchored in Tatar jadīdism and promoted by Tatar intellectuals under the leadership of Rafael Khakimov,[11] a political adviser of the Tatarstan President Mintimer Shaimiev (in office 1991–2010).[12]

From the 2000s, in the context of Russia's recentralization under President Vladimir Putin (in office 2000–),[13] the TsDUM, SMR as well as the Coordinating Centre of Muslims of the North Caucasus (KTsMSK),[14] all three of which claimed federal status, have undertaken several attempts at their unification. But the process has been hampered by their leaders' personal rivalries, as well as the emergence of a new type of state-sponsored 'parallel' official Islamic umbrella administration – the Russian Association of Islamic Consensus (RAIS) and the Spiritual Assembly of Muslims of Russia (DSMR), headed by muftīs Muhamatgali Khuzin (b. 1969, in office 2010–13) and Al'bir Krganov (b. 1976, in office 2010–), respectively.[15] In spring 2014, the configuration and politics of Russian Islamic officialdom was also affected by the arrival of a new influential player – the Crimean muftīate under the leadership of muftī Emirali Ablayev (b. 1962), which formally joined the SMR.[16] In August 2014, the Crimea acquired another Kremlin-backed muftīate – the Spiritual Directorate of Muslims of the Republic of Crimea – the Taurida Muftīate (DUMRK-TM) – under the leadership of Ruslan Saitvaliev (b. 1977)[17] which established close links with the TsDUM, DUM RT and the muftīate of Chechnya.

The chapter begins by examining the politics of the Ufa-based federal muftīate under the leadership of muftī Talgat Safa Tadzhuddin. It pays special attention to Tadzhuddin's theological views and his relations with the Kremlin and Russian Orthodox Church (ROC). It then discusses the formation and organizational and doctrinal evolution of the Moscow-based SMR-DUM RF under the leadership of muftī Ravil Gaynutdin and his political and religious tactics aimed at gaining the official Islamic supremacy in European Russia. The following section deals with Russia's largest regional muftīate of Tatarstan. It examines its relations with the Tatar national movement, official Kazan, on the one hand, and the TsDUM and the SMR-DUM RF on the other. The chapter then analyses the free-standing 'parallel' muftīates – the RAIS and DSMR and their relations with other muftīates and the state. It proceeds to discuss non-institutionalized Islamic organizations and their influence among Turco-Tatar Muslims. The final section deals with a relatively new phenomenon – the Islamic leadership in the Russian North.

DUMES/TsDUM

At the end of the Soviet era the DUMES as the legal successor of the Orenburg Mohammedan Spiritual Assembly was the sole official representative of the Muslims of central Russia and Siberia. Since 1980 it has been headed by muftī Talgat Safa Tadzhuddin, one of the best educated and charismatic Islamic leaders and a skilful politician. In 1989, Talgat Tadzhuddin further strengthened his religious and national credentials by organizing the celebration of the 1100th anniversary of Volga Bulgaria's Islamization and by forging an alliance with the Tatar national movement under the leadership of the All-Tatar Public Centre (VTOTs), the *Millī Mejlīs* (National Council) and the *Ittifāq* Party.[18] The celebration was accompanied by the opening of many new mosques in Ufa, Kazan, Naberezhnye Chelny and Nizhnekamsk; by 1990 the DUMES oversaw 1,103 mosques, compared to 392 mosques in 1985.[19] However, in 1992, in the context of the centrifugal turmoil of the 'parade of sovereignties', spearheaded by President Boris Yeltsin (in office 1991–99), Talgat Tadzhuddin's religious monopoly was undermined by the emergence of a plethora of self-proclaimed muftīs, some of whom were his former subordinates, students or relatives. In Ufa, alongside the DUMES, there appeared another muftīate – the Spiritual Directorate of Muslims of the Republic of Bashkortostan (DUM RB) – under the leadership of the 'young imām' and Tadzhuddin's former deputy Nurmuhamet Nigmatullin (in office 1992–2019),[20] who allied with the Moscow-based Higher Coordinating Centre of Spiritual Directorates of Muslims of Russia (VKTs) and SMR under the leadership of Ravil Gaynutdin. In response, muftī Tadzhuddin authorized the establishment in Ufa of the Regional Spiritual Directorate of Muslims of Bashkortostan (RDUMB), affiliated to DUMES.

Still, against the background of the succession of organizational and political cataclysms the DUMES (renamed as TsDUM in 1994) under Tadzhuddin's leadership – who in 1996 also assumed the titles of supreme muftī and sheikh al-Islām – has remained the largest Russian federal muftīate in terms of the number of affiliated regional muftīates and local Muslim communities. The DUMES/TsDUM's religious centre has continuously been the Ufa Cathedral mosque,[21] Russia's oldest mosque belonging to the Orenburg Mohammedan Spiritual Assembly. In 2020 muftī Tadzhuddin controlled 21 regional muftīates and seven representative organizations in various regions of Russia and other parts of the former USSR. Under the TsDUM's jurisdiction has been the Russian Islamic University of Riza Fahretdin (RIU), established in 1999 in Ufa on the basis of the madrasah which was opened in 1989. Until 2017, RIU, alongside the Moscow Islamic Institute (MII), the Islamic Institute of Khusain Faizkhanov in Nizhny Novgorod (NII) and the Russian Islamic Institute (RII)[22] in Kazan, was a major training centre of imām-khatybs and imām-muhtasibs for Russia, Kyrgyzstan, Kazakhstan and other ex-Soviet states. In 2017 Tadzhuddin acted as the leading co-founder of the Bulgar Islamic Academy (BIA),[23] which was geared towards the training of imāms along the lines of Russian 'traditional' Islam. Talgat Tadzhuddin has also retained his supremacy in representing Russia's Muslim clergy at the Organization of Islamic Cooperation (OIC), the Islamic Council of Europe, UNESCO and other major international organizations and forums. Unlike the theologically weak Gaynutdin, Tadzhuddin has been actively involved in Arabic-based international Islamic discourse, reflected in TsDUM's website www.cdum.ru which runs in three languages – Arabic, Tatar and Russian. The website contains recordings of Tadzhuddin's weekly Friday prayers in Arabic, Tatar and Russian. TsDUM's newspaper *Magliumat al-Bulgar* (The Bulgar News) is similarly trilingual.

Talgat Tadzhuddin's impressive longevity as a Muslim leader has been due to his Islamic scholarly competence, Ṣūfī charisma and political and diplomatic skills. Throughout his 40-year-long religious career he has been an adamant *gosudarstvennik* (an advocate of the strong state) and an unconditional supporter of the state's policies, including Russia's military involvement in Syria and the Kremlin's negative stance on the wearing of the hijāb by Muslim women in Russia.[24] He has adhered to the idea of the Russian unitary centralized muftīate as a function of the centralized Russian state. He has also long held the conviction that there is a theological affinity between Islam and Russian Orthodox Christianity while recognizing the ROC's superiority over DUMES/TsDUM because of its being the Church of the Russian majority. He has had close personal relations with the ROC's leaders, Patriarchs Alexy II (1929–2008) and Kirill (b. 1946), and shared their views regarding the merger of ethnicity with religion – that is, the merger of Russian-ness with Orthodox Christianity and Tatar-ness and Bashkir-ness with Islam, respectively. Accordingly, Tadzhuddin restricts his constituency to ethnic Tatars and Bashkirs and opposes Islamic proselytism as well as the conversion to Islam of

Russians and other Slavs. In his prayers and speeches he often uses Christian Orthodox terminology; for example, in 2003, during the United States-led invasion of Iraq he described America and its allies as 'the Antichrist of the world' and issued a highly controversial fatwā calling for jihād against Western invaders. In the same year Tadzhuddin attempted, albeit unsuccessfully, to rename the TsDUM of Russia into the TsDUM of Holy Rus. In 2015 he put forward the idea of 'Russia as a Caliphate of Holy Rus', in which Orthodox and Muslim believers live peacefully side by side, although on the former's terms – that is, Muslims being the younger brothers of Orthodox believers.[25]

DUM RF-SMR

As mentioned earlier, in 1992 Tadzhuddin's authority was denounced and rejected by a number of 'young imāms' who stood up against his alleged authoritarian and confrontational style of leadership, excessive ecumenism and his supposed mental instability.[26] The actual reasons behind their 'disobedience' were multiple and included their personal leadership ambitions, their quest for direct access to external Islamic funds and other foreign Islamic assistance emanating from various government and non-government Islamic organizations and charities based in Saudi Arabia, the Gulf, Turkey and elsewhere. By the late 2010s, one of these new muftīs, Ravil Gaynutdin, had achieved near parity with Talgat Tadzhuddin in the number of Muslim communities and Islamic educational institutions he controlled. Under his jurisdiction are the Moscow Islamic Institute (MII), the Moscow-based Islamic college and madrasah, as well as the Islamic Institute of Khusain Faizkhanov (NII) and the madrasah 'Mahinur' in Nizhny Novgorod. In terms of publishing capacity and media and online visibility Gaynutdin has even surpassed his former boss. The DUM RF's own publishing house 'Medina' (www.medina.ru) produces the multivolume *Encyclopedia of Islam in the Russian Federation*, the journal *Islam in the Modern World* and the newspaper *Minbar Islama*, while its Russian-language website www.dumrf.ru has superior thematic coverage and technological sophistication. Among key factors behind Ravil Gaynutdin's speedy career progression have been his theatrical training, his Moscow location and his undoubted political shrewdness and tactical skills.

Gaynutdin's ascendance to power began in 1994, when as imām-khatyb of the Moscow Cathedral mosque, he orchestrated his election by the Constituent Mejlīs of Muslim Regional Associations and Communities of Russia as the chairman of the Spiritual Directorate of Muslims of Central European part of Russia (the DUMTsER/DUMER), affiliated to the Cathedral mosque.[27] This he achieved with the active support of the Moscow-based Higher Coordinating Centre of Spiritual Directorates of Muslims of Russia (VKTs) and the Islamic Cultural Centre (IKTs), the former created by muftīs Gabdulla Galiullin, Mukaddas Bibarsov and Nafigulla Ashirov, the latter by a political and religious opportunist, Abdel Wahid Niyazov (b. 1969).[28] In 1996 Gaynutdin strengthened his gains by being 'elected' as chairman of the new umbrella Islamic organization – the Council of Muslims of Russia (the SMR). The SMR united the newly formed muftīate of Tatarstan, Bashkortostan, Asian Russia, the Volga region, 'Association of Mosques', the Orenburg oblast', Nizhny Novgorod and Nizhny Novgorod oblast', Ulyanovsk and Ulyanovsk oblast', as well as Chuvashia. Having consolidated his control over the

SMR, Gaynutdin gradually disposed of his old allies and added to his official title self-designations as 'sheikh' and 'spiritual leader of Russian Muslims'.[29] In 2014, Gaynutdin masterminded the renaming of DUMER into DUM RF which led to the latter's de facto absorption of the SMR, a move that signified the power shift from an originally collegial SMR towards a centralized DUM RF. In order to secure his leadership Ravil Gaynutdin has surrounded himself by his younger protégés Damir Mukhetdinov (b. 1977), Rushan Abbyasov (b. 1981) and Shamil Alyautdinov (b. 1974), who have their own rivalry for the succession, which has made them unlikely to unite against him.[30] Another well-educated contender, Ildar Alyautdinov (b. 1978), has been neutralized through his appointment as muftī of Moscow (Spiritual Directorate of Muslims of Moscow) and chairman of the charity fund 'Zakat', based in the Moscow Cathedral mosque.

Throughout the 1990s, Gaynutdin benefitted from his Moscow location to forge special relations with President Boris Yeltsin and Moscow Mayor Yury Luzhkov (in office 1992–2010) by attuning his religious and political message to their liking, enabling him to create his lobbies within the presidential and mayoral administrations. In March 2000, with the mayor's implicit approval, Gaynutdin asserted control over the second largest mosque in Moscow, the Historical Mosque (*Istoricheskaia Mechet'*), which was previously under the TsDUM's jurisdiction. Since the 2000s, Gaynutdin has significantly 'corrected' the contents of his preaching and public and media statements to conform to President Putin's line on the state's recentralization and social conservatism. In particular, his previous declarative adherence to the globalized Islamic concept of *al-wasaṭīyyah* (moderation) has been replaced by his staunch adherence to traditional Ḥanafīsm. Since 2016, in response to the introduction of anti-terrorist legislation, known as 'the Yarovaya Set of Legislative Amendments',[31] Gaynutdin began to denounce religion – especially, Islam-related terrorism and extremism – and to promote 'Russian Islam' – one of the four government-endorsed traditional religions (Orthodox Christianity, Islam, Buddhism and Judaism).

Unlike the theologically competent Tadzhuddin, Gaynutdin has shunned in-depth theological deliberations and, instead, prioritized his participation in major Islam-related national and international conferences by drawing on the expertise of Moscow-based Arabists and other Islamic Studies specialists from the Institute of Oriental Studies, the Institute of Asia and Africa and other relevant institutions. He has also been a regular contributor to nationwide philosophical, social and political science debates.[32] In order to reach out to non-Tatar Muslims in Russia, and Moscow in particular, and to compensate for his poor knowledge of Arabic, Gaynutdin has embarked on the Russification of original Islamic terminology by purifying it of Arabic and Persian borrowings and replacing them by Christian Orthodox terms. For example, in his sermons and other speeches Allah has been often referred to as *Bog* ('God', in Russian), *Sozdatel'* (Creator) or *Vsevyshnii* (Exalted); the Qur'ān as *Zakon Vsevyshnego* (The Law of Exalted); *mir'āj* (Prophet Muḥammad's spiritual journey) as *voznesenie* (ascension); *namāz* as *molitva* (prayer) and *ḥajj* as *palomnichestvo* (pilgrimage).[33] In January 2015, Gaynutdin caused a stir among Muslim clergy by issuing a *Rozhdestvenskoe Poslanie* ('Christmas Greeting') to believers on the Prophet Muḥammad's birthday.[34] At the same time, compared to the ecumenical Tadzhuddin, Gaynutdin has distanced himself from the ROC and criticized the introduction in schools of the course on 'the Foundation of Orthodox Culture', the creation of the institute of Orthodox chaplaincy in the army and the Church's interference in the construction of new mosques.

Like Tadzhuddin, Gaynutdin has been involved in the Kremlin's Islam-related politics. He played an important role in securing the relatively smooth transfer of the Crimean muftīate under muftī Emirali Ablayev from Ukraine to Russia. Gaynutdin has acted as Russia's soft power influencer by strengthening relations with Tatar Muslim communities outside Russia; for example, the SMR began to send imāms to Finland at the request of the local Tatar community[35] (Bekkin 2020: 285). Gaynutdin has been an enthusiastic supporter of Russia's closer relations with Turkey and has developed close personal relations with Turkey's President Erdoğan (in office 2014–), who, alongside Palestine's President Mahmoud Abbas (in office 2005–), attended the opening of the Moscow Cathedral mosque in September 2015. It is worth noting that during the short-term breakdown of Russian–Turkish relations over the downing by Turkey of a Russian military plane in Syria in November 2015, Gaynutdin refrained from joining the nationwide anti-Turkish campaign. In general, however, muftī Gaynutdin, arguably true to his theatrical background, has been more concerned with his public performance as a muftī than with being a muftī in a normative sense. Furthermore even his formal authority as muftī has been limited to around 800,000 Tatars who have been residing in Moscow for several centuries. Moscow Tatars, however, constitute a minority within the over 3 million-strong Muslim community dominated by labour migrants from Central Asia and the Caucasus. These are associated primarily with over 30 Muslim groups led by unofficial mullahs and imāms – also migrants – who are not subordinate to Ravil Gaynutdin, even if some of them gather at Moscow's Cathedral mosque and Memorial Mosque (est. 1997).[36]

DUM RT

Among most influential regional muftīates which emerged in the early 1990s has been the Spiritual Directorate of Muslims of the Republic of Tatarstan – the DUM RT. It was created on the wave of the rising Tatar national movement organized by the VTOTs, Millī Mejlīs and Ittifāq, leaders of which regarded a muftīate as an important attribute of Tatarstan's national sovereignty.[37] As mentioned earlier, initially, Tatar nationalists collaborated with DUMES muftī Tadzhuddin, a Kazan Tatar. Their alliance broke up, however, when Tadzhuddin rejected the nationalists' call to relocate the DUMES from Ufa to Kazan, which they perceived as Russia's Muslim capital. The Tatar nationalists then increased pressure on official Kazan to endorse the establishment of the muftīate of Tatarstan, so in the summer of 1992 they joined forces with Tadzhuddin's disgruntled colleagues and created the DUM RT under the leadership of Gabdulla Galiullin,[38] a member of the anti-Tadzhuddin alliance and a co-founder of the Moscow-based VKTs and SMR. Until the mid-1990s the DUM RT was effectively subordinated to the Tatar national movement and exercised limited religious functions.

Muftī Tadzhuddin, who refused to recognize Galiullin's legitimacy as Tatarstan's muftī, nominated Gabdulhamit Zinnatullin[39] and, subsequently, Farid Salman

(Khaidarov), as his representatives in Tatarstan. Until 1995 Tadzhuddin's appointees presided over an alternative muftīate – the Spiritual Directorate of Muslims of Tatarstan (the DUMT) – which controlled a significant number of Muslim communities and Kazan's major Islamic institutions – the Marjani mosque and Muḥammadīyyah madrasah.[40] The official Islamic authority's duplicity came to an end in February 1998 at the Unifying Islamic Congress supported by the Shaimiev government.[41] The Congress de-selected the independently minded Galiullin and elected a more 'manageable' muftī, Gusman Iskhakov (in office 1998–2011), who openly positioned himself as Shaimiev's protégé.[42] In Tatarstan's Religious Law of 1999 the DUM RT was named as the single lawful Islamic organization in the republic. Gabdulla Galiullin and Farid Salman, who had lost their legitimacy, attempted to reverse the situation by organizing an opposition movement, 'Muslims of Tatarstan' (1998–99), which soon morphed into the political party *Omet* (Hope), as well as by reinstating the DUMT. However, by 2001 they accepted their defeat and retreated to the educational and scholarly sphere.[43]

Since 1998 the Tatarstan government, which under the 1994 Bilateral Treaty enjoyed greater autonomy from Moscow, has been directly involved in the muftīate's funding and its cadre and educational policies.[44] It also implicitly encouraged the DUM RT's federal ambitions, the Tatarstani authorities turning a blind eye to the establishment in 2000 in Kazan of the Association of Muslim Religious Organizations 'Kazan Muftīate' (2000–11) under the leadership of an influential Islamic scholar and deputy muftī Valiulla Yakupov (1963–2012). The 'Kazan Muftīate' sought to absorb Tatar Muslim communities outside Tatarstan, especially in Ulyanovsk and Kirov oblasts. However, during the 2000s, in the framework of Putin's power vertical, official Kazan gradually lost its special status in its relations with the Kremlin and was forced to curtail the activities of the 'Kazan Muftīate' outside the republic. In 2011 the DUM RT under the leadership of muftī Ildus Faizov (in office 2011–13) disbanded the 'Kazan Muftīate' and restricted the DUM RT's activities to the territory of Tatarstan.[45] Meanwhile, within the Tatarstani government a Department for Religious Affairs was created, modelled on the Soviet-era CARC, and similarly tasked with the muftīate's control.

Throughout its existence the DUM RT has been a key player in all Russian Muslim politics, one reason for which has been its jurisdiction over a large number of Muslims; in 2020 it oversaw 1,415 Muslim communities (Bekkin 2020: 234). Another factor has been its financial advantages due to its greater government funding. It has also benefitted from its location in Kazan – the spiritual centre of all Tatars – and the existence in Tatarstan of the two major Islamic educational centres – the BIA and the Russian Islamic Institute (RII), as well as its Tatar-tailored online and media activity. DUM RT runs the website www.dumrt.ru, produces a journal *Shurah* (Council) and a newspaper *Ummah* and has its own radio programme *Azan* (Call for prayer) and a TV channel *Khuzur*, all of which are in Tatar and Russian. Since 2013, a contributing factor to the DUM RT's religious authority has been the theological competence of its muftī Kamil Sigmatullin (in office 2013–),[46] who has achieved the muftīate's de facto independence from both the DUM RF and TsDUM.

Tatar Trans-regional Independent Muftīates

In the late 2000s, the dichotomy between federal and regional muftīates was complicated by the emergence of two trans-regional free-standing Islamic organizations – the RAIS (2010–13) and the Spiritual Assembly of Muslims of Russia (DSMR, 2016–). These were positioned by their leaders as independent Muslim governing structures, not affiliated to either the TsDUM or the DUM RF, which they accused of over-centralization, bureaucratization and clannism.[47]

The Russian Association of Islamic Consensus

The establishment of the RAIS occurred during the intensified dialogue between Russia's federal muftīates – the TsDUM, the DUM RF and the Coordinating Centre of Muslims of the North Caucasus (KTsMSK) – regarding their potential unification. As in the past, the dialogue was instigated by muftī Talgat Tadzhuddin. A possible catalyst was the rise of Ramzan Kadyrov, the head of Chechnya and son of the late charismatic muftī Akhmad Kadyrov, who began to claim a pan-Russian Islamic authority.[48] A number of senior Tatar and other Muslim clerics of Turkic ethnic origins, however, saw it as the opportunity to establish a new type of centralized Islamic organization. Among them were Muhamatgali Khuzin, Farid Salman and Al'bir Krganov, who, in different times, had been removed by Talgat Tadzhuddin from leading positions within the TsDUM for their alleged disloyalty. They hoped to capitalize on the growing disquiet among some Muslim clergy and ordinary Muslims about muftī Tadzhuddin's excessive ecumenism, behavioural extravagance[49] and his alleged grooming of his son Muḥammad as his successor. In the case of Krganov (a Mishar Tatar) and Muhametgali Khuzin (a Bashkir) and their supporters, a contributing factor was the domination of Kazan Tatars over both the TsDUM and DUM RF.[50]

In April 2010 several Tatar Muslim clerics under the leadership of Muhamatgali Khuzin, muftī of the independent muftīate of the Perm krai, Farid Salman and Muḥammad Rakhimov, muftī of the newly established muftīate of Stavropol' krai, secured the Kremlin's approval for the creation of the RAIS. At its constituent conference in December 2010, the RAIS claimed to also include the muftīate of Mordovia, the muftīate of Ural and the muftīate of the city of Ryazan. For tactical reasons RAIS was nominally headed by muftī Muḥammad Rakhimov (b. 1956), the muftī of Stavropol' krai,[51] but the actual decision-makers were Muhamatgali Khuzin and Farid Salman, who presided over the Executive Committee and the Council of 'Ulamā', respectively. At the theological level, the RAIS was a staunch promoter of 'traditional' Ḥanafī Islam and of the close relationship with the ROC as Russia's dominant Church. It campaigned for the cleansing of the Russian Islamic establishment and the DUM RF, in particular, from alleged Arab and Turkish presence and influences.[52] At the political level, the RAIS claimed its unconditional loyalty to the Kremlin and advocated a tougher military approach towards so-called Wahhābīs, Salafīs, Islamists and other 'non-traditional' Muslims. The RAIS's activity was soon paralysed by the personal rivalry between Rakhimov, Khuzin and Salman and at the end of 2013 the organization disintegrated.

Rakhimov, as muftī of Stavropol' krai, returned under the jurisdiction of the KTsM SK. Khuzin was deselected as muftī of the Perm muftīate, which was reabsorbed by the TsDUM, and Salman retreated to scholarship by heading the Centre for the Study of the Qur'ān and Sunnah.[53]

The Spiritual Assembly of Muslims of Russia

In late 2016 several senior Muslim clerics under the leadership of Al'bir Krganov,[54] muftī of Chuvashia, established in Moscow the Spiritual Assembly of Muslims of Russia – the 'Moscow Muftīate' (the DSMR), which consisted of 10 Mishar-dominated regional muftīates which had broken away either from the TsDUM or the DUM RF. Since then, muftī Krganov has been Russia's most 'political' muftī, with close links to President Putin's administration. In this respect he has not been much different from Talgat Tadzhuddin and has shared the latter's subservience towards the ROC. Krganov has vigorously promoted the Kremlin's policies aimed at the de-radicalization of home-grown Wahhābīs and jihādīs, the enhancing of patriotism and Russian values among Muslim youth and the strengthening of intercultural and inter-confessional dialogue in multi-ethnic Russia. Al'bir Krganov's theological views have been rather peculiar. For example, he has not regarded Salafīs as part of *Ahl al-Sunnah wa al-Jamā'ah* (People of the Sunnah and Community) and perceived Ṣūfism as the core of 'traditional' Islam. It is symptomatic that he subscribed to the 2016 'Grozny Fatwā' on the definition of 'true' Islam, which was opposed by both Gaynutdin and Tadzhuddin.[55] Muftī Krganov's political rather than theological profile has been reflected in the DSMR's website www.rosmuslim.ru which is available in Russian, Tatar, Arabic, Turkish, English and French versions. The website abounds with video and audio recordings of the muftī's political statements while having very limited theological content. Unlike the TsDUM or DUM RF, the 'Moscow Muftīate' barely possesses any infrastructure, although it has close links with the 'Yardam' mosque in the Otradnoe district in Moscow.

Unofficial Islamic Leadership

The weakening and fragmentation of the Tatar official Islamic leadership in the late Soviet and the early post-Soviet periods has occurred alongside the rise of various unofficial Islamic authorities that are both indigenous and foreign in nature.

Faizrakhmanists

Faizrakhmanists are followers of imām Faizrakhman Sattarov (Nasrulla-bai, 1929–2015),[56] who in 1976 quit the allegedly theologically corrupt DUMES where he worked as qāzī with the aim of creating an authentic *firqah* (Islamic community) based exclusively on the Qur'ān. In an interview with the author, Faizrakhman positioned himself as a Messenger of the Prophet Muḥammad and a leader of the only true firqah out of the existing 73. Faizrakhman's religious teaching was eclectic. On the one hand, it had similarities with Salafī, or ever takfīrī perceptions, including the rejection of the divisions into Sunnīs and Shī'a, the division into followers of the four madhhabs within Sunnī Islam, the negative attitude to Ṣūfīsm and the rejection of mawlīd and other 'invented' religious festivals. On the other hand, Faizrakhmanists have displayed tolerance towards folk wake rites and ijtihād. Of special significance was their emphasis on the indigenous roots of their beliefs and their opposition to any association with foreign Muslim authorities, Salafī and non-Salafī.[57]

Unlike his bureaucratized ex-colleagues from the DUMES, Faizrakhman actively proselytized his teaching in grassroots communities, as well as among worshippers in the Kazan mosques of Marjani and Zakabannaia and in the mosques of Naberezhnye Chelny. In 1996, in the village of Torfiano on the outskirts of Kazan, Faizrakhman established a settled community of his adepts which also included women and children. In 1997 it acquired its own madrasah which functioned as a boarding school for around a dozen *shakirds* (students). The teaching in the madrasah was conducted on the basis of books either written or compiled by Sattarov himself. The shakirds combined theological studies with heavy agricultural and other physical work on the community's site. Faizrakhmanists were obliged to pay compulsory zakāt amounting up to two-thirds of their income for the needs of the community. Faizrakhman himself commanded great religious authority among his Kazan- and Naberezhnye Chelny-based followers, the number of whom barely exceeded a hundred. However, his religious fervour and independent stance provoked harsh criticism and administrative pressure from Islamic officialdom and the regional authorities. In the middle of the 2000s, the Faizrakhmanists were forced to scale down their proselytism and to self-isolate. In 2012, during the anti-extremist campaign triggered by the assassination of deputy muftī Valiulla Yakupov, the Faizrakhmanist community was qualified as extremist and banned. In 2015, following Faizrakhman's death, a small number of his followers went deep underground.

Turkish Islamic Influences

Between the late 1980s and the early 2000s Muslims of the Volga-Urals, alongside those in Central Asia, Azerbaijan and the Crimea, were exposed to notable Islamic influence emanating from Turkey. Tatarstan, in particular, witnessed the proliferation of the Qādirī ṭarīqah, linked to the Turkey-based Qādirī murshid Haydar Bash. Until the middle of the 1990s the centre of local Qādirīs was the Nurulla Mosque in Kazan.[58] Another, and more visible, presence among Tatars and other Turkic Muslims of Russia and other parts of the former USSR were the followers of the teachings of the Turkish Islamic scholars Badiuzzam Said Nursi (1876–1960) and the aforementioned Muhammed Fethullah Gülen. A major medium for the dissemination of their ideas was the seven Tataro-Turkish schools – lyceums which were opened in the early 1990s across the Volga-Ural region. The Nursists and Gülenists gained especially strong positions in the educational, mass media and publishing spheres in Naberezhnye Chelny.[59] In 2007 the Russian authorities recognized Said Nursi's books as being of an extremist nature. In 2008 the activity of both Nursists and Gülenists in Tatarstan and other parts of Russia was criminalized and most Turkish teachers were deported to Turkey. Therefore the expulsion of Gülenists from Russia was not linked to the break-up of relations between Fethullah Gülen and Recep Erdoğan – the factor which triggered the crackdown on Gülenists in Azerbaijan and most of Central Asia. It is worth noting however that Gülenists have retained an indirect influence, albeit limited, through the medium of those graduates of Turkish lyceums who acquired high positions in government and educational institutions, as well as the muftīate in Tatarstan.

Transnational Salafī Influences

During the same period a relatively small number of young Tatar and other Turkic Muslims embraced transnational Salafī Islam promoted by foreign preachers and activists, as well as their local adepts. An important factor was the financial and educational assistance of various Islamic charities based in Saudi Arabia, Kuwait and other Gulf countries. As in other Muslim regions of the former USSR, representatives of the Muslim Brotherhood, Hizb al-Taḥrīr and other Islamist organizations propagated their message through skilful preaching and various social projects, as well as print, audio-, internet- and social media-based materials. Unlike registered Islamic clerics, Salafīs were not afraid of exposing corruption and other improper practices which were rampant among the government, law enforcement and official Islamic leadership. They also managed to penetrate several local official madrasahs, as well as to create a network of underground Salafī madrasahs. According to some commentators, in Tatarstan alone, there were around 20 such madrasahs.[60] By the middle of the 2000s the Salafīs' activities were drastically curtailed as a result of the 2003 official ban on foreign Islamic organizations on the territory of the Russian Federation.[61] Most foreign Islamic preachers, educators and activists, including Nursists and Gülenists, were deported while their local associates were charged with terrorism and imprisoned. However, some Islamists continued their proselytism outside the Islamic infrastructure; in Moscow, for example, they have been active in gyms and fitness centres. According to some insiders, these premises were also used for recruitment for Daesh.[62]

The Arctic Muslim Leadership

Since the late 1990s the configuration of the Russian ummah and its leadership has been affected by the emergence of the over 20,000 strong Muslim immigrant community in Russia's Arctic oil- and gas-rich regions of Khanty-Mansi and Yamalo-Nenets. A large segment of this new multi-ethnic Muslim community is made up of Siberian Tatars and Bashkirs, alongside Tajiks, Chechens, Dagestanis and other Muslims from the North Caucasus. Initially, the local Muslim clergy were affiliated to the DUM AChR and subsequently to the SMR/DUM RF. In 2005, in the city of Novyi Urengoi, the SMR-controlled muftīate of Yamalo-Nenets Autonomous *Okrug* (District) under the leadership of muftī Khaidar Khafizov (b. 1970) was established. Later on, however, the legal 'ownership' of Arctic Muslims became contested between the SMR, the TsDUM and the muftīates of Chechnya and Dagestan, which began to send imāms to their respective ethnic jamāʿahs. However, due to the region's remoteness from the federal muftīates, as well as the greater financial and material input of local wealthy Muslim businessmen in the Arctic Muslim domain, the role of the TsDUM and the DUM RF in the region has been limited.[63]

Conclusion

Over the 30 years since the break-up of the USSR and the disintegration of its political, economic and ideological structures the muftīate-based system of state–Muslim relations, which had been introduced by Catherine the Great in Ufa in 1788, has retained its viability. In the Tatar-dominated Muslim regions of European Russia this system has been modified to include two federal muftīates, one independent trans-Russian Tatar muftīate and over two dozen regional muftīates, all of which function as official representative bodies of Russian Muslim communities. These muftīates have been headed by muftīs who, unlike their iftā'-centred counterparts in the Middle East or other parts of the Muslim world, continue to act as Muslim bureaucrats at the service of the Kremlin or its regional governments. On the other hand, post-Soviet Russian muftīates, unlike the Soviet-era DUMES, have acquired their own Islamic educational institutions tasked with training future imāms along the lines of 'traditional' Tatar, Russian and Eurasian Islam. In terms of religious authority, with the exception of Talgat Safa Tadzhuddin, they have been significantly weaker than their imperial Russian and Soviet predecessors, as they have been widely perceived as corrupt, self-centred and detached from the real religious and social needs of ordinary Muslims, some of whom began to seek religious guidance elsewhere.

Throughout the 1990s a relatively small number of young Tatars and other Muslims residing in central and eastern Russia were attracted to various Salafī preachers and activists, including tahrīrīs. Some others embraced the Nurcular and Gülenist version of Islam which was promoted through a network of Turkish colleges operating in Tatarstan and Bashkortostan. In the early 2000s, following the official ban in Russia of Ḥizb al-Taḥrīr and other 'non-traditional' Islamic organizations the activity of 'non-traditional' Islamic preachers and educators has significantly declined. At the same time in the conditions of globalization it has been replaced by 'digital' imāms, predominantly of Salafī or even jihādist orientation, who have been more user-friendly and easily available online and in social media. In the early 2010s under their influence several dozen young Tatar Muslims embraced jihādism and joined Daesh.[64]

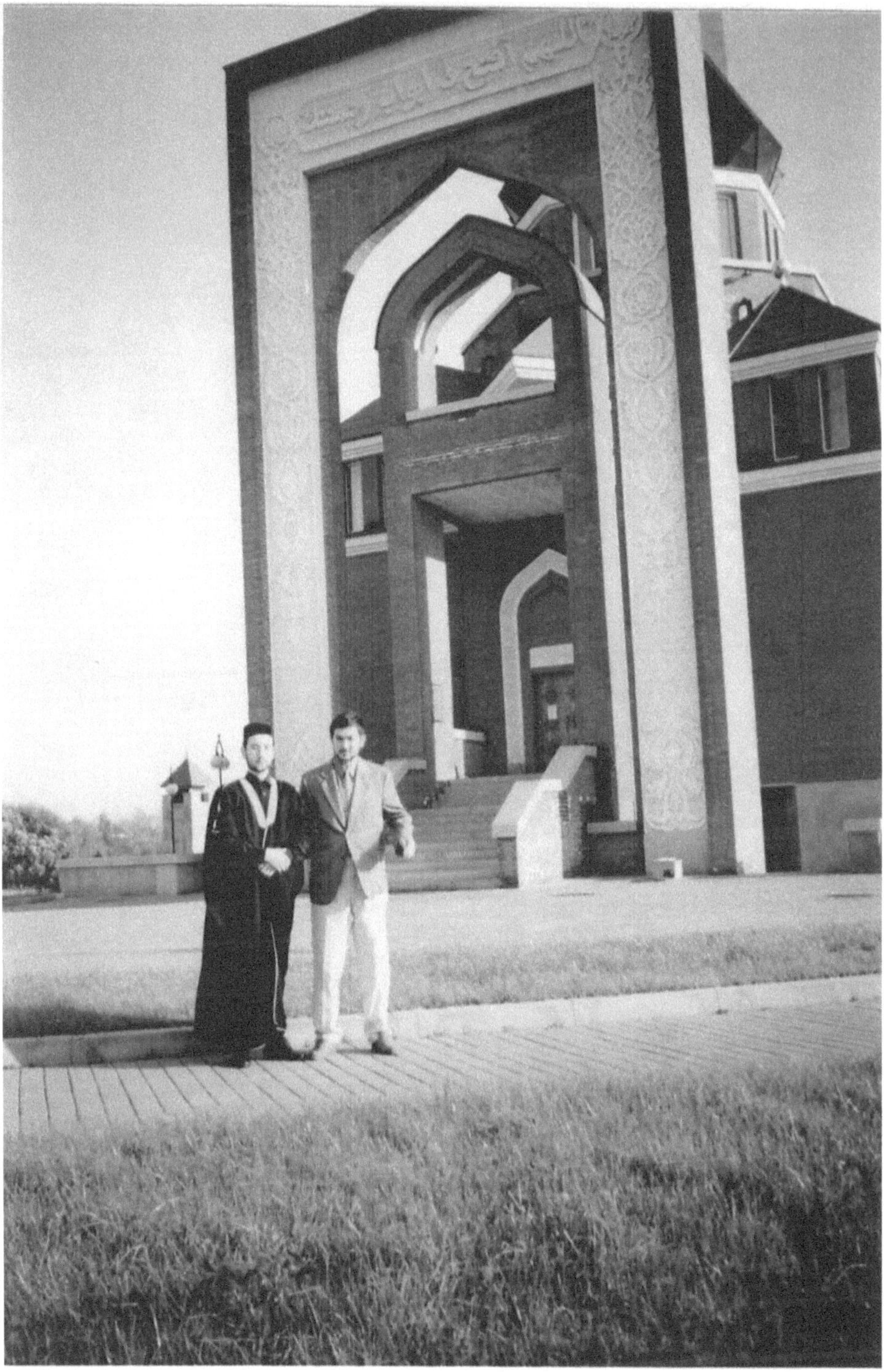

Figure 10.1 Mosque 'Yardam' and its leaders, Moscow.

Figure 10.2 Muftī A'lbir Krganov, Moscow.

Figure 10.3 Rashida-Abystai, Kazan, Tatarstan.

Figure 10.4 Mosque 'Taubah', Naberezhnye Chelny, Tatarstan.

Figure 10.5 Inside the Moscow Cathedral mosque.

Chapter Eleven

THE CAUCASUS

Introduction

After 1991 the main shapers of Islamic trajectories in the Caucasus were the continued 'Islamic revival', the Russo-Chechen wars of 1994–99 and 1999–2009 and, in the case of Azerbaijan, the Nagorno-Karabakh conflict. The 'Islamic revival' led to the increased presence of Islam in both the public and private spheres. The Russo-Chechen wars enhanced the proliferation in the region of radical Islamism and globalized jihādīsm, while the protracted Azerbaijan–Armenia conflict over NagornyKarabakh (1988–2020) was conducive to increased Turkish influences, both ethnonational and Islamic, in Azerbaijan. Against the backdrop of these developments there emerged new official and unofficial Islamic leaders. In 1989 in the North Caucasus the regional muftīate (DUM SK) was disbanded and replaced by a plethora of ethnonational muftīates, headed by 'young imāms'. By the mid-1990s there were six muftīates in the Russian North Caucasus, as each autonomous republic of the region acquired its own muftīate. In the north-east, the muftīates became dominated by Ṣūfīs of Shāfi'ī madhhab, while in the north-west, by Ḥanafī traditionalists. By comparison, in Azerbaijan, the Baku-based muftīate largely remained intact due to the continuation of its leadership.

Across the wider Caucasus the authority of muftīs and the validity of the muftīate-based system of state–Muslim relations has been challenged by unofficial Islamic leaders, mostly Salafīs, who have campaigned for the greater presence of Islam in the social and political spheres. In Chechnya radical Islamists succeeded in seizing power and creating an Islamic state, albeit for a short period. An important factor in the proliferation in the region of Salafīsm, Islamism and jihādism was the financial, theological and practical assistance provided by various government and non-government Islamic funds, organizations and networks based in Saudi Arabia, the UAE, Kuwait, Egypt, Syria, Turkey, Malaysia and other Muslim countries.

The chapter consists of three main sections corresponding to the Caucasus' north-eastern, north-western and southern parts, which have had distinctive Islamic trajectories that affected the nature and role there of the Islamic leadership. The first section analyses the specifics of Islamic official and unofficial leadership in Dagestan, which has been the regional centre of the 'Islamic revival'. It examines the theological views, activities and political engagement of both Ṣūfī sheikhs and Salafī leaders. The chapter then discusses the impact of the Russo-Chechen military conflict on Chechnya's Ṣūfī and Salafī/jihādist leadership, paying special attention to the role of Chechen muftī Akhmad Kadyrov (1951–2004) and his son, the current head of Chechnya, Ramzan Kadyrov (b. 1976), in the state-managed re-Islamization of post-war Chechnya along the lines of

Qādirī Ṣūfīsm. The chapter proceeds to discuss the Islamic dynamic and Islamic leadership in Ingushetia. The second section addresses the official and unofficial leadership in Russia's autonomous republics of Kabardino-Balkaria (KBR), Karachaevo-Cherkessia (KChR) and Adygea (RA), giving special attention to the religious role in the region of the Circassian diaspora from Kosovo, Syria and Turkey. The third section deals with historically Shī'ī Azerbaijan, discussing the triangular relations between the official Islamic clergy, unofficial Islamic leaders of both Shī'ī and Sunnī Salafī orientation, and the state.

The North-Eastern Caucasus: Dagestan

Official Islamic Leadership

During perestroika Dagestan experienced the most intensive Islamic resurgence.[1] In May 1989 the head of the Buinaksk-based Spiritual Directorate of Muslims of the North Caucasus (DUM SK), muftī Mahmud Gekkiev (1935–2007, in office 1978–89), was forced to step down under pressure from the 'young imāms' who accused him of corruption and moral laxity.[2] Following the muftīate's demise, Avar, Kumyk, Dargin, and Lak 'young imāms' attempted to create their own ethnic muftīates. By 1994 the Kumyk and Avar 'young imāms', who dominated the Muslim discourse, agreed to establish in Makhachkala a unified muftīate – the Spiritual Directorate of Muslims of the Republic of Dagestan (DUM RD). Unlike the DUM SK's clergy, who officially denounced ṭarīqatism as a form of religious obscurantism, DUM RD's leaders openly embraced it. By the mid-1990s Dagestan had over two dozen officially recognized Ṣūfī sheikhs[3] who oversaw the various *wirds* (ṭarīqah branches) affiliated to the Naqshbandī, Shādhilī, Jazulī (a Shādhilī branch) and Qādirī ṭarīqahs. The most numerous among them have been the Naqshbandī and Shādhilī wirds, while *murīds* (disciples) of Avar Naqshbandī/Shādhilī sheikh Sayid Chirkeiskii/Chirkawi (Atsaev, 1937–2012) de facto established their control over the DUM RD and acquired a notable presence within Dagestan's legislative and executive bodies. Dagestani Naqshbandī sheikhs have been protective of their respective 'spheres of influence' and treated foreign Naqshbandī sheikhs as *mutasheikhs* (spurious sheikhs). For example, they displayed hostility towards the Cyprus-based Naqshbandī sheikh Nāẓim al-Ḥaqqanī who in summer 1997 visited Dagestan, where he left *ijāzah* (permission) to local Sūfīs, Ismail Burguyev and Abd al-Wahid Abdullayev.[4] The election in February 2006 of Mukhu Aliyev, an ethnic Avar (b. 1940, in office 2006–10), as the first president of Dagestan signalled the establishment of the Avars' both official religious and political supremacy in the republic. It is significant that the Dagestani authorities, which hung on to the Soviet political structures much longer than their counterparts in other parts of the ex-USSR (with the exception of Belarus), retained the Government Department for Religious Affairs as the key agency of state control over the religious sphere.

Under muftīs Sayid-Magomed Abubakarov (1959–1998, in office 1996–98) and Akhmad Abdullayev (b. 1959, in office 1998–), both Avars and murīds of Sayid Chirkeiskii, DUM RD has been an ardent promoter of ṭarīqatism, which has been equated with Islamic traditionalism and the Dagestanis' national identity. In doing so,

DUM RD's leadership has tactically allied itself with the Dagestani authorities against local Salafīs and Islamists. At the same time, the muftīate's clergy and members of Dagestan's Council of 'Ulamā' and Council of Imāms have safeguarded their considerable autonomy from the government, with which they have disagreed on the level of Islamization of Dagestani society. In particular, the muftīate's clergy have pushed for the pronouncing of Islam as the official religion of Dagestan, the designation of Friday as a holiday, the reintroduction of sharī'ah norms into Dagestan's legal system, as was the case in the 1920s, the inclusion of the study of Islam into the school curriculum, the creation of *ḥalāl* ('permissible' in Islam) meat production and distribution network, the imposition of restrictions on the sale of alcohol, erotic literature and TV programmes, and the enforcement of the Islamic dress code for women.[5] By the middle of the 1990s, registered Muslim clergy had effectively achieved the prevalence of sharī'ah over civic norms in dealings with property and family disputes in Tsumadinskii, Shamil'skii and Levashinskii *raions* (districts) of Dagestan.[6]

By the 2010s, the DUM RD had asserted itself as Russia's largest and politically most influential muftīate. As of 2020, it controls over 1,600 Muslim communities, nine Islamic universities and institutes, situated in Makhachkala, Buinaksk, Derbent, Khasaviurt and Kyzyliurt. DUM RD publishes the newspaper *Assalam* and the journal *Islam*; runs the websites islamdag.ru and islam.ru and has its own TV channel HHT.[7] From 2016 the DUM RD has been independent from the Cherkessk-based Coordinating Centre of Muslims of the North Caucasus (KTsM SK), which since 1998 has united the region's muftīates and acted as the third federal muftīate, alongside the Ufa-based TsDUM and Moscow-based DUM RF. It has also asserted its control over Dagestani migrant workers in the Russia's North.[8] But it should be noted that, given Dagestan's ethnic and Ṣūfī diversity, DUM RD has been unable to represent and administer all Dagestani traditionalist Muslim communities, some of which have continued to elect their imāms independently from it.[9]

Salafī and Jihādīst Leadership

The other side of the 'Islamic revival' was the emergence of pro-Salafī Islamic political activists who campaigned for Muslims' greater political involvement. Among their charismatic leaders was Akhmad-qāḍī Akhtayev (1942–1998), the leader of the Dagestani branch of the USSR-wide Islamic Renaissance Party (IRP).[10] From 1992 Akhtayev also headed the all-Russian Islamic organization *Al-Islāmīyyah* and the Islamic Movement of the Caucasus, which had a considerable following among young Avars in Makhachkala and Gunib district. Akhtayev was a moderate Islamic reformer and his political views were close to the programme of the Muslim Brotherhood. He advocated the peaceful societal re-Islamization of Dagestan and the wider Muslim Caucasus through democratic elections and a dialogue with the Dagestani government. Importantly, Akhtayev opposed the employment of the concept of *takfīr* (excommunication) towards government officials and ṭarīqatists and rejected armed jihād against Russia on the grounds of the perceived civilizational affinity between Orthodox Russia and the Muslim Caucasus. Initially, Akhmad-qāḍī Akhtayev and his supporters allied with the 'young imāms' within the wider anti-establishment front which also included members of the Islamic Democratic Party (IDP, 1990–94) under the leadership of Abdurashid Saidov. Following the institutionalization of the DUM RD and the sidelining of unaffiliated Islamic clergy and activists, Akhtayev and his followers became increasingly marginalized and isolated. His death in 1998 dealt a fatal blow to adherents of moderate Salafīsm and subsequently contributed to the rise of radical Salafīsm and jihādism.

Among the leaders of radical Salafīsm (locally termed Wahhābīsm) were the earlier mentioned Bagauddin Kebedov (Bagauddin Dagestani) and his brother Abbas Kebedov (b. 1953).[11] At first, both professed moderate Salafīsm and focused on promoting knowledge of Arabic, the Qur'ān, ḥadīth, fiqh and other fundamentals of Islam among the Dagestani youth. In the late 1970s, in the village of Pervomaisk in the Khasaviurtovskii raion, they created an educational Salafī group that later evolved into an Islamic jamā'ah which acquired branches in Khasaviurtovskii, Kyzyliurtovskii, Gunibskii and Tsumadinskii raions. Bagauddin's jamā'ah had its own underground madrasah and a publishing house, *Santlanda*, which produced Salafī literature and textbooks authored by Bagauddin Kebedov and Magomed Tagaev.[12] For a short time the Kebedov brothers collaborated with Akhmad-qāḍī Akhtayev but in the early 1990s their alliance broke up due to the Kebedovs' increasingly radical stance. Consequently, Bagauddin's jamā'ah was transformed into a semi-militarized group of radical Islamists – *mujāhidīn* (Islamic warriors) – who were prepared to use force against ṭarīqatists and other religious and political opponents whom they accused of takfīr, *shirk* (polytheism) and *bid'ah* (unlawful innovation), and to wage an armed jihād against the Russian federal centre. Their goal was the reunification of Dagestan and Chechnya into an Islamic state based on sharī'ah law. Alongside Bagauddin's jamā'ah, which was dominated by ethnic Khvarshins and Avars, in Buinakskii raion there was formed a Dargin-majority Islamist centre – the Kadar zone – under the leadership of Dzharulla Radzhbaddinov, Mukhtar Atayev and Muhammad-Shafi Dzhangishev.[13]

At the end of 1997, following a failed attack against Russian troops in Buinaksk, Bagauddin and several hundred radical Islamists fled to break-away Chechnya (Ichkeria[14]), where they merged with Chechen and Chechnya-based international jihādīs. An important factor in their hijrah to Chechnya was the criminalization of Wahhābīsm by official Makhachkala. In August–September 1999, Dagestani radical Islamists participated in a failed jihādīst invasion of Dagestan from the territory of Chechnya – the invasion which triggered the Second Russo-Chechen war resulting in the elimination of the Kadar zone in Dagestan and Chechnya's reintegration within Russia. Since the early 2000s some Dagestani Wahhābīs, who numbered between 20,000 and 50,000,[15] have gone underground, while others dispersed across the Caucasus and beyond. In Dagestan, they changed their tactics in favour of sporadic terrorist assaults against representatives of law enforcement and government agencies and ṭarīqatīsts.[16]

Between 1997 and 1999 Bagauddin Kebedov, who forged close links with Saudi Arabian-born Ibn al-Khaṭṭāb (1969–2002) and Abū 'Amr al-Saif (1968–2005), acted as a leading ideologist of Chechnya-based radical Islamists. As well as his Saudi connections Bagauddin also had links with such Chechens as Zelimkhan Yandarbiyev (1952–2004), Ichkeria's second president; Movladi Udugov (b. 1962), Ichkeria's Minister of

Information; and Chechen warlord Shamil Basayev (1965–2006). In Ichkeria, Bagauddin and his associates oversaw a process of official 'Salafīzation': Salafī Islam was made the state religion and the Criminal Code was modelled on the sharī'ah criminal codes in Sudan. Accordingly, ṭarīqatīsm and ziyārats, in particular, were pronounced shirk, while Ṣūfī clerics were marginalized and some physically eliminated. Ichkeria's leadership endorsed a military jihād against Moscow and pro-Moscow regional governments and the creation in Chechnya of a network of militarized jihādist camps administered by Chechen warlords and foreign jihādīs with international experience going back to the 'Afghan jihād' of 1979–89.[17] It is noteworthy that an important factor in the Islamization of the Chechen national cause and its transformation into a constituent part of global jihādīsm was the existence in the Middle East of the vast Chechen and other North Caucasus diaspora which generated a notable number of Chechen mujāhidīn. Following the abortive jihādist invasion of Dagestan in 1999 Bagauddin Kebedov, as well as his brother Abbas,[18] went into hiding while a small number of their followers resorted to sporadic terrorist activities on the territory of Chechnya, Dagestan, the wider Caucasus and central Russia.

From the middle of the 2000s Dagestan witnessed the emergence of a new generation of Salafīs of both moderate and radical orientation. Moderates have had a greater presence in urban areas, and radical Islamists in the mountains and forests. Like their predecessors from the 1990s, moderate Salafīs have refrained from politics, albeit they have differed from Akhmad Akhtayev and his like by directly participating in the re-Islamization of Dagestani society through Islamized business activities and social welfare provision. By comparison, Islamists have adopted a jihādist stance. In 2007 they joined the underground jihādīst cross-regional organization – the *Imarat Kavkaz* (Caucasus Emirate, IK, 2007–16) – which was headed by the Chechen warlord Doku Umarov (1964–2013). Under the IK, Dagestan, alongside some other regions of Muslim Eurasia, was divided into a number of virtual wilāyahs, headed by regional and local amīrs who perceived their jihād against Russia in the Caucasus as part of a global jihād. Following Doku Umarov's death in 2013, the IK's leadership shifted to Dagestani (Avar) jihādīs Aliaskhab Kebekov (a.k.a. Abū Muḥammad) and Rustam Asilderov (a.k.a. Abū Muḥammad Kadarskī) who established links with Al-Qaeda's leader, Ayman al-Ẓawāhirī (b. 1951). Theologically, they adhered to a simplified version of Salafīsm centred on the one-sided interpretation of some Qur'ānic verses and Ḥadīths, the concept of takfīr and an emphasis on military skills rather than Islamic theological competence. In late 2014, Rustam Asilderov, Suleiman Zainalabidov, amīr of the Aukhov jamā'ah, and Islam Muradov, amīr of the Khasaviurt jamā'ah, pledged their allegiance to Abū Bakr al-Baghdādī (1971–2019), the leader of the Daesh and a self-proclaimed caliph. In 2015, Abū Bakr al-Baghdādī appointed Rustam Asilderov amīr of Daesh's Caucasus Wilāyah. According to various sources, by 2017 between 1,500 and 4,000 Dagestani jihādīs and members of their families had joined al-Baghdādī's caliphate. It should be noted the idea of the caliphate also appealed to some non-jihādist Dagestani conservative Muslims on the grounds of Dagestan's past existence as part of the Umayyad and Abbasid Caliphates and the centrality of the concept of caliphate (rather than imāmate) in the Dagestani Islamic reformist discourse from the early twentieth century onwards.[19] After the fall of Daesh a small number of Dagestani jihādīs and their families returned to Dagestan, while the majority went into hiding in Turkey and Europe, or chose to continue to fight on other fronts of the global jihād.[20]

Chechnya and Ingushetia

The trajectories of the Islamic dynamic in Chechnya and Ingushetia, which until 1991 were united within a single Chechen-Ingush autonomous republic, have been shaped by the ethnocultural affinity between Chechens and Ingush, on the one hand, and their differing political histories and positions during the Russo-Chechen wars, on the other. Thus, both Chechens and Ingush are ethnic Vainakhs and largely adhere to Ṣūfī Islam of Qādirī and Naqshbandī ṭarīqahs. Compared to the majority of Dagestanis, however, the bulk of them belong to Kunta-hajjee wird of the Qādirī ṭarīqah and there are no living Ṣufī sheikhs in both autonomies.[21]

Muftīs

Chechnya

In the summer of 1991, following the dissolution of Chechen-Ingushetia, Chechnya, or the Chechen Republic of Ichkeria, acquired its own muftīate. The first muftī was Magomed-Bashir Arsanukaev (1913–1998), a Naqshbandī ustādh and a highly respected 'ālim, who however had reservations about the direction of the Chechen national resurgence under the leadership of General Dzhokhar Dudayev. For that reason in 1992 muftī Arsanukaev was replaced by muftī Mahmud Garkayev (in office 1992–93), who was followed by muftī Muhammad Alsabekov (b. 1958, in office 1993–95),[22] both of whom supported General Dudayev. In 1995, under pressure from Dudayev, muftī Alsabekov declared a jihād against Russia. Given the communist and atheistic background of General Dudayev and his entourage and their ethnonational rather than Islamic, political agenda, the key rationale behind the 'jihādization' of their struggle was to solicit financial and other support from Saudi Arabia and other wealthy Muslim countries. Furthermore, the mobilization of the 'Chechen jihād' largely occurred along *taip* (ethno-territorial community) and wird lines rather than through pan-Islamic solidarity. Dudayev's key supporters came from his own taip Yal'khoi and its associated taips Ma'lkhi, Albakov and Merzhoev, as well as from members of the Qādirī Kunta-hajjee wird, to which Dudayev belonged by birth, as well as the Qādirī wirds of Chimmirza and Vis-hajjee.[23] Of special benefit to Dudayev was the backing of Akhmad Kadyrov,[24] a respected Islamic cleric from the Kunta-hajjee wird and a member of the powerful Benoi taip. In 1993 Akhmad Kadyrov became deputy to muftī Alsabekov and in 1995 he became Ichkeria's muftī. Akhmad Kadyrov, who initially supported an anti-Russian jihād, forged close relations with Shamil Basayev, Ruslan Gelaev (1964–2004) and other leading Ichkeria field commanders. But most of Chechnya's Naqshbandīs distanced themselves from the pro-jihād Dudayev leadership and muftī Kadyrov. Under the influence of Ichkeria's increased Salafīzation and de-Ṣūfīzation under presidents

Yandarbiyev (in office 1996–97) and Aslan Maskhadov (1951–2005, in office 1997–2005) muftī Kadyrov abandoned jihād and turned against the Chechen and Chechnya-based Islamists and jihādīs, and during the Second Russo-Chechen war he openly sided with the Russian federal troops.

In 2000, President Putin appointed Akhmad Kadyrov (in office 2000–4) as head of the Chechen Republic of the Russian Federation. Formally, Kadyrov gave up his official position of muftī of the Spiritual Directorate of Muslims of the Chechen Republic (DUM ChR). However, he de facto combined religious and political leadership while the new Chechen muftī, Akhmad-hajjee Shamayev (b. 1949, in office 2000–5),[25] assumed a subordinate position by focusing on administrative, educational and ritual matters. Kadyrov disavowed the Salafīst religious, legal and political reforms of his predecessors in favour of the institutionalization of the Qādirī wird of Kunta-hajjee as the traditional religion of Chechens and a pillar of their national identity and post-war consolidation. This policy has persisted under Ramzan Kadyrov (in office 2007–) who integrated sharī'ah norms, Kunta-ḥajjee's Islamic practices and Chechen 'adats into Chechnya's political and legal system. From the 2010s Ramzan Kadyrov has been seeking all-Caucasus and even all-Russia Islamic leadership by challenging the authority of the Coordinating Centre of Muslims of the North Caucasus (KTsM SK) under muftī Ismail Berdiyev and the Ufa-, Kazan- and Moscow-based Tatar Islamic leadership. Under Kadyrov's pressure, in 2012 Chechnya's muftī Sultan Mirzayev (b. 1964, in office 2005–14) announced the DUM ChR's departure from the KTsM SK. In 2016, with Ramzan Kadyrov's encouragement, muftī Salah Mezhiyev (b. 1977, in office 2014–) organized the collective issuing of the 'Grozny Fatwā' which equated true Islam with Ṣūfīsm. The fatwā' was supported by most muftīs of the North Caucasus, as well as by the Moscow-based Tatar muftī Al'bir Krganov.[26]

Ingushetia

Despite Ingushetia's entanglement with war-torn Chechnya it has been relatively politically stable. Among the reasons for this has been Ingushetia's different history of relationship with Russia, the conciliatory and restrained policies of its political leadership under president Ruslan Aushev (in office 1993–2002) and Murat Ziazikov (in office 2002–8), and the stronger positions of its taip elders and Qādirī authorities. Due to the coordinated efforts of the Ingush political, taip and Islamic leadership under muftī Sulambek Evloyev (1937–2008, in office 1991–2003) the advance of radical Salafīsm and jihādīsm, as happened in neighbouring Chechnya, was prevented. However, in the 2010s the relationship between the political authorities and the muftīate – the Spiritual Centre of Muslims of the Republic of Ingushetia (DTsM RI) – worsened as muftī Isa-ḥajjee Khamkhoyev (in office 2004–19) began to challenge the leadership of Ingushetia's president and army general Yunus-Bek Yevkurov (in office 2008–19) on both religious and political matters.[27] In 2018 President Yevkurov attempted to abolish the muftīate and replace it with a governmental department of religious affairs. In response the muftīate under muftī Isa-ḥajjee Khamkhoyev expelled Yevkurov from the Ingush Muslim community. Following Yevkurov's ensuing resignation, Ingushetia's next leader Mahmud-Ali

Kalimatov (in office 2019–) restored collaborative relations with the muftīate under the leadership of muftī Khamkhoyev who in August 2020 yet again assumed the position of muftī of Ingushetia.[28]

Salafī and Jihādīst Leadership

Chechnya

As discussed above, in the middle of the 1990s the Chechen nationalist movement was hijacked by radical Islamists, jihādīsts and warlords from Chechnya, Dagestan, other ex-Soviet Muslim regions and the Middle East. Among their key leaders were the Chechens Zelimkhan Yandarbiyev, Movladi Udugov, Isa Umarov, Islam Khalimov, Il'man Yusupov, Abdul Wahhab Khusainov and Shamsutdin Batukayev; a Dagestani, Bagauddin Kebedov; and the Arabs, Ibn al-Khaṭṭāb, Ibn ʿAmr al-Ghāmidī and Abū Zaid. During the inter-war period of 1996–99 they presided over the division of Ichkeria into Islamist jamāʿahs and the creation of a network of training camps in southern Chechnya and in the Pankisi Gorge in Georgia. The camps were run by amīrs who were appointed by Ichkeria's leaders and who combined military and religious functions, routinely issuing fatwās calling for jihād against kāfirs (non-believers) who included Russians and Ṣūfī Chechens, especially influential Qādirīs, and justifying kidnapping for ransom and other criminal and terrorist activities. It is estimated that around 1,600–2,500 jihādīs – Chechens, Arabs, Dagestanis, Balkars, Ingush, Azerbaijanis and Central Asians – were trained in these camps.[29] In the aftermath of the Second Russo-Chechen war, the Pankisi Gorge turned into a stronghold of Ichkerian militants under the leadership of Jordanian-born Abū Hafṣ al-Urdunī (1973–2006), the leader of the Arab mujāhidīn in Ichkeria, and Ruslan Gelayev (1964–2004), a notorious Chechen warlord. They formed the core of the so-called Eastern Front of Ichkeria's resistance under the command of Ibn ʿAmr al-Ghāmidī (1967–2004).

Subsequently, in 2007, surviving Chechen and other Ichkeria jihādīs joined the Caucasus Emirate (*Imarat Kavkaz*, IK) under the leadership of Doku Umarov. Unlike the Islamists of Bagauddin Kebedov's generation, who possessed an Islamic theological background and were mainly concerned with the liberation of the Muslim Caucasus from Russian rule, Doku Umarov and his associates were above all warlords who prioritized military and organizational skills over Islamic theological competence. A corollary was the weakening of the religious and political authority of the IK leadership. The establishment of the Islamist caliphate by al-Baghdādī in June 2014 triggered the mass hijrah of Chechen and other IK mid-level commanders and rank-and-file militants and their families to Iraq and Syria. Their exodus was facilitated by aggressive online propaganda on behalf of both Al-Qaeda and Daesh on the one hand, and the Russian federal and regional authorities' policy of squeezing radical Islamists beyond the borders of the North Caucasus on the eve of the 2014 Sochi Winter Olympic Games on the other. At the forefront of the IK's defectors to Daesh were Chechens from Georgia's Pankisi Gorge, who accounted for the biggest number of non-Arab Chechen (Shishanī) commanders of jihādist formations operating in Iraq and Syria, such as *Katībat al-Mujāḥidīn* (The Brigade of Fighters for Islam), *Jaish al-Muhājirīn wa al-Anṣār* (The Army of Migrants and Helpers) and *Jabhat Fatah al-Shām* (Front of Liberation of Syria), known as *Jabhat al-Nuṣrah* (Front of Supporters).

Ingushetia

In comparison to Chechnya, the religious and political influence of Salafīs and jihādīs has been marginal in Ingushetia. Nevertheless, in 2004–6 it witnessed an upsurge of Islamist violence against its law enforcement officials, military and local authorities. Its perpetrators were members of the Ghalghaiche jamā'ah which was founded in 2000 by Il'as Gorch'khanov, an Ingush (1967–2005) who also fought in Ichkeria. The violence was triggered by the authorities' brutal and indiscriminate 'mopping-up' operations against genuine and alleged Islamists hiding in Chechen refugee camps. Gorch'khanov's successor Akhmed Yevloyev (a.k.a. Emīr Magas, b. 1974), also an ethnic Ingush, headed the IK military wing. Following Yevloyev's capture in 2010 by government forces, the Ghalghaiche jamā'ah ceased to exist, albeit a low level of Islamist insurgency on the territory of Ingushetia has persisted.

The North-Western Caucasus

Official Islamic Leadership

Kabardino-Balkaria

In August 1990 'young imāms' under the leadership of Sharafutdin Chochayev (b. 1960, in office 1990–92), an ethnic Balkar,[30] declared their disengagement from the legacy of the state-controlled DUM SK and established the muftīate of Kabardino-Balkaria (DUM KB). However, as in Dagestan, they soon abandoned their oppositional stance and turned back to the old model of state–Muslim relations. Under muftīs Shafig Pshikachev (in office 1992–2002),[31] Anas Pshikachev (1967–2010, in office 2002–10) and Khizratali Dzhasezhayev (b. 1964, in office 2010–),[32] all ethnic Kabardians, DUM KB has allied with the KBR's authorities and mostly supported their crackdown on 'Wahhābīs'. The level of collaboration between the muftīate and the authorities has varied however under different administrations. It has been higher under presidents/heads Valery Kokov (in office 1992–2005), Yury Kokov (in office 2014–18) and Kazbek Kokov (in office 2018–) compared to the presidency of Arsen Kanokov (in office 2005–13) due to the latter's indiscriminate anti-Islamic campaign in the aftermath of the Islamist attacks in Nal'chik in October 2005. By the late 2010s the DUM KB controlled 125 Muslim communities. It administers the North Caucasus Islamic University of Abū Ḥanīfa which has a Faculty of Finance and Economics and a Faculty of Islamic Studies. It publishes the newspaper *Svet Islama* (Light of Islam) and runs the website www.kbrdum.ru.[33] Since 1999 DUM KB's muftīs have been part of the pro-Kremlin Coordinating Centre of Muslims of the North Caucasus (KTsM SK) and since 2007, they have participated in the Moscow-based All-Russia Fund for Support of Islamic Culture, Scholarship and

Education which has been geared towards the revival of Russian Islamic scholarship. It has also established close links with Adyghe (Cherkess) organizations based in Turkey, Syria, Jordan and the United States.[34] At the theological level, KBR muftīs and their entourage have declaratively adhered to the local version of Ḥanafī Islam, referred to as 'traditional Islam' and 'mosque Islam'. However, in practice, under the influence of externally educated young Muslim clerics, they have been deviating towards Salafī Islam; in particular, they have denounced such local Muslim traditions as the morning prayer for a deceased person and the wakes on the 30th and 52nd day after a death.[35]

Karachaevo-Cherkessia

The muftīate of Karachaevo-Cherkessia and Stavropol' krai (DUM KChR) was created in January 1991 by 'young imāms' under the leadership of Ismail-hajjee Berdiyev (b. 1957, in office 1991–). Since then the muftīate's politics have been shaped by its closer links with the Karachai national movement and muftī Berdiyev's position as the head of the KTsM SK. From the middle of the 1990s, which marked the beginning of the Karachai political supremacy in the republic, the relations between the muftīate and the political authorities have resembled those in the neighbouring KBR, albeit they have been affected by a higher level in the KChR of Islamist activism and Islamist-motivated violence. By the late 2010s the DUM KChR controlled 110 Muslim communities and the Cherkessk-based Islamic Institute.[36]

Adygea

The Muftīate of the Republic of Adygea and Krasnodar Krai (DUM RA KK) was formed in April 1991. Contrary to its counterparts in the KBR and KChR, it was dominated by foreign Muslim clerics of Salafī orientation. Its first two muftīs came from the Cherkess diaspora in Jordan and Syria, respectively. From 1997 Adygea's muftīs started to be elected from local Muslim clerics, who were educated in Islamic institutions in the Middle East. This factor accounted for the muftīate's initial complex relationship with folk Muslim clergy and their ambivalence towards 'traditional' Islam. The situation began to change with the election in 2000 of muftī Enver Shumaf (Shumafov, b. 1954, in office 2000–2),[37] a native of Adygea. Shumaf curtailed the muftīate's dependence on the diaspora's Muslim cadre and methodological assistance in favour of closer links with the muftīs and 'ulamā' of the North Caucasus. This policy has persisted under muftīs Nurbii Emizh (b. 1960, in office 2002–12) and Askarbii Kardanov[38] (b. 1968, in office 2012–), both of whom were also born in Krasnodar Krai. Consequently, the theological and political position of Adygea's official clergy has been aligned with the official Russian Islamic discourse of 'traditional Islam'. From the mid-2000s official Islamic politics have been influenced by Ramzan Kadyrov, who provided the muftīate with financial and material assistance through the medium of the Grozny-based Akhmad Kadyrov Foundation. By the late 2010s the DUM RA KK controlled 47 Muslim communities, was publishing the newspaper *Svet* (Light, est. 2005) and running the website www.dumraikk.ru and a TV programme *Azan*.[39]

Unofficial Islamic Leadership

Kabardino-Balkaria

Unlike in Dagestan and Chechnya, the number of Salafīs and Islamists in Kabardino-Balkaria and other parts of the north-western Caucasus has been relatively small. Furthermore, until the early 2000s they primarily pursued an educational and cultural agenda and were prepared to collaborate with the KBR's political and official Muslim authorities. Throughout the 1990s the leading figures among the local Salafīs, who were also known as 'new Muslims', were Musa Mukozhev, Anzor Astemirov and Rasul Kudayev, all three ethnic Kabardians. They were theologically competent as they had studied in Islamic institutions in Saudi Arabia. In 1995, in Nal'chik, they set up an Islamic Centre with the aim of promoting knowledge of Arabic and Islam among local youth. They were critical of local old imāms for their poor knowledge of Arabic and Islam and their allegedly non-Islamic practices related to funereal and other major events of Muslims' lives. Significantly, for a considerable time they managed to contain the Islamic radicalization of their followers by uniting several Salafī groupings into a centralized jamā'ah.

In the context of the Second Russo-Chechen war the KBR authorities opted for an administrative and political crackdown on Salafīs and other Muslims who were not affiliated to the muftīate. The 'Islamic Centre' and the jamā'ah were forced to shut down and its members were jailed or went underground. One result was an upsurge of radical Islamism among some aggrieved youth. In August 2004 the Islamist jamā'ah *Yarmuk* under the leadership of Muslim Atayev (a.k.a. Emir Saifulla, 1973–2005), an associate of Chechen warlord Ruslan Gelayev, initiated jihad on the territory of the KBR. In October 2005, Yarmuk's members under the command of the radicalized Anzor Astemirov (1976–2010) carried out a series of coordinated attacks against the police, military and security forces leaving 49 people dead and over 240 wounded.[40] As a result of the government's harsh anti-Islamist operations jamā'ah Yarmuk was fragmented, many of its members were killed or jailed while its leaders first joined Ichkeria's Eastern Front, then the Caucasus Emirate, where Anzor Astemirov assumed the position of Supreme Qāḍī. In 2014 the remnants of KBR's jihādīs joined Daesh. Inside the republic, since the 2010s the proliferation of Salafī Islam has occurred through social media, such as WhatsApp, Telegram and YouTube, as well as, indirectly, through the activity of *Ihsān* and other Islamic charity organizations which also distributed pro-Salafī Islamic books and leaflets published in Saudi Arabia.[41]

Karachaevo-Cherkessia

From the late 1980s the Islamists of Karachaevo-Cherkessia were closely linked to Karachai nationalists from the *Dzhamagat* (Community) movement which sought the secession of the Karachai from the KChR. Their leader was Muhammad Bidzhiev (a.k.a. Muhammad Karachai),[42] a member of the USSR-wide IRP. He was an advocate of the peaceful societal and political re-Islamization of Karachai and the wider Caucasus. In November 1991, Bidzhiev and his followers undertook to create an Islamic state – *Imarat*

Karachai (Karachai Emirate) – encompassing several Karachai-majority raions of the KChR. However, his initiative, which met strong opposition from the muftīate and other traditional Muslim clergy, failed to gain sufficient popular support and, perhaps more significantly, financial backing from external Islamic sponsors. The following year Bidzhiev attempted, yet again unsuccessfully, to transform the Karachai Emirate into an Islamic educational organization – *Al-Islāmīyyah*.[43]

In the 1990s, among other influential unofficial pro-Salafī Islamic authorities was imām Ramazan Borlakov, a *mudarris* (teacher) of the Uchkeken madrasah, which was formally affiliated to the DUM KChR. Imām Borlakov acquired a notable following among young Karachais, a well as some Cherkess, Nogai and Abaza Muslims. Although Borlakov himself opposed the concepts of takfīr and violent jihād, some of his pupils and followers formed radical Islamist jamā'ahs which established links with regional and international jihādist networks and became engaged in terrorism against 'kāfir' military personnel and civilians. In September 1999, an Islamist jamā'ah under the leadership of Achemez Gochiyaev (b. 1970), a disciple of Borlakov, was allegedly behind the explosions of apartment blocks in Moscow and Volgodonsk which killed 293 civilians – events that triggered the Second Russo-Chechen war.

Since the 2000s, several underground jihādist jamā'ahs have been involved in targeted attacks on law enforcement officials and senior official Muslim clergy. In August 2006 they killed Abdulkerim-hajjee Bairamukov, imām-khatīb of Karachaevsk and a former deputy muftī. Most notorious in terms of fatal terrorist attacks was the jamā'ah under the leadership of Rustam Ionov (a.k.a. Abū Bakr. d. 2007), an ethnic Abaza. At the end of 2006, the majority of the remaining jihādīs of Karachaevo-Cherkessia joined Ichkeria's 'Eastern Front' and, in 2007, the Caucasus Emirate. In 2014 sixteen of them joined Daesh.[44] There were also reports that between 2018 and 2020 the KChR harboured a number of cells of the international Islamist organization *Al-Takfīr wa al-Hijrah*, which were liquidated by special forces in October 2020.[45]

Adygea

The scale of pro-Salafī opposition activism in Adygea has been much lower than in KBR and KChR due to the republic's small size and its sandwiched location in the Russian-dominated Krasnodar Krai. Furthermore, the small number of ethnic Adygeis in Adygea's population accounted for the centrality of national rather than Islamic political and cultural discourses in the republic. Unlike in KBR and KChR, in Adygea up until the 2000s relations between the pro-Salafī muftīate and unofficial Salafī leaders and activists had been congenial. Among these leaders were Faiz Autlev, Ramadan Tsei, Nazhmuddin Abazi and Alexander (Zakir) Arteev. At the Maikop Cathedral mosque, Faiz Autlev, an Islamic scholar from the Cherkess diaspora in Syria, established an educational Islamic Centre where he taught on Islam and ḥadīths which he translated into Russian. Ramadan Tsei, an Islamic teacher from the Cherkess diaspora in Kosovo, ran another Islamic study group, also based at the Maikop Cathedral mosque, and launched a local Islamic newspaper *Chitai* (Read). It is significant that both Autlev and Tsei distanced themselves from Chechen and Dagestani Islamists, who they criticized for their alleged doctrinal rigidity and their neglect of centuries-long local and national traditions such as *Adyghe Habze* (Adygh Customs).[46] In contrast, Nazhmuddin Abazi and Zakir Arteev, both from Kosovo, sympathized with the Islamists of Chechnya, Kabardino-Balkaria and other parts of the Caucasus. In 2007, Arteev pledged his allegiance to the leader of the Caucasus Emirate, Doku Umarov. In 2014, 22 natives of Adygea were reported to be fighting on the side of Daesh.[47]

The South Caucasus: Azerbaijan

Official Islamic Leadership

Since Azerbaijan's independence in 1991 and throughout the three following decades sheikh-ul-Islām Allashukur Hummat Pashazadeh (b. 1949, in office 1980–) has remained in charge of the Baku muftīate which in 1992 was named the Directorate of Muslims of the Caucasus (*Qafqaz Musulmanlari Idaresi*, QMI). With the exception of the short presidency of Abulfaz Elchibey (in office 1992–93) the Pashazadeh-led QMI has been an integral part of Azerbaijan's political system defined by presidents Heydar Aliyev (in office 1993–2003) and Il'ham Aliyev (in office 2003–). Accordingly, it has attuned its theological and political position to the official political discourse, at the centre of which has been Azerbaijan's conflict with Armenia over Nagorno-Karabakh, and has refrained from politically sensitive issues. Within the QMI's jurisdiction have been such administrative and logistical matters as the registration of mosques and the appointment of its imāms, the organization of local Muslims' ḥajj to Saudi Arabia and Iran, and Azerbaijan's representation in the Muslim world. As in the Soviet era, Pashazadeh, a Shī'ī himself, has overseen the more numerous Shī'ī communities, while his deputy, muftī Ḥajjee Salman Musayev (b. 1958, in office 1989–), has dealt with the Sunnī communities. The QMI's activity has been coordinated and monitored by the State Committee for Work with Religious Organizations, which has combined features of the Soviet-era CARC and the Turkish *Diyanet* (Directorate of Religious Affairs). In 2020, the QMI administered 480 Muslim communities, both Shī'ī and Sunnī. It publishes the newspaper *Haqqin Nuru* (The Light of Truth) and runs a website http://qafqazislam.com.[48] The QMI has been only marginally involved in Islamic education, provided by the state-controlled Baku Islamic University (BIU) and the Theological Faculty of the Baku State University. It is worth noting that among the lecturers at the BIU branches in Zakataly and Sheki have been followers of the Turkish Naqshbandī sheikh Osman Nuri Topbaş (b. 1942).[49] Until 2014 Islamic educational discourse was influenced by followers of the Turkish Islamic preacher Fethullah Gülen (b. 1941) who created a network of Gülenist colleges in Azerbaijan.[50]

Unofficial Islamic Leadership

Given the QMI's close entanglement with the political establishment the 'Islamic revival' in late Soviet and early post-Soviet Azerbaijan occurred primarily within the unofficial Islamic domain. It was associated with several young charismatic Islamic leaders, both Shīʿa and Sunnī, some of whom embraced Islāmism. Among the Shīʿī activists of the early period were Alikram Aliyev (1940–2011) and Ḥajjee Vakif, who acquired adherents in the village of Nardaran near Baku. They established the Azerbaijan Islamic Party (*Azerbaycan Islam Partiyasi*, AIP) which sought a gradual transformation of Azerbaijan into an Islamic republic modelled on the Islamic Republic of Iran through peaceful propagation of Islamic culture and law.[51] In 1995 the AIP was banned on the basis of its alleged ties with Iran, while the party's leaders, members and sympathizers were jailed or forced underground. In the early 2000s, the AIP re-emerged under the leadership of Movsum Samadov (b. 1965)[52] who modified the party's programme by linking Azerbaijan's societal re-Islamization with its political democratization, while downplaying the importance of the Iranian model. However, Samadov's continuing critique of Il'ham Aliyev's government on both Islamic and political grounds led to his imprisonment in 2011. Since then the AIP has been effectively inactive.

Another popular Shīʿī leader was Ilgar Ibrahimoglu Allahverdiyev (b. 1975),[53] a founder of the Islamic society *Icheri Sheher* (Inner City), based at the Baku historical Juma Mosque, which was not affiliated to the QMI. Throughout the 1990s and the early 2000s Ilgar Ibrahimoglu delivered *khutbah*s (Friday sermons) which attracted a considerable following among Azerbaijani youth due to their social and political relevance. Of significance was Ibrahimoglu's establishment of the Centre for Protection of Religious Belief and Freedom of Conscience (known as DEVAMM) which promoted religious freedoms within the context of wider human rights. Since the 2010s, Ibrahimoglu has moderated his anti-government stance and become de facto co-opted within the official Islamic establishment. The role of Shīʿī opposition leader then shifted to Taleh Baghirzadeh (b. 1980),[54] the founder of the unregistered Movement for Muslim Unity, who has accused official Baku and QMI of anti-Islamic policies. A particularly contentious issue was the government's ban on wearing the *ḥijāb* in Azerbaijan. Since 2011 Baghirzadeh has been imprisoned three times on accusations of terrorism.[55]

Among the charismatic Salafī Sunnī preachers was Qamet Suleymanov,[56] imām-khatīb of the Abū Bakr mosque in Baku. Suleymanov combined his theologically clear and socially topical *khutbah*s with educational and social activities, such as the running of classes in Arabic, *tajwīd* (rules of the Qur'ān's recitation), *tafsīr* (interpretation of the Qur'ān), *ʿilm al-Ḥadīth* (studies of prophetic traditions) and *ʿilm al-fiqh* (Islamic jurisprudence).[57] Unlike Shīʿī preachers who mainly attracted ethnic Azerbaijanis, Suleymanov also gained popularity among representatives of ethnic minorities and Russian-speaking Azerbaijanis. Suleymanov's avoidance of political engagement enabled him to form non-confrontational relations with official Muslim clerics, though some politicians and journalists repeatedly accused him of Wahābīsm. Under the influence of Suleymanov and his likes, as well as due to the Gülenists' educational proselytism, the historically Shīʿī Azerbaijan witnessed a growing 'Sunnization'. Importantly, Suleymanov distanced himself from over two dozen Azerbaijani jihādīs who in 2014 joined Daesh.[58]

Conclusion

Since the break-up of the USSR in 1991 the Muslim Caucasus, alongside the Ferghana valley in Central Asia, has been the centre of Islamic resurgence which has generated different types of new Islamic leadership and affected state–Muslim relations in the region. In the north-eastern Caucasus, it led to the institutionalization of the Naqshbandī/Shādhilī wird of Sayid Chirkawi and the Qādirī wird of Kunta-ḥajjee as the new face of Islamic officialdom, while in the north-western Caucasus it prompted an ethnic and generational reshuffle of the official Islamic leadership who formally subscribed to Ḥanafīsm-based Islamic traditionalism while de facto endorsing Salafīsm. Nevertheless across the whole Caucasus, official Muslim clergy have presided over the system of state–Muslim relations, which was not dissimilar from its Soviet analogue. By comparison, the unofficial Islamic sphere has witnessed the arrival of Salafī leaders who advocated a radical change of the existing model and sought the Muslim Caucasus' reintegration within the global ummah. The violent Russo-Chechen conflict, which attracted foreign mujāhidīn, contributed to the radicalization of Salafīsm and the ascendance of jihādist leaders. Between 2007 and 2014 they were affiliated to the underground jihādist polity – the Caucasus Emirate. Subsequently, many of them relocated to Syria and Iraq under the auspices of Daesh, although some have continued with low-intensity insurgency in the region. Alongside radical Islamists there has also been some increase in the number of young Muslims who have embraced moderate, apolitical Salafīsm and who have promoted Islamic ethics and norms in their business and financial practices.

In the north-western Caucasus, the radicalization of Salafī leaders occurred considerably later, in the middle of the 2000s and largely as a result of the authorities' indiscriminate crackdown on 'non-traditional' Muslims. Since then local Islamists, like their counterparts across the region and wider Muslim Eurasia, have adhered to the regional and global jihādist networks. At the same time, compared to the north-eastern Caucasus, their authority among Muslim youth has been significantly weaker due to the stronger positions in the region of the Adyghe Habze and other non-Islamic customary norms. In Azerbaijan, which has remained the most secularized Muslim polity in the region, the role of the non-official Islamic leadership, both Shī'ī and Sunnī, has been very limited. Furthermore, the protracted Azerbaijan–Armenia conflict over Nagorno-Karabakh has channelled Azerbaijanis' consolidation more along national rather than Islamic lines. Still, the notable number of Daesh fighters who came from across the Caucasus suggests the continuing attractiveness of Islamism among some strata of Caucasian Muslim youth.

Figure 11.1 Cathedral mosque, Makhachkala, Dagestan.

Figure 11.2 At the entrance of the Cathedral mosque, Makhachkala.

Figure 11.3 Cathedral mosque, Babugent, Kabardino-Balkaria.

Figure 11.4 Inside the Babugent Cathedral mosque, Babugent, Kabardino-Balkaria.

Figure 11.5 Cathedral mosque, Cherkessk, Karachaevo-Cherkessia.

Figure 11.6 Imām of the Gubden mosque, Gubden, Dagestan.

Figure 11.7 Inside the Cathedral mosque, Makhachkala.

Figure 11.8 Ismail Bostanov, Sharafutdin Chochayev and Akhmad-ḥajjee Tagaev.

Figure 11.9 Juma mosque, Shemakhi, Azerbaijan.

Chapter Twelve

CENTRAL ASIA

Introduction

The 1991 dissolution of the Soviet Union faced Central Asia's political leaders with the existential challenge of ensuring the political and economic survival of their suddenly independent states of Uzbekistan, Tajikistan, Kazakhstan, Kyrgyzstan and Turkmenistan. This Herculean task was aggravated by the demise of communist and internationalist ideologies which had underpinned their countries' societal cohesion – ideologies that were replaced by nationalism and Islam. In Uzbekistan, Kazakhstan and Turkmenistan the former Communist Party leaders managed to retain their power by repackaging themselves as their countries' national leaders and by including Islam in their national discourse. Internationally, they distanced themselves from 'democratizing' and 'liberalizing' impulses emanating from Moscow and moved closer to Turkey and other countries of the Muslim world. In Kyrgyzstan, however, the Communist Party leadership was replaced by new, non-nomenklatura leaders who pursued the Russia-like liberalization and multifaceted engagement with the West, with equally devastating consequences. In Tajikistan, the break-up of the USSR triggered a bloody Civil War (1992–97) which acquired an Islamic dimension and attracted radical Islamists from other parts of Muslim Eurasia and the Middle East. The divergent political trajectories of the new Central Asian states have determined the pace of their 'Islamic revival', the nature and specific forms of state–Muslim relations and the influence of their Islamic official and non-official leadership.[1]

The chapter contains five sections corresponding to the five Central Asian states. It begins by addressing the 'Islamic revival' in Uzbekistan, the region's most populous country and the historical heart of Central Asian Islamic civilization. It discusses the theological and political stance of the 'young imāms' and other official Muslim clerics, as well as the 'unofficial' Salafī preachers who were active in the Ferghana valley throughout the 1990s. It pays special attention to government policy towards the pro-Salafī and pro-jihādist Islamic opposition and the impact of the Tajik Civil War. The following section examines the role of the leaders of the pro-Salafī Islamic Renaissance Party of Tajikistan (IRPT) during the Civil War and in the post-war period. It then discusses their relationship with official Dushanbe and with Tajikistani Islamic officialdom. The role of the international Ismā'īlī organization – the Aghā Khān Foundation (AKF) – in Tajikistan's Gorno-Badakhshan region is also addressed. The third section deals with the Islamic dynamic in Kazakhstan, explaining the factors behind the initially slow pace of 'Islamic revival' there and analysing the evolution of the Kazakhstani official Islamic leadership and the factors in their partial 'Azharization'. The role of the unofficial Islamic leadership of Ṣūfī and Salafī orientation is also addressed. The fourth section turns to Kyrgyzstan and examines its official and unofficial Islamic leadership and their relationship with the state. It is particularly concerned with the religious and social implications of the educational and proselytizing activism in the country of the *Tablīghī Jamā'ah* (Society of Preachers)[2] and some other pro-Salafī foreign Islamic organizations. The final section discusses the specifics of the 'Islamic revival' in Turkmenistan which has been the region's most closed country. It is particularly concerned with the prophetic claims of Turkmenistan's leaders and the role of Islamized tribal authorities.

Uzbekistan

Official Islamic Leadership

Uzbekistani 'young imāms' were at the forefront of the campaign for a radical cadre shake-up of the Tashkent-based Soviet muftīate – SADUM – and for the greater role of Islam in the country's social, political and legal spheres. Among their leaders was Muhammad Sodiq ibn Muhammad Yusuf (Mamayusupov, 1952–2015), a highly respected 'ālim.[3] In February 1989 the SADUM muftī Shamsuddinkhon Bobokhon (1937–2003, in office 1982–89)[4] was forced to resign and, two years later, the SADUM's structures were transformed into the Spiritual Directorate of Muslims of Uzbekistan (*Uzbekiston Musulmonlari Idaresi*, UzMI) under newly elected muftī Muhammad Sodiq Yusuf (in office 1991–93). At the theological level, Muhammad Sodiq Yusuf positioned himself between Central Asian Islamic traditionalism and Salafīsm. He recognized the historical role of al-Māturīdīyyah, the Central Asian version of Sunnī Ḥanafī tradition intertwined with Ṣūfīsm,[5] but at the same time he claimed adherence to the *Ahl al-Sunnah wa al-Jamā'ah* (People of Sunnah and Consensus) who opposed *ziyōrat* (Ṣūfī visitation) and other Ṣūfī practices. At the political and social levels, Muhammad Sodiq Yusuf advocated the participation of Muslim leaders in state politics, the restoration of *waqfs* (endowments) on the pre-1917 scale, the introduction of the study of Islam into state schooling and the development of Islamic publishing. He argued that the spread of radical Islamic ideology among young Uzbeks was due to the absence of Islamic education in state schools. In only a short period of time Muhammad Sodiq Yusuf's theological competence, eloquence and persuasive power earned him a notable following among Uzbek Muslims. At the same time, his independent stance and outspoken critique of President Karimov's suppression of any manifestations of Islamic belief and practice predetermined his removal from the post of muftī.[6]

All Muhammad Sodiq's successors, including the present muftī, Usmonkhon Alimov (b. 1950, in office 2006–),[7] have reverted to the Soviet model of state–Muslim relations which implied their subordination to the Government Committee for Religious Affairs and their cooperation with the security services.[8] Theologically, they have stressed their adherence to al-Māturīdīyyah-based Central Asian Islamic traditionalism. Furthermore, unlike the SADUM's last two muftīs, they have distanced themselves from the legacy of Uzbek jadīds and denounced Salafīsm. Instead, they have participated in the official discourse on 'Uzbek Islam' which included the glorification of Bahā' al-Dīn Naqshband and other great Central Asian Ṣūfīs of the past, while at the same time denouncing their contemporary followers.[9] In 1995, the Uzbekistani authorities established the International Centre for the Study of Islam with the purpose of advising (or instructing) the muftī on the contents of his fatwās and other sermons and on the curricula of the Tashkent Islamic Institute, the Mir-i Arab madrasah in Bukhara and other registered madrasahs. Similar to SADUM, the UzMI has been mainly concerned with its diplomatic and public relations mission, the organization of *ḥajj* and the standardization of Islamic rituals and dietary requirements, rather than with important social and theological issues. Muftī Alimov and other representatives of UzMI have refrained from debating any controversial doctrinal or legal issues. For example, in October 2020, during the rising criticism in the Muslim world of French President Macron's handling of the Prophet Muhammad's cartoons situation, the muftīate called on Uzbekistan's Muslims to stay away from it.[10] The UzMI has promoted its agenda and views through its website www.Muslim.uz which is available in Uzbek, Russian, English and Arabic.

The UzMI has had a steadily diminishing role in the sphere of Islamic education. In 1999, the Karimov government established the Tashkent Islamic University as a secular alternative to the Tashkent Islamic Institute. The University's staff consisted of secular lecturers and researchers who taught Islamic subjects alongside the social sciences, IT, foreign languages and other humanities disciplines. In 2018 the university was transformed into the International Islamic Academy of Uzbekistan (IIAU)[11] which has been projected as the major training institution for future Muslim clerics. Unlike the UzMI-controlled Tashkent Islamic Institute, the IIAU has been part of the state-administered Islamic educational and research system which has also included, among other institutions, the Government Centre for the Study of Islamic Civilizations and the Institute of Oriental Studies. At the centre of Uzbekistani Islamic Studies has been research into Central Asian medieval Islamic manuscripts and archaeological artefacts rather than the contemporary Islamic legal issues debated by Yūsuf al-Qaraḍāwī (b. 1926) and other global muftīs.[12]

Salafī and Jihādīst Leadership

Outside Tashkent, the main protagonists of the 'Islamic revival' were young pro-Salafī preachers and activists who had either been educated in or linked to underground *ḥujrah*s (cells)[13] (see Chapter 8). From the late 1980s and throughout the 1990s they were most active in the Namangan, Andijan and Margilan oblasts of the Ferghana valley. Like their counterparts in the North Caucasus and other parts of Muslim Eurasia, Salafī preachers – also known as 'ḥajjees'[14] – challenged elderly traditionalist mullahs because of their allegedly poor knowledge of the fundamentals of Islam and their promotion of Ṣūfī practices, as well as their condoning of 'non-Islamic' funeral and wake ceremonies. Although the number of Salafī preachers was relatively small compared to traditionalist clerics they had greater appeal among young people due to their educational, propagandist and economic resources. Some of them were involved in various semi-legal business networks, while others received funding from Islamic charities and institutions based in Saudi Arabia, the Gulf, Afghanistan, Pakistan, Egypt and Turkey. Salafī preachers conducted their sermons in existing and newly founded mosques and distributed translated excerpts from works by Ibn Taymīyyah, Ḥasan al-Bannā, Sayyīd Quṭb, Abū A'la Maudūdī, Taqī al-Dīn al-Nabhānī, Ḥasan al-Turābī, 'Abd al-'Azīz ibn Bāz and other Salafī thinkers from the Middle East and South Asia.[15]

The proselytizing of Salafī preachers was paralleled by the activism of Uzbek Islamists who formed a number of opposition parties and groupings, including the Uzbekistani branch of the Islamic Renaissance Party, *Baraka* (Blessing), *Tauba* (Repentance), *Adolat* (Justice) and *Islam Lashkarlari* (Warriors of Islam). The Islamists combined the propagation of Islamic rule over Uzbekistan with security provision and welfare support to the impoverished populations of the Andijan and Namangan oblasts. In the early 1990s, radical Islamists under the leadership of Tohir Yoldoshev (Yoldosh) and Juma Khodjiyev (Namangani) directly challenged the secular regime of Islam Karimov by conducting armed attacks against government and law enforcement representatives whom they accused of kufr. In the mid-1990s, under the radicalizing impact of the ongoing Tajik Civil War, Yoldoshev and Khodjiyev formed the Islamic Movement of Uzbekistan (IMU), which united several hundred Islamist fighters, many of whom were trained in jihādist camps in Afghanistan, Pakistan and Chechnya. The IMU began a guerrilla war with the goal of replacing the Karimov government and of establishing an Islamic state in Uzbekistan. Only by the early 2000s, after several years of armed confrontation, did the Uzbekistani authorities manage to defeat the IMU Islamists,[16] many of whom were physically eliminated or jailed, while others joined Islamist insurgents in the Tavildara valley of Tajikistan and in northern Afghanistan. Subsequently, such prolonged violent conflict between official Tashkent and the radical Islamist opposition has defined the particularly tough official approach towards unsanctioned Islam and Muslims, as well as the format of state–Muslim relations.

In the 2000s, some of the IMU's younger affiliates joined the Islamic Party of Turkestan and other trans-regional and international jihādist structures. For example, Najmeddin Djalilov, a native of Andijan, and Suhail Buranov (Sulaiman Abu Hudhaifa), a native of Tashkent, formed an international jihādist group – the *Ittiḥād Islāmī-Jihād* (IJJ, Islamic Jihād Union) – in Pakistan's North Waziristan. Although the IJJ was dominated by ethnic Uzbeks, it also included jihādīs from other parts of the former Soviet Union and recruits from Turkey, Germany, Pakistan, Libya and other Arab countries. Accordingly, the IJJ's declared aim was an armed jihād against Karimov's regime, as well as against other 'kāfir' governments across the world.[17] It was reported that the IJJ was linked to Al-Qaeda and the jihādīst Ḥaqqānī network,[18] which was allied with the Taliban. From 2014 many IJJ militants and other former IMU members and sympathizers joined Daesh in Iraq and Syria.[19] According to unofficial sources, their number exceeded five hundred.[20]

From the early 1990s, the Ferghana valley also witnessed the proliferation of moderate Salafīsm, associated with the international Islamist organization, Ḥizb al-Taḥrīr al-Islāmī (HTI).[21] The HTI messengers in the region were 'Isām Abū Maḥmūd Qiyadatī and 'Abd al-Qādim Zallūm, both from Jordan. They presided over the creation of a network of underground *ḥalaqahs* (cells) consisting of local supporters of the taḥrīrīs' programme. In Uzbekistan the HTI leaders were Abdulhafiz Nasyrov and Mamasadyk Kadyrov. The taḥrīrīs' appeal among local youth derived from their skilful adaptation of their general anti-Western discourse to the local conditions. In particular, they critiqued the rampant corruption and arbitrariness of regional police and officials and called for the creation of a caliphate in the Ferghana valley as the panacea for its post-Soviet territorial fragmentation, economic collapse and the perceived lack of justice. They propagated their ideas through preaching and the distribution of the HTI's printed, audio and video materials. In addition they provided material support to those who were particularly hard up.[22]

In 1996, Akrom Yuldoshev (1963–2011),[23] an ex-taḥrīrī, formed a separate Islamist organization, *Al-Akromīyyah*, which soon established cells in Andijan, Namangan and Kokand oblasts, as well as in Osh oblast of Kyrgyzstan. Unlike the HTI, Al-Akromīyyah's cells were organized along family and mahallah lines. According to some estimates, by the end of 1998 the total membership of the HTI and Al-Akromīyyah exceeded 6,000; by 2003 their number rose to around 15,000.[24] Throughout the 1990s, taḥrīrīs and akromites claimed their adherence to peaceful tactics and expressed their willingness for dialogue with official Tashkent. However, given the Karimov government's indiscriminate military crackdown on Islamists in the aftermath of the 1999 bombings and its backing of the US-led invasion of Afghanistan in October 2001, the taḥrīrīs began to condone violence against the Uzbekistani authorities. In May 2005 Al-Akromīyyah was implicated in disturbances in a prison in Andijan which provoked a second brutal crackdown on both real and perceived Islamists by the Karimov government which left several hundred dead.[25] Since then any unsanctioned manifestations of Islam and Islamic activism have been criminalized, while Islamist ideologists and their followers have either fled the country or gone deep underground.

Tajikistan

Official Islamic Leadership

In post-Soviet Tajikistan, for more than a decade, the role of both the official and unofficial Islamic leadership was significant due to their direct involvement in the Tajik Civil War and the post-war reconciliation process. Unlike in other parts of Central Asia where the 'young imāms' and other anti-SADUM Muslim clerics distanced themselves from Islamist opposition while allying with the secular ruling regimes, Tajikistan's muftī Hoji Akbar Turajonzoda (Kakhorov, b. 1954, in office 1988–93)[26] joined Islamists from the IRPT under the leadership of Said Abdullo Nuri (1947–2006)[27] and other opposition forces who rose against the government of the ex-Communist Party leader, Rahmon Nabiyev (1930–93, in office 1991–92). Moreover, in Tajikistan there was no clear-cut correlation between the Islamic establishment and Islamic traditionalism on the one side, and the Islamic opposition and Salafism on the other. For example, Akbar Turajonzoda and some other IRPT members were Ṣūfīs and adamant critics of Salafīs. In 1993 Turajonzoda alongside Said Abdullo Nuri became key figures in the United Tajik Opposition (UTO) which established links with the Afghan *mujāhidīn* and other radical Islamist groupings in the region. After the end of the war in 1997 and in accordance with the National Accord Agreement Turajonzoda became the first deputy prime minister of

Tajikistan, while Nuri remained the IRPT leader. However, in 2005 Turajonzoda was forced out of the government as a result of the growing anti-IRPT campaign orchestrated by President Emomali Rahmon (Rahmonov, b. 1952, in office 1994–). Turajonzoda, as a member of *Majlisi Milli* (National Assembly), became co-opted within the ruling regime, while the new leader of the IRPT became Muhiddin Kabiri (Kabirov, b. 1965, in office 2006–15).[28]

From the middle of the 2000s Tajikistan's religious policy has been largely aligned with that of other Central Asian states. The muftīate of the time of Turajonzoda was replaced by a much more subservient High Council of the 'Ulamā' of Tajikistan (HCUT), controlled by the Government Committee for Religious Affairs. The Muftī and other official Muslim clerics were put on the government payroll and were made to promote official 'Tajik traditional Islam' based on the teaching of Abū Ḥanīfa, and to participate in the state campaign against 'Islamic extremism'. The latter included a ban on wearing the *ḥijāb* in schools and mosque attendance by children, the recall of Tajik students from foreign Islamic universities and the imposition of various restrictions on Tajiks' interaction with co-religionists abroad. HCUT provided mosque imāms with a list of permissible topics for fatwās and sermons. In 2011, at the government's request, the HCUT carried out a re-registration of mosques with the aim of eliminating those that were run by independent imāms. As a result, 3,434 mosques were re-registered, while over 1,500 were shut down under various pretexts.[29] Especially targeted were mosques in the Gorno-Badakhshan region where Ismā'īlī Pamiris maintained a stronger allegiance to Aghā Khān IV than to the official Islamic authorities. The HCUT's trumpeting of 'Tajik traditional Islam' has occurred alongside its actual attacks on Ṣūfī practices and such Tajik Islamic customs as lavish wakes on the 3rd, 7th and 40th days after a person's death, as well as conspicuous spending during weddings. Among the main reasons for this discrepancy has been the Tajikistani government's continuing and substantial reliance on Islamic cash from Saudi Arabia, Qatar and other Islamic states and foundations which adhere to Salafī Islam.

Salafī and Jihādīst Leadership

As noted above, during the Tajik Civil War the boundaries between traditionalist and Salafī Islamic leaders were fuzzy as they fought together and in alliance with other representatives of Tajikistan's disadvantaged south against the pro-government forces of the north. Meanwhile the brutal logic of the war and the UTO's military and ideological engagement with Afghan mujahidin and other regional and international jihādīs predetermined the greater authority of the Tajik jihādist leadership. Later on, however, with the end of the war and the formation of the coalition government the leadership shifted to moderate Salafīs from the IRPT, some of whom acquired positions in the government and parliament. At the same time, the co-optation of IPPT leaders into the political establishment forced some of their more radically oriented followers to switch their allegiance to the HTI and other Islamist groupings operating underground. In 2015, after years of gradual encroachment, moderate Salafīsm was defeated and the IRPT was banned. The party's activists were either arrested or put under surveillance; the party's newspaper, *Najod*, website and other media were closed down; and the party's leader, Muhiddin Kabiri, was forced into exile. Among the implications of the destruction of moderate Salafī leadership has been the rise in authority among some young Tajiks, especially from the diaspora, of various underground and digitalized 'imāms' with questionable theological credentials. A corollary has been the proliferation among Tajiks, especially among those from the diaspora, of radical Islamic and jihādīst ideology, as was evidenced by over a thousand Tajiks who in 2016 joined the jihādīst *Jabhat al-Nuṣrah* (Front of the Supporters) in Syria. Daesh's commanders included Colonel Gulmorod Halimov, the former Tajikistan Special Police Forces Commander, and Abu Holid Kulobi, a native of the Kulyab region of Tajikistan.[30]

Kazakhstan

Official Islamic Leadership

For historical and ethnocultural reasons the 'Islamic revival' in Kazakhstan during the late Soviet and early post-Soviet period was more symbolic than substantive. In the case of the Kazakhstani official Islamic leadership, the break-up of the SADUM in 1989 led to its considerable political and theological decline. The main reasons for this were the severance of links with their Uzbek counterparts and the Bukhara- and Tashkent-based Islamic educational centres; the loosening of state control over the religious sphere; and the gradual replacement of ethnically Uzbek and Tatar imāms by ethnic Kazakhs within the country-wide 'kazakhization' campaign. In 1990, Kazakh Muslim clerics under the leadership of one of the anti-SADUM 'young imāms' and, subsequently, the first muftī, Ratbek-kajy Nysanbai-uly (b. 1940, in office 1990–2000),[31] formed the Spiritual Directorate of Muslims of Kazakhstan (DUMK) on the basis of the former Kazakhstani *qāzīyāt* (regional branch). Throughout the 1990s, Ratbek-kajy, who assumed the title of supreme muftī, was preoccupied with the new muftīate's cadre and organizational issues related to ḥajj and *'umrah* (small ḥajj), and with public relations activities.[32] Of particular significance was Ratbek-kajy's educational reorientation of the new muftīate away from the Central Asian Islamic institutions towards al-Azhar and Islamic universities in Turkey, Pakistan and other Muslim countries.

The 'Azharization' of the Kazakh Muslim establishment persisted under Ratbek-kajy's successor, muftī Absattar-kajy Derbisali (b. 1947, in office 2000–13),[33] who presided over the opening in 2003 in Almaty of the Kazakh-Egyptian Islamic University 'Nur' under the directorship of an Egyptian professor of Sharī'ah Law, Maḥmūd Faḥmī al-Ḥijāzī.[34] It is symptomatic that the University's core subjects have been *'aqīdah* (Islamic creed), *fiqh* (Islamic jurisprudence), *Ḥadīth* (Prophet Muḥammad's sayings), *sīrah* (Prophet Muḥammad's biography) and *tajwīd* (rules of recitation of the Qur'ān), while the courses on Ṣūfīsm and its Kazakh variations have been only optional. In 2013, the theologically feeble muftī Derbisali was replaced by Yerjan Mayamerov (b. 1972), an al-Azhar graduate and a former member of the fatwā department of the muftīate in Egypt. From 2017, the DUMK has been headed by Serikbai-kajy Oraz Satybaldy-uly (b. 1975), another graduate of al-Azhar, as well as the pro-Salafī International Islamic University in Islamabad. An accompaniment of the muftīate's changed educational preferences and cadre shifts has been the growing theological divergence on the part of externally and internally pro-Salafī-educated young Kazakh clerics from 'Kazakh Islam' intertwined with *khojah* Ṣūfīsm and shamanism. This divergence has occurred against the background of the official discourse on 'traditional Kazakh Islam' which has been endorsed by the country's authorities.

Unofficial Islamic Leadership and Influences

In the 1990s, in the context of the official policy of religious liberalism, Kazakhstan witnessed an influx of Islamic preachers and Islamic proselytizers from Turkey, Egypt, Kuwait, Saudi Arabia, the UAE and Pakistan. Particularly active in the country were representatives of the Saudi-based World Assembly of Muslim Youth (WAMY) and *Al-Waqf al-Islāmī*, the Kuwait-based *Al-Khairīyyah* (Benevolence) Foundation and *Jamā'ah al-Iṣlāh al-Ijtimā'i* (Society for Social Reform); the Pakistan-based Tablīghī Jamā'ah; and the UK-based *Aḥmadīyyah* movement,[35] alongside other foreign government and non-government Islamic funding and proselytizing organizations which became involved in the construction of mosques, the opening and staffing of madrasahs, the provision of Islamic scholarships and the distribution of Islamic books, most of which were of Salafī orientation.[36]

Special mention should be made of the emissaries of the Turkish Muslim preacher Fethullah Gűlen who established the Turkey-funded International Kazakh-Turkish University of Aḥmad Yasāwī in Turkistan, the Suleyman Demirel University in Almaty and a network of over 25 Gűlenist colleges across the country, as well as launching the Turkish-Kazakh newspaper *Zaman* (Times). On the theological level, the transnational Gűlen movement *Hizmet* (Service) positioned itself as moderate and inclusive while its members emphasized their alleged altruism and duty of service to the nation and the wider world. At the political level, however, they acted as an agency of Turkey's soft power penetration into Kazakhstan and other Turkic-majority parts of the former Soviet Union. As discussed in Chapter 9, after the break-up of the alliance between Fethullah Gülen and Turkey's President Recep Erdoğan in 2013, Gülenists began to pursue their proselytizing projects independently from official Ankara. Another contributing factor to the rise of Turkey's Islamic influence in Kazakhstan was the arrival of Süleymancis (Süleymancilar), followers of the Turkish Naqshbandī Mujaddidī sheikh Süleyman Hilmi Tunahan (1888–1959), as well as *murīds* (disciples) of the contemporary Turkish Naqshbandī sheikhs 'Abd al-Bāki Ḥuseyn, Aḥmad Afand and Maḥmud Usta Osmanoglu. The Süleymancis, in particular, were involved in running several madrasahs and in Islamic publishing.[37]

From the 2000s, Kazakhstan began to witness the limited resurgence of indigenous Ṣūfīsm and Salafīsm. Among the Kazakh Ṣūfīs were members of the Naqshbandī group of Ibrahim-Hazrat (1928–2009), who belonged to the Ḥusaynīyyah's branch of the Mujaddidī Naqshbandīyyah, and the Yasāwī/Qādirī group of pir Ismatulla Abdugappar. The majority of Ibrahim-Hazret's murīds were in the Turkistan region of southern Kazakhstan, while Abdugappar's followers were concentrated in Almaty and the Almaty region. The former led a secretive existence and refrained from public life, while the latter were engaged in business, educational and media activities. Both groups were regarded unfavourably by both the government and the muftīate, which treated their members as promoters of 'untrue Islam'.[38] The local Salafīs were represented by so-called Qur'ānists who rejected the Ṣūfīsm-infused Kazakh Islam, regarded the Qur'ān as the only source of the faith, observed Ramaḍān, abstained from alcohol and adhered to Islamic dietary requirements. It is worth noting that the Qur'ānists, albeit disguised, were present among students, young professionals and state officials. There was also a small number of Kazakhs who joined the regional Islamist networks consisting of members of HTI, the Islamic Renaissance Party, IMU and their splinter groups. In the 2010s ethnic Kazakhs were also reported as being involved in some regional and transnational radical Islamist and jihādist structures, such as *Jamā'ah al-Mujāhidīn* (Community of Islamic Warriors) of Central Asia, the Islamic Party of Turkestan, *Al-Takfīr wa al-Hijrah*, *Jund al-Caliphate* (Soldiers of the Caliphate), Al-Qaeda and Daesh. Thus, over three hundred ethnic Kazakhs, including women, formed the Daesh Kazakh jamā'ah.[39] From the 2010s, the Kazakhstan authorities under President Nursultan Nazarbayev (b. 1940, in office 1989–2019)[40] abandoned their previously liberal religious policy and introduced tight state control over the religious sphere. As in other parts of Muslim Eurasia, all Islamist organizations on the territory of Kazakhstan were criminalized and their leaders either jailed or forced into exile.

Kyrgyzstan

Official Islamic Leadership

In Kyrgyzstan, the 1989 break-up of SADUM, together with the near absence of a state religious policy and the free run in the country of foreign Islamic proselytizers, accounted for the particular weakness of the official Islamic leadership. A major contributing factor was the continuing political instability in Kyrgyzstan which since 1991 underwent several regime changes. At the institutional level, in 1991 Kyrgyz Muslim clerics acquired their own muftīate – the Spiritual Directorate of Muslims of Kyrgyzstan (DUMKyr) – based on the Kyrgyzstani *qāzīyāt* and headed by muftī Kimsanbai-aji Abdurahmanov (b. 1940, in office 1991–96 and 2000–2), who was one of the 'young imāms'.[41] DUMKyr, which was situated in Bishkek, established its own newspaper, *Ummah*, and later on its website https://muftiyat.kg, in Kyrgyz and Russian. At the societal level, however, the influence among the believers of muftī Kimsanbai-aji, and especially his successors, has been minimal due to their preoccupation with internal rivalries, which has led to the muftīs' frequent rotation. Thus, since 1991 Kyrgyzstan has had eight muftīs.[42] Official clerics have squabbled over the external Islamic funding and control over unscrupulous businesses related to the organization of ḥajj and 'umrah, the selling of counterfeit *ḥalāl* licences and of bottles of 'zamzam water'. Some have even been involved in public scandals and violence.

At the theological level, most Kyrgyzstani muftīs, with the exception of Kimsanbai-aji, have been educated abroad and have lacked an adequate knowledge of Kyrgyz Islamic traditions, which contain many elements of Ṣūfīsm and shamanism. For this reason, some of them in their *fatwās* denounced as 'non-Islamic' such traditional religious practices as lavish funerals with distribution of meat and other food among numerous relatives and guests, as well as the custom of burying their deceased three or four days after the death. The current muftī Toktomyshev (b. 1973, in office 2014–),[43] while publicly adhering to 'Kyrgyz traditional Islam', has been condoning the proselytizing activities in Kyrgyzstan of the Tablīghī Jamā'ah.[44] Their emissaries de facto control a significant number of madrasahs in the south of the country where Kyrgyz students are taught to view their Islamic traditions as *bid'ah* (unlawful innovation).[45] In parallel, the muftīate, for a long time, legitimized a network of madrasahs which were run by followers of the Turkish Naqshbandī sheikh Sűleyman Hilmi Tunahan in Osh, Jalal-Abad, Bishkek and Narin.[46] It could be argued that the low religious and moral credentials of the official Muslim clergy have pushed pious young Kyrgyz to seek guidance from various unofficial Islamic preachers, including those of radical Salafī and jihādist orientation, as well as from online and social media Islamic and Islamist sources. This has been particularly the case among the numerous Kyrgyz labour migrants in Russia and in other non-Muslim parts of the former Soviet Union.

Unofficial Islamic Authorities

The prolonged state non-interference in the religious sphere, which persisted till the 2010s, was conducive to the greater presence in Kyrgyzstan of various foreign Islamic foundations, educators and proselytizers. As a result, by the mid-1990s, a relatively small country with a population of less than 5 million had acquired over 2,000 mosques, over 200 madrasahs and over a dozen Islamic institutes. Some of these Islamic institutions, especially in southern Kyrgyzstan, were unregistered and run by pro-Salafī imāms and mudarrises from Egypt, Jordan, Saudi Arabia, Syria, Pakistan and Turkey who used the curricula and teaching materials of their original institutions which treated local Islamic beliefs and practices as corrupt. Of significance was the emergence in Kyrgyzstan of co-educational as well as exclusively female madrasahs. In the Jalal-Abad oblast' such madrasahs were dominated by the aforementioned Tablīghī Jamā'ah. The girls attending them were required to wear the ḥijāb which was historically alien to nomadic Kyrgyz women.[47] The other major foreign provider of Islamized education was the Turkish Gülen movement Hizmet. As in Kazakhstan, the Gülenists formed a network of Kyrgyz-Turkish colleges across the country and established the Kyrgyz-Turkish University in Bishkek. These colleges and the university have remained open despite the persistent pressure from the Erdoğan government for their closure following the break-up of the relationship between Recep Erdoğan and Fethullah Gülen in 2013.

In the 1990s, a limited number of young Muslims in southern Kyrgyzstan, especially of Uzbek ethnic origins, supported the IMU and other Islamist organizations which operated in the Ferghana valley. In the 2000s, some Kyrgyz also joined the HTI which was active in the Jalal-Abad, Osh and Batken oblasts. In the 2010s, in the context of the globalization of radical Islamism, dozens of disenchanted young Kyrgyz youth became members of the Islamic Jiḥād Union, the Islamic Party of Turkestan and other regional jiḥādīst organizations. It was also reported that ethnic Kyrgyz dominated in the jihādīst jamā'ah – the *Jaish al-Mahdī* (Army of the Righteous Ruler) – under the leadership of Sovetbek Islamov (1972–2011), an ethnic Kyrgyz from Chui oblast'.[48] The increasing Islamic radicalization of some Kyrgyz, both male and female, was evidenced by over two hundred Kyrgyz fighters who joined Daesh.[49]

Turkmenistan

Islam within the Official National Discourse

Unlike other Central Asian republics, Turkmenistan was barely affected by perestroika. Following the break-up of the USSR, the Turkmenistan Communist Party leader Saparmurat Niyazov (1940–2006) fenced in the country from destabilizing influences emanating from Moscow and its neighbours and, alongside Belarus' leader Alexander Lukashenko, opted for the preservation of the core features of the Soviet economic and political system despite their terminological de-Sovietization and de-Russification. At the ideological level, however, President Niyazov (Turkmenbashi, in office 1990–2006) replaced Marxism–Leninism with Islamized Turkmen tribal nationalism centred on his own personality.[50] Under this approach an 'Islamic revival' was stifled, while selected Islamic activities and symbols became integrated into the official national discourse. In 1992, the Turkmenbashi became the first among the Central Asian presidents to conduct ḥajj to Mecca and to activate Turkmenistan's membership of the OIC. The government proclaimed Ḥanafī Islam as an integral part of Turkmen-ness and funded the construction of the spectacular Geok Tepe Grand Mosque for 5,000 worshippers, as well as over three hundred smaller mosques. The mosque and the mausoleum of the great Ṣūfī sheikh Yūsuf Ḥamaḍānī (1062–1141) in Merv, as well as over 30 Ṣūfī *mazārs* (Ṣūfī visitations), were lavishly renovated and turned into official Ṣūfī shrines.

With this background of the country's symbolic Muslim-ness, any spontaneous manifestations of Islamic religiosity in the country were suppressed or monitored by the much expanded security services. Islamic or Islam-related organizations were required to undergo thorough 'anti-Wahhabi' checks prior to their registration by the Council for Religious Affairs (*Gengesh*), which reported directly to the Turkmenbashi. Those imāms and a small number of Islamic activists who dared to venture beyond the designated remit were persecuted or locked up in the infamous Owadandepe prison, located 70 kilometres north of the capital Ashgabat. The Turkmen's foreign travels, including those related to hajj, were drastically reduced.[51] At the same time, within Ashgabat's initial foreign policy reorientation towards the Muslim world, the country became open to the proselytizing activities of Saudi, Pakistani, Iranian and Turkish preachers. For example, on the outskirts of Ashgabat, the Saudis opened an orphanage and built a mosque where they propagated a stricter version of Sunnī Islam, based on the Ḥanbalī madhhab. Particularly active were Fethullah Gülen's emissaries and other missionaries and educators from Turkey who benefitted from their ethnolinguistic affinity with Turkmen.

A contributing factor was the appointment of Ahmet Calik, an intimate of Fethullah Gülen, as an adviser to the Turkmenbashi.[52] Gülenists created a network of their colleges for around 3,000 students,[53] while the Turkish government funded the establishment in Ashgabat of the International Turkmen-Turkish University and the Lycée Turgut Özal.

Especially significant for Islam in Turkmenistan was the elevation to the status of the Qur'ān of the book *Ruhnama* (Book of the Spirit), which presented a collection of the Turkmenbashi's thoughts on Turkmen history and culture. The Ruhnama was included in school curricula and excerpts from it were placed in public spaces and mosques. In accordance with the Ruhnama, Turkmen's Islamic beliefs and duties became secondary to their duty to the Turkmenbashi and to their tribal genealogy-related Turkmen symbols and festivals dedicated to Turkmen horses, carpets and melons. The state's similar approach towards Islam and Muslims has largely persisted under President Gurbanguly Berdymahamedov (Arkadag, b. 1957, in office 2006–), albeit the Ruhnama was replaced with his own books on Ahal-Tekke horses, carpets and medicinal plants.

Muslim Leadership

In the late 1980s Turkmenistan's 'young imāms', who were predominantly ethnic Uzbeks, were involved in the anti-SADUM movement. Their leader was qāẓī Nasrullah ibn Ibadullah (b. 1947),[54] also an ethnic Uzbek. In 1991 he became the first Turkmenistani muftī, although the Niyazov government prevented him from upgrading the Soviet-era qāzīyāt to muftīate. Like other 'young imāms' Ibadullah campaigned for the greater role of Islam in the Turkmenistani society and state. However, in 1994 his freedom of manoeuvre was significantly curtailed when he was made a Gengesh member and a civil servant on the state payroll. In 1997 and 2000, Ibadullah was pressurized to organize the re-registration of mosques and madrasahs, as a result of which almost half of the allegedly 'problematic' mosques and two out of a total of three madrasahs were closed down. Advanced Islamic Studies were permitted for only a small number of students in the Theology Department of the Makhtumkuli State University.[55] Ibadullah's relations with the ruling regime took a turn for the worse when, as a member of Gengesh, he had to participate in the destruction of over 40,000 copies of the Qur'ān in Turkmen on the grounds of alleged anti-Turkmen commentaries made by the translator, Hajaahmet Orazklychev.

In 2004, Ibadullah's position became untenable when he refused to recognize the Ruhnama as being equal to the Qur'ān and to urge imāms to refer more to the Ruhnama than to the Qur'ān in their sermons. Muftī Ibadullah was sacked and sentenced to 22 years in jail on the basis of his alleged involvement in an assassination plot against the Turkmenbashi.[56] Since then the qāīyāt has been headed by muftī Kakagel'dy Vepayev, an ethnic Turkmen and a staunch loyalist of the regime. Muftī Vepayev has been directly involved in the government's promotion of codified Turkmen Islamic practices and the 'de-radicalization' campaign which started in 2013. The authorities and the qāzīyāt have especially targeted Turkmenistan's small Shī'ī minority, comprising of Azeris, Iranians and Kurds, who have been portrayed as religious extremists. Overall, under the state's tight control of the Islamic sphere any unsanctioned Islamic activity has been virtually impossible. Nevertheless, according to some unverified accounts, a number of ethnic Turkmen have been members of the HTI, Tablīghī Jamā'ah, *Atageldi-Agha*, *Murad-Agha* and some other Salafī and Islamist groupings which have operated deep underground. Over three hundred Turkmenistan nationals were also reported to be among Daesh's fighters in Iraq and Syria.[57]

Conclusion

The 1991 disintegration of the USSR signalled the end of Muslim Central Asia's over a century-long inclusion within the historically Christian Russian Empire and atheistic Soviet Union. The newly independent states of Uzbekistan, Tajikistan, Kazakhstan, Kyrgyzstan and Turkmenistan established closer relations with the Muslim world, while their peoples were able to reconnect with their ethnic brethren and co-religionists in Afghanistan, Turkey, Iran and China. The Central Asian republics experienced different degrees of the 'Islamic revival' which produced new leaderships within both the established Islamic structures, affiliated to the deceased SADUM, and among independent Islamic preachers and activists. The relationship between the newly emerged national governments, the post-Soviet muftīs and unofficial Islamic leaders, as well as their respective authority among ordinary Muslims has varied significantly between the five countries. In Uzbekistan, which in the 1990s witnessed a prolonged confrontation between the political authorities and the pro-Salafī Islamist leadership, the Karimov government finally prevailed and imposed its tight control over the Islamic sphere. The Islamist leadership was destroyed or forced into exile. In the case of the muftīate, the short period of its relative independence under muftī Muhammad Sodiq Yusuf was superseded by the muftīate's subordination to the Uzbekistani authorities under presidents Karimov and Shavkat Mirziyoyev (in office 2016–), who de facto followed the Soviet model of state–Muslim relations. They even developed it further by withdrawing Islamic education from the muftīate's jurisdiction and blocked the latter's interaction with ḥujrah-based Ṣūfī and Salafī Islamic authorities. In Turkmenistan, the state has introduced its total control over the Islamic sphere by turning Muslim clerics into civil servants. Independent Islamic thinkers and activists have been jailed or fled the country.

In Tajikistan, the government's armed conflict with the Islamist leadership led to a 1997 power-sharing agreement which, at least until 2015, allowed the Islamists from the IRPT to participate in the political process. The subsequent criminalization of the IRPT was accompanied by Dushanbe's campaign against 'Islamic extremists' – that is, Islamist, as well as Islamic leaders – who were not affiliated to the state-controlled High Council of the 'Ulamā' of Tajikistan. Meanwhile Tajikistani Islamic officialdom, despite its formal adherence to 'Tajik Ḥanafī Islam', has been characterized by theological and financial ambiguity leading to their endorsement of non-Tajik Islamic practices. A similar pattern emerged in Kyrgyzstan where the official Islamic leadership, with the exception of Kimsanbai-aji, has been theologically inadequate and financially corrupt, and has been largely detached from grassroots Muslim communities which have been subjected to the educational activities of the Tablīghī Jamā'ah and other foreign Muslim proselytizers. In Kazakhstan, the near absence of domestic Islamic scholarly tradition

Figure 12.1 Remains of the 'Old mosque', Isfana, Batken region, Kyrgyzstan.

resulted in the moulding of the muftīate along the lines of 'normative' Islam which has been at odds with Kazakh Islamic tradition imbued with Ṣūfīsm, shamanism and nomadic 'adats. A corollary has been the state-sponsored formation of a new type of official Muslim cleric who treats 'Kazakh Islam' as bid'ah. Despite the differences outlined, all the Central Asian republics, as well as other Muslim regions of the former USSR, have experienced the growing influence among some sectors of their youth of online preachers, especially of Salafī or even jihādist orientation, who encourage them to prioritize their allegiance to 'the global ummah'. Their influence has been particularly noticeable among Central Asian labour migrants in Russia and other parts of non-Muslim Eurasia.

Figure 12.2 Central mosque, Khujand, Tajikistan.

Figure 12.3 At the Naqshbandī khānqāh, Qushi-Ata, Kazakhstan.

Figure 12.4 Madrasah's teachers and the author, Karakol, Kyrgyzstan.

Figure 12.5 Imām of the Central mosque, Karakol, Kyrgyzstan.

Figure 12.6 Hazrat Sultan mosque, Nur-Sultan, Kazakhstan.

Chapter Thirteen

EURASIAN ISLAMIC LEADERSHIP WITHIN THE GLOBAL CONTEXT

Introduction

As shown in Parts I and II, the nature and specific forms of Islamic authority and leadership across Eurasia have historically been defined by three major factors. First was the early arrival of Islam in the Caucasus, Central Asia and the Volga region and its particular fusion with distinctive indigenous cultures, rooted in the Iranian and Bulgar civilizational heritage and, in the mountainous Caucasus and parts of Central Asia, with local 'adats. An outcome of this fusion was the proliferation of Ṣūfīsm in the north-eastern Caucasus and Central Asia. The second major factor was the inclusion of most of Eurasia in a sequence of nomadic Turkic and Turco-Mongol empires resulting in the prevalence in the Volga-Urals, Central Asia and the north-western Caucasus of Ḥanafī madhhab of Sunnī Islam and the emergence of regional forms of Ṣūfī Islam intertwined with Tengrism, animism, shamanism and other nomadic beliefs and customs. By contrast, the Iranian Safawid rule over the southern Caucasus accounted for the dominance of Shī'ī Islam among the peoples of present-day Azerbaijan. The third factor was the separation of the Muslims of Eurasia from the ummah because of the region's inclusion within the Russian Empire in the nineteenth century and, later on, in the Soviet Union. The imperial Russian and Soviet periods were responsible for the formation of a distinctive Russian/Soviet official Islamic leadership represented by state-controlled muftīs and other registered Muslim clergy who coexisted or overlapped with folk imāms, Ṣūfīs and other unregistered Islamic authorities. Most importantly, due to comprehensive Sovietization, Islam to a large extent was dissolved within particular secular national cultures, and the Muslim clergy and other representatives of Muslim leadership ceased to play a notable social and political role. In Central Asia and the north-eastern Caucasus, however, there remained a few 'ulamā' and Ṣūfī sheikhs who operated underground and who ensured the perpetuation of Islamic knowledge among a small number of followers.

In 1991, the demise of the USSR and the collapse of official atheist and internationalist ideology triggered a return of Islam into the public domain. Muslim Eurasia witnessed the emergence of a new type of Islamic leadership, both within the muftīate-based structures and outside them. Some of them advocated a much greater societal and political role for Islam, while some others even aspired to create an Islamic state. Of special significance was the reconnection of Eurasian Muslims and their religious leaders with their co-religionists in the Middle East and other parts of the Muslim world and the arrival in the region of foreign Islamic preachers, educators and other proselytizers – a process which occurred under the conditions of the post-Soviet states' considerable withdrawal from the religious sphere in the first decade after the dissolution of the USSR. However, by the 2000s, most national governments across post-Soviet Muslim Eurasia had reasserted their control over religion through the system of the de facto Soviet institutions of the muftīate and the securitizing policy towards 'unofficial' Islam and its leaders and adherents. Still, under the conditions of globalization, internet and social media interconnectedness the state's control over the hearts and minds of its citizens has been compromised. The authority of muftīs and other official Muslim clergy has been challenged by various unofficial Muslim preachers and activists, including of Islāmist and jihādist orientation, who have operated underground, online or through social media. An indication of their influence was the participation of several thousand Eurasian Muslims in Daesh's jihādist project in Iraq and Syria. The underlying conditions for the appeal of the unofficial and internet-based Islamist and jihādist leaders and activists among some strata of the Eurasian Muslim youth have been not dissimilar from those in other parts of the Muslim world, as well as among Muslims in the West. Thus, among the triggers of Islamic radicalization have been persistent socio-economic hardship, unemployment, lack of social mobility and the rampant corruption of the ruling elites, as well as the social and cultural alienation of some Central Asian and Caucasian Muslim labour migrants in the predominantly Christian Orthodox Far East, the Urals and central Russia.

The chapter situates the discussion of the Islamic leadership and authorities and their relationship with the bearers of political power in post-Soviet Eurasia within the wider geographical and Islamic context. It undertakes to compare the past and contemporary religious authority and political influence of Muslim leadership across Muslim Eurasia with those in the Middle East and Western Europe on the basis of these three regions' geographical, cultural and political entanglement. In doing so, it seeks to identify the key historical factors contributing to the divergence of Islamic trajectories in Eurasia from those in the Middle East, on the one hand, and Western Europe, on the other. With regard to the Middle East, the chapter outlines the major shifts in the religious–political axis since the fall of the Arab caliphates. It pays special attention to the enduring legacy of the region's nineteenth-century colonization or semi-colonization by Great Britain, France and some other European powers. Of interest also are the implications for the Islamic leadership of the USSR-backed advance of secular nationalism and proto-socialism in parts of the Middle East after the Second World War. With regard to Western Europe of particular relevance is the case of southern Spain which had been Islamized at roughly the same period as the southern Caucasus and Central Asia's Ferghana valley, but which subsequently rejected its Islamic religious identity in favour of state-sponsored Catholicism. While discussing the post–Second World War period the chapter outlines the specifics of the emergence of Muslim communities, the ethnocultural and theological profile of Islamic leaders in countries with substantial Muslim minorities and their relations with their constituencies, host states and the centres of Islamic scholarship and financing in the Middle East and other Muslim-majority parts of the world. The chapter concludes by assessing the dominant trends in the evolution of the Islamic leadership and authorities across post-Soviet Eurasia and the impact on them of particular states' domestic and international political preferences, as well as global Islamic influences.

Islamic and National Leadership in the Middle Eastern Context

From the Era of Rāshidūn to the Second World War

As we saw in Chapter 1, ever since the Prophet Muḥammad's death in 632 CE the relationship between Muslim political and Islamic leaders has defined the nature of polities and societies in the Middle East and other parts of the Muslim world. The early period of Arab caliphates witnessed a significant overlap between the political, military and religious authority of caliphs who, nevertheless, did not claim prophetic knowledge. From the tenth century, the rise of the Kurdish, Iranian, Turkic and Turco-Mongol Muslim dynasties was accompanied by a greater separation between political and religious authorities, as non-Arab sovereigns preferred ruling titles such as mālik, sulṭān, shāh or khān, rather than caliph. The Buyyīds, in particular, began to prioritize the concept of the state over that of the caliphate. At the same time Muslim political leaders continued to appeal to Islam for legitimization of their power and included 'ulamā' and Ṣūfī sheikhs into their entourages. Under the Sunnī Ottoman Turks the title of caliph was appropriated by the Turkish sulṭāns who institutionalized Islamic authorities by establishing the office of Muftī of Istanbul – the model which was subsequently followed, albeit with significant modification, by imperial Russia. By comparison, in Shī'ī Safawid, Afshar and Qajar Iran, senior religious leaders – the *marja'-i taqlīd* – enjoyed considerable political clout independently from the political rulers – the shāhs.

Beginning in the late eighteenth century the expansion in the Middle East of the British, French and some other Christian European empires introduced significant changes into the relationship between regional political leaders, many of whom became subjugated to foreign non-Muslim powers, and influential Islamic thinkers who appealed to Islam as both the spiritual and political force capable of reviving Islamic civilization. Egypt, which from the sixteenth century had been the intellectual harbour of the Islamic world, turned into the epicentre of the Islamic reformist movement, hosting Jamāl al-Dīn al-Afghānī (1839–1897), Muḥammad 'Abduh (1849–1905), Rashīd Riḍā'(1865–1935) and other Islamic reformers who followed in the footsteps of the forefather of Salafīsm, Ibn Taymīyyah.[1] They called for Islam's 'purification' from an assumed stagnant traditionalism and for the revival of *ijtihād* (independent judgement) as the means of societal and economic revival and their particular countries' political liberation from European domination. As we have seen, their ideas resonated among their contemporaries in Muslim Eurasia, especially among the Tatar Muslims, most of whom, however, pursued Islamic reform in the context of the Russian state political and economic modernization.

While most Islamic reformists operated within the boundaries of theological debate, some turned to political action by calling for popular resistance to the Western presence in the region. In Sudan, in the 1880s, Islamic revivalists under the leadership of Muḥammad Aḥmad ibn 'Abd Allah (1844–1885), who proclaimed himself *Mahdī*, waged an Islamic liberation war against the British and Khedivian Egyptian forces. Such politicized Islamic reformers found themselves in the same anti-Western camp with some Ṣūfīs and other representatives of 'impure' Islam. In Algeria, for example, it was 'Abd al-Qādir (1808–1883), a Ṣūfī, who led a popular armed struggle against the French – the struggle which became a precursor of the Algerian War of Independence (1554–62).[2] Islamic credentials were invoked even by the Ottoman sulṭān Abdülhamid II (1842–1918, r. 1876–1909) who attempted to reassert his claims to the caliphate as a medium of pan-Islamic solidarity and defence against European expansion in the Ottoman lands.[3] At the elitist cultural level, however, the encounter with European scientific and technological achievements, as well as the ideas of the Enlightenment, contributed to the germination in Egypt and wider Syria of the cultural Renaissance movement *al-Nahḍah* (lit. 'Awakening'). Among its leading representatives were Rifā'a al-Ṭahṭawī (1801–1873), Aḥmad Fāris al-Shidyāq (1805–1887), Buṭrus al-Bustānī (1819–1883) and Jurjī Zaydān (1861–1914), who combined their adherence to the pan-Arabist agenda with the promotion of the productive scientific and cultural synthesis between Christian and Islamic civilizations.[4]

In the first half of the twentieth century the Islamized response to Western domination gained further momentum. It also produced a new type of Muslim leader who embraced politics. In Egypt, a leading figure among them was Ḥasan al-Bannā' (1909–1942), a revivalist preacher who in 1928 established the Islamist organization *Al-Ikhwān al-Muslimūn* (the Muslim Brotherhood), which sought the structural and moral re-Islamization of Egyptian society and politics and their ridding of perceived Western decadence and corruption. The Muslim Brothers denounced the pro-Western stance of the political elite and the passivity of the established Muslim clergy and called for popular action towards the establishment of an Islamic state centred on Egypt. It is significant that the position of al-Azhar University on the Muslim Brotherhood was ambivalent, as some of its scholars were implicitly sympathetic to it.[5] By the middle of the twentieth century the Muslim Brotherhood had turned into an important political force numbering over half a million members in Egypt and across the Middle East and some other parts of the world.[6] The Muslim Brotherhood would establish its organizational presence in Western Europe, while in post-Soviet Muslim Eurasia its offshoots – *Ḥizb al-Taḥrīr al-Islāmī* (The Party of Islamic Liberation) and *Al-Takfīr wa al-Ḥijrah* (Excommunication and Emigration), alongside the *Tablīghī Jamā'ah* (Society of Preachers), would become the recognizable faces of unofficial Islam.

Meanwhile, in a few Muslim countries which were spared colonial subjugation the relationship between political and religious Islamic leadership exhibited significant differences. Thus, in the eighteenth century, Arabia's Najd region came under the Islamic rule of the northern Arabian tribal dynasty of 'Āl Sa'ūd (Al Saud) which allied with Sunnī purists under the leadership of Muḥammad ibn 'Abd al-Wahhāb (1703–1792),[7] who was also of Adnanite descent.[8] In the 1920s the Sa'ūdī-Wahhābī Islamic government imposed its control over Hejāz, where the holy cities of Mecca and Medina are situated. Following the establishment in 1932 of the Islamic Kingdom of Saudi Arabia, which occupied most of the Arabian Peninsula, the Sa'ūdīs turned into the main custodians of Salafī Islam and the centre of global *da'wah* (Islamic proselytism). However, most of Yemen from the ninth century until 1962 was governed by

Shīʿī Zaydī imāms and other indigenous Shīʿī and Sunnī rulers.[9] Zaydī imāms were deposed only in 1962 in the course of a military coup, followed by the establishment of the Yemen Arab Republic (1962–90). By contrast, Aden and adjacent territories, between 1839 and 1967, were under the colonial rule of the British, who divided the area into several puppet sultanates and emirates, headed by local tribal leaders. During the Cold War period, Yemen's different pasts would contribute to the conflicting political and external orientations of its southern and northern parts. Subsequently, they would also manifest themselves during the Yemeni Civil War (2014–), when the Yemeni Ḥūthīs would appeal to the Zaydī teaching against the alleged injustice, pervasive corruption and pro-Saudi and pro-American policies of Sunnī presidents ʿAlī ʿAbdullāh Ṣāliḥ (1942–2017, in office 1990–2012) and ʿAbdrubbuh Manṣūr Hādī (b. 1945, in office 2012–).

Arab Nationalism versus Islamism

In the aftermath of the Second World War Arab Islamists acquired a powerful rival in their quest for leadership over the anti-Western liberation struggle in the form of the Arab nationalist movement. Paradoxically, the movement's leaders came from the military and intellectual elite whose members had been shaped by national and cultural paradigms generated in the West and rooted in al-Nahḍah's legacy. Arab leaders sought to decolonize and reunite the externally fragmented Muslim Middle East within the historical borders of Arab caliphates, albeit on national rather than Islamic terms. The rise of Arab nationalism was safeguarded by the political, economic, educational and military backing of the USSR and other countries of the Eastern bloc which sought to counterbalance the Western presence in the Middle East according to the post–Second World War logic of the bipolar world order. The key figure among the Arab national leaders was Jamāl ʿAbd al-Nāṣir (Gamal Abdel Nasser, 1918–1970), who in 1952 headed an anti-British revolution resulting in the nationalization of the Suez Canal in 1956. In the 1960s and 1970s, Arab nationalists, who subscribed to a variety of socialist or quasi-socialist ideologies, ran governments in Egypt, Syria, Iraq, Libya, South Yemen and Algeria. The Arab nationalists' political and ideological antagonism towards Islamists predetermined their largely acrimonious relations resulting in the Islamists' persecution, imprisonment or even execution. In 1966, the Nāṣir government's crackdown on the Muslim Brotherhood culminated in the execution of its leading ideologist, Sayyīd Quṭb (1906–1966). At the same time Arab nationalist leaders at large rejected Soviet atheism and, despite their proclaimed adherence to secularism, did not significantly interfere in the religious sphere. As a result, the vast majority of the population, especially in rural regions, were barely affected by the official secularist discourse and retained their Islamic way of life.

Of relevance to our discussion is Jamāl ʿAbd al-Nāṣir's stand on al-Azhar University. Unlike the leaders of Tunisia and Morocco, who chose to marginalize these countries' respective Islamic universities of al-Zaytuna and al-Qarawiyyin – the other traditional major centres of Islamic scholarship – al-Nāṣir opted for al-Azhar's reform aimed at turning it into the authoritative Islamic counterweight to the Muslim Brotherhood at home and the Islamic agency of Egypt's leadership in the Arab and the wider Muslim world. In 1961, the Egyptian government nationalized al-Azhar and instructed its authorities to add to the university's three core Islamic faculties three other secular faculties of engineering, economics and medicine. Under the new arrangements the Sheikh al-Azhar and other leading 'ulamā' were encouraged to secure legal endorsement to official policies at home and to provide Islamic theological guidance to Muslims across the world. The government began to fund al-Azhar's international scholarships, which were offered to students from across the global ummah. Among the implications of al-Azhar's reform was the emergence of the discourse of moderate Islam, or *al-Wasaṭiyyah*, which differed significantly from that of Ibn Taymīyyah. According to it, for example, the Shī'ah, Alawites and Druses, who were previously regarded as *munāfiqūn* (hypocrites), were recognized as mainstream Muslims.[10] Later on al-Azhar would embark on its educational and ideological mission, and the promotion of al-Wasaṭiyyah in particular, in Muslim-majority parts of the former USSR.

Alongside Nāṣirist Egypt, the camp of the USSR-backed Arab progressist nationalist and other leftist pro-secular regimes included Syria, Iraq, Libya, South Yemen and Algeria as well as the umbrella Palestine Liberation Organization (PLO) under the leadership of Yāsir 'Arafāt (1929–2004). In the early 1960s Syria and Iraq came under the rule of the leaders of the Arab Socialist Ba'ath Party,[11] while Algeria became governed by the pro-socialist *Front De Liberation Nationale* (FLN), headed by Aḥmad Ibn Bella (1916–2012, in office 1963–65) and Howārī Būmedīn (Houari Boumédiène, 1932–1978, in office 1965–78), the leaders of the Algerian armed struggle against the French colonizers. In Libya in the late 1960s the Arab revolutionaries under the leadership of Mu'amar al-Qadhāfī (1942–2011, in office 1969–2011) established a peculiar socialist state – *Jamāhirīyyah* (lit. 'The State of Masses') – while in South Yemen, the leaders of the pro-Marxist National Liberation Front, which waged a successful armed struggle against the British occupation, established the People's Democratic Republic of Yemen (PDRY) with its capital in Aden.

The Arabs' defeat in the Six Day War of June 1967 dealt a major blow to Nāṣir's Egypt and other progressist forces in the Middle East. The combination of their ensuing decline and the oil-based economic growth of Wahhābī Saudi Arabia, which shook the world by imposing an oil embargo against the United States and its Western allies following the Arab-Israeli war of 1973, paved the way for the advance of theological and political Salafīsm across the Middle East. An important agency of the Salafī (Wahhābī) proselytism in the region and beyond became the Islamic University of Medina (IUM) which was established by the Saudi government in 1961. The IUM, which received lavish state funding, was geared towards educating foreign Muslim students along the lines of Wahhābī Islam. It should be noted that three decades later, in the 1990s, a notable number of IUM graduates would be natives of various Muslim regions of the former Soviet Union. At more or less the same time political Salafīsm in Egypt underwent further radicalization which occurred when the Muslim Brotherhood renounced violence in the 1970s. Egyptian radical Islamists began to call for the overthrow of the regime of Anwar al-Sādāt (1918–1981, in office 1970–81), which succeeded Nāṣir's rule, on the grounds of its alleged 'un-Islamic' governance and its peace deal with the arch-enemy Israel.[12] In 1981 the Islamist organization *al-Jihād al-Islāmī al-Miṣrī* (Egyptian Islamic Jihād (1979–), under the leadership of Muḥammad 'Abd al-Salām Faraj (1954–1982), who did not have a theological background, carried out al-Sādāt's assassination in retaliation for his 'treacherous' 1978 peace deal with Israeli Prime Minister Menachem Begin (1913–1992, in office 1977–83) and his crackdown on the country's Islamists. Throughout the 1990s another major Islamist organization *Al-Jamā'ah al-Islāmīyah* ('The Islamic Group' 1992–98), founded by 'Amr 'Abd al-Raḥman ('The Blind Sheikh', 1938–2017), who was *ālim*, educated at al-Azhar, waged Islamized insurgency against the pro-Western secularist government of Ḥosnī Mubārāk (1928–2020, in office 1981–2011), during which over 1,200 lost their lives. The Islamists particularly targeted the military, law enforcement servicemen, pro-Western politicians and academics, and Western tourists.[13]

In 1979 the Soviet invasion of Afghanistan became a major catalyst for the transformation of Egypt-centred radical Islamism into global jihādism involving radical Muslim fighters – *al-mujāhidūn* – from across the Muslim world. The anti-Soviet Islamized resistance was propped up by Saudi Arabia and the intelligence services of Pakistan and the United States.[14] The theological basis for the rise of global jihād was provided in a fatwā by 'Abdullah Yūsuf 'Azzām (1941–1989), an influential Palestinian Salafī jurist, who would later become a mentor of Osāma binLāden (1967–2011), the leader of Al-Qaeda. In his fatwā, which was endorsed by Saudi Arabia's Muftī 'Abd al-Azīz ibn Bāz (1910–1999), sheikh 'Azzām qualified both the Afghan and Palestinian resistance to the Soviets and Israelis, respectively, as a legitimate jihād. The fatwā therefore also paved the way for the Islamization of the Palestinian struggle against the Israeli occupation and for the increased political influence of pro-Islamist Palestinian groupings compared to the pro-secular PLO under the leadership of Yāsir 'Arafāt and Maḥmūd 'Abbās (b. 1935, in office 2005–). In 2007, the Islamists of Ḥamās challenged the authority of the PLO and established their rule in the Gaza Strip.

In the 1970s Islamists also went on the offensive in Iran, where Shī'ī imāms under the leadership of Mūsawī Khomīnī (Ayatollah Ruhollah Khomeini, 1902–1989) were able to mobilize the masses against the pro-Western secularist rule of Shāh Mohammad Reza Pahlavi (1919–1980, r. 1941–79), leading to the 1978–79 Islamic Revolution under the slogan 'Independence, Freedom and an Islamic Republic' (*Estiqlal, Azadi, Jumhuri-ye Eslami*). The revolution's participants, who also included representatives of the liberal and democratic opposition, rose against the rampant corruption and ill-considered economic policies of the Pahlavi government; its irreligion and subservience to the United States, the UK, Israel and other Western powers; and called for Iran's return to true Islamic governance. Ideologically, the revolution's leadership fused the Shī'ī legal principle of *marja'-i taqlīd* (supreme religious authority) both with the radical concept of *velāyat-e faqīh* (guardianship of the Islamic jurists), formulated by Khomeini and Islamist sociologist 'Alī Sharī'atī Mazīnānī (1933–1977), and the idea of *Gharbzadegi* (Westoxification), introduced by the Iranian socialist Jalāl Āl-e-Ahmad (1923–1969). Following its creation in 1979 the Islamic Republic of Iran turned into a main backer of the Shī'ah across the world, while al-Mustafa International University and other Iranian Islamic universities have trained Shīʿī clerics in Shīʿah-majority parts of the Muslim world, including the southern Caucasus.

The withdrawal of Soviet troops from Afghanistan in 1989, followed by the demise in 1991 of the USSR, sealed the fate of the Arab progressist regimes as they lost the backing of their patron-state. Direct US-led Western military aggression against Iraq and Libya (as well as Afghanistan), alongside its later indirect interference in Syria, contributed to plunging these countries into humanitarian and economic catastrophe, while South Yemen has been destroyed by Saudi Arabia, armed by the UK and the United States. The overthrow of the pro-secular regimes was accompanied by the emergence in Iraq, parts of Syria, Libya and some other parts of the Muslim world of a new generation of populist Islamist and jihādist leaders, associated with the Muslim Brotherhood, Ḥizb al-Taḥrīr, Al-Qaeda, Daesh and their like. Between 1991 and 2002, Algeria was engulfed in a bloody conflict between government forces and the Islamist opposition. Following the forcible removal in 2011 of Muʿamar Qadhāfī Libya became fractured and mired in violence involving various Islamist formations. In 2012, the Muslim Brotherhood's Muḥammad Morsī (1951–2019, in office 2012–13) was elected president of Egypt. In 2014, on the territory of war-torn Iraq and Syria, radical Islamists under the leadership of Abū Bakr al-Baghdādī (1971–2018) established a quasi-caliphate which attracted thousands of self-proclaimed mujāḥidīn from across the Middle East and the wider ummah.

Among other outcomes of the forcible removal of five out of seven pro-secular regimes was the strengthening of pro-Western conservative Muslim regimes, especially Saudi Arabia and other Gulf states, which turned into major sponsors of *daʿwah* and Islamism across the world, including in post-Soviet Muslim Eurasia and Europe. From the late 1990s Saudi-backed religious proselytism on the ground would be supported by Saudi Islamic propagation online, the main Saudi-sponsored internet platforms being Islam Q&A (www.islam-qa.com) and Fatwa-Online (www.fatwa-online.com).[15] At the grassroots level, the large-scale destruction of the material and economic infrastructure in Iraq, Syria, Libya and some other parts of the Middle East and Africa in the course of external bombing and civil wars prompted the mass exodus from these countries of civilians who moved to Europe, thus creating a major refugee crisis there and straining to the limits the liberalism of Western liberal society.

Islamic Leadership in the European Context

From the Early History to the 1970s

Unlike in the Middle East and Muslim Eurasia, the Islamic leadership in Western Europe is a relatively recent temporal phenomenon due to the region's different religious history. The only exceptions were Iberia's al-Andalus (Andalusia),[16] which during almost eight centuries was ruled by a succession of Muslim dynasties – the Umayyads, Almoravids, Almohads and Naṣrids – and Sicily and Malta, which were governed by the Muslim dynasty of Aghlabids from the mid-ninth century until the end of the eleventh century, when the Catholic Christians put an end to the Muslim presence and Islamic culture on both islands. The same fate awaited Muslim Andalusia, which in 1492 was conquered by the

Catholic Christian troops of King Ferdinand II of Aragon (1452–1516, r. 1479–1516) and his wife, Queen Isabella I of Castille (1451–1504, r. 1474–1504), who completed the unification of Spain as a mono-religious Catholic country. As a result, Iberia's Muslims, alongside its Jews, were forced either to convert to Catholicism or to flee the country. Their exquisite culture and Islamic scholarly heritage were nearly destroyed, while their distinctive Moorish Islamic architecture was vandalized by being remodelled into Catholic cathedrals and churches.[17]

The medieval political and cultural history of the rest of Western Europe was shaped by Catholicism which, following the 1054 East–West Schism, was centred on the authority of the Rome-based pope. The period between the eleventh and thirteenth centuries witnessed the ruthless papacy-instigated campaign against heretics across Europe, as well as a series of Rome-directed crusades to the Middle East with the aim of 'liberating' Jerusalem from Islamic rule. From the fifteenth century the supremacy of the papacy's obscurantism began to be challenged culturally by the Renaissance movement and, from the sixteenth century, religiously by the Protestant Reformation as well. Subsequently, the Scientific Revolution and the Enlightenment, which began in the seventeenth century, paved the way for accelerated technological breakthrough and a reason-based world view. The Industrial Revolution, which began in England in the late eighteenth century and soon spread across most of Western Europe, ensured Europe's technological and military advantage over the Ottoman Empire and other parts of the Muslim world and enabled Great Britain and France, and to a lesser extent Italy and Spain, to impose their direct or indirect rule over most of the Muslim Middle East. Following the 1916 Sykes–Picot Agreement the Arab provinces of the Ottoman Empire were effectively divided between Britain and France, where the former asserted its control over southern Iraq and wider Palestine, and the latter over northern Iraq and wider Syria. Subsequently, the British oversaw the establishment of two new polities – Jordan and Israel – on the territory of historical Palestine, while the French presided over the creation of Lebanon on the territory of Greater Syria. Additionally, Britain retained its upper hand in Egypt and Sudan, France in Algeria, Tunisia and most of Morocco, while Italy and Spain gained control over parts of Libya and Morocco, respectively. The borders between the newly formed polities were often drawn with no regard to the religious and ethnocultural homogeneity of their inhabitants. Following the post–Second World War political decolonization of the Middle East these borders became international.

It was in the process of post–Second World War economic and social reconstruction that secular Britain, Germany, France, Belgium and some other European countries acquired their sizeable Muslim populations.[18] Initially, the majority of Muslim migrants in Britain were from Pakistan, Kashmir and Bangladesh; in France and Belgium from Algeria and Morocco; and in Germany from Turkey. From the 1990s, in the context of violent conflicts and economic hardships in Chechnya, Kosovo, Afghanistan, Iraq, Syria, Libya, Palestine, Yemen and Somalia many other countries of the European Union (EU) have also been receiving a growing number of Muslim economic migrants and refugees. By 2020 Muslim communities across Western Europe have been characterized by considerable ethnolinguistic, cultural and social diversity. The exact size of Europe's Muslim population is debatable due to a lack of accurate data regarding increasingly large-scale illegal immigration; but according to official statistics, as of 2016, Western Europe's Muslim population was around 25.8 million (under 5 per cent of the total population), including 5.7 million in France (around 9 per cent of the total population), 5 million in Germany (over 6 per cent of the population) and 4.1 million in the UK (over 6 per cent of the population).[19]

In the light of the fragmentation and diversity of Muslims in Europe it is difficult to generalize on the Islamic leadership and authorities there, albeit it is plausible to identify some of their dominant patterns as well as modes and forms of their interaction with the host state. Among key factors which shaped Islamic leadership in any individual European state were the country of the Muslims' descent, the length of their European experience and the individual state's official policy towards immigration and Islam. The country of descent was especially significant for the first and, to a somewhat lesser extent, second generations of French, German and British Muslims as they largely continued to be guided by Muslim authorities in their countries of origin. Most imāms in mosques established by Turkish, Maghrebian or Pakistani migrants were often recruited from Muslim clergy in Turkey, Algeria/Morocco and Pakistan. They therefore tended to treat their Muslim constituencies in Europe as if they were in their home countries, thus perpetuating the ethnocultural distinctiveness of the various Muslim communities and their *otherness* in relation to the rest of the population. Imāms also contributed to the dogmatic fragmentation of Muslims in any particular European country. For example, in Britain, some imāms belonged to Deobandi, Tablīghī Jamā'ah, Ahl al-Ḥadīth and other pro-Salafī schools of Sunnī Islam while others were Barelvis[20] or adherents of other Ṣūfism-centred beliefs. An individual Muslim's traditional religious beliefs were also reinforced by his or her strong family, financial and property ties with the country of origin. Consequently, many Muslims of the first generation paradoxically combined their participation in the host country's socio-economic and civil life with religious and family life still very much belonging to their country of origin. At the same time there developed a cacophony of Islamic creeds and practices and, consequently, the fragmentation and weakness overall of Islamic leadership.

The Making of 'European Islam' and Islamic Leadership

In the 1970s the outlook of Muslim communities in Germany, France, Britain and some other European countries began to change as they became dominated by Muslims of the second and successive generations, who were born, educated and socialized in these countries. Unlike their grandparents and parents, many of them started to identify themselves as German, French, British and other European Muslims. These identity shifts were accompanied by the emergence of a new type of mosque imām and other Muslim clergy who either came from the Arab Middle East or were European nationals who had received Islamic training in international centres of Islamic learning such as the IUM or al-Azhar. Unlike traditional imāms they theologically distanced themselves from various 'ethnonational' Islams in favour of 'pure' Salafī Islam. While accepting the Western political and economic system, they prioritized Muslims' moral and cultural autonomy from their host liberal societies.[21] Although the majority of these imāms abstained from politics, some embraced radical Salafīsm and Islāmism and established links with the Muslim Brotherhood, Ḥizb al-Taḥrir al-Islāmī and other Islamist organizations, most of which, unlike in Eurasia, operate there legally. A vivid example is the London-based imām Abū Ḥamza al-Maṣrī (b. 1958),[22] who between 1997 and 2003 conducted pro-jihādist sermons in Finsbury Park Mosque and who was closely linked to the Islamist organization al-*Muhājirūn* (Emigrants, est. 1986), which until 2005 had legal status.

Alongside the new generation of mosque imāms there also emerged Muslim jurists specializing in European fiqh, or *fiqh al-aqalīyyāt* (minorities' fiqh) as well as secularized Muslim scholars who advocated 'European Islam'. Most of the former either resided outside Europe or were of recent immigrant background, while the latter were representatives of the second and third generations of Europe's Muslims.[23] Among influential protagonists of fiqh al-aqalīyyāt have been al-Azhar scholars Yūsuf al-Qaraḍāwī (b. 1926) and Ṭaha Jābir 'Alwānī (1935–2016), who have made the juridical case for fiqh's adjustment, or the creation of a new branch of fiqh, which would bring together Muslims of different legal traditions and accommodate religious rulings to the specific conditions of Muslim communities in Europe.[24] Furthermore, al-Qaraḍāwī, who is based in Qatar, has positioned himself as a 'global muftī' by offering his pronouncements to Muslims in both Muslim-minority and -majority contexts through his English/Arabic websites www.islamonline.net and www.qaradawi.net. The leading figure among proponents of 'European Islam' has been the Oxford Professor of Islamic Studies, Ṭāriq Ramaḍān (b. 1962), a Swiss national and a grandson of Ḥasan al-Bannā. Ramaḍān has argued in favour of the development of a special brand of 'European Islam', which would be fully compatible with the values and norms of secularized liberal democratic societies.[25]

Since the 2000s the religious authority of al-Qaraḍāwī, Ramaḍān and other publicly well-known Muslim theologians and Islamic Studies scholars has been supplemented, or even challenged, by the internet-based self-proclaimed and anonymous *mujtāhidūn* (practitioners of *ijtihād*) who have made pronouncements and issued fatwās in response to online petitioners. Unlike conventional muftīs whose pronouncements have been endorsed by al-Azhar or other authoritative Islamic institutions, the givers of e-fatwās have ventured their own interpretations of ijtihād.[26] It could be argued that the e-muftīs' plurality and anonymity, as well as their detachment from any particular ethnonational context, have furthered the proliferation of Salafī interpretations of Islamic beliefs and practices which have worked against Muslims' full-fledged integration within particular European societies.

European Islamic Structures and Organizations

At a structural level, the growing 'Europeanization' of Muslims in major European countries has been accompanied by the creation of pan-European and national European Islamic organizations, most of them of Salafī orientation and financially supported by Saudi Arabia and other Gulf countries. In 1973 the Islamic Council of Europe (ICE) was established in London, acting as the coordinating centre for Muslim organizations across Europe and claiming to provide unified and ethnicity- and region-neutral theological guidance to Europe's Muslim individuals seeking arbitration, reconciliation or mediation over various family, interpersonal and financial issues.[27] Alongside the ICE, the Federation of Islamic Organizations in Europe (FIOE), which was theologically close to the Muslim Brotherhood, was formed in 1989, in Brussels. In 1997, the FIOE initiated the creation of the European Council for Fatwā and Research (ECFR), which consisted of over 30 Muslim scholars most of whom resided in Europe and North America. Since its inception, the Dublin-based ECFR has been presided over by the aforementioned al-Qaraḍāwī. Among the FIOE's other affiliated bodies have been the Forum of European Muslim Youth and the European Forum of Muslim Women, while its largest national constituent organizations have included the Union of Islamic Organisations of France (*Union des Organisations Islamiques de France*, UOIF, est. 1983), the Islamic Community of Germany (*Islamische Gemeinschaft in Deutschland*, IGD, est. 1982) and the Muslim Association of Britain (MAB, est. 1997), all of which have allegedly been linked to the Muslim Brotherhood. Compared to the theology-centred FIOE and ECFR, the Brussels-based Muslim Council for Cooperation in Europe (MCCE, est. 1996) has embodied a pan-European Muslim bureaucratic structure which was designed by Belgian, French, Italian, Spanish and British bureaucrats of Muslim heritage as the Muslim representative body within the EU.

At a national level, in Germany the largest Islamic organization has been *Millî Görüş* (National Vision, est. 1969), which by the middle of the 2000s united around 50,000 of Germany's Turks and over 30,000 Turks residing in other European countries. The organization was founded by the former prime minister of Turkey, Necmettin Erbakan (1926–2011), who adhered to moderate Islamism critical of Europe's perceived secularism, advocating the moral and social advantages of Islam-based political systems. In France, the main Islamic representative organization has been the aforementioned pro-Salafī UOIF, which unites around two hundred mosques. By comparison, the UK's major Muslim umbrella organization, the Muslim Council of Britain (MCB, est. 1997), which comprises over five hundred mosques and affiliated educational and charitable associations, has been run by technocrats of Islamic heritage[28] and has been integrated within the British political landscape. It has received government funding for its educational and other projects and has been active in parliament, especially in regard to alleged Islamophobia in the Conservative Party. The UK's other major educational Islamic organization has been the pro-Salafī Islamic Foundation (est. 1973) in Leicester. The London-based Aghā Khān Foundation (AKF, est. 1967) and the affiliated Institute of Ismā'īlī Studies (IIS, est. 1977) are agencies of the Aghā Khān Development Network (AKDN) operating in over 30 countries in Africa, the Middle East and Asia. The AKDN is headed by Karīm al-Ḥuseynī (the Aghā Khān IV, b. 1936), the 49th imām of the Shī'ī Nizārī Ismā'īlī imāmate. The AKDN combines the implementation of generously funded economic, health and educational projects with Ismā'īlī proselytism. In 2000 the Aghā Khān IV signed an agreement with the governments of Tajikistan, Kyrgyzstan and Kazakhstan on the establishment of the Aghā Khān University of Central Asia which opened its branches in Tajikistan, Kyrgyzstan and Kazakhstan. The AKF has been particularly active in the Ismā'īlī-majority region of Badakhshan in mountainous Tajikistan where the Aghā Khān's authority surpasses that of Tajikistan's Islamic officialdom.

The degree of Muslims' societal integration and their political representation has been affected by the type of state–Muslim relations and the nature of citizenship in any particular European country. Arguably, it has been relatively higher in the UK and other states which have subscribed to the policy of multiculturalism than in France and some other countries which have prioritized an assimilationist approach towards Muslims and other minorities.[29] By comparison, Germany and some other European countries have adhered to a hybrid approach towards the governance of Muslims, which has produced mixed results in terms of their integration into the host society.[30] Overall, in the context of the dominant secularism and the primacy of individual rights most Muslims have silently accepted the separation between public and private space and curtailed their public religious observance, while mosques have undergone a degree of 'churchification'. On the other hand, a small Muslim minority have opted to reject Western social and cultural norms and appealed to Salafīsm and, in some cases, to Islamīsm or even jihādīsm, as evidenced by the considerable number of European jihādīs among Daesh's recruits. The ethnolinguistic and cultural diversity of Europe's Muslim communities has also enhanced the role in their pious strata of Yūsuf al-Qaraḍāwī and other global Salafī muftīs. In terms of state–Muslim relations, unlike in the Middle East and Eurasia, there has been an implicit essentialization of Islam and Muslims as the *other*, alongside the state's largely non-interference into the theological orientations and activities of Islamic organizations as well as of imāms' training – the sphere which has been largely controlled by governments or non-government Islamic foundations based in Turkey, Saudi Arabia, Algeria, Pakistan and other major Muslim countries. External Islamic influences have gone beyond the religious sphere as representatives of the ruling elites of Saudi Arabia, the Gulf and other Islamic countries have been involved in funding Islamic Studies centres and chairs at secular universities across Europe. Meanwhile, in relation to the Islamist and jihādist minority the state's dominant approach has been that of securitization, prevention of violent extremism (PVE), for example, 'Prevent' in Britain, or 'Aarhus' in Denmark, and de-radicalization and re-education programmes. In this respect it has some commonalities with relevant state policies across post-Soviet Eurasia.

The Muslim Refugee Crisis

From the early 2000s the Muslim demographics and leadership in Europe have been affected by the steady influx of Muslim economic migrants and refugees fleeing violent conflicts and economic hardships in Iraq, Libya, Syria and other parts of the Muslim Middle East, Asia and Africa. As a result, Germany, France and the UK, which already had relatively integrated Muslim communities, acquired ethnically, culturally and socially diverse Muslim residents of the first generation. In the 2010s Germany alone accommodated over a million refugees from the Middle East. Furthermore, as a result of the new wave of migration the Netherlands, Sweden, Norway, Denmark, Switzerland, Austria, Spain and some other countries acquired notable Muslim communities of the first generation. The growing Islamic self-awareness of Europe's Muslims of the third and fourth generations, especially among the economically and socially disadvantaged strata, together with the persistent influx into Europe of Muslim refugees from war zones in the Middle East – and, as a reaction, the development of anti-immigration populism – have strained the existing models of state–Muslim relations in Europe. Individual European countries have witnessed the rise of Islamist radicalism on the one hand and further official securitization of Islam and Muslims on the other. Among the extreme hallmarks of societal ruptures and apparent failure of the official policies of 'adaptation' and 'domestication' of Islam[31] have been Islamist attacks in Madrid in May 2004, in London in July 2005, in Belgium in 2014–18, in France in January and November 2015, and in Vienna in November 2020. These acts of Islamized terrorism were masterminded by a new type of Islamist political activist who perceived themselves as part of international jihādīst networks which have been coordinated through the internet and social media. They have also actively used new communication and video technologies, including YouTube, as mobilizing tools for a 'global jihād' against the West and its 'immorality' and 'criminal' foreign policies in Muslim Iraq, Libya and Afghanistan, as well as its explicit and implicit backing of Israel's continuing aggression against Palestinians. It is symptomatic that, in 2014–17, such visual online jihādīst propaganda played a pivotal role in the recruitment to Daesh of many hundreds of European Muslims.

Post-Soviet Islamic Leadership between Europe and Asia

Islamic Leadership in the Democratic Context

The fall of the Iron Curtain and the break-up of the USSR in the late 1980s/early 1990s set in motion major political, societal and religious transformations across the post-communist and post-Soviet space. At the geopolitical level, it created a new division between Russia and other countries of the Moscow-spearheaded Eurasian Economic Union (EAEU)[32] on the one hand, and the formerly communist Central and Eastern European countries, most of which joined the EU and NATO, on the other. Under the new political dispensation, the ex-Soviet Baltics were absorbed into the Western economic, political and military alliances, while Georgia and, to some degree, Ukraine have been moving in this direction. These geopolitical and cultural shifts have affected the nature and forms of Islamic leadership and state–Muslim relations across the post-Soviet lands, although the extent and trajectories of the ensuing changes have varied significantly from one post-Soviet country to another. At the same time, a comparative analysis of the post-Soviet Islamic dynamic has been hampered by the epistemological inclusion of Islam in the Baltics, Ukraine and, to a lesser degree, Georgia within the category of 'European Islam', while Islam in Russia, Azerbaijan and Central Asia has been dealt with as narrowly understood 'Eurasian Islam' or as a part of Middle Eastern Studies.

As discussed in Chapter 9, the pro-Western political reorientation of Lithuania and, to some extent, of Ukraine has accounted for the organizational and religious separation of their respective Muslim communities from their Muslim brethren in Russia and in most other ex-Soviet regions. In Lithuania, Lithuanian Tatars and some other autochthonous Muslims, who in the past had been formally affiliated to the Ufa-based

DUMES, acquired their own Vilnius muftīate, which found itself in competition with Tatar national organizations based in Vilnius and Kaunas. On the other hand, some of Lithuania's Muslim immigrants and converts came to be represented by the Klaipeda-based Salafī centres which were more active in online *da'wah* (Islamic proselytism).[33] Most importantly, from the 1990s, Lithuania's Muslims were transformed from being a part of the multimillion Eurasian ummah characterized by historical, ethnic and religious commonalities into a tiny religious (ethnic) minority numbering just under 0.3 per cent of the Catholic-dominated population. Lithuania's religious legislation, state–Muslim relations and Muslim representative bodies were remoulded along European lines. Accordingly, its Muslims, along with other non-ethnic Lithuanians, were accorded the status of an ethnic (religious) minority within the state, where the rights of ethnic Lithuanians have been privileged. The Tatar-dominated Vilnius muftīate and a few affiliated mosques which were recognized by the state as 'traditional' underwent a process of churchification, while the official policy towards radical Salafīs was defined by the securitization discourse which has been prevalent in Europe since the early 2000s.[34] Among the implications of these legislative, political and discursive shifts have been the increased assimilation of Lithuania's Muslims and their linguistic and cultural Lithuanization. A similar process of gradual assimilation of Muslim Adjarians (around 5 per cent of the total population) into the dominant Christian Orthodox Georgian population has been occurring in Georgia, which since 2003 has adhered to a pro-Western political course.

By comparison, geographical, political and cultural divisions within modern Ukraine have accounted for the coexistence there of 'European' and 'Eurasian' forms of Muslim leadership and representation. Ukraine's liberal religious legislation and the state's non-interference in the Islamic sphere (unlike in the domain of the Christian Orthodox Church) have facilitated an influx into the country of Muslim immigrants from the Middle East and Muslim Eurasia. As a result, Ukraine has acquired a plethora of muftīates and other Muslim organizations of traditionalist, Ṣūfī, Salafī and Shī'ī orientation. Many of these organizations have been headed by immigrants of the first generation. Until 2014, Gűlenists had been exerting considerable influence on the Crimean Tatars. As in the case of Lithuania, Ukraine's political separation from Russia and other former Soviet states with sizeable autochthonous Muslim populations has turned its Muslims into a small religious minority numbering just less than 1 per cent of Ukraine's overwhelmingly Christian population. By the 2010s, the demographics of Ukraine's Muslim community had changed as it became dominated by immigrants from the Middle East, Central Asia and the Caucasus. Some of them were taḥrīrīs and other Islamists fleeing persecution in their home countries. On the other hand, the inclusion in 2014 of the Crimea into the Russian Federation has been accompanied by the reintegration into the Eurasian ummah of the bulk of Crimean Tatars affiliated to the Crimean muftīate under the leadership of Emirali Ablayev. In Belarus, which since 1991 has retained close links with Russia and other former Soviet states with large Muslim populations, members of the Tatar-dominated Muslim community, though making up only less than 2 per cent of the total population, have maintained ties with the Eurasian Muslim community. At the same time, due to their ethnic and historical affinities with Muslims in Ukraine and Lithuania as well as their relatively small number, they have similarly experienced some linguistic and cultural Belorusification and have been dependent on foreign providers of Islamic education.

Islamic Leadership in the Authoritarian Context

From the 2000s, after a decade of relatively liberal religious legislation, the governments of the Muslim-majority Central Asian republics, Azerbaijan and Russia, which had large Muslim populations of around 20 million (over 15 per cent of the total population), have de facto returned to the imperial Russian/Soviet model of state–Muslim relations based on the institution of the state-controlled muftīate. The degree of effectiveness of this model has varied significantly across different parts of Muslim Eurasia. It could be argued that in Uzbekistan the muftīate has become well integrated into the system of governance and ensured the separation of Islam from politics and the perpetuation of Uzbek and, broadly understood, Central Asian Islam defined by al-Māturīdīyyah and Ṣūfīsm. In Turkmenistan the level of the state's co-optation of Islamic structures has even exceeded that of Soviet times, as, unlike in other Central Asian republics, the Soviet-era Turkmen qāzīyāt was not upgraded to the muftīate and Turkmenistani Muslim clergy were made civil servants. The state has established its direct control over the much reduced Islamic education and fused Turkmen Muslimness with Turkmen tribal nationalism and sacralized loyalty to Turkmenistan's political leadership. In Kazakhstan, the formal return to the Soviet model of state–Muslim relations has been accompanied by the negation of Kazakh traditional Ṣūfī Islam, intertwined with tribal customs, and the transformation of the muftīate into the official centre of re-Islamization of Kazakhstani Muslims along Salafī lines. Among the implications of this process have been the marginalization of unofficial Ṣūfī authorities, the 'Salafīzation' of mosque imāms and the growing association by young people of their Muslim-ness with Salafīsm. In Kyrgyzstan and Tajikistan, albeit for different reasons, the legal and political authority of the official Muslim clergy has been low, even in comparison with Soviet times. Instead, Islamic perceptions and practices among some young Kyrgyz and Tajiks have been shaped by unofficial Muslim preachers and educators from the Tablīghī Jamā'ah, the Hizmet movement and other foreign organizations and groupings of both Salafī and Ṣūfī orientation.

In Azerbaijan, the continuity of the de facto Soviet system of state–Muslim relations has been ensured by sheikh-ul-Islām Allashukur Hummat Pashazadeh who has been in charge of the Azerbaijani muftīate since 1980. Pashazadeh, as an insider of the Aliyev ruling dynasty, has been involved in the implementation of official Baku's secularist policy by emphasizing the apolitical, cultural and trans-sectarian aspects of Azerbaijani Islam. An important factor which has underpinned Azerbaijani secularized Islam has been the establishment of a close relationship between historically predominantly Shī'ī Azerbaijan and Sunnī Turkey, which positions itself as the model of the secularist Muslim state in the Turkic world. Since the 2000s, Turkish and Azerbaijani leaders have subscribed to the principle of 'One Nation-Two States' and the two countries have been united by a strategic partnership. Among the channels of Turkish Islamic proselytism in Azerbaijan was a chain of Gülenist colleges which operated in the country between 1991 and the 2010s. Another major factor has been the centrality of the Nagorno-Karabakh conflict in the Azerbaijani national discourse, which channelled popular mobilization along Turkic national rather than Shīʿī Islamic lines. A corollary has been the relatively limited influence in Azerbaijan of unofficial Islamic authorities of both Shīʿī and Sunnī orientation.

By contrast, in the Russian North Caucasus, the authority and popular influence of both official and unofficial Islamic leadership has been on the rise. This has been due to the region's Muslim majority, the greater intensity of the 'Islamic revival' and, in the case of the north-eastern Caucasus, the prevalence of the stricter Shāfiʿī madhhab of Sunnī Islam. In 1991, all seven Muslim autonomies of the North Caucasus acquired their own ethnonational muftīates modelled on the Soviet-era DUM SK. In the north-eastern Caucasus muftīates have been dominated by ṭarīqatīsts and in the north-western Caucasus by Ḥanafī Muslim traditionalists. As in the past, muftīs and other official Muslim clergy have been subordinated to the political authorities and participated in the government's crackdown on unofficial Islamist and jihādīst leadership and Islamized militants. Compared to the Soviet times, however, they have established control over higher Islamic education provided by the newly established Islamic universities in Dagestan and Karachaevo-Cherkessia. In Chechnya, state–Muslim relations have been affected by Ramzan Kadyrov's claims to both political and religious authority and the government-spearheaded societal and partially legal re-Islamization of the republic. Across the region, the notable influence of unofficial Islamic traditionalist and Islamist leadership has been perpetuated by continuing socio-economic hardships, the rampant corruption of the ruling political elites and the authorities' uncompromising and heavy-handed approach towards its opponents.

The official Islamic leadership and state–Muslim relations in Russia's Volga-Urals, which are largely populated by Muslim Tatars and Bashkirs, have been characterized by personal rivalries within the official Muslim clergy whereas the authority of the Soviet-era DUMES muftī Talgat Tadzhuddin has been challenged by his younger subordinates, who have established over a dozen regional muftīates. At the theological level, some of them have claimed their adherence to 'traditional' Islam, while implicitly embracing Salafī Islam due to their financial and educational dependence on Wahābī and Salafī organizations and charities in Saudi Arabia and other Gulf countries. From the 2010s, the Russian federal government as well as the Tatar and Bashkir regional authorities have re-established their tight control over the muftīates and have participated in the creation of a number of Islamic universities, based in Bulgar, Kazan, Moscow and Nizhny Novgorod. These Islamic educational institutions, which have included both secular and Muslim scholars teaching Islamic and secular subjects, have been intended to break the methodological and doctrinal dependence of future generations of the Russian Muslim clergy on Islamic universities in the Middle East and to become the main centres of Islamic education for Eurasian Muslims. Overall, the Moscow-, Ufa- and Kazan-centred muftīates, as well as other regional Tatar-dominated muftīates, have been either directly or indirectly incorporated within the system of government bodies. Their authority among ordinary Muslims, however, has remained relatively low. The same applies to various unofficial Islamic and Islamist leaders whose religious authority has been restricted to a relatively small stratum of their respective Muslim communities.

Conclusion

As demonstrated in Chapters 10–12, the nature and forms of Islamic leadership and state–Muslim relations in Muslim-majority and other parts of post-Soviet Eurasia have remained largely defined by the early Islamization of the Caucasus, Central Asia and the Volga region, Eurasia's Christian–Islamic civilizational identity compared to Western Europe's Christianity-centred culture and ethics, the persistence of the muftīate-based system of state management of Islam and Muslims and the continuing legacy of Sovietized secularism[35] intertwined with societal conservatism. Due to the lengthy period of Soviet atheism the degree of secularization there has been much higher than in the Muslim Middle East and on a par with most of Western Europe. On the other hand, there have been considerable similarities between the Muslim Middle Eastern and Eurasian countries in terms of the state's relationship with Islam and Muslims. Across Eurasia, muftīates have acted as agencies of state religious policy in Muslim communities. As in the imperial Russian and Soviet past, modern muftīs have derived their legitimacy from their recognition by the state rather than from their spiritual authority among ordinary Muslims. Accordingly, they have been involved in the state-endorsed promotion of safe and apolitical 'traditional' Islam and have provided legal justifications for the de-legitimization and criminalization of any forms of 'untraditional' Islam, some adherents of which were prepared to challenge the existing social and political order. In Russia, where the state has explicitly prioritized the Russian Orthodox Church (ROC) as the main 'traditional' religion, muftīs, in their capacity as 'younger traditional brothers', have collaborated with Orthodox hierarchs within the framework of Russia's ethnic pluralism and perceived trans-confessional spirituality. In doing so they have been primarily concerned with matters pertinent to post-Soviet Eurasia and have been only barely engaged in the wider Islamic scholarly discourse on the relationship between globalized post-modernity and Islam, the legality and limits of ijtihād, and other critical theological issues which have preoccupied 'ulamā' and Islamologists in the Middle East and Western Europe. On the other hand, unlike in Europe, the state in Russia, Azerbaijan and Central Asia has been directly involved in Islamic theological debate as the primary agent for the authoritative interpretation of tradition – that is, in defining 'traditional' and 'untraditional' Islams – as well as in the curricula of Islamic universities, institutes and madrasahs and, albeit indirectly, in the choice of imāms and other Muslim clergy.

Across most of Eurasia, official Islamic leaders have coexisted with their unofficial counterparts. Those have included theologically knowledgeable local Sunnī or Shī'ī Islamic authorities who have not been affiliated to muftīates. The second and largest group of unofficial Islamic leadership has been represented by various folk Muslim authorities, both male and female, who, despite lacking a structured Islamic education, have possessed charisma and commanded popular respect in rural and mountainous areas of Muslim Central Asia and the Caucasus. Historically, it has been these unofficial and folk Muslim authorities who played the central role in perpetuating a variety of regional versions of Eurasian Islam infused with ethnic and tribal cultures and customs, disengaged from politics. It is significant that there has been no dichotomy between the official and unofficial Islamic leadership as their leading representatives often came from the same venerated Islamic dynasties and substantiated their true Muslim-ness by the same dogmatic references. The third category of unofficial leaders has been represented by pro-Salafī Islamists and jihādīs who have opposed the existing political and social order and the system of state–Muslim relations and have advocated its replacement by an ideational Islamic state. Unlike the first two categories of unofficial Islamic leaders, they have been linked to Islamist and jihādīst authorities and networks outside Eurasia. In the 1990s, in the Ferghana valley, they became directly involved in an armed confrontation with the Uzbekistani ruling regime of Islam Karimov, while in Chechnya they succeeded in establishing short-term Islamic rule. By the 2000s, jihādīs were militarily defeated across Eurasia. Their remainder were either forced underground or fled to Turkey or Western Europe and North America. With the establishment in 2014 of the so-called Islamic State of Iraq and al-Shām (ISIS, Daesh) most members of the Caucasus Emirate and other Eurasian underground jiḥādīst formations relocated to the Middle East. Following the fall of Daesh in 2019, most of those who survived have been prevented by governments from returning to Eurasia. The only exception was several dozen women and over a hundred children who were repatriated from Syria's northern city of Raqqa to Chechnya by Ramzan Kadyrov's government.

Meanwhile, the physical destruction or expulsion of many Eurasian jiḥādīs has not ended the appeal of the Islāmist project among some sectors of Eurasian Muslims. It has continued to resonate among those who have felt economically and socially disadvantaged at home, or ethnically and culturally alienated in non-Muslim host societies. This has been especially the case among some Central Asian and North Caucasian immigrants in Moscow, other major cities of central Russia, the southern Urals and the Far East. Here, Salafī Islam has played the role of a trans-ethnic unifying identity among some groups of Muslim immigrants, while a comparatively small number of them became receptive to the caliphate utopia. Important sources for their re-Islamization along de-territorialized fundamentalist, as well as radical lines, have been sermons and comments by e-imāms and other self-proclaimed digital Muslim authorities available on WhatsApp, YouTube, *MoiMir* (MyWorld), Twitter, Facebook Messenger and other predominantly Russian-language social media. This phenomenon has not been very different from the patterns of Salafīzation and Islamic radicalization in Western Europe, although due to language barriers the role of al-Qaraḍāwī and other Arabic and English-speaking global digital muftīs and imāms in Muslim Eurasia has remained minimal. Overall, in the longer run, the sustainability of the distinctly Eurasian type of Islamic leadership and state–Muslim relations will depend on the ability of Eurasian countries to safeguard their distinctive Eurasian culture defined by intrinsic polyethnicity, polyconfessionalism and social solidarity in the face of the global commodification of values, beliefs and politics.

NOTES

INTRODUCTION

1 See, for example, Galina M. Yemelianova, *Russia and Islam: A Historical Survey* (London: Palgrave, 2002); Galina M. Yemelianova and Hilary Pilkington, eds, *Islam in Post-Soviet Russia: Public and Private Faces* (London: RoutledgeCurzon, 2003); Galina M. Yemelianova, ed., *Radical Islam in the Former Soviet Union* (London: Routledge, 2010); Galina M. Yemelianova, *Muslims of Central Asia: An Introduction* (Edinburgh: Edinburgh University Press, 2019) and Galina M. Yemelianova and Laurence Broers, eds, *Routledge Handbook of the Caucasus* (London: Routledge, 2020).

2 Here the term 'jihādism' describes the global Islamist movement which unites Islamized militants waging an armed *jihād* against perceived *kufarā'* (unbelievers) among both non-Muslims and Muslims with the purpose of the establishment of an Islamic state.

3 For an in-depth analysis of the process of 'churchification' of Islam in Eastern Europe, see Egdūnas Račius, *Islam in Post-communist Eastern Europe: Between Churchification and Securitization* (Leiden: Brill, 2020).

4 I apply the term 'Salafī' (lit. 'successors' to Prophet Muḥammad) as synonymous with the term 'fundamentalist' (*uṣūlī*, in Arabic) in relation to representatives of the first three generations of Muslim jurists (specialists in jurisprudence – *uṣūl al-fiqh*) and dialecticians (scholars of religion – *uṣūl al-dīn*), as well as in relation to any advocates of return to the fundamentals of early Islam. For a fuller discussion on the notion of Salafīsm, see Youssef Choueiri, *Islamic Fundamentalism: The Story of Islamist Movements* (London: Bloomsbury, 2010).

5 I use the terms 'clerics' and 'clergy' in relation to muftīs, qāḍīs, imāms and other Muslim functionaries largely for the sake of utility and simplicity since they are problematic due to their Christian origins.

6 Here I employ the term 'official Islam' in relation to *fatwā*s, Islamic sermons and other pronouncements and written works by muftīs and other Muslim clergy, affiliated to state-controlled muftīates. Consequently, I use the term 'unofficial Islam' in relation to teachings and works by independent Muslim authorities, while acknowledging the theological and personal entanglement of representatives of 'official' and 'unofficial' Islams.

7 Here the term 'Islamism' relates to an Islamized political action or movement.

8 I use the inherently Greco-Roman temporal categories of 'antiquity', 'middle ages' and 'modern era', as well as the Gregorian calendar, for the purposes of convention and simplicity, while recognizing that most of Central Asia and a large part of the Caucasus from as early as the second millennium BCE belonged to the Iran-centric *oikoumene* (cultural habitat), and from the late eighth till the early nineteenth centuries CE to the Islamic East, characterized by other temporal divisions as well as the *Ḥijrī* (lunar), Julian and other non-Gregorian calendars.

9 Here I use a narrow definition of Central Asia corresponding to the present-day states of Uzbekistan, Kazakhstan, Tajikistan, Kyrgyzstan and Turkmenistan. The broader definition of Central Asia (also referred to as Inner Asia, or Central Eurasia) might also encompass Xinjiang, Mongolia, eastern Russia, southern Caucasus, Tibet, north-eastern Iran, northern Afghanistan, northern Turkey, north-western Pakistan and northern India. On the terms and notions of 'Central Asia', see Svetlana Gorshenina, *L'invention de Asie centrale: Histoire du concept de la Tartarie à l'Eurasie* (Paris: Librarie Droz, 2014).

10 SADUM stands for *Sredne-Aziatskoe Dukhovnoe Upravlenie Musul'man*, in Russian.

Chapter One AUTHORITY AND LEADERSHIP IN ISLAM: A HISTORICAL AND COMPARATIVE PERSPECTIVE

1 AH stands for *Anno Herirae* (*Hijrī* calendar) in Latin. Hijrī calendar consists of 354/5 days divided into 12 months which are: *Muḥarram, Ṣafar, Rabīʿ al-awwal, Rabīʿ al-thānī, Jumādā al-ūlā, Jumādā al-ākhirah, Rajab, Shaʿbān, Ramaḍān, Shawwāl, Dhū al-Qaʿdah* and *Dhū al-Ḥijjah.*

2 Here I employ the term 'secularism' to denote the political doctrine of secularism which emerged in modern Western Europe and the United States rather than the separation between religious and secular institutions in government and irreligious public space. On the political doctrine of secularism, see Talal Asad, *Formations of the Secular: Christianity, Islam, Modernity* (Stanford, CA: Stanford University Press, 2003).

3 Patrick Cockburn, 'War with ISIS', *Independent,* 16 November 2016. Accessed 1 November 2019, https://www.independent.co.uk/news/world/middle-east/war-with-isis-islamic-militants-have-army-of-200000-claims-kurdish-leader-9863418.html.

4 Gianluca P. Parolin, *Citizenship in the Arab World: Kin, Religion and Nation-State* (Amsterdam: Amsterdam University Press, 2009), 30.

5 Here and afterwards, the dates related to Muḥammad's life, revelations and activities are indicative rather than certain as they are based on traditional Muslim sources which remain debatable among academics. On some problematic issues of Muslim sources, see Hugh N. Kennedy, *The Prophet and the Age of the Caliphates: The Islamic Near East from the Sixth to the Eleventh Century,* 3rd edn (London: Routledge, 2016).

6 *Ṣaḥābah* comprised *Muhājirūn, Anṣār* and other individuals who knew Muḥammad personally, believed in him and died as Muslims. John L. Esposito, *The Oxford Dictionary of Islam* (Oxford: Oxford University Press, 2003), 301.

7 According to the Shīʿī tradition, for the first time this title was assumed by ʿAlī ibn Abī Ṭālib, the fourth Righteous caliph.

8 On *al-Khawārij,* see Annie C. Higgins, 'Kharijites, Khawarij'. In *Encyclopaedia of Islam and the Muslim World,* vol. 1, edited by Richard C. Martin (London: Macmillan, 2004), 48–67.

9 On the Shīʿī doctrine, see Moojan Momen, *An Introduction to Shiʿi Islam* (London: George Ronald, 1985).

10 On Central Asia within the Arab Caliphate, see Chapter 4.

11 In Roman sources, Mawarannahr, or *Mā Warāʾ al-Nahr,* was referred to as Transoxiana.

12 'Caucasian Albania' is an exonym which appeared in Greco-Latin sources. In Armenian sources the region was known as 'Aghwank', in Parthian sources as 'Ran', in Sasanian sources as 'Ardan' and in Arabic sources as 'Arrān'. Caucasian Albania, which existed from the second century BCE till the eight century CE, included the lands corresponding to the present-day Republic of Azerbaijan and southern Dagestan. Its rulers adopted Christianity in the fourth century CE. On Caucasian Albania, see Alison Vacca, *Non-Muslim Provinces under Early Islam: Islamic Rule and Iranian Legitimacy in Armenia and Caucasian Albania* (Cambridge: Cambridge University Press, 2017).

13 On the Volga Bulgars' conversion to Islam, see Chapter 2.

14 Between the ninth and eleventh centuries Sicily and Malta were governed by the Muslim dynasty of North African Aghlabids who conquered these islands from the Byzantines in the context of the wider Arab-Byzantine confrontation.

15 On al-Andalus and the Spanish Reconquista, see Hugh Kennedy, *Muslim Spain and Portugal: A Political History of al-Andalus* (London: Longman, 1996) and Joseph F. O'Callaghan, *Reconquest and Crusade in Medieval Spain* (Philadelphia: University of Pennsylvania Press, 2004).

16 Kennedy, *Muslim Spain,* 131.

17 The term 'Moorish' derives from 'Moors' which is an exonym first used by Christian Europeans to designate Muslim inhabitants of the Maghreb, the Iberian Peninsula, Sicily and Malta during the Middle Ages. The term was later also applied in the West to Arabs and Arabized Iberians.

18 Abū al-ʿAbbās gained the nickname of al-Saffāḥ (The Blood-Shedder) for his ruthlessness and cruelty towards Umayyads and their supporters.

19 More than a millennium later, in 2010, black flags would be re-enacted by followers of Daesh under the leadership of Abū Bakr al-Baghdādī (r. 2010–19).

20 On specifics of Central Asian Islam, see Chapter 4.

21 On Islamic scholarship in medieval Dagestan, see Chapter 3.

22 On the Volga Bulgaria, see Chapter 2.

23 Vacca, *Non-Muslim Provinces*, 7–9.

24 The 'Mamlūk Sulṭānate' is a modern term. Historically, during the Bahrī rule, it was referred to as *Dawlat al-Atrāk* (State of Turks) and during the Burjī rule as *Dawlat al-Jarākisah* (State of Circassians).

25 *Muʿtazilīs* (lit. 'Those who withdrew'), whose spiritual leader was Wāṣil ibn ʿAtāʾ (d. 748), promoted *kalām* – a scholastic approach to both the Qur'ān and Ḥadīth. They did not perceive the Qur'ān as uncreated and co-eternal with Allah and believed in reason as a source of knowledge and an effective means for determining what was just and religiously sanctioned. Muʿtazilīs became politically influential during the reign of the Abbasid caliphs al-Ma'mūn (r. 813–33), al-Muʿtaṣim (r. 833–42) and al-Wāthiq (r. 842–47). By contrast, their opponents – *Atharīs* (lit. 'Followers of the traditionalist narrative'), whose most influential representative was Aḥmad ibn Ḥanbal (780–855) – insisted on the strict literal (*ẓāhir*) interpretation of the Qur'ān and Ḥadīth, both of which they considered the sole authorities in matters of belief and law. Subsequently, Atharīs formed the movement *Ahl al-Ḥadīth* (People of Ḥadīth). Muʿtazilīs' other critiques were *Ashʿarīs*, followers of Abū al-Ḥasan al-Ashʿarī (d. 936), a native of Basra, who believed that reason was subordinated to revelation and that Islam had a mystical component. Among their leading representatives was the great Ṣūfī luminary Abū Ḥāmid al-Ghazālī (d. 1111). On Atharīs, Mu'tazilīs and Ashʿarīs, see Jonathan P. Berkey, *The Formation of Islam: Religion and Society in the Near East, 600–1800* (Cambridge: Cambridge University Press, 2003); Richard C. Martin, Mark R. Woodward and Dwi S. Atmaja, *Defenders of Reason in Islam: Muʿatazilism from Medieval School to Modern Symbol* (London: Oneworld, 1997).

26 On Sunnī legal theories and juristic schools, see Wael B. Hallaq, *A History of Islamic Legal Theories: An Introduction to Sunnī Uṣūl Al-Fiqh* (Cambridge: Cambridge University Press, 1997).

27 On Ibn Taymiyyah, see Abdul Hakim I. al-Matroudi. *The Hanbali School of Law and Ibn Taymiyyah: Conflict and Conciliation* (London: Routledge, 2006).

28 On the Imarat Kavkaz, see Chapter 11.

29 Over time Twelvers developed into the largest Shīʿī group. At present they make up the majority in Iran, Azerbaijan, Iraq, Lebanon and Bahrain. There are also significant Twelver minorities in India, Pakistan, Afghanistan, Saudi Arabia, Bangladesh, Kuwait, Oman, UAE, Qatar, Nigeria, Chad and Tanzania. On Twelvers, see Andrew J. Newman, *Twelver Shiʿism: Unity and Diversity in the Life of Islam, 632 to 1733* (Edinburgh: Edinburgh University Press, 2013).

30 By the late tenth century the Buyyīds de facto controlled Abbasid Baghdad and dominated most of present-day Iran, Iraq, Syria, Kuwait, eastern Arabia, Turkey, Afghanistan and Pakistan. On Buyyīds, see John J. Donohue, *The Buwayhid Dynasty in Iraq 334H/945 to 403H/1012: Shaping Institutions for the Future* (Leiden: Brill, 2003).

31 Between 1920 and 1936 Alawites had their own state on the territory of Syria under the French Mandate (1920–43). At present Alawites make up about 12 per cent of Syria's population; a significant Alawite minority also exists in the region of Antakya in southern Turkey. The family of Syria's current president, Bashar al-Assad (in office 2000–), is affiliated to the Alawites. On Alawites, see Yaron Friedman, *The Nuṣayrī-ʿAlawīs: An Introduction to the Religion, History and Identity of the Leading Minority in Syria* (Leiden: Brill, 2010).

32 The Zaydī imāmate was established in 898 in the Yemeni city of Sa'adah by the imām al-Hādi Yahya ibn al-Ḥusayn (r. 898–911). The leading positions in the imāmate were occupied by sayyīds and sharīfs. At the theological level, Zaydīs were closer to Mu'atazilīs and Ibāḍīs, as

they opposed fatalism and the eternal nature of the Qur'ān and believed in an individual's capacity and will to act against any form of injustice, even if it came from a caliph, sulṭān, shāh or any other ruler. In terms of fiqh, Zaydīs had many similarities with Sunnī Ḥanafīs. On Zaydīs in Yemen, see Galina M. Yemelianova [Udalova]. *Yemen v Period Pervogo Osmanskogo Zavoevaniia (1538–1635)* (Moscow: Nauka, 1988) and Caesar E. Farah, *The Sultan's Yemen: Nineteenth-Century Challenge to Ottoman Rule* (London: I.B. Tauris, 2002).

33 On Ismā'īlīs, see Farhad Daftary, *The Ismailis: Their History and Doctrine* (Cambridge: Cambridge University Press, 2007).

34 Fāṭimids bore the title of caliph on the basis on their claims to the genealogical link to Prophet Muḥammad via his youngest daughter Fāṭimah. At the peak of its power the Fāṭimid Caliphate included Egypt, Sudan, the Levant, Hejaz, parts of the Maghreb and Sicily. It is worth noting that it was the Fāṭimids who laid the foundation of the al-Azhar Mosque which would subsequently evolve into the al-Azhar University, a major global centre of Islamic learning and scholarship. On Fāṭimids, see Michael Brett, *The Fatimid Empire* (Edinburgh: Edinburgh University Press, 2017).

35 The name *Ṣūfism*, or *Taṣawwuf*, is likely to originate from *ṣūf* (wool) which was associated with woollen clothes worn by Muslim ascetics and mystics. On Ṣūfīsm and Ṣūfī ṭarīqahs, see J. Spencer Trimingham, *The Sufi Orders in Islam* (Oxford: Oxford University Press, 1998).

36 The *dhikr* (recollection of Allah) is the central Ṣūfī practice which constitutes the pivot of mysticism. It consists of the repeated recitation of litanies founded on the Qur'ān and fixed phrases. Some ṭarīqahs (e.g. the Naqshbandīyyah) practise a quiet, internal dhikr (*dhikr-i khāfī*), while some others (e.g. al-Qādirīyyah) conduct loud dhikr (*dhikr-i zhahrī*). Alexandre Bennigsen and S. Enders Wimbush, S. Enders, *Mystics and Commissars. Sufism in the Soviet Union* (London: Hurst, 1985), 78–83.

37 *'Adats* is a generic term for unwritten customary norms which also play an important social role among various peoples of Central Asia.

38 On the Naqshbandīyyah in Central Asia and the North Caucasus, see Chapters 3 and 4.

39 Egdūnas Račius, and Antonina Zhelyazkova, 'Introduction: Rational of the Book'. In *Islamic Leadership in the European Lands of the Former Ottoman and Russian Empires: Legacy, Challenges and Change*, edited by Egdūnas Račius and Antonina Zhelyazkova (Leiden: Brill, 2017), 1–11.

40 Muhammad K. Masud, Brinkley Messick and David Powers, 'Muftis, Fatwas, and Islamic Legal Interpretation'. In *Islamic Legal Interpretations: Muftis and Their Fatwas*, edited by Muhammad K. Masud, Brinkley Messick and David Powers, 3–32 (Cambridge, MA: Harvard University Press, 1996).

41 Jacob Skovgaard-Petersen, 'Historical Retrospective on Muftiship: Muftis, State and Official Muftis'. In *Islamic Leadership in the European Lands*, 14.

42 For more on the Mongol Empire, see Chapter 4.

43 The Ottomans are called after Osman I (1258–1323), a bey from the Oghuz Turkic tribe of Kayi in Anatolia. On the Ottomans, see Colin Imber, *The Ottoman Empire, 1300–1650: The Structure of Power* (New York: Palgrave Macmillan, 2009); Halil Inalcik, *The Ottoman Empire: The Classical Age, 1300–1600* (London: Weidenfeld and Nicholson, 1973); Daniel Goffman, *The Ottoman Empire and Early Modern Europe* (Cambridge: Cambridge University Press, 2002) and Donald Quataert, *The Ottoman Empire, 1700–1922* (Cambridge: Cambridge University Press, 2000).

44 It should be noted that not all 'ulamā' accepted him as caliph, insisting that the caliph should be a Muslim Arab from the Qurayshī tribe of the Prophet Muḥammad. Incidentally, the idea of restoration of the Arab caliphate would be invoked in the early twentieth and twenty-first centuries.

45 Richard C. Repp, *The Mufti of Istanbul: A Study in the Development of the Ottoman Learned Hierarchy* (London: Ithaca Press, 1986), 73.

46 Ibid., 193, 297.

47 Ibid., 26, 28, 63, 123.

48 On Islamic authorities in the Crimea and the north-western Caucasus, see Chapters 2 and 3.
49 Many Safawids originated from an Oghuz Turkic confederation of *Aqquyunlu* (White Sheep, 1378–1501), which alongside its rival, *Qaraquyunlu* (Black Sheep, 1375–1468), dominated parts of Iran, Turkey and the Caucasus.
50 The Qizilbash acquired this name due to their wearing of red 12-pleated hats (*tajs*).
51 The Safawids had three successive capitals: Tabriz (1501–55), Qazvin (1555–98) and Isfahan (1598–1736).
52 Newman, *Twelver Shi'ism*, 17.
53 Arif Yunusov, *Islam v Azerbaidzhane* (Baku: Zaman, 2004), 80.
54 Ibid., 81, 92.
55 Keiko Sakurai, 'Making Qom a Centre of Shi'i Scholarship: Al-Mustafa International University'. In *Shaping Global Islamic Discourses: The Role of al-Azhar, al-Medina and al-Mustafa*, edited by Masooda Bano and Keiko Sakurai (Edinburgh: Edinburgh University Press, 2015), 43.
56 See Chapter 13.

Chapter Two ISLAMIC LEADERSHIP AMONG TATARS AND OTHER TURKIC PEOPLES PRIOR TO AND DURING RUSSIAN RULE

1 The name 'Tatar' is likely to have originated among Mongolic-speaking nomads in the north-eastern Gobi desert in the fifth century CE. Between the thirteenth and nineteenth centuries, 'Tatar' was the exonym which referred to various sedentary and semi-nomadic Qipchaqs (north-western Turkic people) who inhabited the Volga-Urals, Siberia, parts of the northern Caucasus and Crimea. Among the proto-Tatars' ancestors were Biars, a Turkic people, who populated the river basins of the Oka, Volga and Kama (Chulman). On the Tatars' ethnic origins, see Abrar G. Karimullin, *Tatary: Etnos i Etnonim* (Kazan: Tatarskoe Knizhnoe Izdatel'stvo, 1988).
2 The name 'Bashkir' originates from the endonym 'Bashkort' (Wolf-head) which had been used by semi-nomadic Qipchaqs in the southern Urals at least from the ninth century CE. On the Bashkirs' ethnic origins, see Togan Validi, *Istoriia Bashkir*. Translated from Turkish by Amir M. Yuldashbaev (Ufa: Kitap, 2010).
3 The name 'Russian' derives from the endonym 'Rus' related to the principality of Kievan Rus' (882–1240). On the notions of 'Rus' and 'Russian', see Oleg N. Trubachev, *Rus'. Rossiia. Ocherki Etimologii Nazvaniia* (Moscow: RAN, 2005).
4 On the notion of 'Tartars' and 'Tartaria' in European sources, see Svetlana Gorshenina, *L'invention de Asie centrale: Histoire du concept de la Tartarie à l'Eurasie* (Paris: Librarie Droz, 2014).
5 The Ruriks were a Varangian/Viking dynasty (859–1598), which first ruled over the Kiev-centred political formation – Kievan Rus – and later over the early Russian state. It is believed that its founding fathers were the chieftains Sineus, Trevor, Askold and Rurik. Galina M. Yemelianova, *Russia and Islam: A Historical Survey* (London: Palgrave, 2002), 5.
6 Tengrism or Tengrianism is an ancient belief system among various Turkic- and Mongolic-speaking peoples of Eurasia who sought to achieve harmony with their surrounding world. It contains elements of shamanism, animism, totemism, Zoroastrianism and Buddhism, as well as monotheism and polytheism.
7 On Volga Bulgaria and the Kazan Khānate, see Il'iaz B. Muslimov, ed., *Na Styke Tsivilizatsii* (Moscow: Insan, 1996).
8 On the Khazar Khaganate, see Peter B. Golden, *Turks and Khazars: Origins, Institutions and Interactions in pre-Mongol Eurasia* (Farnham: Ashgate, 1980).
9 *Nowruz* marks the day of vernal equinox and symbolizes the beginning of spring. It was widely celebrated for over 3,000 years among various peoples of Iran, Central and western Asia, the Caucasus, the Black Sea region and the Balkans.

10 Muslimov, *Na Styke Tsivilizatsii*, 31; Zufar Z. Miftakhov, *Kurs po Istorii Tatarskogo Naroda* (Kazan: Dom Pechati, 1998), 223–24.
11 Rafik Mukhametshin, *Tatary i Islam v XX veke* (Kazan: Fen, 2003), 24.
12 Galina M. Yemelianova, *Muslims of Central Asia: An Introduction* (Edinburgh: Edinburgh University Press, 2019), 21.
13 Yuri V. Sochnev, 'Khristianstvo v Zolotoi Orde'. In *Iz Istorii Zolotoi Ordy*, edited by Damir Iskhakov (Kazan: Fond im. Sultan-Galieva, 1993), 110.
14 The Great *Yasa* consisted of two parts: the *Yasa* proper and the *Bilik* (Wisdom). The former included 58 customary administrative, criminal, civic and family rulings, while the latter contained 30 moral pronouncements based on Genghiz Khān's sayings.
15 Yemelianova, *Muslims of Central Asia*, 33–34.
16 Muslimov, *Na Styke Tsivilizatsii*, 675–76, 683, 686.
17 Renat Bekkin, '"Parallel" Muftiates as the "Third Force" among Spiritual Administrations of Muslims in Russia'. *Journal of Muslims in Europe* 8: 1–21 (2019): 55.
18 Muslimov, *Na Styke Tsivilizatsii*, 680–81.
19 Lithuania officially adopted Christianity in 1387.
20 Daša Slabčanka, 'Belarus'. In *Islamic Leadership in the European Lands of the Former Ottoman and Russian Empires: Legacy, Challenges and Change*, edited by Egdūnas Račius and Antonina Zhelyazkova (Leiden: Brill, 2017), 260; Egdūnas Račius, 'Lithuania'. In *Islamic Leadership in the European Lands*, 273; Egdūnas Račius, *Muslims in Eastern Europe* (Edinburgh: Edinburgh University Press, 2018), 26.
21 On the Astrakhan Khānate, see Ilia V. Zaitsev, *Astrakhanskoe Khanstvo* (Moscow: Vostochnaia Literatura, 2004).
22 Zaitsev, *Astrakhanskoe Khanstvo*, 183–85, 189.
23 On the Nogai Horde, see Vadim V. Trepavlov, *Istoriia Nogaiskoi Ordy* (Moscow: RAN, 2002).
24 Between the mid-sixteenth and the late nineteenth centuries the Russian state (since 1721, the Russian Empire) and the Ottoman Empire, which were territorially contiguous to each other, fought many wars for the control of the Black Sea zone, the Caucasus, Crimea and parts of Central Asia. These wars were accompanied by numerous border changes, population exchanges and contributed to the proliferation of the Ottoman version of Islam in the north-western Caucasus, Batum (present-day Adjara) and the Crimea. The first internationally recognized border between the Russian and Ottoman empires was established only in 1878 in the aftermath of Russia's victory in the Russo-Ottoman war of 1877–78. According to the Treaties of San Stefano and Berlin, both of 1878, St. Petersburg acquired jurisdiction over most of the Caucasus and the Black Sea region of Ardahan, Kars and Batum. In the midst of the First World War, the Bolshevik government of Russia signed the Brest-Litovsk Treaty with Germany and other Central Powers, according to which Ardahan, Kars and Batum were ceded to Turkey. On the Ottoman policy in the Caucasus and the Crimea, see Bayram Balci and Thomas Liles, 'Turkey and the Caucasus: Mutual Interests and Influences in the post-Soviet Era'. In *Routledge Handbook of the Caucasus*, edited by Galina M. Yemelianova and Laurence Broers (London: Routledge, 2020), 331–46.
25 On the Crimean Tatars and the Crimean Khānate, see Alan W. Fisher, *The Crimean Tatars* (Stanford, CA: Hoover Institution Press, 2014) and Dariusz Kolodziejczyk, *The Crimean Khanate and Polish-Lithuania: International Diplomacy on the European Periphery (15th–18th Centuries). A Study of Peace Treaties. Followed by Annotated Documents* (Leiden: Brill, 2011).
26 Halil Inalcik, *The Ottoman Empire: The Classical Age, 1300–1600* (London: Weidenfeld and Nicholson, 1973), 106.
27 In 1774, in the aftermath of the Russo-Ottoman war of 1768–74, the Crimea gained a short independence before being annexed to Russia in 1783.

28 Among the peninsula's centres of Islamic learning was the Solkhat madrasah. Andrei Yakubovych, Vitalii Shchepanskyi and Ayder Bulatov, 'Ukraine'. In *Islamic Leadership in the European Lands*, 315.
29 On the ethnic origins of Mishar Tatars, see Ramziia G. Mukhamedova, *Tatary-Mishari: Istoriko-Etnograficheskoe Issledovanie* (Moscow: Nauka, 1972).
30 Galina M. Yemelianova, *Russia and Islam: A Historical Survey* (London: Palgrave, 2002), 34.
31 On the Sibir Khānate, see Hadi Atlasi, *Istoriia Sibiri* (Kazan: Tatarskoe Knizhnoe Izdatel'stvo, 2005).
32 On Islamic beliefs and practices among Kazakhs, see Chapter 4.
33 In 2005, this mosque was rebuilt and named after Sayyīd Kul Sharif (tat. Qol Sharif) who died in 1552 defending Kazan against the troops of Ivan IV.
34 Mukhametshin, *Tatary i Islam*, 31.
35 Ibid., 32.
36 Renat Bekkin, *People of Reliable Loyalty* [...] *Muftiates and the State in Modern Russia*, PhD Dissertation (Stockholm: Elanders, 2020), 96–97.
37 On the role of Genghizids in Russian history, see Yemelianova (2002).
38 Old Believers (rus. *Starovers*) were the followers of original Eastern Orthodox liturgical and ritual practices, which dominated in Russia prior to Patriarch Nikon's reforms (1652–66) aimed at accommodating Russian Orthodox rituals to the contemporary forms of Greek Orthodox worship.
39 Robert Landa, *Islam v Istorii Rossii* (Moscow: Vostochnaia Literatura, 1995), 125.
40 Originally the muftīate was established in Ufa. Between 1796 and 1802, the muftīate was based in the city of Orenburg in southern Siberia. Although in 1802 it returned to Ufa, it retained its name as the Orenburg Mohammedan Spiritual Assembly (rus. OMDS). On the OMDS, see Michael Kemper, *Sufii i Uchenye v Tatarstane i Bashkortostane: Islamskii Diskurs pod Russkim Gospodstvom* (Kazan: RII, 2008); Aidar Khabutdinov, *Istoriia Orenburgskogo Magometanskogo Dukhovnogo Sobraniia* (Nizhny Novgorod: Medina, 2010) and Ildus Zagidullin, *Orenburgskoe Magometanskoe Dukhovnoe Sobranie i Dukhovnoe Razvitie Tatarskogo Naroda v Poslednei Chetverti XVIII – Nachala XX Veka* (Kazan: IIAN RT, 2011).
41 Bekkin, *People of Reliable Loyalty*, 79.
42 Ibid., 5.
43 Bekkin, *People of Reliable Loyalty*, 100; Khabutdinov, *Istoriia*, 111.
44 Evgeny Khamidov, 'O Neizvestnoi Rukopisi Sheikha Zainully Rasuleva'. *Kazan Islamic Review* 1 (2015): 106.
45 Bekkin, *People of Reliable Loyalty*, 362.
46 On the Russian conquest of the Kazakh Steppe, see Chapter 4.
47 Taurida (also known as Tavrika, or Tauria) was the ancient Greek name for the Crimean Peninsula, which was used until the creation of the Crimean Khānate in the fifteenth century. In the middle of the nineteenth century over 85 per cent of the nearly half a million Crimean population were Crimean Tatars, while other sizeable communities included Greeks and Armenians. Yaroslav E. Vodarskii, Olga I. Eliseeva and Vladimir M. Kabuzan, *Neselenie Kryma v Kontse XVIII- Kontse XX Vekov* (Moscow: Institut Rossiiskoi Istorii, 2003).
48 In the course of the Crimean War (1853–56), the Russo-Ottoman War (1877–78) and Russia's annexation of the Crimea (1783) nearly half of the 500,000-strong population of the Crimean Tatars emigrated to Turkey. Vodarskii, Eliseeva and Kabuzan, *Neselenie Kryma.*
49 Galina M. Yemelianova, 'Russia's Umma and its Muftis', *Religion, State and Society* 31, no. 2 (2003): 139–50; Mustafa Tuna, *Imperial Russia's Muslims: Islam, Empire and European Modernity, 1788–1914* (Cambridge: Cambridge University Press, 2015).
50 Joseph Schacht, *An Introduction to Islamic Law* (Oxford: Clarendon Press, 1982), 71.
51 Among influential pro-jadīd Tatar Islamic scholars were Musa Bigi, Ziauddin Kamali, Ubaydulla Bubi, Jarullah Bigi, Galimzhan Galeev and Zaki Kadiri. On Tatar Muslim

reformists, see Tuna, *Imperial Russia's Muslims* and Danielle Ross, *Tatar Empire: Kazan's Muslims and the Making of Imperial Russia* (Bloomington: Indiana University Press, 2020).

52 *Tercuman* (1883–1918), which was published in Turkī, was the most influential and popular Muslim periodical in Russia. Under its influence, Turkī became the dominant language of Muslim periodicals which appeared in the Crimea and Central Asia at the beginning of the twentieth century.

53 A comparatively small number of jadīds favoured Tatar and other Turkic peoples' reunification under the auspices of the Ottoman Turkey. Among these were, for example, Yusuf Akchura, Mehmet Akif (Ersoy), Ahmed Aga-oglu (Agaev) and Galimzhan Idrisi. Galina M. Yemelianova, 'The National Identity of the Volga Tatars at the Turn of the 19th Century: Tatarism, Turkism and Islam'. *Central Asian Survey* 16, no. 4 (1997): 553.

Chapter Three ISLAM AND ISLAMIC LEADERSHIP IN THE CAUCASUS

1 On the ethno-linguistic diversity of the Caucasus, see John Colarusso, 'Peoples, Languages and Lore'. In *The Routledge Handbook of the Caucasus*, edited by Galina M. Yemelianova and Laurence Broers (London: Routledge), 32–51.

2 Arif Yunusov, *Islam v Azerbaidzhane* (Baku: Zaman, 2004), 43.

3 On the Islamization of Central Asia, see Yemelianova (2019): 13–17.

4 Alison Vacca, *Non-Muslim Provinces under Early Islam: Islamic Rule and Iranian Legitimacy in Armenia and Caucasian Albania* (Cambridge: Cambridge University Press, 2017), 31.

5 Ibid., 25, 31.

6 In 1122 the Emīrate of Tiflis was finally defeated by the Georgian king, David IV, who re-asserted the supremacy of the Orthodox Church over Tiflis.

7 Yunusov, *Islam v Azerbaidzhane*, 45, 47, 51.

8 Until the early nineteenth century Azerbaijan was a single region situated in northern Iran. By the treaties of Gulistan (1813) and Turkmanchai (1828) the northern part of Azerbaijan, alongside other territories to the north of the Aras River, were transferred to Russia. The territory of the modern Republic of Azerbaijan roughly corresponds to this part of historic Azerbaijan. See Chapter 7.

9 Vacca, *Non-Muslim Provinces*, 44.

10 Ahmad Baladhuri, *Kniga Zavoevaniia Stran* (Baku: Obshchestvo Obsledovaniia I Izucheniia Azerbaidzhana, 1927), 20.

11 Ahmed I. Osmanov, ed., *Istoriia Dagestana s Drevneishykh Vremen do Nashykh Dnei*, vol. 1 (Moscow: Nauka, 2004), 185–86.

12 Yūsuf ibn Ḥusain al-Lakzī is the likely author of *Darband-Nameh* (History of Darband) which provides an invaluable account of Islam and Islamic scholarship in medieval Dagestan. Stanislav M. Prozorov, 'Al-Lakzī Yūsuf'. In *Islam na Territorii Byvshei Rossiiskoi Imperii*, no. 1 (Moscow: Vostochnaia Literatura, 1998), 15.

13 Kaflan Khanbabaev, 'Islam and Islamic Radicalism in Dagestan'. In *Radical Islam in the Former Soviet Union*, edited by Galina M. Yemelianova (London: Routledge, 2010), 85.

14 *Ahl al-Ḥaqq*'s members regarded the fourth righteous caliph 'Alī to be superior to the Prophet Muḥammad. At the same time they worshiped fire and believed in reincarnation, and that God could be incarnated in human beings. Yunusov, *Islam v Azerbaidzhane*, 55.

15 Vacca, *Non-Muslim Provinces*, 7.

16 For a fuller account of the Caucasus' Islamization and the role of 'adats, see Galina M. Yemelianova and Svetlana I. Akkieva, 'The Muslim Caucasus: The Role of *'ādat*s and *shari'ah*'. In *The Routledge Handbook of the Caucasus*, edited by Galina M. Yemelianova and Laurence Broers (London: Routledge, 2020), 68–84.

17 Khanbabaev, 'Islam and Islamic Radicalism in Dagestan', 85–87.

18 Anna Zelkina, *In Quest of God and Freedom* (London: Hurst, 2000), 33–34.
19 In the first millennium BCE the Circassian (Adyghe) people formed four major subgroups: the Abkhaz, the Abazas, the Ubykhs and the Circassians *per se*.
20 Walter Richmond, *The Northwest Caucasus: Past, Present, Future* (London: Routledge, 2008), 28–30.
21 Ruslan Baramidze, *Islam i ego Osobennosti v Adzharii* (Heinrich Böl Stiftung, 2005), https://ge.boell.org/en/2005/01/16/islam-i-ego-osobennosti-v-adzharii.
22 For a detailed discussion of Abū Bakr al-Darbandī and his Ṣūfī encyclopaedia *Raiḥān al-Ḥaqāiq*, see Alikber K. Alikberov, *Epokha Klassicheskogo Islama na Kavaze* (Moscow: Vostochnaia Literatura RAN, 2003).
23 The Naqshbandī ṭarīqah is named after Ṣūfī sheikh (khwājah) Bahā' al-Dīn Naqshband (1318–1389), a Persianized Bukharan, who followed the Ṣūfī tradition of khwājah Yūsuf Ḥamadanī (d. 1147). At its core were the principles of 'reclusion in the community', 'externally amongst people' and 'internally with God', as well as the practice of silent dhikr (*dhikr-i khāfī*). More on the Naqshbandīyyah, see Chapter 4.
24 The Mujaddidīyyah (from 'tajdīd', lit. 'modernization', in Arabic) phase in the development of the Naqshbandī tarīqah was initiated by sheikh Aḥmad al-Farūqī al-Sirhindī (1564–1624), a leading reformist Naqshbandī sheikh from India.
25 Zelkina, *In Quest of God*, 84, 93.
26 Khanbabaev, 'Islam and Islamic Radicalism in Dagestan', 87.
27 Alexander Knysh, 'Contextualizing the Salafi – Sufi Conflict (from the Northern Caucasus to Hadramawt)'. *Middle Eastern Studies* 43, no. 4 (2007): 515.
28 On Ingush attitudes to the Russo-Chechen conflict in the 1990s, see Chapter 11.
29 Qādirī ṭarīqah is named after 'Abd al-Qādir Gīlānī (1078–1166), a Persian native of Gīlān, who adhered to the Ḥanbalī madhhab. In the fifteenth-sixteenth centuries the Qādirī ṭarīqah was introduced to Syria and Egypt and, in the early seventeenth century to Istanbul, from where it might have spread to the Caucasus. J. Spencer Trimingham, *The Sufi Orders in Islam* (Oxford: Oxford University Press, 1998), 41, 44.
30 Vahit Akaev, 'Islam and Politics in Chechnya and Ingushetia'. In *Radical Islam in the Former Soviet Union*, edited by Galina M. Yemelianova (London: Routledge, 2010), 66.
31 Magomed Abdullayev, *Iz Istorii Filosofskoi i Obshchestvenno-Politicheskoi Mysli Dagestana* (Makhachkala: Yupiter, 1993), 80.
32 Khanbabaev, 'Islam and Islamic Radicalism in Dagestan', 106.
33 Yasawī ṭarīqah is named after Ṣūfī sheikh (*khojah*) Aḥmad Yasawī (1093–1166), a Turkic native of Turkestan in present-day southern Kazakhstan. He followed the Ṣūfī tradition of Yūsuf Ḥamadānī (d. 1141) via *khwājah* 'Abd al-Khaliq Gijduvanī (d. 1179) from Bukhara. He was also the first Ṣūfī sheikh to use the Turkī language in his Ṣūfī teaching and poetry. Subsequently, the Yasawī ṭarīqah became an important medium of Islamization among various Turkic peoples.
34 Kubrawī ṭarīqah was named after Naj al-Dīn Kubrā (d. 1221) from Khwārazm.
35 Mamaikhan A. Aglarov, *Sel'skaia Obshchina v Nagornom Dagestane v VII- nachale XIX v* (Moscow: Nauka, 1988), 6.
36 Among the influential Chechen tukhums were the Nokhchakhkhoy, the Akkhiy, the Tierloy, the Chebarloy, the Sharoy, the Ma'lkhiy, the Shuotoy, the Chiantiy and the Ershtkhoy. Saipudi A. Nataev, 'K Voprosu ob Institute 'Tukhum/Tokhum/Tuk'um/Tukkham' u Narodov Kavkaza'. *Gumanitarnye, Sotsial'no-Ekonomicheskie i Obshchestvennye Nauki* 6 (2015): 38–59.
37 'Adat courts were called *maslahat* among some Dagestanis, *tёre turg'an* among the Karachai-Balkars, *mekhk-khel* among the Ingush, *kheisha* among the Circassians and other names among different peoples. Khadzhi-Murad Khashaev, *Pamiatniki obychnogo prava Dagestan XVII–XIX vv* (Moscow: Nauka, 1965), 54.
38 Boris M. Kharsiev, *Ingushskie adaty kak fenomen pravovoi kul'tury* (Nazran': Piligrim, 2009), 55.
39 Irina L. Babich, *Evolutsiia pravovoi kul'tury adygov (1860–1990-e gody)* (Moscow: Nauka, 1999), 66.
40 Valentin K. Gardanov, *Gardanov V.K. – Istorik i Etnograf* (Nal'chik: El'-Fa, 2004), 205.

41 Yemelianova and Akkieva, 'The Muslim Caucasus', 74.
42 On the socio-cultural and political implications of Genghizid rule over most of Eurasia, see Yemelianova (2019): 33–34.
43 Vladimir O. Bobrovnikov, *Musul'mane Severnogo Kavkaza: Obychai, Pravo, Nasilie* (Moscow: Vostochnaia Literatura RAN, 2002), 5.
44 Zelkina, *In Quest of God*, 205, 207.
45 Ibid., 209–11.
46 Andarbek D. Yandarov, *Sufizm i Ideologiia Natsional'no-Osvoboditel'nogo Dvizheniia* (Alma-Ata: Nauka, 1975), 127.
47 Bobrovnikov, *Musul'mane Severnogo Kavkaza*, 23.
48 According to sharī'ah, a caught thief had his or her right hand amputated for the first time, the left for the second, the right leg for the third, the left for the fourth and finally beheading for the fifth. Zelkina, *In Quest of God*, 221–22.
49 An important centre of Christian proselytizing in the Caucasus was the Society for the Restoration of Orthodoxy in the Mountains, which was established by the Caucasian Viceroy Aleksandr Bariatinsky (1815–1879). Elena Shavlokhova, 'Khristianizatsiia Naseleniia Narodov Severnogo Kavkaza Kak Etap Vkliucheniia v Administrativno-Pravovuiu Sistemu Rossii'. *Istoricheskaia i Sotsial'no-Obrazovatel'naia Mys*l' 8, nos. 6/1 (2016): 120.
50 In Turkey, Caucasian muhājirs from different ethnic groups, including the Chechens and Dagestanis, became referred to as 'Cherkess'.
51 Timothy K. Blauvelt, 'The Caucasus in the Russian Empire'. In *The Routledge Handbook of the Caucasus*, edited by Galina M. Yemelianova and Laurence Broers (London: Routledge, 2020), 116.

Chapter Four ISLAM, ISLAMIC AUTHORITY AND LEADERSHIP IN CENTRAL ASIA

1 For a detailed discussion of the role of Sogdians and Samanids in the Islamization of Central Asia, see Galina M. Yemelianova, *Muslims of Central Asia: An Introduction* (Edinburgh: Edinburgh University Press, 2019) and Chapter 1.
2 The special place of Khorāsān in the region's Islamization is reflected in the formation within Daesh of the so-called 'Khorāsān wilāyah' (2015–18) on the territory of present-day Afghanistan and Pakistan.
3 The Battle of Talas put an end to China's westward expansion and secured Central Asia's Islamic destiny.
4 Rustam T. Shodiyev, *Sufism v Dukhovnoi Zhizni Narodov Srednei Azii (IX-XIII vv)* (Tashkent: Institut Filosofii, 1993), 14.
5 Nāṣir Khusraw served at the Ghaznavid court and, following the arrival of the Seljūqs, embarked on travels across the Middle East. He converted from Sunnī Islam to Isma'īlism in Fāṭimid Egypt. On Nāṣir Khusraw, see Alice C. Hunsberger, *Nasir Khusraw, the Ruby of Badakhshan: A Portrait of the Persian Poet, Traveller and Philosopher* (London: I.B. Tauris, 2003).
6 The origins of the term 'Tajik' are debated. Some link it to the Persian word 'Tazi', meaning 'Arab', which was used by locals to describe newly arrived Muslim settlers. Others derive it from the word 'Tat', which was used from the eleventh century by Turkic speakers in relation to Iranian speakers.
7 On the Islamic debate in post-Soviet Kazakhstan, see Chapter 12.
8 Later on, the title of 'khwājah' would become the hallmark of Central Asian Naqshbandīs, who were also known as *Tariqa-i-Khwajagan* (Order of Khwājahs).
9 On Qara Khitais, see Michal Biran, *The Empire of the Qara Khitai in Eurasian History: Between China and The Islamic World* (Cambridge: Cambridge University Press, 2005).
10 Ibid., 182.

11 On the Ghaznavids, see Clifford E. Bosworth, *The Later Ghaznavids: Splendour and Decay in Afghanistan and Northern India 1040–1186* (New York: Columbia University Press, 1977).
12 The Seljūqs had several successive capitals which reflected their territorial expansion. These were Nishapur (1037–43), Rey (1043–51), Isfahan (1051–1153), Merv (eastern capital, 1118–53) and Hamadan (western capital, 1118–94).
13 In 1055 the Abbasid Caliph al-Qā'im granted the Seljūq sultan Toghrül Beg the title of *Mālik al-Mashriq wa al-Maghrib* (King of the East and West) in gratitude for Seljūqs' liberation of Baghdad from the control of the Shī'ī Būyyīds. By that time, however, the political and religious authority of Abbasid caliphs was nominal.
14 New Persian (also referred to as Modern Persian) became prevalent in present-day Iran and adjacent regions from the ninth century.
15 Among Samarqand's magnificent Timūrid hallmarks are, for example, Registan, consisting of the madrasahs of Ulugh Bek, Tilia-Kori and Sher-Dor, Bibi-khanum's mosque and Shahi-Zinda's necropolis.
16 Subsequently, Timūr's descendants, including Babur, the founder of the Mughal Empire (1526–1857), also bore non-Genghizid titles such as 'amīr' or 'sulṭān'. This was the case with the Shaybānids and the Bukharan rulers who preferred the title of 'emīr'.
17 In 1377 Ibn Khaldūn wrote the *Muqaddimah* (*Prolegomena*) which arguably laid the foundation for the modern disciplines of sociology, historiography, economics and demography.
18 Yemelianova, *Muslims of Central Asia*, 25.
19 The origins of the name 'Uzbek' are debated, although it is most likely to derive from Uzbek (d. 1341), khān of the Golden Horde.
20 This madrasah was named after the sheikh Mir-i-Arab, who was the Ṣūfī mentor of 'Ubaidallah (r. 1533–39), a Shaybānid ruler.
21 *Ziyārat* (a Ṣūfī pilgrimage site) was locally known as *ziyōrat.*
22 Makhdūm-i A'zam authored over 30 books on Islamic theology, philosophy, history, ethics and Ṣūfīsm. His *Mujmū'at al-Rasā'il* (*Collection of Papers*) became a key textbook of Central Asian practical Ṣūfīsm.
23 Svat Soucek, *A History of Inner Asia* (Cambridge: Cambridge University Press, 2000), 158.
24 Yemelianova, *Muslims of Central Asia*, 27.
25 The Afshārīds was an Iranian dynasty that originated from the Turkic tribe of Afshār which was centred on Khorāsān. Its founder was Nādir Shāh (Nader Shah, r. 1736–47).
26 On Shī'ī communities in Central Asia, see Ashirbek Muminov, 'Shiitskiie Kul'turnye Vliianiia na Tsentral'nuiu Aziiu'. In *Ars Islamica*, edited by Mikhail B. Piotrovsky and Alikber K. Alikberov (Moscow: Vostochnaia Literatura, 2016), 647–728.
27 For a fuller discussion of the khānates of Bukhara and Khiva, see Seymur Becker, *Russia's Protectorates in Central Asia: Bukhara and Khiva, 1865–1924* (London: RoutledgeCurzon, 2004).
28 The Kokand's Mings were unrelated to the Ming dynasty in China.
29 On the Kokand Khānate, see Bakhtiyar Babadzhanov, *Kokandskoe Khanstvo. Vlast', Politika, Religiia* (Tokyo-Tashkent: TIAS, 2010).
30 Soucek, *A History of Inner Asia*, 187.
31 Yemelianova, *Muslims of Central Asia*, 13, 43–44.
32 On specifics of Islam among Kazakhs, see Bruce G. Privratsky, *Muslim Turkistan: Kazak Religion and Collective Memory* (Richmond: CurzonPress, 2001).
33 Due to Iran's proximity the Turkmen's Islamic beliefs and practices were influenced by Shī'īsm.
34 During the imperial Russian and the early Soviet period the Kazakhs were referred to as the Kirghiz, and the Kyrgyz as the Qara-Kirghiz (lit. 'Black Kyrgyz').
35 By that time the Kichi Juz also included the Bukey Juz (Inner Juz) which was formed in 1801 in the area between the Ural and Volga rivers by the decree of Tsar Paul I (r. 1796–1801).
36 Yemelianova, *Muslims of Central Asia*, 40.

37 For a detailed account of the Russian conquest of Central Asia, see, for example, Becker, *Russia's Protectorates*; Robert D. Crews, *For Prophet and Tsar: Islam and Empire in Russia and Central Asia* (Cambridge, MA: Harvard University Press, 2006); Naftula A. Khalfin, *Prisoedinenie Srednei Azii k Rossii (60–90-e gody XIX v.)* (Moscow: Nauka, 1965) and Mehmet Saray, 'Russian Conquest of Central Asia'. *Central Asian Survey* 1, nos. 2/3 (1982): 1–30.

38 On the Great Game, see Evgeny Sergeev, *The Great Game, 1856–1907: Russo-British Relations and East Asia* (Washington, DC: Woodrow Wilson Center Press, 2013).

39 For a discussion of the Russian civilizational discourse in Turkestan, see Robert P. Ceraci, *Window on the East: National and Imperial Identities in Late Tsarist Russia* (Ithaca, NY: Cornell University Press, 2008); Svetlana Gorshenina, *L'invention de Asie centrale: Histoire du concept de la Tartarie à l'Eurasie* (Paris: Librarie Droz, 2014); Andreas Kapeller, *The Russian Empire: A Multi-Ethnic History* (London: Routledge, 2001) and Vera Tolz, *Russia's Own Orient: The Politics of Identity and Oriental Studies in the Late Imperial and Early Soviet Periods* (Oxford: Oxford University Press, 2011).

40 On the Andijan revolt of 1898, see Bakhtiyar Babadzhanov, 'Andizhanskoe Vosstanie 1898 goda i "Musul'manskii Vopros" v Turkestane (Vzgliady "Kolonizatorov" i "Kolonizirovannykh"'. In *Musul'mane v Novoi Imperskoi Istorii*, edited by Vladimir O. Bobrovnikov et al. (Moscow: SADRA, 2017), 104–55.

41 The name 'basmach' originates from the Turkish verb 'basmak' which means 'to attack'. Originally it was used by the Russians in relation to Muslim raiders on their positions in Central Asia. On the basmachi movement, see Glenda Fraser, 'Basmachi'. *Central Asian Survey* 6, no. 1 (1987): 1–73.

Chapter Five THE VOLGA-URALS

1 The nature of the events in October 1917 in Petrograd is debated by scholars in Russia and internationally. While some view them as a genuine social revolution which was hijacked by the Bolsheviks, others regard them as a Bolshevik coup d'état.

2 Compared to the Russian Empire, Bolshevik Russia/USSR did not include Finland and the Baltics in the north and the towns of Kars, Kagyzman, Ardahan, Olty and Artvin in the south.

3 Musa Bigi's Islamic reformist stance gained him the reputation of being the 'Luther of Islam'.

4 Galina M. Yemelianova, *Russia and Islam: A Historical Survey* (London: Palgrave, 2002), 92.

5 More on *Olash Orda*, see Chapter 8.

6 Following the collapse of Idel-Ural state, Sadri Maksudi, Zeki Velidi Togan and Ayaz Ishaki fled Russia. Maksudi escaped to Finland. Togan first fled to Central Asia where he headed the anti-Bolshevik 'National Union of Turkistan' which allied with the *basmachis*. In 1923, following the basmachis' defeat, he emigrated to Turkey and subsequently to Germany. Iskhaki first emigrated to Germany and in 1939 left for Turkey where he lived till his death in 1954. See Adile Aida, *Sadri Maksudi Arsal* (Ankara: Kültür Balkanliği, 1991) and Ayaz Ishaki, *Idel-Ural* (London: Society for Central Asian Studies, 1988).

7 The establishment of Bolshevik rule in the Crimea was accompanied by Red Terror which lasted almost three years. During it about 150,000 people were killed and dozens of villages were burnt. Yemelianova, *Russia and Islam*, 108.

8 On Turkestan autonomy, see Chapter 7.

9 In 1931 the journal was renamed *Yana Milli Yol* (New National Road).

10 Sergei Kirov was an influential member of Stalin's inner circle. Between 1921 and 1925 he headed the Communist party of Azerbaijan. From 1926 until 1934 he was in charge of the Communist party of Leningrad (formerly Petrograd/St. Petersburg). His assassination in December 1934 triggered the first wave of Great Purges, during which many Muslim leaders were executed or sent to the Gulag.

11 Aidar Khabutdinov, *Istoriia Orenburgskogo Magometanskogo Dukhovnogo Sobraniia* (Nizhny Novgorod: Medina, 2010), 112; Vladislav Romanenko, *Sotrudnichestvo Sovetskoi Diplomatii i Musul'manskogo Dukhvenstva v Dvatsatye Gody XX veka* (Nizhny Novgorod: Medina, 2005), 66–67.

12 Yemelianova, *Russia and Islam*, 106; see also Chapter 9.

13 Il'nur Minnullin, *Politika Sovetskogo Gosudarstva v Otnoshenii k Musul'manskomu Dukhovenstvu v Tatarstane v 1920–1930-e Gody*. PhD Dissertation (Kazan: Institute of History, 2003).

14 Many Communists in the Middle East were charged with espionage on behalf of Britain or links with the Zionists or the Trotskyists and executed. Galina M. Yemelianova, 'The National Identity of the Volga Tatars at the Turn of the 19th Century: Tatarism, Turkism and Islam'. *Central Asian Survey* 16, no. 4 (1997): 43–572.

15 During this war, which played a key role in the defeat of Nazism, over 27 million Soviet people from different ethnonational groups lost their lives.

16 Alexei Malashenko, *Islamskoe Vozrozhdenie v Sovremennoi Rossii* (Moscow: Carnegie Endowment, 1998), 57.

17 Here and elsewhere, I use the more commonly known Russian abbreviation –DUMES, which stands for *Dukhovnoe Upravlenie Musul'man Evropeiskoi* [*chasti Rossii* – GY] *i Sibiri*, rather than its English abbreviation – SDMES (Spiritual Directorate of Muslims of the European [part of Russia – GY] and Siberia).

18 Both the CARC and the CRA were infiltrated by the security services and were headed by Ivan Poliansky (in office 1944–57), Alexei Puzin (in office 1957–65) and Vladimir Kuroedov (in office 1965–93). For the analysis of the CARC and CRA's documents and activities, see Yaacov Ro'i, *Islam in the Soviet Union: From the Second World War to Gorbachev* (London: Hurst, 2000) and Mark Saroyan and Edward Walker, eds, *Minorities, Mullahs and Modernity: Reshaping Community in the Former Soviet Union* (Berkeley: University of California Press, 1997).

19 Yemelianova, *Russia and Islam*, 128.

20 Following muftī Gabdrahman Rasulev's death in 1950 the Ufa muftīate was headed by muftīs Shakir Khiyaletdinov (in office 1951–74), Gabdel'baryi Isaev (in office 1975–80) and Talgat Tadzhuddinov (Tadzhuddin, in office 1980–present).

21 In the 1950s the DUMES's international status was weakened as a result of the increased foreign engagement of Moscow-based official Muslim clergy.

22 The author's interview with Marat Safarov, a historian of the Muslim community of Moscow, 4 September 2016, Moscow.

23 On SADUM, see Chapter 8.

24 On DUMZ, see Chapter 7.

25 For a detailed discussion of the 'Islamic revival' in the late Soviet and early post-Soviet periods, see Yemelianova (2010).

26 Here and elsewhere, I use the more commonly known Russian abbreviation – DUMES, which stands for *Dukhovnoe Upravlenie Musul'man Evropeiskoi* [*chasti Rossii* – GY] *i Sibiri*, rather than its English abbreviation – SDMES (Spiritual Directorate of Muslims of the European [part of Russia – GY] and Siberia).

27 On the detailed biography of Talgat Tadzhuddin, see Ayslu B. Yunusova, *33 Goda Sluzheniia Istine i Otechestvu: Verkhovnyi Muftii Rossii* (Ufa: GUP UPK, 2013). Yunusova (2013).

28 Renat Bekkin, *People of Reliable Loyalty … Muftiates and the State in Modern Russia*. PhD Dissertation (Stockholm: Elanders, 2020), 25.

29 All Soviet children and young people were automatically affiliated to the ideologically driven scout-like organisations of *Little Octobrists* (7- to 9-year-olds), *Young Pioneers* (10- to 14-year-olds) and *Komsomol* (14- to 28-year-olds). *Komsomol* was an abbreviation for All-Russian Leninist Young League which acted as a de facto subdivision of the Communist Party.

30 In 1991 DUM SK moved from Buinaksk to Makhachkala.

Chapter Six THE NORTH CAUCASUS

1 Special relations between Russian and Kabardian ruling elites were forged in 1557 and cemented in 1560 by the marriage of Ivan the Terrible to the daughter of the Kabardian prince Temriuk Indarko. Walter Richmond, *The Northwest Caucasus: Past, Present, Future* (London: Routledge, 2008), 42.

2 Dagestanis is a collective term for the multi-ethnic inhabitants of Dagestan, which is the toponym deriving from the combination of the Turkic word 'dag' (mountain) and the Persian word 'stan' (locality).

3 On the linguistic history of the Caucasus, see John Colarusso, 'Peoples, Languages and Lore'. In *The Routledge Handbook of the Caucasus*, edited by Galina M. Yemelianova and Laurence Broers (London: Routledge, 2020), 32–51.

4 On Shamīl's imāmate, see Chapter 3.

5 Richmond, *The Northwest Caucasus*, 28, 30.

6 Timothy K. Blauvelt, 'The Caucasus in the Russian Empire'. In *The Routledge Handbook of the Caucasus*, 118–19.

7 Amir R. Navruzov, 'Gazeta "Jaridat Dagistan" (1913–1918) – unikal'nyi obrazets araboiazychoi publitsistiki nachala XX veka'. *Islamovedenie* 2 (2009): 92–106.

8 Akhmet Yarlykapov, 'Metody obucheniia i propaganda idei dzadidizma v Severokavkazskikh medrese v deiatel'nosti A. Akaeva (nach. XX v.)'. In *Abu Sufian Akaev. Epokha, zhizn', deiatel'nost': sbornik statei, perevodov i materialov*, edited by Gasan M.-R. Orazaev (Makhachkala: Dagestanskoe Knizhnoe Izdatel'stvo, 2012), 62.

9 Shamil Shikhaliev, 'Musul'manskoe reformatorstvo v Dagestane (1900–1930 gg.)'. *Gosudarstvo, Religiia, Tserkov' v Rossii i za Rubezhom* 3, no. 35 (2017): 138.

10 The All-Russia Party of Progress (*Partiia Progressistov*, 1912–17) represented big business. Politically, it was of liberal and centrist orientation and it was close to the Kadets.

11 In May 1921 the Bolsheviks renamed Dagestan's city of Petrovsk-Port as Makhachkaka in honour of 'Makhach'.

12 On divisions at the First and Second All-Russia Muslim Congresses, see Chapter 5.

13 Sheikh Ḥasan Ḥilmī al-Qaḥī was a follower of sheikh Maḥmud al-Almānī who opposed Shamīl's ghazawāt. See Chapter 3.

14 Kaflan Khanbabaev, 'Islam and Islamic Radicalism in Dagestan'. In *Radical Islam in the Former Soviet Union*, edited by Galina M. Yemelianova (London: Routledge, 2010), 89.

15 Gadzhikurban Kakagasanov and Adilgerei Gazhiev, *Akushinsky-Sheikh-ul-Islam Dagestana, Patriot i Mirotvorets* (Makhachkala: Yupiter, 1998), 10.

16 Vahit Akaev, *Sufiiskaia Kul'tura na Severnom Kavkaze* (Grozny: Knizhnoe Izdatel'stvom, 2011), 109.

17 General Anton Denikin led the 270,000-strong Armed Forces of Southern Russia (*Vooruzhennye Sily Yuga Rossii*, 1919–20) which consisted of his Volunteer Army and the Cossack-dominated All-Great Don Army (*Vsevelikoe Voisko Donskoe*). Denikin's headquarters were in the city of Taganrog in south-western Russia. On the Russian White movement, see Oleg G. Goncharenko, *Tainy Belogo Dvizheniia: Poteri i Porazheniia 1918–1922* (Moscow: Veche, 2004).

18 On the Democratic Republics of Azerbaijan, Armenia and Georgia, which existed in the southern Caucasus between 1918 and 1921, see Arsène Saparov, 'Between the Russian Empire and the USSR: The independence of Transcaucasia as a socio-political transformation'. In *The Routledge Handbook of the Caucasus*, 121–35.

19 According to other accounts, it was Uzun-ḥajjee's successor sheikh Darvīsh Muḥammad who accepted Bolshevik rule.

20 In 1924, the Mountain Autonomous Soviet Socialist Republic was disbanded and its territory was divided between the North-Ossetian, Chechen and Ingush oblasts, the Sunzhen Cossack district and the city of Vladikavkaz (as an independent administrative unit) of Soviet Russia.

21 In the mid-1920s 'Alī-ḥajjee Akushinsky turned against the Bolsheviks in response to their encroaching on Dagestani *waqfs* and sharī'ah courts. Akushinsky's religious authority persisted

after his death in 1931. Until the present his grave in the village of Akusha has been a popular *ziyārat* (Ṣūfī pilgrimage site).

22 OGPU stands for *Ob'edinennoe Gosudarstvennoe Politicheskoe Upravlenie*, in Russian.

23 Khadzhi Murat Donogo, *Najmuddin Gotsinsky* (Makhachkala: IAE DNTs, 2011), 385.

24 Iosif Stalin, 'Vystuplenie na S'ezde Narodov Dagestana'. *Sochinenia*, vol. 4 (Moscow: OGIZ, 1947), 396–97.

25 On the relationship between the Bolshevik state and Ṣūfī leaders, see Imanutdin Sulaev, *Musul'manskoe Dukhovenstvo i Sovetskaia Vlast: Bor'ba i Sotrudnichestvo* (Makhachkala: Institut Istorii, 2004).

26 Vladimir O. Bobrovnikov, *Musul'mane Severnogo Kavkaza: Obychai, Pravo, Nasilie* (Moscow: Vostochnaia Literatura RAN, 2002), 220; Alexei Malashenko, *Islamskoe Vozrozhdenie v Sovremennoi Rossii* (Moscow: Carnegie Endowment, 1998), 49.

27 Among those were, for example, the Kumyk-language *Musāwāt* (Equality), *Tāng Cholpān* (Morning Star), *Īshchī Khalk* (Working People) and the Lak-language *Īlchī* (Bulletin), and *Channah Tsuku* (Morning Star).

28 Dibirov was executed by OGPU, while Kaiaev and Akaev were sent to a Gulag.

29 In the 1920s, Soviet ethnologists introduced the ethnonyms 'Cherkess' and 'Adygei' to describe the Adyghe of Karachaevo-Cherkessia and Adygea, respectively.

30 On Soviet nationality policy, see Jeremy Smith, *Red Nations: The Nationalities Experience in and after the USSR* (Cambridge: Cambridge University Press, 2013).

31 More on *Oktobrist*, Young Pioneers and Komsomol organizations, see Chapter 5.

32 In the early 1930s, 961 mullahs out of a total of 1,468, 961, and 552 qāḍīs out of a total of 632 refused to perform their religious duties. Khanbabaev, 'Islam and Islamic Radicalism in Dagestan', 89.

33 Ibid.

34 NKVD stood for *Narodnyi Komissariat Vnutrennikh Del* (1934–46); KGB was an abbreviation of *Komitet Gosudarstvennoi Bezonasnosti* (1954–91).

35 Among perceived mutasheikhs (*mutashayyikhūn*) was, for example, the Cyprus-based Naqshbandī sheikh Nāẓim al-Ḥaqqānī (1922–2008), who derived his *silsilah* (a chain of transmission) from the Dagestani sheikh 'Abdurahman al-Sughurī (1792–1882). Galina M. Yemelianova, 'Transnational Islam versus Ethnic Islam in Eastern Europe: The Role of Mass Media'. In *Muslim Networks and Transnational Communities in and across Europe*, edited by Stefano Allievi and Jorgen Nielsen (Leiden: Brill, 2003), 274.

36 Richmond, *The Northwest Caucasus*, 114; Jeremy Smith, 'The Soviet Caucasus, 1920–91: Resistance and Accommodation'. In *The Routledge Handbook of the Caucasus*, 136–53.

37 On the numbers of representatives of different ethnic groups from the North Caucasus who fought in the Soviet Army during the Great Patriotic War, see Svetlana I. Akkieva, *Sotsiokul'turnye Transformatsii Deportirovannykh Narodov Severnogo Kavkaza v 1940–1990-e Gody* (Nal'chik: IGI KBNTs RAN, 2019).

38 Outside the North Caucasus other deportees included Meskhetian Turks, Crimean Tatars, Volga Germans, Kurds, Greeks and Bulgarians.

39 Isabelle Kreindler, 'The Soviet Deported Nationalities: A Summary and Update'. *Soviet Studies* 38, no. 3 (1986): 387.

40 On ethno-national mobilization in post-Soviet Caucasus, see Chapter 11.

41 Yaacov Ro'i, *Islam in the Soviet Union: From the Second World War to Gorbachev* (London: Hurst, 2000), 409; Alexandre Bennigsen and S. Enders Wimbush, *Mystics and Commissars: Sufism in the Soviet Union* (London: Hurst, 1985), 75.

42 Khanbabaev, 'Islam and Islamic Radicalism in Dagestan', 89.

43 Ro'i, *Islam in the Soviet Union*, 116.

44 Khanbabaev, 'Islam and Islamic Radicalism in Dagestan', 94, 107.

45 Interview with Muhammad-Rasul Mugumayev, 18 June 1999, Makhachkala.

46 More on the movement of 'young imāms', see Chapter 5.

47 In June 1991, the All-National Congress of the Chechen People under the leadership of General Dudayev established the Chechen Republic, separate from Ingushetia. See Chapter 11.

48 Shafig Pshikachev was educated at the Mir-i Arab madrasah in Bukhara, the Islamic University in Amman (Jordan) and the Institute of *al-Da'wah al-Islāmīyyah* in Damascus. Since 2004 he has headed the Moscow-based pro-government 'International Islamic Mission' and acted as the official representative of the Coordinating Centre of Muslims of the North Caucasus (KTsM SK, in Russian) in Moscow.

49 Ismail-ḥajjee Berdiyev was educated in the Mir-i Arab madrasah and the Islamic Institute in Tashkent. Between 1991 and 2003 he was muftī of Karachaevo-Cherkessia and Stavropol' krai. Since 2003 he has headed the KTsM SK.

50 In late Soviet and post-Soviet Eurasia Salafīs were incorrectly termed Waḥḥābīs.

51 Both Akhmad-qāḍī Akhtayev and Bagauddin Kebedov commanded high Islamic authority among some Avar Muslim youth. Their growing popularity was a cause for concern among Dagestani political and religious officials. Akhtayev's sudden death at the age of 58 prompted speculations about his possible poisoning. More on Akhmad-qāḍī Akhtayev and Bagauddin Kebedov, see Chapter 11.

52 Dmitrii Makarov and Rafik Mukhametshin, 'Official and Unofficial Islam'. In *Islam in Post-Soviet Russia: Public and Private Faces*, edited by Hilary Pilkington and Galina M. Yemelianova (London: RoutledgeCurzon, 2003), 150.

53 Alexander Ignatenko, *Islam i Politika* (Moscow: Institute of Religion and Politics, 2004), 93.

54 For example, the manuscript fund of the Centre of Oriental Studies at the Makhachkala-based Dagestani branch of the Russian Academy of Sciences contains over 3,900 manuscripts authored by renowned Middle Eastern and Dagestani 'ulamā' over a period of more than 900 years. Khanbabaev, 'Islam and Islamic Radicalism in Dagestan', 106.

Chapter Seven THE SOUTH CAUCASUS

1 Michael Chamberlain, *Chislennost' naseleniia SSSR na 17 yanvaria 1939* (Moscow: Gosplanizdat, 1941).

2 For the pre-Soviet period, the ethnonyms 'Azeri' and 'Azerbaijani' are used interchangeably. Following the establishment of the Azerbaijan Soviet Socialist Republic (AzSSR), 'Azerbaijani' is used in relation to AzSSR's Azeris. It is worth noting that the imperial Russian authorities referred to Russia's Azeris as 'Tatars', 'Shirwan Tatars', 'Russian Turks', 'Azerbaijani Turks' or just 'Muslims.' Timothy K. Blauvelt, 'The Caucasus in the Russian Empire'. In *The Routledge Handbook of the Caucasus*, edited by Galina M. Yemelianova and Laurence Broers (London: Routledge, 2020), 110.

3 Russia's annexation of Kartli-Kakheti was preceded by the 1783 Treaty of Georgievsk which established the Russian protectorate over it. The Treaty was signed by the ruler of Kartli-Kakheti, Erekle II (Heraclius II, r. 1762–98), who was faced with persistent threats of Iranian and Ottoman aggression.

4 Rashad Guseinov, 'Istoriia islamskikh institutov v Azerbaidjane'. *Kavkaz i Globalizatsiia* 1, no. 2 (2014): 87.

5 In Azerbaijan, mullahs were referred to as 'mollahs'.

6 Anastasiya Ganich, ed., *Dukhovnye Pravleniia Musul'man Zakavkaz'ia v Rossiiskoi Imperii: XIX-Nachalo XX v.* (Moscow: Mardzhani, 2013), 9.

7 Guseinov, 'Istoriia islamskikh institutov', 89.

8 Tadeusz Swietochowski, *Russia and Azerbaijan: A Borderland in Transition* (New York: Columbia University Press, 1985), 33.

9 Rufat Sattarov, 'Islamic Revival and Islamic Activism in post-Soviet Azerbaijan'. In *Radical Islam in the Former Soviet Union*, edited by Galina M. Yemelianova (London: Routledge, 2010), 152.

10 Among Gummet's leaders were Mammad Emin Rasulzadeh (1884–1955), Sultan Mejid ogly Efendiyev (1887–1938), Asadulla Jawad ogly Akhundov (1873–1927), Mohammad Gasan Jafarquli ogly Gadzhinsly (1875–1931) and Adjar Melikov (1889–1921). Gummet also had branches in Dzhul'fa (Julfa), Elizabethpol, Nakhchivan, Shusha and Shemakhi. On Gummet and other left-wing organizations in the South Caucasus in the early twentieth century, see Irada S. Bagirova, *Politicheskie Partii i Organizatsii Azerbaidzhana v Nachale XX veka* (Baku: Elm, 1997).

11 For a detailed account of Transcaucasia's political transformation during the Russian Civil War, see Arsène Saparov, 'Between the Russian Empire and the USSR: The Independence of Transcaucasia as a Socio-political Transformation'. In *The Routledge Handbook of the Caucasus*, edited by Galina M. Yemelianova and Laurence Broers (London: Routledge, 2020), 121–35.

12 Swietochowski, *Russia and Azerbaijan*, 133.

13 On the ADR's religious politics, see Sevinj I. Aliyeva, 'Azerbaidzhanskaia Demokraticheskaia Respublika i Gorskaia Respublica: Proekty Obrazovaniia Edinogo Gosudarstva'. *Caucasus Survey* 3, no. 1 (2015): 58–75.

14 Arif Yunusov, *Islam v Azerbaidzhane* (Baku: Zaman, 2004), 148–49.

15 Among the Shī'a, Shakhsei-Vakhsei processions were traditionally held on *'Āshūrā'* – the tenth day of the month of Muḥarram in commemoration of the death on that day of imām Ḥuseyn.

16 It is believed that this mosque was built on the burial place of the sister of the eighth Shī'ī imām, 'Alī al-Riḍā (766–818).

17 Sattarov, 'Islamic Revival', 153–54.

18 Yunusov, *Islam v Azerbaidzhane*, 151.

19 Subsequently, the Soviet invasion of Iran in 1941 paved the way for the creation in northern Iran of the pro-Moscow Azerbaijani Democratic Government (1945–46).

20 In 1944 the Meskhetian Turks, who were historically linked to Turkey, were 'preventively' deported from Georgia's Meskheti, Javakheti and Adjara regions to Central Asia.

21 Yaacov Ro'i, *Islam in the Soviet Union: From the Second World War to Gorbachev* (London: Hurst, 2000), 105.

22 Guseinov, 'Istoriia islamskikh institutov', 91.

23 For example, in 1957 there were only 50 Azerbaijani ḥajjees to Karbala and 28 hajjees to Meshed. Ro'i, *Islam in the Soviet Union*, 173.

24 Yunusov, *Islam v Azerbaidzhane*, 158.

25 Dmitrii Yu. Arapov, *Islam i Sovetskoe Gosudarstvo (1944–1991): Sbornik Dokumentov*, vol. 3 (Moscow: Mardzhani, 2011), 67.

26 Ro'i, *Islam in the Soviet Union*, 381.

27 *Marthiahs* were mourning songs which were traditionally performed by the Shī'ah during *'Āshūrā'*.

28 Among the most visited were the Holy site of Bibi Heybar near Baku; the Imām-zadeh (Goy-Imām) mausoleum near Kirovobad (Ganja); the pīrs of Rahim-Hanim, Sayyid, Ataga and Ali Aiagy in Absheron peninsular; pīrs of Askhab-i Kahf, Imām-zadeh, Ibrahim-efendi and Nusnus in Nakhchivan ASSR; pīrs of Sayyid Ahmed, Jamala, Sheikh Zahid, Babagil, Gyzylagach and Hanega in Lankaran-Masalli zone; pīrs of Pirsaat, Dadagiunash, Veis-Baba, Hajjee-Baba, Goy-Imām and Imām-zadeh in central Azerbaijan; pīrs of Soltan-halach and Aglib-Baba in the north-east; and pīrs of Aldada, Hajjee-efendi, Babaratma and Mamed-efendi in the north-west of the country. Yunusov, *Islam v Azerbaidzhane*, 175–76; Bayram Balci, *Islam in Central Asia and the Caucasus since the Fall of the Soviet Union* (London: Hurst, 2018), 31–32.

29 Ro'i, *Islam in the Soviet Union*, 375.

30 Mawlānā Rūmī (1207–1273) was an influential Islamic scholar, Ṣūfī mystic and poet from Greater Khorāsān.

31 Yunusov, *Islam v Azerbaidzhane*, 167.

32 Ibid., 171.

33 Tom Trier and Andrei Khanzhin, eds, *The Meskhetian Turks at a Crossroads: Integration, Repatriation or Resettlement?* (New Brunswick, NJ: Transaction, 2007), 2–4.

34 In the post-Soviet period the main articulator of the Meskhetian Turks' national concerns has been *Vatan* (Homeland), an organization established in 1990 in Moscow under the leadership of Yusuf Sarvarov. It subscribes to the Turkic identity of Meskhetian Turks in opposition to their Georgian identity promoted by the Meskhetian organization *Khsna* (Salvation) under the leadership of Khalil Umarov (Gozalishvili).

35 Ruslan Baramidze, *Islam i ego Osobennosti v Adzharii* (Berlin: Heinrich Böl Stiftung, 2005), https://ge.boell.org/en/2005/01/16/islam-i-ego-osobennosti-v-adzharii.

36 On the role of Turkey in the Islamic dynamic of post-Soviet Azerbaijan, see Chapter 11.

37 For a detailed analysis of the Armenia–Azerbaijan conflict over Nagorno-Karabakh, see Laurence Broers, *Armenia and Azerbaijan: Anatomy of a Rivalry* (Edinburgh: Edinburgh University Press, 2019).

38 The Azerbaijani religious leaders' passivity during the early stages of the Nagorno-Karabakh conflict contrasted with the religious and political activism of Armenian Catholicos Vazgen I (in office 1955–94). Yunusov, *Islam v Azerbaidzhane*, 181.

39 In November 2020, following two months of intensive fighting, the Azerbaijani armed forces restored their control over most of Azerbaijan's territory and Moscow returned to the region as the sole security guarantor by deploying two thousand peacekeepers along the conflict's front lines for a period of five years.

40 Abdul Abdulov was a former criminal who turned to Islam in prison in repentance for his crimes. Sattarov, 'Islamic Revival', 206.

41 Ibid., 162–63.

42 Here and afterwards, the problematic term 'ethnic Muslims' denotes various peoples of historically Muslim regions of the USSR and it is equally applied to atheists, secularists and practising Muslims.

43 Sattarov, 'Islamic Revival', 156; Arapov, *Islam i Sovetskoe Gosudarstvo*, 69.

44 Yunusov, *Islam v Azerbaidzhane*, 172, 174.

Chapter Eight CENTRAL ASIA AND KAZAKHSTAN

1 In the USSR, the region was referred to as Middle Asia and Kazakhstan (*Sredniaia Aziia i Kazakhstan*). See introduction.

2 Thus, in the late 1930s, even after a notable drop in the region's population due to the casualties of the Russian Civil War, hunger, the exodus abroad and Stalinist collectivization and purges, Central Asia's population numbered over 20 million. According to the 1939 census, the population of Kazakhstan was 9.3 million; of Uzbekistan 8 million; of Kyrgyzstan 2 million; of Tajikistan 2 million; and of Turkmenistan of 1.5 million. Michael Chamberlain, *Chislennost' naseleniia naseleniia SSSR na 17 yanvaria 1939* (Moscow: Gosplanizdat, 1941).

3 More on *hujūm*, see Chapter 7 and Marianne Kamp, *The New Woman in Uzbekistan: Islam, Modernity, and Unveiling under Communism* (Seattle, WA: University of Washington Press, 2006).

4 In 1914, during the First World War, in which Russia confronted Germany, St. Petersburg was renamed Petrograd.

5 On Central Asian Muslim reformers, see Chapter 4.

6 On the Kokand Autonomy, see Paul Bergne, 'The Kokand Autonomy 1917–1918'. In *Central Asia: Aspects of Transition*, edited by Tom Everett-Heath (London: Psychology Press, 2003), 30–44.

7 During the Second World War, Mustafa Chokay collaborated with the Germans who entrusted him to lead the so-called 'Turkestan Legion' which was designated for Germany's advance into Central Asia. The 'Legion' included Soviet military prisoners of Turkic descent who were held in German concentration camps.

8 Seymur Becker, *Russia's Protectorates in Central Asia: Bukhara and Khiva, 1865–1924* (London: RoutledgeCurzon, 2004), 304.

9 In August 1931 Ibrahim Bek was executed by the Bolsheviks in Tashkent.

10 Adeeb Khalid, *Islam after Communism: Religion and Politics in Central Asia* (Berkeley: University of California Press, 2007), 57.

11 Becker, *Russia's Protectorates*, 301.

12 In the late imperial Russian and the early Soviet periods, present-day Kazakhs were externally referred to as 'Kyrgyz' and the modern Kyrgyz as 'Qara-Kyrgyz' ('Black Kyrgyz').

13 Galina M. Yemelianova, *Muslims of Central Asia: An Introduction* (Edinburgh: Edinburgh University Press, 2019), 62.

14 On asharshylyk, see Robert Kindler, *Stalin's Nomads: Power and Famine in Kazakhstan* (Pittsburgh: Pittsburgh University Press, 2018).

15 The League of Militant Godless was officially dissolved in 1947.

16 The SADUM's first residence was in Eshon Bobokhon's private house in the *mahalla* (neighbourhood community) of Khazret-i Imām. The house, which in 1928 was confiscated by the Bolsheviks, was returned to the Bobokhon family.

17 Yaacov Ro'i, *Islam in the Soviet Union: From the Second World War to Gorbachev* (London: Hurst, 2000), 279.

18 Roman A. Silantiev, *Musul'manskaia Diplomatiia v Rossii: Istoriia i Sovremennost'* (Moscow: Rema, 2009), 166.

19 In Tashkent, between 1956 and 1961, there also functioned the Barakhon madrasah.

20 The journal was published in Russian, Uzbek, Persian, Arabic, English and French.

21 Biacheslav A. Akhmadullin, 'Osobennosti Sovetskoi Dvukhurovnevoi Podgotovki Islamskikh Kadrov'. *Islam v Sovremennom Mire* 11, no. 2 (2015): 158.

22 Shami Domullo refuted Central Asian Sūfīsm as bid'ah and advocated the Central Asians' return to the Islam of Prophet Muḥammad and the Four Righteous Caliphs. He disseminated his teaching through the underground group *Ahl-i Ḥadīth* (People of Ḥadīth). Yemelianova, *Muslims of Central Asia*, 66.

23 Ro'i, *Islam in the Soviet Union*, 360–62.

24 Among the most popular mazārs of regional importance were Takht-i Sulayman (Solomon's Throne) in Osh, Kyrgyzstan; the Baha al-Dīn mausoleum in Bukhara; the Shoh-i Zinda in Samarqand; the Shoh-i Mardon in Ferghana oblast'; the Sultan-Baba in the Karakalpak ASSR of Uzbekistan; and the tomb of Aḥmad Yasawī in Turkistan in Kazakhstan.

25 Ro'i, *Islam in the Soviet Union*, 365–72.

26 The term 'ishān' or 'ishōn' derives from the Persian plural meaning 'they' and was used as a form of respect. In Central Asia ishānism was synonymous with Ṣūfīsm.

27 Ro'i, *Islam in the Soviet Union*, 395.

28 From 1957 Ismā'īlīs worldwide have been subordinated to Aghā Khān IV (Prince Shān Karim al-Husseini, b. 1936), a grandson of Aghā III (Sir Sulṭān Magomed Shāh). See Chapter 12.

29 Ashirbek Muminov, 'Shiitskiie Kul'turnye Vliianiia na Tsentral'nuiu Aziiu'. In *Ars Islamica*, edited by Mikhail B. Piotrovsky and Alikber K. Alikberov (Moscow: Vostochnaia Literatura, 2016), 647–728.

30 On Hindustoniy's life, thinking and his pupils, see Vitaly V. Naumkin, *Radical Islam in Central Asia: Between Pen and Rifle* (Lanham, MD: Rowman & Littlefield, 2005).

31 On Islamists in the Ferghana valley in the post-Soviet period, see Chapter 12.

Chapter Nine BELARUS, UKRAINE AND LITHUANIA

1 I have not included Estonia and Latvia in the discussion due to the very small size of their Muslim communities. For an account of Islam and Muslim communities across the Baltic, see Harry Norris, *Islam in the Baltic: Europe's Early Muslim Community* (London: I.B. Tauris, 2009).

2 Thus, in the 2010s, in Belarus there were around 20,000 Muslims (Tatars, Azerbaijanis, Turkmen and some others) who made up under 0.2 per cent of the total population; in Ukraine around 250,000 Muslims (Tatars, Azerbaijanis, Arabs and others) who accounted for around 0.8 per cent of the population; and in Lithuania under 3,000 Muslims (Tatars, Lithuanians and others), corresponding to under 0.15 per cent of the population. Egdūnas Račius, *Muslims in Eastern Europe* (Edinburgh: Edinburgh University Press, 2018), 155.

3 On Gengizid Khānates, see Chapter 2.

4 In 1791 the Polish–Lithuanian Commonwealth was renamed the Commonwealth of Poland.

5 Egdūnas Račius, 'Lithuania'. In *Islamic Leadership in the European Lands of the Former Ottoman and Russian Empires: Legacy, Challenges and Change*, edited by Egdūnas Račius and Antonina (Leiden: Brill, 2017), 274.

6 Ibid., 275.

7 Aleksandr A. Kovalenya et al. 2004, *Velikaia Otechestvennaia Voina Sovetskogo Naroda* (Minsk: BGU, 2004), 99; Valentin I. Kravchenko and Petr P. Panchenko, *Ukraina vo Vtoroi Mirovoi Voine (1939–1945)* (Donetsk: TsPA, 1998), 75.

8 Agata S. Nalborczyk, 'Poland'. In *Islamic Leadership in the European Lands*, 302.

9 In June 1944 muftī Szynkiewicz fled to Germany where he stayed until the end of the war. Subsequently, he moved to Egypt and in 1956 to the United States.

10 On DUMES, see Chapter 10.

11 Račius, 'Lithuania', 279.

12 *Demoscop weekly*, nos. 859–60, 18–20 May 2020, http://www.demoscope.ru/weekly/ssp/sng_nac_79.php. Accessed 9 June 2020.

13 Since the presidential elections in August 2020 the legitimacy of Lukashenko's continuous rule has been challenged by opposition forces under the leadership of Sviatlana Tikhanovskaya (b. 1982).

14 MRS stands for *Musul'manskoe Religioznoe Soobshchestvo*, in Russian.

15 Daša Slabčanka, 'Belarus'. In *Islamic Leadership in the European Lands*, 264, 266.

16 Ibid., 262.

17 See, for example, Ibn Taymīyyah's seminal work *Al-Aqīdah al-Wasaṭīyyah*. On the meaning of al-Wasaṭīyyah in Islam, see Mohammad H. Kamali, *The Middle Path of Moderation in Islam: The Qur'anic Principle of Wasatiyyah* (Oxford: Oxford University Press, 2015).

18 The Tatar international organization – 'The World Congress of Tatars' (WCT) – was established at the First World Congress of Tatars, which was convened in June 1992 in Kazan with the aim of Tatars' national, cultural and spiritual consolidation worldwide.

19 Slabčanka, 'Belarus', 265, 270.

20 *Demoscop weekly*, nos. 859–60, 18–20 May 2020, http://www.demoscope.ru/weekly/ssp/sng_nac_79.php. Accessed 9 June 2020.

21 These figures represent an average of various estimates due to the lack of reliable data on the number of Ukraine's Muslims, which includes a considerable number of unaccounted for illegal Muslim immigrants.

22 Račius, *Muslims in Eastern Europe*, 62–63.

23 The muftīate's official name is the Centralized Religious Organization – The Spiritual Directorate of Muslims of the Crimea and Sevastopol.

24 Emirali Ablayev, a Crimean Tatar, was born in the Tashkent *oblast'* of Uzbekistan. In 1988 he and his family returned to the Crimea. He has a limited Islamic education based on his one-year-long studies at a Turkish madrasah.

25 On SMR, see Chapter 10.

26 Račius, *Muslims in Eastern Europe*, 63.

27 Ibid., 65.

28 Originally, the DUMU united Arab and other Muslim students who had come to study in Ukraine. In the 1970s, sheikh Tamīm acquired a degree in Technical studies before switching to Islamic studies.

29 Mykhaylo Yakubovych, Vitalii Shchepanskyi and Ayder Bulatov, 'Ukraine'. In *Islamic Leadership in the European Lands*, 320.

30 Ibid., 323.

31 Rais Suleymanov, 'Za chto voiuiut v Donbasse opolchentsy iz Tatarstana'. *Nezavisimaya Gazeta*, 25 March 2015.

32 Yakubovych, Shchepanskyi and Bulatov, 'Ukraine', 322.

33 Other presidents of Al-Rāid were Farūq 'Ashūr (in office 2000–5), Ismā'īl Qāḍī (in office 2005–12) and Vasiil Mareei (in office 2013–16). Since 2017, Al-Rāid has been headed by Seyran Arifov.

34 See more in Munster, Anna. *The Changing Face of Islam in post-Soviet Ukraine: A Study of Arraid in the Light of Social Movement Theory*. PhD Thesis. London: SOAS, 2011.

35 On Hizmet activities in post-Soviet Eurasia, see Bayram Balci, *Missionnaires de l'Islam en Asie central, les écoles turques de Fethullah Gűlen* (Paris: Maisonneuvre et Larose y Institut français d'etudes anatoliennes, 2003) and Bayram Balci, *The Gűlen Movement and Turkish Soft Power* (Washington, DC: Carnegie Endowment for International Peace, 2014), https://carnegieendowment.org/2014/02/04/g-len-movement-and-turkish-soft-power-pub-54430.

36 Following Erdoğan's visit to Kiev in February 2020, Ukraine's President Volodymyr Zelensky (in office 2019–) issued an official ban on the Gűlenist schools in the country in 'appreciation' of Ankara's support for the territorial integrity of Ukraine.

37 By the 1980s, HT, which emphasizes its peaceful and non-violent tactics, evolved into a truly international organization with members in the Middle East, North Africa, the Indian subcontinent, Indonesia, as well as the United States, Western Europe and Australia. In the late 1980s, during the Gorbachevian perestroika, HT made inroads in Central Asia and some other Muslim-dominated parts of the USSR. On HT in Central Asia, see Chapter 12.

38 The organization Al-Takfīr wa al-Ḥijrah was founded in the 1960s in Egypt by Shukrī Muṣṭafā (1942–1978), a former member of the Muslim Brotherhood. Takfīrīs believe that many parts of the Muslim world have reverted to a state of *jāhilīyyah* (ignorance) and need to be returned to Islam either by peaceful means or by force. Importantly, they apply the concept of takfīr (excommunication) to those Muslims whom they accuse of deviation from true Islam.

39 Račius, *Muslims in Eastern Europe*, 64.

40 *Naselenie SSSR: Po dannym vsesoiuznoi perepisi naseleniia 1989 g* (Moscow: Finansy i Statistika, 1989).

41 According to the 1995 Religious Law, Lithuania's other traditional religions are Roman Catholicism (dominant), Orthodox Christianity, Evangelical Lutherans, Evangelical Reformed, Greek Catholicism, Old Believers, Judaism and Karaites.

42 Račius, *Muslims in Eastern Europe*, 69.

43 Račius, 'Lithuania', 287.

44 Muftī Romualdas Krinickis was educated in a madrasah in Ufa (Bashkortostan, Russia) and Islamic college in Istanbul, while muftī Romas Jakubauskas received his training in an Islamic college in Lebanon.

45 Two mosques are located in the district of Vilnius, one in Raiziai and another one in the district of Alytus. *Islamas vigiems*, http://en.islamasvisiems.lt/mosques-islamic-centres-and-tourist-place. Accessed 18 January 2021.

46 Račius, 'Lithuania', 282.

47 Muftī Ramadan Yaqoob does not have any Islamic education.

48 The very low religious observance among Lithuania's Muslims has been congruent with that in the other two Baltic states of Estonia and Latvia. For an overview of Muslim minorities in the Baltics, see Ingvar Svanberg and David Westerlund, eds, *Muslim Minorities in the Baltic Sea Region* (Leiden: Brill, 2016).

49 Račius, 'Lithuania', 289.

50 For a detailed discussion of Muslims' 'churchification' in post-communist Eastern Europe, see Egdūnas Račius, *Islam in Post-Communist Eastern Europe: Between Churchification and Securitization* (Leiden: Brill, 2020).

Chapter Ten EUROPEAN RUSSIA

1 In 1994, DUMES was renamed TsDUM, which stands for *Tsentral'noe Dukhovnoe Upravlenie Musul'man* (Central Spiritual Directorate of Muslims).

2 Muftī Talgat Tadzhuddinov/Tadzhuddin is a native of Kazan. He graduated from Mir-i Arab madrasah in Bukhara and al-Azhar University (Faculty of Islamic Theology) in Cairo. More on Tadzhuddinov, see Chapter 5.

3 Ravil Gaynutdin (Gaynutdinov), a Kazan Tatar and a member of Talgat Tadzhuddin's clan through his marriage to Talgat's cousin. He studied at the Theatrical Institute and was referred to as an *artist* (actor) by other members of the Russian Islamic establishment. In the 1980s he studied at the Mir-i-Arab madrasah in Bukhara, though, unlike Talgat Tadzhuddin, he does not have a higher Islamic education. Galina M. Yemelianova, 'Russia's Umma and Its Muftis'. *Religion, State and Society* 31, no. 2 (2003): 139–50.

4 In 1998 the DUMTsER was renamed the DUMER (Spiritual Directorate of Muslims of European part of Russia). In 2014 the DUMER changed its name to the DUM RF (Spiritual Directorate of Muslims of the Russian Federation).

5 Gabdulla Galiulla (Galiullin), a Kazan Tatar and a member of Talgat Tadzhuddin's clan. In 1983 he graduated from the Mir-i-Arab madrasah in Bukhara and continued his studies at the Islamic Institute in Tashkent. Between 1987 and 1992 he was imām-khatyb at the Nurulla mosque in Kazan.

6 Gusman Iskhakov, a Kazan Tatar and a member of Talgat Tadzhuddin's clan. In 1982 he graduated from the Mir-i-Arab madrasah and in 1984–85 studied at the Sharī'ah Faculty at the Islamic University in Tripoli, Libya. Between 1985 and 1994 he was imām-khatyb at the Central mosque in the town of Oktiabrskii in Bashkortostan.

7 Until 1997 the DUM AChR was known as the Spiritual Directorate of Muslims of Siberia and the Far East (DUM SDV). In 1998 the DUM AChR was formally absorbed into the SMR.

8 Nafigulla Ashirov, a Siberian Tatar, was born in the city of Tobol'sk in Siberia. In the 1970s he spent five years in jail for burglary and hooliganism. Subsequently, he studied at the Mir-i-Arab madrasah and the Islamic Institute in Algeria where he got involved with Algerian Islamists. His second wife is Algerian. In 1991–92 he worked as Tadzhuddin's deputy.

9 Mukaddas Bibarsov, a Siberian Tatar, was born in Penza oblast'. He graduated from the Ufa madrasah where he was taught by Talgat Tadzhuddin. Between 1987 and 1992 he was imām-khatyb of the Saratov mosque.

10 In Western Europe the concept of Euro-Islam was coined in 1988 by a Swedish academic Carl E. Olivestam to describe Islam in England, France and Germany and some other European countries which have substantial immigrant Muslim populations. In the late 1990s the concept was further developed by the Swiss Muslim academic, Tariq Ramadan, and the Syrian-German academic, Bassam Tibi. For a fuller discussion of European Islam, see Nielsen (1999).

11 On Tatar Euro-Islam, see Khakim Rafael, *Gde Nasha Mecca?* (Kazan: Magarif, 2003).

12 Rafik Mukhametshin, 'Islamic Discourse in the Volga-Urals Region'. In *Radical Islam in the Former Soviet Union*, edited by Galina M. Yemelianova (London: Routledge, 2010), 54.

13 Between 2008 and 2012 Putin was nominally prime minister under the presidency of Dmitry Medvedev (b. 1965). Following the 2012 presidential elections Putin resumed the presidency while Medvedev became prime minister (in office 2012–20).

14 The KTsM SK was established in 1998. Since then it has been continuously headed by Ismail Berdiyev (b. 1954), muftī of Karachaevo-Cherkessia. See Chapter 11.

15 Renat Bekkin, '"Parallel" Muftiates as the "Third Force" among Spiritual Administrations of Muslims in Russia'. *Journal of Muslims in Europe* 8 (2019): 1–21.

16 On the Crimean muftīate, see also Chapter 9.

17 Ruslan Saitvaliev, a Crimean Tatar, was born in Uzbekistan. In 1989 together with his family he resettled in the Crimea. He obtained a degree in Islamic Theology from the Kievan Islamic

University and also studied in Tunisia and Turkey. In the 2000s he was imām-khatyb of the Bakhchysarai mosque.

18 Among key figures of the Tatar national movement were Fandas Safiullin and Zaki Zaynullin, who were leaders of VTOTs; Aydar Halim, the chairman of Millī Mejlīs, and Fauzia Bayramova, the leader of the Ittifāq Party.

19 Renat Bekkin, *People of Reliable Loyalty … Muftiates and the State in Modern Russia*. PhD Dissertation (Stockholm: Elanders, 2020), 182.

20 Nigmatullin was the only ethnic Bashkir among the DUMES' senior Muslim clergy, most of whom were Kazan Tatars.

21 The Ufa Cathedral Mosque was built in 1830 on the initiative of the Orenburg muftī Gabdessalam Gabdrahimov (in office 1825–40) with the financial support of Tatar merchant Mukmin Hoziaseitov.

22 The RII was established in Kazan in 1998. Since then it has been headed by Rafik Mukhametshin (b. 1955), a professional philosopher and Islamic Studies specialist.

23 The BIA, which was situated on the site of historical Volga Bulgaria in modern Tatarstan, was co-founded by the TsDUM, DUM RT and DUM RF. Since its establishment it has been closely monitored by the Tatarstan and Russian federal authorities. Since 2019 it has been headed by Daniyar Abdrahmanov (b. 1980), a professional sociologist with no Islamic education.

24 Bekkin, *People of Reliable Loyalty*, 276.

25 Ibid., 269.

26 At some point Tadzhuddin, who was accused by his former subordinates of schizophrenia, was forced to obtain a medical certificate stating his mental adequacy. Alexei Malashenko, *Islamskoe Vozrozhdenie v Sovremennoi Rossii* (Moscow: Carnegie Endowment, 1998), 123.

27 The Moscow Cathedral mosque was originally built in 1904 near the present-day Olympic complex with the money of Tatar merchant Salih Yerzin (1833–1911). In 2015 it was comprehensively renovated and turned into one of the largest mosques in Russia and Europe. In total, there are four mosques in Moscow.

28 Abdel Wahid Niyazov (formerly, Vadim Medvedev), a Siberian Tatar, was born in the city of Omsk in western Siberia. In the late 1980s he converted to Islam. Niyazov lacks an Islamic education, though he does have a criminal record. In 1998 he created the *Refah* (Prosperity) Party which joined the pro-Putin block *Yedinstvo* (Unity), which ensured him a seat in the Duma. In 2001 he headed the pro-government Political Council of the 'Eurasian Parties – the Union of Patriots of Russia'. He has been notoriously unscrupulous in his activities, which have been defined by his anticipated financial and political gains. Galina M. Yemelianova, 'Russia's Umma and Its Muftis', *Religion, State and Society* 31, no. 2 (2003): 147.

29 Bekkin, *People of Reliable Loyalty*, 280, 294.

30 Damir Mukhetdinov (b. 1977) is Gaynutdin's first deputy. He is also the MII's rector and the head of the Medina Publishing House. Gaynutdin's other deputies are Rushan Abbyasov and Shamil Alyautdinov.

31 The 2016 Russian anti-terrorist legislation was named after Irina Yarovaya, the Duma deputy, who was one of its key authors.

32 For example, Ravil Gaynutdin has been critical of the 'anti-religious' nature of the West, which was allegedly rooted in the Renaissance, Enlightenment and, in particular, the Frankfurt School of Social Research, represented by Max Horkheimer, Theodor Adorn, Herbert Marcuse, Walter Benjamin and Eric Fromm. Gulnaz Sibgatullina, 'Translating Islam into the Language of the Russian State and the Orthodox Church'. *Religion, State and Society* 47, no. 2 (2019): 234–47.

33 Ibid.

34 Ravil Gaynutdin, 'Rozhdestvenskoe poslanie Muftiia Rossii Gainutdina', 27 January 2015, http://www.dumrf.ru/common/speech/8925. Accessed 7 July 2020.

35 Bekkin, *People of Reliable Loyalty*, 285.

36 Interview with Farid Asadullin, a historian of 'Moscow Islam' and an insider of the SMR. Moscow, 25 August 2016.

37 For a detailed discussion of the relationship between the Tatar national movement and Tatar Muslim 'clergy', see Galina M. Yemelianova, 'Islam and Power'. In *Islam in Post-Soviet Russia: Private and Public Faces*, edited by Hilary Pilkington and Galina M. Yemelianova (London: RoutledgeCurzon, 2003), 61–116.

38 Gabdulla Galiulla and Talgat Tadzhuddin are related via their wives who are daughters of Rashida Abystai (Iskhakova, 1924–2016), an influential unofficial female Islamic authority. Rashida Abystai was also mother of muftī Gusman Iskhakov who in 1998 succeeded Galiullin as muftī of the RT.

39 Prior to this appointment Gabdulhamit Zinatullin, a Tadzhuddin disciple, worked as imām-khatyb of the Zelenodol'sk mosque.

40 In January and October 1995 the conflict between the DUM RT and DUMT acquired violent form when muftī Galiullin, together with his associates, stormed the Marjani mosque and Muhammadiyya madrasah and imposed DUM RT's control over them.

41 According to Gabdulla Galiullin, President Shaimiev tasked the heads of raion administrations and local security services with ensuring the election of Gusman Iskhakov. Each pro-Iskhakov voter was paid between 100,000 and 200,000 rubles, disguised as 'subsistence payment', while security servicemen checked voters' 'correct' choice of the candidate. Interview with Gabdulla Galiullin, Kazan, 20 April 1999.

42 Interview with Farid Salman, Kazan, 20 April 1999.

43 In 2007 Farid Salman founded the Islamic publishing house *Esma* which specializes in producing Muslim calendars and commentaries to works of famous 'ulamā' and Ṣūfī sheikhs in Tatar and Russian languages.

44 The Shaimiev government gave the DUM RT an interest-free credit of 500 million rubles and established an Islamic fund of 3 billion rubles for the development of Islamic sphere. Interview with Gabdulla Galiullin, Kazan, 20 April 1999.

45 This move reflected a compromise between the Tatarstan authorities and the federal government where, in exchange for Moscow's non-interference in the confessional situation in Tatarstan, the Tatarstani muftīate's jurisdiction would not exceed Tatarstan's borders. Bekkin, *People of Reliable Loyalty*, 301.

46 Sigmatullin is a graduate of a number of Islamic institutions, including a madrasah in Istanbul, the North Caucasian Islamic University and the Sharī'ah Faculty of the Russian Islamic Institute. He is fluent in Arabic and Turkish and bears the title of *ḥāfiẓ* (memorizer of the Qur'ān).

47 Interview with the DSMR muftī Al'bir Krganov, Moscow, 1 September 2016.

48 On Akhmad Kadyrov's religious policy, see Chapter 11.

49 In December 1999 muftī Tadzhuddin alienated many devout Muslims by kissing Patriarch Alexy II's hand as a symbolic gesture of his subservience to the ROC.

50 Interview with the DSMR muftī Al'bir Krganov, Moscow, 1 September 2016.

51 Until April 2010 Muḥammad Rakhimov was affiliated with the Spiritual Directorate of Muslims of Karachaevo-Cherkessia and Stavropol' *krai* (DUM KChR). His election as RAIS's muftī was determined by his non-involvement in personal confrontation with Talgat Tadzhuddin, as was the case with muftīs Khuzin and Salman.

52 Muhametgali Khuzin ne upustil vozmozhnosti v teleefire pozhalovat'sia pravoslavnym na musul'man'. *Golos Islama*, 7 February 2013, https://golosislama.com/news.php?id=14846. Accessed 15 July 2020.

53 Since 2019 Farid Salman has also held the position of imām of the Kazan-based Belaia mosque (White mosque), affiliated to the DUM RT.

54 Al'bir Krganov was born in Chuvashia. He holds a degree in Chuvash philology. He is also a graduate of a Kazan madrasah, the Islamic Institute of Riza Fahretdin and the

TsDUM-affiliated Islamic University. Between 2005 and 2012 he was the first deputy of muftī Tadzhuddin and his representative in Moscow.

55 Bekkin, *People of Reliable Loyalty*, 348.

56 Faizrakhman Sattarov, a Kazan Tatar, received his theological training in Mir-i-Arab madrasah in Bukhara in 1955–64. Prior to leaving the DUMES, he worked, successively, as imām-khatyb in Leningrad (St. Petersburg), Rostov-upon-Don and Oktiabrsk and as the DUMES qāzī. It is likely that his breaking away from the DUMES was a result of his failed attempt to become muftī after the death in 1974 of muftī Khiyaletdinov.

57 Interview with Faizrakhman Sattarov, in the village of Torfianoi (near Kazan), 22 April 1999.

58 Rafik Mukhametshin, *Tatary i Islam v XX veke* (Kazan: Fen, 2003), 298.

59 Valiulla Yakupov, *Neofotsial'nyi Islam v Tatarstane: Dvizheniia, Techeniia, Sekty* (Kazan: Iman, 2003), 13.

60 Gleb Postnov, 'Tatarskie Bratia-Musul'mane Ukhodiat v Podpol'e'. *Nezavisimaya Gazeta*, 11 November 2011, https://www.ng.ru/regions/2011-11-15/1_tatarstan.html. Accessed 22 July 2020.

61 Among other banned foreign Islamic organizations, which had a limited presence in the region, were *Al-Aḥmadīyyah* and *Tablīghī Jamā'ah*.

62 If an informer, who asked not to be named, is to be believed, Daesh recruiters combined their Islamist message with an upfront payment of $ 30,000 to a signed-in individual. Moscow, 27 June 2017.

63 Marlene Laruelle and Sophie Hohmann, 'Polar Islam: Muslim Communities in Russia's Arctic Cities'. *Problems of Post-Communism* (2010). Online version, https://www.tandfonline.com/doi/full/10.1080/10758216.2019.1616565.

64 Joanna Parashiuk, 'Islamisty groziat Tatarstanu', *Radio Free Europe/Radio Liberty*, 10 February 2015, https://www.svoboda.org/a/26837871.html. Accessed 23 July 2020.

Chapter Eleven THE CAUCASUS

1 On the Islamic revival in Dagestan in the late Soviet period, see Chapter 6.

2 Paradoxically, in 2008 the KTsMSK posthumously awarded muftī Gekkiev (1935–2007) the order 'For the Service to the Ummah'.

3 In the 1990s, the most influential sheikhs were Sayid Chirkeiskii (Chirkawi/Atsaev), Magomed-Amin (Gadzhiev), Badrudin Botlikhskii, Arsanali Gamzatov (Paraul'skii), Ramazan Gimrinskii, Abdulwahid Kakamakhinskii, Abdulgani Zakatal'skii, Muhammad-Mukhtar Kakhulaiskii, Sirazhudin Khurikskii, Tadzhuddin Khasaviurtskii and Muhadzir Dogrelinskii. Dmitrii Makarov, *Ofitsial'nyi i Neofitsial'nyi Islam v Dagestane* (Moscow: Tsentr Strategicheskikh i Politicheskikh Issledovanii, 2000), 7, 11, 72.

4 Interview with sheikh Abd al-Wahid Abdullayev, *khalifa* (representative) of sheikh Nāẓim in the North Caucasus. 30 June 1999, Makhachkala.

5 Dmitrii Makarov and Rafik Mukhametshin, 'Official and Unofficial Islam'. In *Islam in Post-Soviet Russia: Public and Private Faces*, edited by Hilary Pilkington and Galina M. Yemelianova (London: RoutledgeCurzon, 2003), 141.

6 Amri R. Shikhsaidov, 'Islam v Dagestane', *Central Asia and the Caucasus* 5, https://www.ca-c.org/journal/cac-05-1999/st_18_shihsaid.shtml.

7 *Muftīate Respubliki Dagestan*, http://muftiyatrd.ru. Accessed 15 October 2020.

8 On new Muslim communities in Russia's North, see Chapter 10.

9 Mikhail Roshchin, 'Iz Istorii Islama v Dagestane'. In *Islam na Severnom Kavkaze: Istoriia i Sovremennost'*, edited by Islam Tekushev and Kirill Shevchenko (Prague: Medium Orient, 2011), 19.

10 On the USSR-wide IRP, see Chapter 6.

11 The Kebedov brothers are ethnic Khvarshins (an Avar sub-ethnic group), originating from the village of Santlanda in the Tsumadinskii raion. According to some sources, they studied Islam at Islamic institutions in Saudi Arabia. Kaflan Khanbabaev, 'Islam and Islamic Radicalism in Dagestan'. In *Radical Islam in the Former Soviet Union*, edited by Galina M. Yemelianova (London: Routledge, 2010), 108.
12 On Bagauddin's jamā'ah and his publishing house, see Chapter 6.
13 Between the mid-1990s and 1999 the Kadar zone, which comprised the villages of Kadar, Karamakhi and Chaban-Makhi of Buinakskii raion, acted as a semi-independent Islamic polity.
14 In June 1991, under Dzhokhar Dudayev's leadership Chechnya's official name was changed to the Chechen Republic of Ichkeria. Following Chechnya's reintegration into Russia in spring 2000, it was renamed the Chechen Republic, while the name 'Ichkeria' became associated with anti-government Chechen militants.
15 There are significant discrepancies in the estimated number of Islamic radicals in Dagestan. For example, according to official data for 2004, there were around 2,000 'Wahhābīs', while other sources suggested that their number exceeded 100,000. Kaflan M. Khanbabaev, 'Vozrozhdenie Musul'manskogo Prava v Dagestane: Teoriia i Praktika'. *Islam i Pravo v Rossii* 2 (2004): 130.
16 Among the 'Wahhābīs' high-profile victims were Zahir Arukhov, minister for nationalities; Magomed Omarov, deputy interior minister; Zagid Varisov, a prominent political scientist; muftī Abubakarov; deputy muftī Akhmad Tagaev; and Naqshbandī/Shādhilī sheikh Sayid Chirkeiskii.
17 For a detailed analysis of jihādism in the North Caucasus, see Galina M. Yemelianova, 'Political Islam and Jihad in Eurasia: The Case of the North Caucasus'. In *Exporting Global Jihad: Critical Perspectives from Asia and North America*, vol. 2, edited by Tom Smith and Kirsten E. Schulze (London: I.B. Tauris, 2020), 99–122.
18 In 2007 Abbas Kebedov was deported from Egypt to Dagestan and jailed. In 2010 he rejected jihādism and joined the government's Commission for Islamist de-radicalization.
19 Shamil Shikhaliev, 'Musul'manskoe reformatorstvo v Dagestane (1900–1930 gg.)', *Gosudarstvo, Religiya, Tserkov' v Rossii i za rubezhom* 3, no. 35 (2017): 143. See also Chapter 6.
20 Jean-François Ratelle, 'Transnational Salafi and Jihadist Networks: From Independent Insurgency to a Leaderless Network'. In *The Routledge Handbook of the Caucasus*, edited by Galina M. Yemelianova and Laurence Broers (London: Routledge, 2020), 299.
21 On Kunta-ḥajjee wird, see Chapter 6.
22 Muhammad Alsabekov was born in deportation in Kazakhstan. He studied at Islamic institutions in Syria and Pakistan. Prior to becoming Chechnya's muftī, he worked as imām-khatyb of the Cathedral mosque of Almaty and deputy muftī of Kazakhstan. In 1996, after falling out with the Chechen separatist leadership, Alsabekov returned to Almaty as deputy muftī of Kazakhstan.
23 Vahit Akaev, 'Islam and Politics in Chechnya and Ingushetia'. In *Radical Islam in the Former Soviet Union*, 68.
24 Akhmad Kadyrov was born in deportation in Kazakhstan. In 1957, he and his family returned to the Chechen-Ingush ASSR. He was a graduate of the Mir-i Arab madrasah in Bukhara and the Islamic Institute in Tashkent.
25 Like Akhmad Kadyrov, muftī Akhmad-ḥajjee Shamayev and his successors have been members of the Kunta-ḥajjee wird of Qādirī ṭarīqah.
26 See Chapter 10.
27 Among the main issues of contention was the muftī's criticism of the unpopular 2018 Border Treaty between Chechnya and Ingushetia.
28 Isa-ḥajjee Khamkhoyev was yet again elected as muftī following the death from Covid-19 in April 2020 of muftī Abdurahman Martazanov (in office 2019–20).

29 Ratelle, 'Transnational Salafi and Jihadist Networks', 290.
30 Sharafutdin Chochayev received his Islamic education at the Mir-ir Arab madrasah in Bukhara and the Islamic Institute in Tashkent. Since 1996 he has headed the Islamic Institute of Abū Ḥanīfa which in 2007 was renamed the Islamic University of the North Caucasus.
31 Shafig Pshikachev was educated at the Mir-i Arab madrasah in Bukhara, the Islamic University in Amman (Jordan) and the Institute of *al-Da'wah al-Islāmīyyah* in Damascus. Since 2004 he has headed the Moscow-based pro-government 'International Islamic Mission' and acted as the official representative of the KTsM SK in Moscow.
32 Khazretali Dzhasezhev was educated at the Mir-ir Arab madrasah in Bukhara and the Islamic Institute of Imām Shamīl in Damascus.
33 *Dukhovnoe Upravlenie Kabardino-Balkarskoi Respubliki*, http://www.kbrdum.ru. Accessed 19 October 2020.
34 Interview with muftī Anas Pshikachev, Nal'chik, 8 April 2008 (Courtesy of Svetlana I. Akkieva).
35 Interview with Nazir-ḥajjee Akhmatov, Nal'chik, 10 January 2021 (Courtesy of Svetlana I. Akkieva).
36 *Musul'mane Rossii*, http://dumrf.ru/common/org/2304. Accessed 19 October 2020.
37 Enver Shumaf was born in the village of Uspenskoe in the Armavir raion of Krasnodar Krai. His Islamic education was limited to three-month-long studies at the Islamic Institute in Damascus.
38 Askarbii Kardanov was educated at the Islamic Institute in Damascus and the Cherkessk-based Islamic University of the North Caucasus.
39 *DUM RA i KK*, http://dumraikk.ru. Accessed 20 October 2020.
40 According to some researchers the Nalchik Islamists' attacks and the ensuing violent confrontation between Islamists and government law enforcement forces were orchestrated from above to create a smokescreen for the re-appropriation and re-division of lucrative land and other resources. Author's interview with Professor Svetalna I. Akkieva, Nal'chik, 10 January 2021.
41 Interview with Nazir-ḥajjee Akhmatov, Nal'chik, 10 January 2021 (Courtesy of Svetlana I. Akkieva).
42 Muhammad Bidzhiev received his Islamic education at the International Academy of Islamic Da'wah of Pakistan.
43 In 1993, Bidzhiev gave up his Islamist project in Karachai and moved to Moscow where he joined the Council of Muftīs of Russia under Ravil Gaynutdin. See Chapter 10.
44 *Vykhodtsy s Kavkaza v Riadakh IGIL*. Kavkazskii Uzel, https://www.kavkaz-uzel.eu/articles/251 513. Accessed 23 October 2020.
45 *FSB Otchitalos' o Likvidatsii Yacheek Takfīr wa al-Hijrah v KChR i Dagestane*. Kavkazskii Uzel, https://www.kavkaz-uzel.eu/articles/355663/. Accessed 23 October 2020.
46 Domitilla Sagramoso and Galina M. Yemelianova, 'Islam and Ethno-Nationalism in the North-Western Caucasus'. In *Radical Islam in the Former Soviet Union*, 140.
47 *Vykhodtsy s Kavkaza v Riadakh IGIL*. Kavkazskii Uzel, https://www.kavkaz- uzel.eu/articles/251513/. Accessed 23 October 2020.
48 *Qafqaz Musulmanlari Idaresi*, http://qafqazislam.com/index.php?lang=az&sectionid=23. Accessed 24 October 2020.
49 Bayram Balci, *Islam in Central Asia and the Caucasus since the Fall of the Soviet Union* (London: Hurst, 2018), 50.
50 On Gülenist schools in other parts of post-Soviet Eurasia, see Chapters 9, 10 and 12.
51 Dmitry Trofimov, *Islam in the Political Culture of the former Soviet Union: Central Asia and Azerbaijan* (Hamburg: IFSH, 1995), 52.
52 Movsum Samadov was educated at the Islamic University at Qum, Iran.
53 Ilgar Ibrahimoglu received his theological training at the International University of Imam Khomeini in Qazwin, Iran.

54 Taleh Baghirzade was educated at the Islamic University in Qum, Iran, and at the Islamic University in Najaf, Iraq.

55 For a fuller discussion of the religious-political agenda of Taleh Baghirzade and Ilgar Ibrahimoglu, see Murad Ismayilov, *The Dialectics of Post-Soviet Modernity and the Changing Contours of Islamic Discourse in Azerbaijan* (Lanham: Lexington Books, 2018).

56 Qamet Suleymanov was educated at the International Islamic University in Medina, Saudi Arabia.

57 Rufat Sattarov, 'Islamic Revival and Islamic Activism in Post-Soviet Azerbaijan'. In *Radical Islam in the Former Soviet Union*, 188.

58 'Vykhodtsy s Kavkaza v Riadakh IGIL', *Kavkazskii Uzel*, 28 May 2018, https://www.kavkaz-uzel.eu/articles/251513/#cont_20. Accessed 25 October 2020.

Chapter Twelve CENTRAL ASIA

1 For a detailed discussion of political and societal development in post-Soviet Central Asia, see Galina M. Yemelianova, *Muslims of Central Asia: An Introduction* (Edinburgh: Edinburgh University Press, 2019).

2 Members of the Tablīghī Jamā'at promoted a revivalist version of Islam of the Deobandi school. It originated in the madrasah Dar al-'Ulūm in the city of Deoband in India in the 1860s and was aimed at cleansing Islam of the allegedly corrupting influences associated with British colonialism.

3 Muhammad Sodiq Yusuf, an ethnic Uzbek and a native of Andijan in the Ferghana valley, was educated at the Bukhara Mir-i Arab madrasah, the Tashkent Islamic Institute and the University of *Al-Da'wah al-Islamīyyah* in Libya.

4 Muftī Shamsuddinkhon Bobokhon's membership of the Soviet-era political establishment was evidenced by his later appointment as Uzbekistan's ambassador to Egypt and then to Saudi Arabia.

5 On Abū Manṣūr al-Māturīdī and al-Māturīdīyyah, see Chapter 1.

6 In 1993 Muhammad Sodiq Yusuf fled to Libya where he stayed till 1999 when he was permitted to return to Uzbekistan, albeit in a private capacity. Until his death in 2015 Muhammad Sodiq Yusuf was a member of several high-profile international Islamic organizations including the World Union of Muslim *'Ulamā'*, the World Islamic League and the World Council of *Al-Da'wah al-Islāmīyyah*. It is worth noting that his recorded sermons informally circulated in Uzbekistan throughout the 1990s and 2000s.

7 Usmonkhon Alimov, an ethnic Uzbek and a native of Samarqand region, was educated at the Bukhara Mir-i Arab madrasah, the Tashkent Islamic Institute and the Islamic University of al-Qarawiyyin in Fez, Morocco.

8 In January 2020 Muftī Alimov's service to the state was recognized by President Shavkat Mirziyoyev (in office 2016–), who awarded him the order of *El Yurt Hurmati* (lit. 'To One Respected by People and Motherland').

9 Thus, the Tashkent muftīate distanced itself from Naqshbandīs belonging to the group of Ibrahim-Hazrat. See the section on Kazakhstan.

10 'V Uzbekistane prizvali ne poddavat'sia emotsiiam iz-za karikatur na Muhammada', *Sputnik Uzbekistan*, 28 October 2020, https://uz.sputniknews.ru/society/20201028/15275886/V-Uzbekistane-prizvali-ne-poddavatsya-emotsiyam-iz-za-karikatur-na-Mukhammeda.html. Accessed 5 November 2020.

11 The IIAU teaches MA and PhD programmes in the history of Islam and in Qur'ān, Ḥadīth, fiqh and *kalām* (scholastic theology) studies. Its 'international' status is based on its formal relations with a number of Islamic institutions and research centres from Egypt (Al-Azhar), Saudi Arabia, Morocco, Turkey, Indonesia, Malaysia, Japan, the UK, Kazakhstan and Russia.

12 In particular, the IIAU has run joint projects on the study of the Central Asian Islamic heritage with the OIC Research Centre for Islamic History, Arts and Culture.
13 On the role of ḥujrahs in late Soviet period, see Chapter 8.
14 Local Salafīs were often referred to as 'hajjees' due to their Islamic dress and their positioning of themselves, on the basis of their hajj experience, as the bearers of 'true Islam'.
15 Yemelianova, *Muslims of Central Asia*, 83.
16 The nation-wide crackdown on the IMU and its affiliates was triggered by the alleged involvement of IMU militants in the Tashkent bombing on 16 February 1999, which left 16 people dead and over a hundred wounded.
17 In 2007, the IIJ was involved in planning a series of bombings of an American military base in Rheinland-Pfalts in Germany. Yemelianova, *Muslims of Central Asia*, 86.
18 The Ḥaqqānī network unites jihādīs fighting against the American and other Western presence in Afghanistan. It is named after the network's founder Jalāl al-Dīn al-Ḥaqqānī (1939–2018).
19 On Daesh's fighters from Central Asia, see Erlan Karin, *The Soldiers of the Caliphate: The Anatomy of a Terrorist Group* (Astana: KazISS, 2016).
20 'Skol'ko Uzbekov voiuiut na storone IGIL', *Vesti.Uz*, 9 December 2015, https://vesti.uz/skolko-uzbekov-voyuyut-na-storone-igil/. Accessed 6 November 2020.
21 On the HTI, see also Chapter 9.
22 On the taḥrīrīs' tactics in the Ferghana Valley, see Zumrat Salmorbekova and Galina M. Yemelianova, 'Islam and Islamism in the Ferghana Valley'. In *Radical Islam in the Former Soviet Union*, edited by Galina M. Yemelianova (London: Routledge, 2010), 211–43.
23 Akrom Yuldoshev, a native of Andijan, was a local mathematics teacher without any Islamic education. He outlined his five-stage strategy towards the creation of an Islamic state in the Ferghana valley in his book *Iymonga Yul* (Path to Faith).
24 Michael Fredholm, 'Islamic Extremism as a Political Force'. In *Seeds of Terror*, edited by Gretchen Peters (New York: St. Martin's Press, 2009), 130–33.
25 According to official sources, 187 were killed, while unofficial sources estimated the death toll to be between 700 and 1,500. See, for example, 'Bullets Were Falling like Rain'. *Human Rights Watch*, 2 June 2005, https://www.hrw.org/report/2005/06/06/bullets-were-falling-rain/andijan-massacre-may-13-2005. Accessed 6 November 2020.
26 Hoji Akbar Turajonzoda (Kakhorov), a native of the Kofarnihon region of Tajikistan, received his Islamic education from his father Eshon Turajon, an influential Ṣūfī scholar, at the Bukhara Mir-i Arab madrasah, the Tashkent Islamic Institute and the Sharī'ah Faculty at the Jordan University.
27 Said Abdullo Nuri, a native of the Garm region of Tajikistan, learnt the basics of Islam from his father and Hajjee Domla Hindustoniy (see Chapter 8). In the early 1980s, he campaigned for the greater role of Islam in Tajikistani politics and society and was subjected to state persecution, including imprisonment. Prior to becoming the leader of the IRPT he worked as editor-in-chief of the newspaper *Minbari Islom* (Voice of Islam).
28 Muhiddin Kabiri, a native of the Faizobad region of Tajikistan, lacks a structured Islamic education, albeit he graduated from the Arabic Faculty of the Tajik National University and the Diplomatic Academy in Moscow. During the Tajik Civil War he was engaged in business activity in Moscow.
29 Georgy Rudov, 'Islam v Tsentral'noi Azii: Mashtaby i Perspektivy Vliianiia'. *Obozrevatel'* 6, no. 293 (2014): 63.
30 Noah Tucker, 'Public and State Responses to ISIS Messaging: Tajikistan'. *Central Asian Program*, vol. 11 (Washington, DC: George Washington University, 2016), 2.
31 Ratbek-kajy Nysanbai-uly, a native of southern Kazakhstan, was educated at the Mir-i Arab madrasah in Bukhara and the sharī'ah faculty of the Libyan university. He was the first translator of the Qur'ān into Kazakh.

32 During the 1990s the DUMK founded its own periodicals: *Islam Alemi* (Islamic World), *Imam* (Faith), *Islam Zhane Orkeniyet* (Islam and Civilization) and *Shapagat Nur* (Light of Mercy), as well as its website www.muftyat.kz (in Kazakh and Russian).

33 Absattar Derbisali, a native of southern Kazakhstan, lacked any Islamic education and his elevation to the post of muftī was due to his knowledge of Arabic. In the past he worked as an academic and diplomat. In 2013 he returned to academia as director of the Institute of Oriental Studies.

34 In 2014, al-Ḥijāzī was succeeded by al-Azhar Professor Judah ʻAbd al-Ghanī Basyūnī and since 2018 the 'Nur' University has been headed by Muḥammad al-Shahat al-Jindī.

35 The Aḥmadīyyah Muslim community is an international Sunnī reformist movement that originated in the Punjab, British India, at the end of the nineteenth century. It is named after its founder Mirzā Ghulām Aḥmad (1835–1905) who proclaimed himself mahdī. Aḥmadīs believe in the spiritual rather than the human nature of the caliphate and see their mission as being the peaceful promoters of Islamic teaching and ethics. At present there are between 15 and 20 million Aḥmadīs in over two hundred countries. Since 1984 the movement's headquarters has been in London, and since 2004 their leader has been Mirzā Masrūr Aḥmed (b. 1960). On Aḥmadīyyah, see Simon R. Valentine, *Islam and the Ahmadiyya Jama'at: History, Belief, Practice* (New York: Columbia University Press, 2008).

36 These books were in Russian, Turkish and Arabic and were published in Mecca, Medina, Istanbul, Beirut, Cairo, Karachi and Lahore.

37 Aitzhan Sh. Nurmanova and Asilbek K. Izbairov, 'Islamic Education in Soviet and Post-Soviet Kazakhstan'. In *Islamic Education in the Soviet Union and Successor States*, edited by Michael Kemper, Raoul Motika and Stefan Reichmuth (London: Routledge, 2010), 306; Bayram Balci, *Islam in Central Asia and the Caucasus since the Fall of the Soviet Union* (London: Hurst, 2018), 51.

38 Interview with Nasrettin-qari, son of Ishan-Baba, predecessor of Ibrahim-Hazret. Village of Qushi-Ata, Turkistan, 20 April 2012.

39 Yemelianova, *Muslims of Central Asia*, 111–13.

40 In 2019 Nursultan Nazarbayev was succeeded by Kassym Jomart Tokayev (b. 1953).

41 Kimsanbai-aji, a native of Batken, was educated at the Mir-i Arab madrasah in Bukhara and the sharīʻah faculty of the Islamic University in Jordan.

42 In 1996 muftī Kimsanbai-aji was forced out of office by Moldo Abdusatar-aji Majotov (in office 1999–2000) who, in 2000, was yet again replaced by Kimsanbai-aji (in office 2000–2). The next muftī was Murataaly-aji Jumanov (in office 2002–10), followed by Abdyshukur Narmanov, Suiun Kuliyev and Chubak-aji Jalilov (in office 2010–12), then by Rahmatullo-aji Egemberdiyev (in office 2012–14). Since 2014 the DUMKyr has been headed by muftī Maksatbek-aji Toktomushev.

43 Maksatbek-aji Toktomushev, a native of Osh, studied in a madrasah in Pakistan. His lack of higher Islamic education raises a question about his eligibility for the post of muftī.

44 Members of the Tablīghī Jamāʻah promoted a revivalist version of Islam of the Deobandi school. It originated in the madrasah Dar al-ʻUlūm in the city of Deoband in India in the 1860s and was aimed at cleansing Islam of the allegedly corrupting influences associated with British colonialism.

45 Yemelianova, *Muslims of Central Asia*, 141.

46 Balci, *Islam in Central Asia*, 51.

47 Salmorbekova and Yemelianova, 'Islam and Islamism', 228–29; Yemelianova, *Muslims of Central Asia*, 137.

48 Karin, *The Soldiers of the Caliphate*, 135.

49 Yemelianova, *Muslims of Central Asia*, 138.

50 For a detailed analysis of post-Soviet Turkmenistan's politics and society, see Sébastien Peyrouse, *Turkmenistan: Strategies of Power, Dilemmas of Development* (Armonk, NY: M.E. Sharpe, 2011).

51 For example, by the mid-1990s, only around 450 people had been allowed to go on hajj despite the Saudi-allocated annual quota of 4,600. Peyrouse, *Turkmenistan*, 111.

52 Balci, *Islam in Central Asia*, 60.
53 In 2011, the Berdymuhamedov government decreed the closing of the Gülenist colleges.
54 Nasrulla ibn Ibadulla, a native of Tashauz region of Turkmenistan, was educated at Mir-i Arab madrasah in Bukhara, an Islamic Institute in Syria and Al-Azhar University in Egypt.
55 The remaining madrasah in Ashgabat was closed down during the presidency of Berdymuhamedov. Yemelianova, *Muslims of Central Asia*, 183.
56 It might be that the removal of Nasrulla ibn Ibadulla was part of the Turkmenbashi's campaign of Turkmenization of the ruling political and religious elite. In 2007 Nasrulla ibn Ibadulla was pardoned by President Berdymuhamedov.
57 'Grazhdane Turkmenistana, voevavshye za IG, perekhodiat v riady Svobodnoi Siriiskoi Armii', *Khronika Turkmenistana*, 3 July 2019, https://www.hronikatm.com/2019/07/ex-isis/. Accessed 17 November 2020.

Chapter Thirteen EURASIAN ISLAMIC LEADERSHIP WITHIN THE GLOBAL CONTEXT

1 On Egyptian Islamic reformers, see M. A. Zaki Badawi, *Reformers of Egypt* (London: Croom Helm, 1978).
2 The 'delayed' imposition of French and Spanish control over Morocco, as well as the high religious credentials of the ruling Alawite (*'Alawīyyīn*) who have ruled in Morocco from 1631 accounted for the country's relative political stability through the period discussed.
3 Ş.Tufan Buzpinar, 'Opposition to the Ottoman Caliphate in the Early Years of Abdulhamid II: 1877–1882'. *Die Welt des Islams* 36, no. 1 (1996): 59.
4 On al-Nahḍah, see Jens Hanssen and Max Weiss, eds, *Arabic Thought beyond the Liberal Age: Towards an Intellectual History of the Nahda* (Cambridge: Cambridge University Press, 2016).
5 On theological and political division among al-Azhar's 'ulamā' divisions, see Indira F. Gesink, *Islamic Reform and Conservatism: Al-Azhar and the Evolution of Modern Sunni Islam* (London: I.B. Tauris, 2010).
6 For an analysis of the Muslim Brotherhood, see Richard P. Mitchell, *The Society of the Muslim Brothers* (Oxford: Oxford University Press, 1969).
7 On the Wahhābīs' proselytizing mission, see David Commins, *The Wahhabi Mission and Saudi Arabia* (London: I.B. Tauris, 2006).
8 On the Adnanites, see Chapter 1.
9 The indigenous Yemen ruling dynasties included the Zaydīs (819–1018, 1635–1849, 1911–62), the Ṣulayḥids (1047–1138), the Rasūlids (1229–1454), the Ṭāhirids (1454–1517). Only for a relatively short period was Yemen nominally under external Muslim rule that was under the Egyptian Ayyūbids in the thirteenth century and under the Ottomans, first in the sixteenth century and then in the nineteenth century.
10 Said K. Nasser Aburish, *The Arab Leader* (New York: St. Martin's Press, 2004), 200; Bano Masooda, 'Protector of "al-Wasatiyya" Islam: Cairo's al-Azhar University'. In *Shaping Global Islamic Discourses: The Role of al-Azhar, al-Medina and al-Mustafa*, edited by Masooda Bano and Keiko Sakurai (Edinburgh: Edinburgh University Press, 2015), 77.
11 From 1970 Sunnī-dominant Syria has been governed by the Ba'ath leaders Ḥāfiẓ al-Asad (1930–2000, in office 1970–2000) and his son Bashār al-Asad (b. 1965, in office 2000–), both of the Shī'ī Alawite heritage. The last Ba'athist leader of Shī'ah-dominated Iraq was Ṣaddām Ḥuseyn (1937–2006, in office 1979–2003), of Sunnī affiliation.
12 Dale F. Eickelman and James Piscatori, *Muslim Politics* (Princeton, NJ: Princeton University Press, 1996), 12.
13 Laurence Wright, *The Looming Tower: Al Qaeda and the Road to 9/11* (New York: Alfred A. Knopf, 2006), 258.

14 On the role of Saudi Arabia, Pakistan and the CIA in the mujāḥidīn movement in Afghanistan, see Aisha Ahmad, *Jihad & Co. Black Markets and Islamist Power* (Oxford: Oxford University Press, 2017).

15 Gary R. Bunt, *Islam in the Digital Age: E-Jihad, Online Fatwas and Cyber Islamic Environments* (London: PlutoPress, 2003), 138, 142.

16 On al-Andalus, see Chapter 1.

17 A symbol of such architectural Christianization is the spectacular Great Mosque of Córdoba which was built in 785 on the orders of Umayyad Amīr ʿAbd al-Raḥmān I. In 1236, following Córdoba's capture by the Christian forces of Castile, the Great Mosque was converted into the Cathedral of Our Lady of Assumption and its *miḥrāb* (sacred niche), mosaics and other Islamic artefacts were either destroyed or severely damaged.

18 It should be noted that a comparatively small number of Muslims from the Middle East, North Africa and Asia began to settle in their respective European metropoles during colonial rule.

19 'Muslim population in Europe', Pew Research Center, 29 November 2017, https://www.pewresearch.org/fact-tank/2017/11/29/5-facts-about-the-muslim-population-in-europe/. Accessed 1 December 2020.

20 Barelvis, who number around 200 million in South Asia, follow the teaching of Aḥmad Riḍā Khān al-Baralwī (Ahmad Reza Khan, 1856–1921) who originated in the town of Bareilly in India. Barelvis refer to themselves as *Ahl al-Sunnah wa al-Jamāʿah*, or simply as Sunnīs. They oppose Deobandis and other pro-Salafī groups and position themselves as defenders of Sufism-based Islamic traditionalism.

21 Jocelyn Cesari, *When Islam and Democracy Meet* (London: Palgrave Macmillan, 2004), 157.

22 In 2004 Abū Ḥamza was arrested by British police and charged with inciting racial hatred and terrorism. In 2014 he was extradited from Britain to the United States where he was sentenced to life imprisonment.

23 Egdūnas Račius, *Islam in Post-Communist Eastern Europe: Between Churchification and Securitization* (Leiden: Brill, 2020), 45.

24 Yousuef al-Qaradawi, *Fiqh of Muslim Minorities: Contentious Issues and Recommended Solutions* (Cairo: Al-Falah Foundation for Translation, Publication and Distribution, 2003), 3; Taha Alwani, *Towards a Fiqh for Minorities: Some Basic Reflections* (London: International Institute of Islamic Thought, 2010), 3.

25 Tariq Ramadan, *Western Muslims and the Future of Islam* (Oxford: Oxford University Press, 2004).

26 Bunt, *Islam in the Digital Age*, 135.

27 The ICE's *fuqahāʾ* were largely educated at sharīʿah faculties of the Islamic University of Medina, al-Azhar or other major Islamic universities. As of 2020, ICE's jurists were sheikh Ḥaitham al-Ḥaddād, sheikh Farīd Haibatan, sheikh Abū ʿUbaydah and sheikh Shaqur Rehmān, https://iceurope.org/about-us/our-advisors. Accessed 30 November 2020.

28 For example, since 2016 the MCB has been headed by Harūn Khān (b. 1958) who was trained as an engineer.

29 For an analysis of state–Muslim relations in Western Europe, see Jorgen S. Nielsen, *Muslims in Western Europe* (Edinburgh: Edinburgh University Press, 2004).

30 Račius, *Islam in Post-Communist Eastern Europe*, 62.

31 Ibid., 62, 69.

32 The EAEU was established in 2015. As of 2020, it united Russia, Kazakhstan, Kyrgyzstan, Belarus and Armenia.

33 Račius, *Islam in Post-Communist Eastern Europe*, 159.

34 Ibid.

35 For different perceptions of the secular and secularism and their application to European and Muslim societies, see for example, Talal Asad, *Formations of the Secular: Christianity, Islam, Modernity* (Stanford, CA: Stanford University Press, 2003); Cesari, *When Islam and Democracy Meet*; Olivier Roy, *Secularism Confronts Islam* (New York: Columbia University Press, 2007); Bryan S. Turner, *Religion and Modern Society: Citizenship, Secularisation and the State* (Cambridge: Cambridge University Press, 2011).

BIBLIOGRAPHY

Abdullayev, Magomed. *Iz Istorii Filosofskoi i Obshchestvenno-Politicheskoi Mysli Dagestana*. Makhachkala: Yupiter,1993.

Aburish, Said K. Nasser. *The Arab Leader*. New York: St. Martin's Press, 2004.

Aglarov, Mamaikhan A. *Sel'skaia Obshchina v Nagornom Dagestane v VII-nachale XIX v*. Moscow: Nauka, 1988.

Ahmad, Aisha. *Jihad & Co. Black Markets and Islamist Power*. Oxford: Oxford University Press, 2017.

Aida, Adile. *Sadri Maksudi Arsal*. Ankara: Kültür Balkanliği, 1991.

Akaev, Vahit, 'Islam and Politics in Chechnya and Ingushetia'. In *Radical Islam in the Former Soviet Union*, edited by Galina M. Yemelianova, 62–82. London: Routledge, 2010.

———. *Sufiiskaia Kul'tura na Severnom Kavkaze*. Grozny: Knizhnoe Izdatel'stvo, 2011.

Akhmadullin, Biacheslav A. 'Osobennosti Sovetskoi Dvukhurovnevoi Podgotovki Islamskikh Kadrov'. *Islam v Sovremennom Mire* 11, no. 2 (2015): 145–62.

Akkieva, Svetlana I. *Sotsiokul'turnye Transformatsii Deportirovannykh Narodov Severnogo Kavkaza v 1940–1990-e Gody*. Nal'chik: IGI KBNTs RAN, 2019.

Alikberov, Alikber K. *Epokha Klassicheskogo Islama na Kavaze*. Moscow: Vostochnaia Literatura RAN, 2003.

Aliyeva, Sevinj I. 'Azerbaidzhanskaia Demokraticheskaia Respublika i Gorskaia Respublica: Proekty Obrazovaniia Edinogo Gosudarstva'. *Caucasus Survey* 3, no. 1 (2015): 58–75.

Alwani, Taha. *Towards a Fiqh for Minorities: Some Basic Reflections*. London: International Institute of Islamic Thought, 2010.

Arapov, Dmitrii Yu. *Islam i Sovetskoe Gosudarstvo (1917–1936): Sbornik Dokumentov*. Vol. 2. Moscow: Mardzhani, 2010.

———. *Islam i Sovetskoe Gosudarstvo (1944–1991): Sbornik Dokumentov*. Vol. 3. Moscow: Mardzhani, 2011.

———. *Islam v Rossiiskoi Imperii. Sbornok Dokumentov*. Vol. 1. Moscow: IVRAN, 2001.

Asad, Talal. *Formations of the Secular: Christianity, Islam, Modernity*. Stanford, CA: Stanford University Press, 2003.

Ashmarin, Nikolai. *Ocherki Literaturnoi Deiatel'nosti Tatar-Muhammedan za 1880–95 gody*. Moscow: Lazarevskii Institut Vostochnykh Yazykov, 1901.

Atlasi, Hadi. *Istoriia Sibiri*. Kazan: Tatarskoe Knizhnoe Izdatel'stvo, 2005.

Babadzhanov, Bakhtiyar. 'Andizhanskoe Vosstanie 1898 goda i "Musul'manskii Vopros" v Turkestane (Vzgliady "Kolonizatorov" i "Kolonizirovannykh". In *Musul'mane v Novoi Imperskoi Istorii*, edited by Vladimir O. Bobrovnikov, Igor V. Gerasimov and Sergei V. Glebov, 104–55. Moscow: SADRA, 2017.

———. *Kokandskoe Khanstvo. Vlast', Politika, Religiia*. Tokyo-Tashkent: TIAS, 2010.

Babich, Irina L. *Evolutsiia pravovoi kul'tury adygov (1860–1990-e gody)*. Moscow: Nauka, 1999.

Badawi, M. A. Zaki. *Reformers of Egypt*. London: Croom Helm, 1978.

Bagirova, Irada S. *Politicheskie Partii i Organizatsii Azerbaidzhana v Nachale XX Veka*. Baku: Elm, 1997.

Baladhuri, Ahmad. *Kniga Zavoevaniia Stran*. Baku: Obshchestvo Obsledovaniia i Izucheniia Azerbaidzhana, 1927.

Balci, Bayram. *Islam in Central Asia and the Caucasus since the Fall of the Soviet Union*. London: Hurst, 2018.

———. *Missionnaires de l'Islam en Asie central, les écoles turques de Fethullah Gülen*. Paris: Maisonneuvre et Larose y Institut français d'etudes anatoliennes, 2003.

———. *The Gülen Movement and Turkish Soft Power*. Carnegie Endowment for International Peace (2014), https://carnegieendowment.org/2014/02/04/g-len-movement-and-turkish-soft-power-pub-54430. Accessed on 20 January 2021.

Balci, Bayram, and Liles, Thomas. 'Turkey and the Caucasus: Mutual Interests and Influences in the Post-Soviet Era'. In *Routledge Handbook of the Caucasus*, edited by Galina M. Yemelianova and Laurence Broers, 331–46. London: Routledge, 2020.

Bano, Masooda. 'Protector of "al-Wasatiyya" Islam: Cairo's al-Azhar University'. In *Shaping Global Islamic Discourses: The Role of al-Azhar, al-Medina and al-Mustafa*, edited by Masooda Bano and Keiko Sakurai, 73–90. Edinburgh: Edinburgh University Press, 2015.

Bano, Masooda, and Sakurai, Keiko, eds, *Shaping Global Islamic Discourses: The Role of al-Azhar, al-Medina and al-Mustafa*. Edinburgh: Edinburgh University Press, 2015.

Baramidze, Ruslan. *Islam i ego Osobennosti v Adzharii*. Berlin: Heinrich-Böll-Stiftung, 2005, https://ge.boell.org/en/2005/01/16/islam-i-ego-osobennosti-v-adzharii.

Becker, Seymur. *Russia's Protectorates in Central Asia: Bukhara and Khiva, 1865–1924*. London: RoutledgeCurzon, 2004.

Bekkin, Renat. '"Parallel" Muftiates as the "Third Force" among Spiritual Administrations of Muslims in Russia'. *Journal of Muslims in Europe* 8 (2019): 1–21.

———. *People of Reliable Loyalty … Muftiates and the State in Modern Russia*. PhD Dissertation. Stockholm: Elanders, 2020.

Bennigsen, Alexandre, and Wimbush, S. Enders. *Mystics and Commissars: Sufism in the Soviet Union*. London: Hurst, 1985.

Berger, Peter. *The Desecularization of the World: Resurgent Religion and the World Politics*. Washington, DC: Ethics and Public Policy Center,1999.

Bergne, Paul. 'The Kokand Autonomy 1917–1918'. In *Central Asia: Aspects of Transition*, edited by Tom Everett-Heath, 30–44. London: Psychology Press, 2003.

Berkey, Jonathan P. *The Formation of Islam: Religion and Society in the Near East, 600–1800*. Cambridge: Cambridge University Press, 2003.

Biran, Michal. *The Empire of the Qara Khitai in Eurasian History: Between China and The Islamic World*. Cambridge: Cambridge University Press, 2005.

Blauvelt, Timothy K. 'The Caucasus in the Russian Empire'. In *The Routledge Handbook of the Caucasus*, edited by Galina M. Yemelianova and Laurence Broers, 107–20. London: Routledge, 2020.

Bobrovnikov, Vladimir O. *Musul'mane Severnogo Kavkaza: Obychai, Pravo, Nasilie*. Moscow: Vostochnaia Literatura RAN, 2002.

Bobrovnikov, Vladimir O., and Babich, Irina, L. *Severnyi Kavkaz v Sostave Rossiiskoi Imperii*. Moscow: Novoe Literaturnoe Obozrenie, 2007.

Bosworth, Clifford E. *The Later Ghaznavids: Splendour and Decay in Afghanistan and Northern India 1040–1186*. New York: Columbia University Press, 1977.

Brett, Michael. *The Fatimid Empire*. Edinburgh: Edinburgh University Press, 2017.

Broers, Laurence. *Armenia and Azerbaijan: Anatomy of a Rivalry*. Edinburgh: Edinburgh University Press, 2019.

Bruce, Steve. *God Is Dead: Secularization in the West*. Oxford: Blackwell, 2002.

Bunt, Gary R. *Islam in the Digital Age: E-Jihad, Online Fatwas and Cyber Islamic Environments*. London: PlutoPress, 2003.

Bustanov, Alfried K., and Kemper, Michael. *Islamic Authority and the Russian Language: Studies on Texts from European Russia, the North Caucasus and West Sibiria*. Amsterdam: Pegasus, 2012.

Buzpinar, Ş.Tufan. 'Opposition to the Ottoman Caliphate in the Early Years of Abdulhamid II: 1877–1882'. *Die Welt des Islams* 36, no. 1 (1996): 59–89.

Casanova, Jose. *Public Religions in the Modern World*. Chicago: Chicago University Press, 1994.

Ceraci, Robert P. *Window on the East: National and Imperial Identities in Late Tsarist Russia*. Ithaca, NY: Cornell University Press, 2008.

Cesari, Jocelyne. *When Islam and Democracy Meet*. London: Palgrave Macmillan, 2004.

Chamberlain, Michael. *Chislennost' naseleniia SSSR na 17 yanvaria 1939*. Moscow: Gosplanizdat, 1941.

———. *Knowledge and Social Practice in Medieval Damascus*. Cambridge: Cambridge University Press, 1994.

Choueiri, Youssef. *Islamic Fundamentalism: The Story of Islamist Movements*. London: Bloomsbury, 2010.

Colarusso, John. 'Peoples, Languages and Lore'. In *The Routledge Handbook of the Caucasus*, 2020, 32–51.

Commins, David. *The Wahhabi Mission and Saudi Arabia*. London: I.B. Tauris, 2006.

Crews, Robert D. *For Prophet and Tsar: Islam and Empire in Russia and Central Asia*. Cambridge, MA: Harvard University Press, 2006.

Daftary, Farhad. *The Ismailis: Their History and Doctrine*. Cambridge: Cambridge University Press, 2007.

De Weese, Devin, and Gross, Jo-Ann, eds. *Sufism in Central Asia: New Perspectives of Sufi Traditions, 15th–21st Centuries*. Leiden: Brill, 2018.

Devji, Faisal. *Landscapes of the Jihad: Militancy. Morality. Modernity*. London: Hurst, 2005.

Donogo, Khadzhi Murat. *Najmuddin Gotsinsky*. Makhachkala: IAE DNTs, 2011.

Donohue, John J. *The Buwayhid Dynasty in Iraq 334H/945 to 403H/1012: Shaping Institutions for the Future*. Leiden: Brill, 2003.

Dudoignon, Stéphane A., Hisao, Komatsu and Yasushi, Kosugi, eds. *Intellectuals in the Modern Islamic World: Transmission, Transformation, Communication*. London: Rougledge, 2006.

Eickelman, Dale F., and Piscatori, James. *Muslim Politics*. Princeton, NJ: Princeton University Press, 1996.

Esposito, John L. *The Oxford Dictionary of Islam*. Oxford: Oxford University Press, 2003.

Esposito, John, and Tamimi, Azzam, eds. *Islam and Secularism in the Middle East*. London: Hurst, 2000.

Farah, Caesar E. *The Sultan's Yemen: Nineteenth-Century Challenge to Ottoman Rule*. London: I.B. Tauris, 2002.

Fisher, Alan W. *The Crimean Tatars*. Stanford, CA: Hoover Institution Press, 2014.

Fraser, Glenda. 'Basmachi'. *Central Asian Survey* 6, no. 1 (1987): 1–73.

Fredholm, Michael, 'Islamic Extremism as a Political Force'. In *Seeds of Terror*, edited by Gretchen Peters, 130–33. New York: St. Martin's Press, 2009.

Friedman, Yaron. *The Nuṣayrī-ʿAlawīs: An Introduction to the Religion, History and Identity of the Leading Minority in Syria*. Leiden: Brill, 2010.

Gammer, Moshe. *The Lone Wolf and the Bear: Three Centuries of Chechen Defiance of Russian Rule*. Pittsburgh, PA: University of Pittsburgh, 2006.

Ganich, Anastasiya, ed. *Dukhovnye Pravleniia Musul'man Zakavkaz'ia v Rossiiskoi Imperii: XIX-Nachalo XX V.* Moscow: Mardzhani, 2013.

Gardanov, Valentin K. *Gardanov V.K.- Istorik i Etnograf.* Nal'chik: El'-Fa, 2004.

Gellner, Ernest. *Postmodernism, Reason and Religion*. London: Routledge, 1992.

Gesink, Indira F. *Islamic Reform and Conservatism: Al-Azhar and the Evolution of Modern Sunni Islam*. London: I.B. Tauris, 2010.

Goffman, Daniel. *The Ottoman Empire and Early Modern Europe*. Cambridge: Cambridge University Press, 2002.

Golden, Peter B. *Turks and Khazars: Origins, Institutions and Interactions in pre-Mongol Eurasia*. Farnham: Ashgate, 1980.

Goncharenko, Oleg G. *Tainy Belogo Dvizheniia. Poteri i Porazheniia 1918–1922*. Moscow: Veche, 2004.

Gorshenina, Svetlana. *L'invention de Asie centrale: Histoire du concept de la Tartarie à l'Eurasie*. Paris: Librarie Droz, 2014.

Guseinov, Rashad. 'Istoriia islamskikh institutov v Azerbaidjane'. *Kavkaz i Globalizatsiia* 1, no. 2 (2014): 86–94.

Hallaq, Wael B. *A History of Islamic Legal Theories: An Introduction to Sunnī Uṣūl Al-Fiqh*. Cambridge: Cambridge University Press, 1997.

Hanssen, Jens, and Weiss, Max, eds. *Arabic Thought beyond the Liberal Age: Towards an Intellectual History of the Nahda*. Cambridge: Cambridge University Press, 2016.

Higgins, Annie C. 'Kharijites, Khawarij'. In *Encyclopaedia of Islam and the Muslim World*, edited by Richard C. Martin. Vol. 1, 48–67. London: Macmillan, 2004.

Hoffman, Valerie Jon. *The Essentials of Ibadi Islam*. Syracuse: Syracuse University Press, 2012.

Hunsberger, Alice C. *Nasir Khusraw, the Ruby of Badakhshan: A Portrait of the Persian Poet, Traveller and Philosopher*. London: I.B. Tauris, 2003.

Ignatenko, Alexander, *Islam i Politika*. Moscow: Institute of Religion and Politics, 2004.

Imber, Colin. *The Ottoman Empire, 1300–1650: The Structure of Power*. New York: Palgrave Macmillan, 2009.

Inalcik, Halil. *The Ottoman Empire: The Classical Age, 1300–1600*. London: Weidenfeld and Nicholson, 1973.

Ishaki, Ayaz. *Idel-Ural*. Paris. Reprinted in 1988. London: Society for Central Asian Studies, 1933.

Ismayilov, Murad. *The Dialectics of Post-Soviet Modernity and the Changing Contours of Islamic Discourse in Azerbaijan*. Lanham, MD: Lexington Books, 2018.

Kakagasanov, Gadzhikurban, and Gazhiev, Adilgerei, *Akushinsky- Sheikh-ul-Islam Dagestana, Patriot i Mirotvorets*. Makhachkala: Yupiter, 1998.

Kamali, Mohammad H., *The Middle Path of Moderation in Islam: The Qur'anic Principle of Wa Satiyyah*. Oxford: Oxford University Press, 2015.

Kamp, Marianne. *The New Woman in Uzbekistan: Islam, Modernity, and Unveiling Under Communism*. Seattle, WA: University of Washington Press, 2006.

Kapeller, Andreas. *The Russian Empire: A Multi-Ethnic History*. London: Routledge, 2001.

Karimullin, Abrar G. Tatary: *Etnos i Etnonim*. Kazan: Tatarskoe Knizhnoe Izdatel'stvo, 1988.

Karin, Erlan. *The Soldiers of the Caliphate: The Anatomy of a Terrorist Group*. Astana: KazISS, 2006.

Kemper, Michael. 'Mufti Ravil Gainutdin: The Translation of Islam into a Language of Patriotism and Humanism'. In *Islamic Authority and the Russian Language: Studies on Texts from European Russia, the North Caucasus and West Siberia*, edited by Alfrid K. Bustanov and Michael Kemper, 105–41. Amsterdam: Pegasus, 2012.

———. *Sufii i Uchenye v Tatarstane i Bashkortostane: Islamskii Diskurs pod Russkim Gospodstvom*. Kazan: RII, 2008.

Kennedy, Hugh N. *Muslim Spain and Portugal: A Political History of al-Andalus*. London: Longman, 1996.

———. *The Prophet and the Age of the Caliphates: The Islamic Near East from the Sixth to the Eleventh Century*, 3rd edn. London: Routledge, 2016.

Kepel, Gilles. *Jihad: The Trail of Political Islam*. London: I.B. Tauris, 2002.

Khabutdinov, Aidar Y. *Istoriia Orenburgskogo Magometanskogo Dukhovnogo Sobraniia*. Nizhny Novgorod: Medina, 2010.

Khakim, Rafael. *Gde Nasha Mecca?* Kazan: Magarif, 2003.

Khalid, Adeeb. *Islam after Communism: Religion and Politics in Central Asia*. Berkeley: University of California Press, 2007.

Khalfin, Naftula A. *Prisoedinenie Srednei Azii k Rossii (60–90-e gody XIX v.)*. Moscow: Nauka, 1965.

Khamidov, Evgeny H. 'O neizvestnoi rukopisi sheikha Zainully Rasuleva'. *Kazan Islamic Review* 1 (2015): 106–14.

Khanbabaev, Kaflan. 'Islam and Islamic Radicalism in Dagestan'. In *Radical Islam in the Former Soviet Union*, edited by Galina M. Yemelianova, 82–111. London: Routledge, 2010.

———. 'Vozrozhdenie Musul'manskogo Prava v Dagestane: Teoriia i Praktika'. *Islam i Pravo v Rossii* 2 (2004): 118–45.

Kharsiev, Boris M. *Ingushskie adaty kak fenomen pravovoi kul'tury*. Nazran': Piligrim, 2009.

Khashaev, Khadzhi-Murad. *Pamiatniki obychnogo prava Dagestan XVII–XIX vv*. Moscow: Nauka, 1965.

Kindler, Robert. *Stalin's Nomads: Power and Famine in Kazakhstan*. Pittsburgh: Pittsburgh University Press, 2018.

Knysh, Alexander. 'Contextualizing the Salafi – Sufi Conflict (from the Northern Caucasus to Hadramawt)'. *Middle Eastern Studies* 43, no. 4 (2007): 503–30.

Kolodziejczyk, Dariusz. *The Crimean Khanate and Polish-Lithuania: International Diplomacy on the European Periphery (15th –18th Centuries). A Study of Peace Treaties*. Leiden: Brill, 2011.

Kovalenya, Aleksandr A., et al. *Velikaia Otechestvennaia Voina Sovetskogo Naroda*. Minsk: BGU, 2004.

Kravchenko, Valentin I., and Panchenko, Petr P. *Ukraina vo Vtoroi Mirovoi Voine (1939–1945)*. Donetsk: TsPA, 1998.

Kreindler, Isabelle. 'The Soviet Deported Nationalities: A Summary and Update'. *Soviet Studies* 38, no. 3 (1986): 387–405.

Landa, Robert G. *Islam v Istorii Rossii*. Moscow: Vostochnaia Literatura, 1995.

Laruelle, Marlene and Hohmann, Sophie. 'Polar Islam: Muslim Communities in Russia's Arctic Cities'. *Problems of Post-Communism* (2010). Online version, https://www.tandfonline.com/doi/full/10.1080/10758216.2019.1616565.

Makarov, Dmitrii. *Ofitsial'nyi i Neofitsial'nyi Islam v Dagestane*. Moscow: Tsentr Strategicheskikh i Politicheskikh Issledovanii, 2000.

Makarov, Dmitrii, and Mukhametshin, Rafik. 'Official and Unofficial Islam'. In *Islam in post-Soviet Russia: Public and Private Faces*, edited by Hilary Pilkington and Galina M. Yemelianova, 117–64. London: RoutledgeCurzon, 2003.

Malashenko, Alexei. *Islamskoe Vozrozhdenie v Sovremennoi Rossii*. Moscow: Carnegie Endowment, 1998.

Mandaville, Peter. *Islam and Politics*. London: Routledge, 2014.

Martin, Richard C., Woodward, Mark R. and Atmaja, Dwi S. *Defenders of Reason in Islam: Mu'atazilism from Medieval School to Modern Symbol*. London: Oneworld, 1997.

Masud, Muhammad K., Messick, Brinkley and Powers, David S., eds. *Islamic Legal Interpretations: Muftis and Their Fatwas*. Cambridge, MA: Harvard University Press, 1996.

———. 'Muftis, Fatwas, and Islamic Legal Interpretation'. In *Islamic Legal Interpretations*, 1996, 3–32.

Matroudi al-, Abdul Hakim I. *The Hanbali School of Law and Ibn Taymiyyah: Conflict and Conciliation*. London: Routledge, 2006.

Miftakhov, Zufar Z. *Kurs po Istorii Tatarskogo Naroda*. Kazan: Dom Pechati, 1998.

Minnullin, Il'nur. *Politika Sovetskogo Gosudarstva v Otnoshenii k Musul'manskomu Dukhovenstvu v Tatarstane v 1920–1930-e Gody*. PhD Dissertation. Kazan: Institut Istorii, 2003.

Mitchell, Richard P. *The Society of the Muslim Brothers*. Oxford: Oxford University Press, 1969.

Momen, Moojan. *An Introduction to Shi'i Islam*. London: George Ronald, 1985.

Mukhamedova, Ramziia G. *Tatary-Mishari: Istoriko-Etnograficheskoe Issledovanie*. Moscow: Nauka, 1972.

Mukhametshin, Rafik. 'Islamic Discourse in the Volga-Urals Region'. In *Radical Islam in the Former Soviet Union*, 2010, 31–61.

———. *Tatary i Islam v XX veke*. Kazan: Fen, 2003.

Muminov, Ashirbek. 'Shiitskiie Kul'turnye Vliianiia na Tsentral'nuiu Aziiu'. In *Ars Islamica*, edited by Mikhail B. Piotrovsky and Alikber K. Alikberov, 647–728. Moscow: Vostochnaia Literatura, 2016.

Muminov, Ashirbek, ed. *Sobranie Fetv po Obosnovaniiu Zikra Dzhahr i Sama'*. Almaty: Daik- Press, 2008.

Muslimov, Il'iaz B., ed. 1996. *Na Styke Tsivilizatsii*. Moscow: Insan.

Naselenie SSSR: Po dannym vsesoiuznoi perepisi naseleniia 1989 g. Moscow: Finansy i Statistika.

Nataev, Saipudi A. 'K Voprosu ob Institute "Tukhum/Tokhum/Tuk'um/Tukkham" u Narodov Kavkaza'. *Gumanitarnye, Sotsial'no-Ekonomicheskie i Obshchestvennye Nauki* 6 (2015): 38–59.

Navruzov, Amir. *'Dzharidat Dagistan' – Araboiazychnaia Gazeta Kavkazskikh Dzhadidov*. Moscow: Mardzhani, 2012.

———. 'Gazeta "Jaridat Dagistan"(1913–1918)- unikal'nyi obrazets araboiazychoi publitsistiki nachala XX veka'. *Islamovedenie* 2 (2009): 92–106.

Naumkin, Vitaly V. *Radical Islam in Central Asia: Between Pen and Rifle*. Lanham, MD: Rowman & Littlefield, 2005.

Newman, Andrew J. *Twelver Shi'ism: Unity and Diversity in the Life of Islam, 632 to 1733*. Edinburgh: Edinburgh University Press, 2013.

Nielsen, Jorgen S. *Muslims in Western Europe*. Edinburgh: Edinburgh University Press, 2004.

———. *Towards a European Islam*. London: Palgrave Macmillan, 1999.

Norris, Harry. *Islam in the Baltic: Europe's Early Muslim Community*. London: I.B. Tauris, 2009.

Nurmanova, Aitzhan Sh., and Izbairov, Asilbek K. 'Islamic Education in Soviet and post- Soviet Kazakhstan'. In *Islamic Education in the Soviet Union and Successor States*, edited by Michael Kemper, Raoul Motika and Stefan Reichmuth, 320–68. London: Routledge, 2010.

O'Callaghan, Joseph F. *Reconquest and Crusade in Medieval Spain*. Philadelphia: University of Pennsylvania Press, 2004.

Osmanov, Ahmed I., ed. *Istoriia Dagestana s Drevneishykh Vremen do Nashykh Dnei*. Vol. 1. Moscow: Nauka, 2004.

Parolin, Gianluca P. *Citizenship in the Arab World: Kin, Religion and Nation-State*. Amsterdam: Amsterdam University Press, 2009.

Peyrouse, Sébastien. *Turkmenistan: Strategies of Power, Dilemmas of Development*. Armonk, NY: M.E. Sharpe, 2011.

Pilkington, Hilary, and Yemelianova, Galina M., eds. *Islam in Post-Soviet Russia: Private and Public Faces*. London: RoutledgeCurzon, 2003.

Privratsky, Bruce G. *Muslim Turkistan: Kazak Religion and Collective Memory*. Richmond: Curzon Press, 2001.

Prozorov, Stanislav.M. 'Al-Lakzī Yūsuf'. In *Islam na Territorii Byvshei Rossiiskoi Imperii*. Vol. 1. Moscow: Vostochnaia Literatura, 1998.

Qaradawi al-, Yousuef. al-. *Fiqh of Muslim Minorities: Contentious Issues and Recommended Solutions*. Cairo: Al-Falah Foundation for Translation, 2003.

Quataert, Donald. *The Ottoman Empire, 1700–1922*. Cambridge: Cambridge University Press, 2000.

Račius, Egdūnas. *Islam in Post-Communist Eastern Europe: Between Churchification and Securitization*. Leiden: Brill, 2020.

———. 'Lithuania'. In *Islamic Leadership in the European Lands of the Former Ottoman and Russian Empires: Legacy, Challenges and Change*, edited by Egdūnas Račius and Antonina Zhelyazkova, 272–93. Leiden: Brill, 2017.

———. *Muslims in Eastern Europe*. Edinburgh: Edinburgh University Press, 2018.

Račius, Egdūnas, and Zhelyazkova, Antonina. 'Introduction: Rational of the Book'. In *Islamic Leadership in the European Lands*, 2017, 1–11.

Ramadan, Tariq. *Western Muslims and the Future of Islam*. Oxford: Oxford University Press, 2004.

Ratelle, Jean-François. 'Transnational Salafi and Jihadist Networks: From Independent Insurgency to a Leaderless Network'. In *The Routledge Handbook of the Caucasus*, 2020, 288–302.

Repp, Richard C. *The Mufti of Istanbul: A Study in the Development of the Ottoman Learned Hierarchy*. London: Ithaca Press, 1986.

Richmond, Walter. *The Northwest Caucasus: Past, Present, Future*. London: Routledge, 2008.

Ro'i, Yaacov. *Islam in the Soviet Union: From the Second World War to Gorbachev*. London: Hurst, 2000.

Romanenko, Vladislav. *Sotrudnichestvo Sovetskoi Diplomatii i Musul'manskogo Dukhvenstva v Dvatsatye Gody XX veka*. Nizhny Novgorod: Medina, 2005.

Roshchin, Mikhail. 'Iz Istorii Islama v Dagestane'. In *Islam na Severnom Kavkaze: Istoriia i Sovremennost'*, edited by Islam Tekushev and Kirill Shevchenko, 13–19. Prague: Medium Orient, 2011.

Ross, Danielle. *Tatar Empire: Kazan's Muslims and the Making of Imperial Russia*. Bloomington: Indiana University Press, 2020.

Roy, Olivier. *Globalized Islam: The Search for a New Ummah*, rev. edn. London: Hurst, 2004.

———. *Jihad and Death: The Global Appeal of Islamic State*. Oxford: Oxford University Press, 2017.

———. *Secularism Confronts Islam*. New York: Columbia University Press, 2007.

Rudov, Georgy. *Islam v Tsentral'noi Azii: Mashtaby i Perspektivy Vliianiia'. Obozrevat'l'* 6, no. 293 (2014): 45–69.

Sagramoso, Domitilla, and Yemelianova, Galina M., 'Islam and Ethno-Nationalism in the North-Western Caucasus'. In *Radical Islam in the Former Soviet Union*, 2010, 112–45.

Sahakyan, Naira. 'Language Debate and Visions of the Future in Revolutionary Dagestan'. *Caucasus Survey* 6, no. 2 (2018): 147–62.

Sakurai, Keiko. 'Making Qom a Centre of Shi'i Scholarship: Al-Mustafa International University'. In *Shaping Global Islamic Discourses*, 2015, 41–72.

Salmorbekova, Zumrat, and Yemelianova, Galina. 'Islam and Islamism in the Ferghana Valley'. In *Radical Islam in the Former Soviet Union*, 2010, 211–43.

Saparov, Arsène. 'Between the Russian Empire and the USSR: The Independence of Transcaucasia as a Socio-political Transformation'. In *The Routledge Handbook of the Caucasus*, 2020, 121–35.

Saray, Mehmet. 'Russian Conquest of Central Asia'. *Central Asian Survey* 1, no. 2 (1982): 1–30.

Saroyan, Mark, and Walker, Edward, eds. *Minorities, Mullahs and Modernity: Reshaping Community in the Former Soviet Union*. Berkeley: University of California, 1997.

Sattarov, Rufat, 'Islamic Revival and Islamic Activism in Post-Soviet Azerbaijan'. In *Radical Islam in the Former Soviet Union*, 2010, 146–210.

Schacht, Joseph. *An Introduction to Islamic Law*. Oxford: Clarendon Press, 1982.

Sergeev, Evgeny. *The Great Game, 1856–1907: Russo-British Relations and East Asia*. Washington, DC: Woodrow Wilson Center Press, 2013.

Shavlokhova, Elena, 'Khristianizatsiia Naseleniia Narodov Severnogo Kavkaza Kak Etap Vkliucheniia v Administrativno-Pravovuiu Sistemu Rossii'. *Istoricheskaia i Sotsial'no-Obrazovatel'naia Mysl'* 8, nos. 6/1 (2016): 118–22.

Shikhaliev, Shamil, 'Musul'manskoe reformatorstvo v Dagestane (1900–1930 gg.)'. *Gosudarstvo, Religiia, Tserkov' v Rossii i za rubezhom* 3, no. 35 (2017): 134–69.

Shikhsaidov, Amri. R. 'Islam v Dagestane'. *Central Asia and the Caucasus* 5 (1999), https://www.ca-c.org/journal/cac-05-1999/st_18_shihsaid.shtml.

Shodiyev, Rustam T. *Sufism v Dukhovnoi Zhizni Narodov Srednei Azii (IX-XIII vv)*. Tashkent: Institut Filosofii,1993.

Sibgatullina, Gulnaz. 'Translating Islam into the Language of the Russian State and the Orthodox Church'. *Religion, State and Society* 47, no. 2 (2019): 234–47.

Silantiev, Roman A. *Musul'manskaia Diplomatiia v Rossii: Istoriia i Sovremennost'*. Moscow: Rema, 2009.

———. *Sovet Muftiev Rossii: Istoriia Odnoi Fitny*. Moscow: RISI, 2015.

Skovgaard-Petersen, Jacob. 'Historical Retrospective on Muftiship: Muftis, State and Official Muftis'. In *Islamic Leadership in the European Lands of the Former Ottoman and Russian Empires*, 2017, 12–30.

Skovgaard-Petersen, Jacob, and Gräf, Bettina, eds. *Global Mufti: The Phenomenon of Yusuf al- Qaradawi*. London: Hurst, 2009.

Slabčanka, Daša. 'Belarus'. In *Islamic Leadership in the European Lands of the Former Ottoman and Russian Empires*, 2017, 260–71.

Smith, Jeremy. *Red Nations: The Nationalities Experience in and after the USSR*. Cambridge: Cambridge University Press, 2013.

———. 'The Soviet Caucasus, 1920–91. Resistance and Accommodation'. In *The Routledge Handbook of the Caucasus*, 2020, 136–53.

Sochnev, Yuri V. 'Khristianstvo v Zolotoi Orde'. In *Iz Istorii Zolotoi Ordy*, edited by Damir Iskhakov, 107–18. Kazan: Fond im. Sultan-Galieva, 1993.

Soucek, Svat. *A History of Inner Asia*. Cambridge: Cambridge University Press, 2000.

Stalin, Iosif, 'Vystuplenie na S'ezde Narodov Dagestana'. *Sochineniia*. Vol. 4. Moscow: OGIZ, 1947.

Sulaev, Imanutdin. *Musul'manskoe Dukhovenstvo i Sovetskaia Vlast': Bor'ba i Sotrudnichestvo*. Makhachkala: Institut Istorii, 2004.

Suleymanov, Rais. 'Za chto voiuiut v Donbasse opolchentsy iz Tatarstana'. *Nezavisimaya Gazeta*, 25 March 2015.

Svanberg, Ingvar, and Westerlund, David, eds. *Muslim Minorities in the Baltic Sea Region*. Leiden: Brill, 2016.

Swietochowski, Tadeusz. *Russia and Azerbaijan: A Borderland in Transition*. New York: Columbia University Press, 1985.

Tekushev, Islam, and Shevchenko, Kirill, eds. 2011. *Islam na Severnom Kavkaze: Istoriia i Sovremennost'*. Prague: Medium Orient, 2011.

Tolz, Vera. *Russia's Own Orient: The Politics of Identity and Oriental Studies in the Late Imperial and Early Soviet Periods*. Oxford: Oxford University Press, 2011.

Trepavlov, Vadim V. *Istoriia Nogaiskoi Ordy*. Moscow: RAN, 2002.

Trier, Tom, and Khanzhin, Andrei, eds. *The Meskhetian Turks at a Crossroads: Integration, Repatriation or Resettlement?* New Brunswick: Transaction, 2007.

Trimingham, J. Spencer. *The Sufi Orders in Islam*. Oxford: Oxford University Press, 1998.

Trofimov, Dmitry. *Islam in the Political Culture of the former Soviet Union: Central Asia and Azerbaijan*. Hamburg: IFSH, 1995.

Trubachev, Oleg. N. *Rus'. Rossiia. Ocherki Etimologii Nazvaniia*. Moscow: RAN, 2005.

Tucker, Noah. 'Public and State Responses to ISIS Messaging: Tajikistan'. *Central Asian Program*, no. 11. Washington, DC: George Washington University, 2016.

Tuna, Mustafa. *Imperial Russia's Muslims: Islam, Empire and European Modernity, 1788–1914*. Cambridge: Cambridge University Press, 2015.

Turner, Bryan S. *Religion and Modern Society: Citizenship, Secularisation and the State*. Cambridge: Cambridge University Press, 2011.

Vacca, Alison. *Non-Muslim Provinces under Early Islam: Islamic Rule and Iranian Legitimacy in Armenia and Caucasian Albania*. Cambridge: Cambridge University Press, 2017.

Vaganovich, Ismail. Interview of muftī Vaganovich. The Third International Conference 'The Principle of al-Wasatyya in Islam'. Donetsk, 19 September 2013.

Valentine, Simon R. *Islam and the Ahmadiyya Jama'at: History, Belief, Practice*. New York: Columbia University Press, 2008.

Validi, Togan. *Istoriia Bashkir*. Translated from Turkish by Amir M. Yuldashbaev. Ufa: Kitap, 2010.

Vodarskii, Yaroslav E., Eliseeva, Olga I. and Kabuzan, Vladimir M. *Neselenie Kryma v Kontse XVIII-Kontse XX Vekov*. Moscow: Institut Rossiiskoi Istorii, 2003.

Weber, Max. *Sociology of Religion*. London: Methuen, 1966.

Wright, Laurence. *The Looming Tower: Al Qaeda and the Road to 9/11*. New York: Alfred A. Knopf, 2006.

Yakubovych, Mykhaylo, Vitalii Shchepanskyi and Ayder Bulatov, 'Ukraine'. In *Islamic Leadership in the European Lands of the Former Ottoman and Russian Empires*, 2017, 314–28.

Yakupov, Valiulla. *Neofotsial'nyi Islam v Tatarstane: Dvizheniia, Techeniia, Sekty*. Kazan: Iman, 2003.

Yandarov, Andarbek D. *Sufizm i Ideologiia Natsional'no-Osvoboditel'nogo Dvizheniia*. Alma-Ata: Nauka, 1975.

Yarlykapov, Akhmet. 'Metody obucheniia i propaganda idei dzadidizma v Severokav kazskikh medrese v deiatel'nosti A. Akaeva (nach. XXv.)'. In *Abu Sufian Akaev. Epo kha, zhizn', deiatel'nost': sbornik statei, perevodov i materialov*, edited by Gasan M.-R. Orazaev, 53–75. Makhachkala: Dagestanskoe Knizhnoe Izdatel'stvo, 2012.

Yemelianova, Galina M. 'Alexander Shami. 1893–1838'. In *Neizvestnye Stranitsy Otechestvennogo Vostokovedeniia*, edited by Vitaly Naumkin and Irina Smilianskaya, 39–81. Moscow: Vostochnaia Literatura, 1997.

———. 'Islam and Power'. In *Islam in Post-Soviet Russia*, 2003, 61–116.

———. *Muslims of Central Asia: An Introduction*. Edinburgh: Edinburgh University Press, 2019.

———.'Muslim-State Relations in Russia'. In *Muslim Minority-State Relations: Violence, Integration and Policy*, edited by Robert Mason, 107–32. London: PalgraveMacmillan, 2016.

———. 'The north-eastern Caucasus: Dagestan, Chechnya and Ingushetia'. In *The Routledge Handbook of the Caucasus*, 2020, 203–19.

———. 'Political Islam and Jihad in Eurasia: The Case of the North Caucasus'. In *Exporting Global Jihad: Critical Perspectives from Asia and North America*. Vol. 2, edited by Tom Smith and Kirsten E. Schulze, 99–122. London: I.B. Tauris.

———. *Russia and Islam: A Historical Survey*. London: Palgrave, 2002.

———. 'Russia's Umma and Its Muftis'. *Religion, State and Society* 31, no. 2 (2003): 139–50.

———. 'The National Identity of the Volga Tatars at the Turn of the 19th Century: Tatarism, Turkism and Islam'. *Central Asian Survey* 16, no. 4 (1997): 543–72.

———. 'Transnational Islam versus Ethnic Islam in Eastern Europe: The Role of Mass Media'. In *Muslim Networks and Transnational Communities in and across Europe*, edited by Stefano Allievi and Jorgen Nielsen, 243–80. Leiden: Brill, 2003.

———. [Udalova]. *Yemen v Period Pervogo Osmanskogo Zavoevaniia (1538–1635)*. Moscow: Nauka, 1988.

Yemelianova, Galina M., and Akkieva, Svetlana I. 'The Muslim Caucasus: The Role of *ādat*s and *shari'ah*'. In *The Routledge Handbook of the Caucasus*, 2020, 68–84.

Yunusov, Arif. *Islam v Azerbaidzhane*. Baku: Zaman, 2004.

Yunusova, Ayslu B. *33 Goda Sluzheniia Istine i Otechestvu. Verkhovnyi Muftii Rossii*. Ufa: GUP UPK, 2013.

Yunusova, Aislu, and Azamatov, Danil. *225 Let Dukhovnomu Upravleniiu Musul'man Rossii. Istoricheskie Ocherki*. Ufa: GUP RB, 2013.

Zagidullin, Ildus K. *Orenburgskoe Magometanskoe Dukhovnoe Sobranie i Dukhovnoe Razvitie Tatarskogo Naroda v Poslednei Chetverti XVIII – Nachala XX Veka*. Kazan: IIAN RT, 2011.

Zaitsev, Ilia V. *Astrakhanskoe Khanstvo*. Moscow: Vostochnaia Literatura, 2004.

Zaman, Muhammad Q. *The Ulama in Contemporary Islam*. Princeton, NJ: Princeton University Press, 2002.

Zelkina, Anna. *In Quest of God and Freedom*. London: Hurst, 2000.

Zubaida, Sami. *Law and Power in the Islamic World*. London: I.B. Tauris, 2003.

INDEX

Abbasids 16, 44–45, 56–57
Abbyasov, Rushan 142–43
Abdikeev Ruslan, muftī 134. *See also* Donetsk muftīate
'Abduh, Muḥammad 199
Abdülhamid II 200
Abdullayev, Akhmad, muftī 158–59
Ablayev, Emirali, muftī 132, 134, 139–40, 144. *See also* DUMK
Abū Ḥamza al-Maṣrī 207, 248n22
Abubakarov, Sayid-Magomed, muftī 158–59
Abulkhair 61–62
'Adats 5, 20, 24–25, 49
Adjara 108, 211
Adnanites 2, 200
Adygea 166, 168
'Afghan jihād' 160–61
Afghānī, Jamāl al-Dīn al- 199
Agayev, Ahmet 103–4
Aghā Khān 19–20, 122–23, 184, 208. *See also* Badakhshan
Ahl al-Bayt 13
Ahl al-Ḥadīth 24–25
Ahrār, khwājah 'Ubaydallah 61, 62
Akaev, Abū Sufyān 89–90, 93
Akchura, Yusuf 74
Akhtayev, Akhmad-qāḍī 98, 159–60, 161–62, *See also* IRP
Akromīyyah Al- 183. *See also* Akrom Yuldoshev
Akundzadeh, Mirza Fatali 103–4
Akushinsky, 'Alī-ḥajjee 90–91, 92–93, 230n21
Alash Orda 76–77, 116
Alawites 19, 24–25, 247n2
Aleksandrovich, Ismail, muftī 130
Alexy II, Patriarch 141–42. *See also* ROC
Alimov, Usmonkhon, muftī 180–81, 244n7. *See also* UzMI
Aliyev, Alikram 108–9, 111, 169–70
Aliyev, Heydar 107, 169. *See also* Azerbaijan
Aliyev, Il'ham 169. *See also* Azerbaijan
Aliyev, Mukhu 158. *See also* Dagestan
Alizadeh, Aga 106–7
Almohads 15–16
Almoravids 15
Al-Rāid 133–34. *See also* Ukraine
Alsabekov, Muhammad, muftī 162–63, 242 n22. *See also* Chechnya
Altmysh, Bulgar ruler 29
Alyautdinov, Ildar 142–43. *See also* Russia
Alyautdinov, Shamil 142–43. *See also* Russia
Andalus, al- (Andalusia) 4, 14–16, 24–25, 69, 204
Anṣār 13, 24–25
Arab nationalism 201
'Arafāt, Yāsir 203
'Arctic Islam' 149
Arrān (Caucasian Albania) 11, 14, 24–25, 44–45, 46
Arsanov, Bagautdin 94–95. *See also* Chechnya
Arsanukaev, Magomed-Bashir, muftī 97–98. *See also* Chechnya
Arystanbab 12–13
Ash'arīs 24–25
Ashirov, Nafigulla, muftī 142–43, 238 n8
Astemirov, Anzor 167 *See also* Kabardino-Balkaria
Astrakhan Khānate 31
Atharīs 24–25
Aushev, Ruslan 163–64. *See also* Ingushetia
Autlev, Faiz 168–69. *See also* Adygea
Ayyūbids 17
Azerbaijan 169, 212
Azerbaijan Democratic Republic(ADR), 1918–20 92, 105, 230n18
Azerbaijan Islamic Party (AIP) 109–10, 169–70. *See also* Aliyev, Alikram
Azhar al- 1–2, 3–4, 7–8, 24–25, 185–86
'Azzām, 'Abdullah Yūsuf 203. *See also* 'global jihād'

Badakhshan 19–20, 56–57, 122–23, 184, 208. *See also* Ismā'īlīs
Baghdādī, Abū Bakr al-, *Daesh* leader 24–25, 161–62, 164–65, 204

Baitursynuly, Ahmet 76–77. *See also Alash*
Balādhurī 44–45
Bannā, Ḥasan al- 200, 207. *See also* Muslim Brotherhood
Barelvis 206, 248n20
Barudi, Galimjan, muftī 76, 79
Basayev, Shamil 160–61, 162–63. *See also* Chechnya
Bashrevkom 76–77
basmachis 69, 116–17, 238n41
Behbudi, Mahmud Khoja 68–69
Belarus 130
Berdiyev Ismail-hajjee, muftī 97–98, 166. *See also* Karachaevo-Cherkessia
Berdymahamedov, Gurbanguly 190. *See also* Turkmenistan
Bibarsov, Mukaddas, muftī 139, 142–43. *See also* Russia
Bidzhiev, Muhammad 167–68. *See also* Karachaevo-Cherkessia
Bigi, Musa 74, 228n3
Bobokhon, Eshon, muftī 120–21. *See also* SADUM
Bobokhon, Shamsuddinkhon, muftī 121, 180. *See also* SADUM
Bobokhon, Ziyouddinkhon, muftī 120–21. *See also* SADUM
Borlakov, Ramazan 168. *See also* Karachaevo-Cherkessia
Bukeikhanov, Alikhan 114–15
Bukhara Khānate/Emīrate 62, 63, 68, 117
Bukhārī, Muḥammad al- 18, 57–58
Bulgar Islamic Academy 141. *See also* Tatarstan
Buyyīds 19, 24–25, 199
Byzantium 14

CARC (Council for Affairs of Religious Cults) 82, 84–85, 106–7, 108, 121, 137
Catherine the Great 5, 36
Çelebicihan, Noman 75–76, 77. *See also Millī Firqāh*
Chagatai Khānate 29–30, 60. *See also* Genghizids
'Chechen jihād' 162–63, 164
Chechnya 162, 164, 213
Chirkawi (Chirkeiskii), Sayid, sheikh 158 *See also* DUMRD
Chochayev, Sharafutdin 165–66. *See also* Kabardino-Balkaria
Chokaboyev, Ibrahim-Bek, *kurbashi* 130–31
Chokai, Mustafa 77, 116
'churchification' 138
Comintern 79, 81
Córdoba Caliphate of 15–16, 24–25
Crimean Khānate 33. *See also* Genghizids
Crimean muftīate 132, 133

Daesh (ISIS) 18, 45, 99–100, 150, 161–62, 164–65, 167, 168, 170, 184–85, 190–91, 204, 209, 215. *See also* 'global jihād'
Dagestan 158
Dahadaev, Magomed-'Alī 90, 91
Darband (*Bāb al-Abwāb*) 12–13, 44
Darbandī, Abū Bakr al- 18, 20, 47
deportations 5–6, 82, 87, 95, 108–9, 132
Derbisali, Absattar-kajy, muftī 185–86. *See also* Kazakhstan
Dibirov, Muḥammad-qāḍī 93
Dinya Nazaraty 76, 79
Diyanet 135, 169
'Donetsk muftīate' 134
Donish, Ahmad Makhtum Qalla 68–69
DTsM RI (muftīate of Republic of Ingushetia) 163–64. *See also* Ingushetia
Dudayev, Dzhokhar 87, 95–96, 162–63. *See also* Chechnya
Dukchi Ishān 69. *See also* basmachis
DUMB (muftīate of Belarus) 131. *See also* Belarus
DUMChR (muftīate of Chechen Republic) 163. *See also* Chechnya
DUMES/TsDUM (muftīate of central Russia) 82, 83, 84–85, 127, 129–30, 139, 140. *See also* Russia
DUMK (muftīate of Kazakhstan) 185. *See also* Kazakhstan
DUMKB (muftīate of Kabardino-Balkaria) 165 *See also* Kabardino-Balkaria
DUMKChR (muftīate of Karachaevo-Cherkessia) 166. *See also* Karachaevo-Cherkessia
DUMKyr(muftīate of Kyrgyzstan) 187. *See also* Kyrgyzstan
DUMRA (muftīate of Republic of Adygea) 166. *See also* Adygea
DUMRB (muftīate of Republic of Bashkortostan) 140–41
DUMRD (muftīate of Republic of Dagestan) 158–59. *See also* Dagestan
DUM RT (muftīate of Republic of Tatarstan) 139, 144. *See also* Tatarstan
DUMSK (muftīate of the North Caucasus) 157, 213

DUMU (muftīate of Ukraine) 133, 138. *See also* Ukraine
DUMZ (muftīate of Transcaucasia) 101, 102, 106, 111

Emizh, Nurbii, muftī 166. *See also* Adygea
Enver Pasha, Ottoman Minister of War 116–17
Erbakan, Necmettin 208
Erdoğan, Recep 135, 144, 148–49
Eurasian Economic Union (EAEU) 210
Euro-Islam (European Islam) 139–40, 149
European Union (EU) 2–3, 127, 132, 138, 206, 210
Evloyev, Sulambek, muftī 163–64. *See also* Ingushetia

Fahretdinov (Fahretdin), Riza, muftī 79–80
Faizkhanov, Khusain 39–40
Faizov, Ildus, muftī 145
Faizrakhmanists 147. *See also* Sattarov, Faizrakhman
Fāṭimids 17, 19–20, 24–25
Fihrīds 14–15
Fitrat, Abdurauf 68–69, 117
Fivers (Zaydīs), Shī'ah 19, 24–25, 200
France 200, 205, 208

Galiulla (Galiullin) Gabdulla, muftī 139, 142–43, 144–45. *See also* Tatarstan
Gaspiralī, Ismaīl 39–41. *See also jadīdism, Tercuman*
Gaynutdin (Gaynutdinov) Ravil, muftī 139, 142–43. *See also* SMR
Gekkiev, Mahmud, muftī 97–98, 158
Gengesh 189–90. *See also* Turkmenistan
Genghis Khān 60
Genghizids 60, 128. *See also* Chagatai Khānate, Golden Horde, Ilkhānate and Yan Khānate
Germany 206, 208
Ghazālī, Abū Ḥāmid al- 24–25, 47, 59–60
Ghazawāt 44, 46, 48, 50, 53, 91, 102, 115
Ghaznivids 49
Ghumūqī, Jamāl al-Dīn al- 47–48
Gijduvanī, 'Abd al-Khāliq 58
Girei Khān 61–62
'global jihād' 159, 160–62, 168, 171, 181, 184, 203, 210
Golden Horde 28, 29, 41–42, 50, 60. *See also* Genghizids
Gorch'khanov, Il'as 165. *See also* Ingushetia
Gotsinsky, Najmuddīn 90–91, 92
Granada, Amīrate 15–16. *See also* Andalusia
Grand Duchi of Lithuania (GDL) 128
'Great Game' 67
'Grozny Fatwā' 147, 163
Gülen, Fethullah 1–2, 7–8, 135, 148–49, 186, 188, 189–90

Ḥamadanī, Yūsuf 58, 61
Ḥaramain Al-, Islamic Foundation 99
High Council of the 'Ulamā' of Tajikistan (HCUT) 184. *See also* Tajikistan
Hijrī calendar 24–25
Hindustoniy, Ḥajjee Domla 123
Ḥizb al-Taḥrīr al-Islāmī 1–2, 7–8, 135–36, 182–83, 188
hujūm 106, 113–14, 132

Ibn Khaldūn 60–61
Ibn Taymīyyah 18, 199
Ibrahīm al-Ibrahīm, Islamic foundation 99
Ibrahimoglu, Ilgar (Allahverdiyev) 170. *See also* Azerbaijan
Ibraim, Veli 77, 80–81
Idel-Ural 76–77, 81–82
Ijtihād 16–17, 18–20, 29, 45, 84–85, 121, 199, 207
Ikramov, Akmal 117–19
Ilkhānate 29–30, 60. *See also* Genghizids
Imarat Kavkaz (Caucasus Emirate) 161–62, 164–65, 167, 168–69, 215
Inakids 64. *See also* Khiva (Khwārazm) Khānate
Ingushetia 162, 163, 165
'Iranian intermezzo' 17–18
Ishaki, Ayaz 76–77
Iskhakov, Gusman, muftī 139, 144–45. *See also* Tatarstan
Islamic Jihād Union (IIJ) 182, 188. *See also* 'global jihād'
Islamic Movement of Uzbekistan (IMU) 182. *See also* Uzbekistan
Islamic Renaissance Party (IRP) 98, 159–60
Islamic Renaissance Party of Tajikistan (IPRT) 183–85, 191–92. *See also* Tajikistan
'Islamic revival' 5–6, 83–84, 97, 109, 110–11, 123, 159–60, 189
Ismagilov, Saeed, muftī 133–34
Ismailov, Mustafa-qāḍī 89–90
Israilov, Hasan 95

Ittifāq al-Muslimīn, 1906–17 73, 74, 75–76
Ivan the Terrible 28

Jadīdism 5
among Central Asian Muslims 56, 68–69, 113, 117–18, 180–81
among Tatars and Bashkirs 39, 74, 83, 139
Jaish al-Mahdī 188. *See also* Kyrgyzstan
Jakubauskas, Romas, muftī 136. *See also* Lithuania
Jalil, Musa 82
Jamil, Mustafa 133. *See also* Mejlīs of Crimean Tatars
Janibeg Khān 61–62
Janīds 63–64. *See also* Bukhara Khānate/Emīrate
Jazulī Ṣūfīs 158
Jungars 65, 66–67

Kabardino-Balkaria 165, 167
Kabiri, Muhiddin 184–85. *See also* IPRT
Kadar zone 160. *See also* Dagestan
Kadyrov, Akhmad 146, 162–63. *See also* Chechnya
Kadyrov, Ramzan 146, 163, 167, 213
Kakhibsky, Ḥasan Ḥilmī, sheikh 91, 92, 94
Kaiaev, 'Alī 89–90, 93
Kalimatov, Mahmud-Ali 163–64. *See also* Ingushetia
Kalmyks (Oirats) 32–33
Karabakh 108, 110, 169, 212. *See also* Azerbaijan
Karachaevo-Cherkessia 166, 167
Kardanov, Askarbii, muftī 166. *See also* Adygea
Karimov, Islam 182, 215. *See also* Uzbekistan
Kashgar 56–57, 58
Kaufman, General Konstantin von 67
Kazakh Khānate 34
Kazakhstan 58, 61–62, 65–66, 185–86, 212
Kazan Khānate 30
'Kazan Muftīate' 145
Kebedov, Abbas 160–61
Kebedov, Bagauddin 98, 160–61, 164. *See also* IRP
Kebekov, Aliaskhab 161–62
Khafizov, Khaidar, muftī 149–50. *See also* 'Arctic Islam'
Khakimov, Rafael 139. *See also* Tatarstan
Khalikov, Dalgat 90
Khamkhoyev, Isa-ḥajjee, muftī 163–64. *See also* Ingushetia
Khārijites 13
Khaṭṭāb, Ibn al- 160–61, 164. *See also* Chechnya
Khazars 13–14, 27–28, 29
Khiva (Khwārazm) 64, 68, 117
Khojayev, Faizulla 117, 119. *See also* 'Young Bukharans'
Khomīnī, Mūsawī (Khomeini) 203
Khorāsān 16, 44, 55, 56–57
Khorram-Dinan 45–46
Khusnutdinov, Kanafiya, muftī 134. *See also* 'Kievan muftīate'
Khuzin, Muhamatgali, muftī 139–40, 146–47
Khwārazm 14, 55
'Kievan muftīate' 134
Kimsanbai-aji (Abdurahmanov) muftī 187. *See also* Kyrgyzstan
Kirill, Patriarch 141–42. *See also* ROC
Kokand Autonomy 116
Kokand Khānate 64
Korkmasov, Jelāl al-Dīn 90, 91
Krganov, Al'bir, muftī 139–40, 146, 147. *See also* Russia
Krinickis, Romualdas, muftī 136–37
KTsM SK (Coordinating Centre of Muslims of the North Caucasus) 139–40, 159, 163, 166
Kubrawī Ṣūfīs 32–49, 122
Kunta-ḥajjee, Kishiev 48, 94–95, 163. *See also* Chechnya
Kyrgyzstan 64, 66, 187–88, 212

Lakzī, al- 18, 43, 45
League of the Militant Godless 81–82, 94, 106, 118, 120
Lithuania 136, 210
Lithuanian (Lipka) Tatars 128, 131, 136, 210
Lulashenko, Alexander 130. *See also* Belarus

Maarifchilik 103–4
Macarius, Metropolitan 35–36. *See also* ROC
Maksudi, Sadri 74, 75–76
Malikov-Zardabi, Hasan-bey 103–4
Mamlūks 17–18, 24–25
Mammadguluzadeh, Jalil 103–4
Manghits 63–64. *See also* Bukhāra Khanate/Emīrate
Manṣūr, sheikh 50–51
Marwānids 14–15
Maskhadov, Aslan 162–63. *See also* Chechnya
Māturīdī Abū Manṣūr al- 18, 24, 57–58, 180
Mavraev, Magomed-Mirza 89–90

Mawarannahr 5–14, 16, 55–56
Mayamerov, Yerjan, muftī 185–86. *See also* Kazakhstan
Mazīnānī, 'Alī Sharī'atī 203
Mejlīs of Crimean Tatars 133
Mehdi, Abdureshid 74–75
Meskhetian Turks 108
Mevlevī Ṣūfīs 108
Mezhiyev, Salah, muftī 163
military-popular governance 89
Millī Firqāh 75–76, 77
Mir-i Arab madrasah 62, 65, 118–19, 120–21, 180–81
Mirzayev, Sultan, muftī 163
Mirziyoyev, Shavkat 191
Mitaev, Ali, sheikh 90–91
'Moscow Muftīate' 147. *See also* Krganov, Al'bir
Muhājirūn al- 207
Mukhetdinov, Damir 142–43. *See also* Russia
Mu'āwiyah ibn Abī Sufyān 13
Mufti concept 20–22, 31, 32, 50–51
muhājirūn 12–13, 24–25
muhājirs 18
Mukhetdinov, Damir 142–43. *See also* Russia
Mukhitdin, Abdul Qadir 117. *See also* 'Young Bukharans'
Mukozhev, Musa 167. *See also* Kabardino-Balkaria
Mulūk ul-Ṭawa'if 15–16. *See also* Andalusia
Munawwar Qari 68–69
Musavat, party 73, 105
Muslim Brotherhood 159–60, 200, 206
Muslim Communists 5–6, 77
Muslim World League (MWL) 99
Mustafin, Ahmedzian 83
Mu'tazilīs 18, 24–25, 57–58

Nahḍah al- 200
Nakhchivan 48–49, 108, 111
Namangani, Juma (Khodjiyev) 123, 182. *See also* Uzbekistan
Naqshband, Bahā' al-Dīn 61, 180–81
Naqshbandī Ṣūfīs 20, 32, 47–49, 62, 94–95, 96–97, 122, 158, 186–87. *See also* Naqshband, Bahā' al-Dīn
Narimanov, Nariman 104
Nāṣir Khusraw 56–57
Naṣirī, Abdul Qayum al- 40
Nasrullah ibn Ibadullah, muftī 190–91. *See also* Turkmenistan
Nasser, Gamal Abdel 201
NATO (North Atlantic Treaty Organization) 2–3, 127, 210
Nāẓim al-Ḥaqqānī, sheikh 158
Nigmatullin, Nurmuhamet, muftī 140–41. *See also* DUMRB
Nikon, Patriarch 35–36. *See also* ROC
Niyazov, Abdel Wahid 142–43. *See also* Russia
Saparmurat Niyazov (Turkmenbashi) 189. *See also* Turkmenistan
Nogai Horde 32 *See also* Genghizids
Nuri, Said Abdullo 183–84. *See also* Tajikistan
Nursi, Badiuzzam Said 148–49
Nysanbai-uly Ratbek-kajy, muftī 185. *See also* Kazakhstan

October Manifesto of 1905 73
Organisation of Islamic Cooperation (OIC) 110–11, 141, 189
Orenburg muftīate 38–39, 141
Ottomans 21, 24–25, 33, 52–53

Pankisi Gorge 164–65
Pashazadeh, Allashukur Hummat 107, 110–11, 169, 212. *See also* Azerbaijan
Peter the Great 36–37
Polish-Lithuanian Commonwealth (PLC) 128
Prométhée 77
Pshikachev, Anas, muftī 165–66. *See also* DUMKB
Pshikachev, Shafig, muftī 97–98, 165–66. *See also* DUMKB
Putin, Vladimir 139–40, 143. *See also* Russia

Qahtanites 12
Qadīmists 40–41
Qādirī Ṣūfīs 48–49, 94–95, 148–49, 158, 163
Qaeda Al- 161–62, 164–65, 182, 203. *See also* 'global jihād'
Qarā Khitais 58–59
Qaraḍāwī, Yūsuf al- 181, 207, 215
Qarākhānids 58
Qasimov Khānate 33
Qizilbash 22–23
QMI (muftīate of Republic of Azerbaijan) 169, 170. *See also* Azerbaijan
Quraysh 12, 13
Qursawī, Abū Naṣr al- 39–40
Quṭb, Sayyīd 201. *See also* Muslim Brotherhood

Rahmon, Emomali (Rahmonov) 183–84. *See also* Tajikistan
RAIS (Russian Association for Islamic Consensus) 146. *See also* Russia
Ramaḍān, Ṭāriq 207. *See also* Euro-Islam
Rashida Abystai. *See also* Tatarstan
Rāshidūn 12,199
Rasulev, Gabdrahman, muftī 78–79, 81–82
Rasulev, Zainulla, ishān 38–40
Rasulzadeh, Mammad Emin 105
'Red Mollahs' 105–6
Riḍā', Rashīd 199
Rome papacy 205
Ruhnama 190. *See also* Turkmenbashi
Russia 139–42, 212
'Russian Islam' 41–42, 143–44. *See also* Catherine the Great, Russia
Russian Orthodox Church (ROC) 29–30, 37–38, 81–82, 130–31, 140, 141–42, 146–47, 214

Sādāt, Anwar al- 202
SADUM (muftīate of Central Asia) 83, 113–14, 120, 180, 185
Safawids 22, 24–25, 46–47, 52–53
Ṣaḥābah 12–13, 24–25
Saidov, Abdurashid 159–60. *See also* Dagestan
Salman, Farid 144–45, 146–47. *See also* Tatarstan
Saltinsky, Uzun-ḥajjee 90–91, 92
Sāmānīds 17, 57
Sasanians 27–28, 44, 56–57
Sattarov, Faizrakhman 147. *See also* Faizrakhmanists
Serikbai-kajy, muftī 185–86. *See also* Kazakhstan
Seljūqs 17–18, 46–47, 59
Seveners (Ismā'īlīs), Shī'ah 19–20, 122. *See also* Badakhshan
Seydahmet, Jafer 75–76, 77, 82. *See also* *Millī Firqāh*
Shabanovich, Abu Bekir, muftī 130, 131. *See also* Belarus
Shādhilī Ṣūfīs 48, 96–97, 158
Shamayev, Akhmad-ḥajjee, muftī 163. *See also* Chechnya
Shamīl, *imām* 5, 47–48, 50–52
Sharwānshāhs (Shirwan) 17, 23, 45–46
Shaybānī, Muḥammad 62
Shaybānīds 62, 63–64
Sheripov, Mairbek 95
Shirvani, Seyid Azim 103–4
Shumaf, Enver, muftī 166. *See also* Adygea
Sibir, Khānate 34, 62. *See also* Genghizids
Sigmatullin, Kamil, muftī 145. *See also* DUMRT
Silk Road 55, 57, 63
SMR (Council of Muftīs of Russia) 132, 134, 139–40, 142
Sogdia 56–57
'Soviet Muslims' concept 84, 99–100, 113–14
Ṣūfīsm, concept 20, 24–25
Sufyānids 14
Sughūrī,'Abd al-Raḥmān al- 47–48
Suhrawardī Ṣūfīs 47
Süleymancis 186
Suleymanov, Qamet 170. *See also* Azerbaijan
Sultan-Galiev, Mirsaid 74–75, 77–79, 80–81
Sunnīs of Abū Ḥanīfa madhhab 18, 46–47, 89
Sunnīs of Abū al-Shāfi'ī madhhab 18, 45, 46, 89
Sunnīs of Ibn Ḥanbal madhhab 18, 24–25
Sunnīs of Mālik ibn Anas madhhab 18
Sykes–Picot Agreement 205
Szynkiewicz, Jakub, muftī 128–30

Tablīghī Jamā'ah 1–2, 7–8, 187–88, 190–91, 200
Tadzhuddin(Tadzhuddinov), Talgat, muftī 139, 140, 144–45, 146. *See also* DUMES
Tajikistan 183–84, 212
Takfīr (Al-) wa al-Ḥijrah 135–36, 168, 200
Tamīm, Aḥmad, sheikh 133. *See also* DUMU
taqīyyah 45–46, 48–49, 106
Tarablusi, Shami Domullo al- 121–22
Tatarstan 144
Taurida muftīate 39, 128
Tercuman 40–41. *See also* Gaspiralī, Ismaīl
Tbilisi (Tiflis), Emīrate of 14
Timūr (Tamerlane) 60–61
Timūrids 60
Tirmidhī, Abū 'Īsā al- 57–58
Togan, Zeki Velidi 75–77
Topbaş Osman Nuri, sheikh 169. *See also* Azerbaijan
'traditional' Islam concept 214
Tsalikov, Akhmet-bey 90–91
Tunahan, Süleyman Hilmi, sheikh 186–88. *See also* Kazakhstan, Kyrgyzstan
Turajonzoda, Hoji Akbar, muftī 183–84. *See also* Tajikistan
Turkestan, Russian Governorate 64, 67
Turkmenistan 212189–90

Twelvers (*Ithnā 'Asharīyah*), Shī'ah 4, 19, 22–25, 46–47

Udugov, Movladi 160–61, 164. *See also* Chechnya
Ukraine 132
'Umar ibn al-Khaṭṭāb, Caliph 12–13
Umarov, Doku 161–62, 164–65. *See also* Caucasus Emirate
Umayyads 11, 13–14
United Kingdom 204, 208
United States of America 141–42, 203
United Tajik Opposition (UTO) 183–85. *See also* Tajikistan
'untraditional' Islam concept 214
Uzbekistan 61–62, 64, 180–81
UzMI (muftiate of Uzbekistan) 180, 181. *See also* Uzbekistan

Vahitov, Mullanur 75–76, 77–78. *See also* Muslim Communists
Vepayev, Kakagel'dy, muftī 190–91. *See also* Turkmenistan
Volga Bulgaria 16–17, 28, 29–30, 140–41
Voronovich, Ali, muftī 131. *See also* DUMB
Voronovich, Ismail, muftī 131. *See also* DUMB

Wahhāb, Muḥammad ibn 'Abd al- 200
'War on Terror' 1–2
Wasaṭīyyah al- 143

Xinjiang 56–57, 64, 65

Yamashev, Huseyn 74–75
Yan Khānate 60. *See also* Genghizids
Yandarbiyev, Zelimkhan 160–61, 162–63, 164. *See also* Chechnya
Yakupov, Valiulla 145, 148. *See also* Tatarstan
Yaqoob, Ramadan, muftī 136–37. *See also* Lithuania
Yarāghī, Muḥammad-efendī al- 47–48
Yarmuk 167. *See also* Kabardino-Balkaroa
Yaroslavsky, Yemelyan 81. *See also* League of Militant Godless
Yasa 29–30, 48–49
Yasawī, Aḥmad 58. *See also* Yasawīs
Yasawī Ṣūfīs 34–35, 48–49, 58, 122, 186–87. *See also* Yasawī, Aḥmad
Yevkurov, Yunus-Bek 163–64. *See also* Ingushetia
Yevloyev, Akhmed 165. *See also* Ingushetia
Yoldoshev, Tohir 123, 182
'Young Bukharans' 117–18
'young imāms' 83–84, 97–98, 139, 142, 157, 158, 159–60, 166, 180, 183–84, 185, 187
'Young Khivans' 117
Yuldoshev, Akrom 183. *See also* Uzbekistan
Yusuf, Muhammad Sodiq, muftī 123, 179, 180. *See also* Uzbekistan

Ẓawāhirī Ayman al- 161–62
Ziazikov, Murat 163–64. *See also* Ingushetia

www.ingramcontent.com/pod-product-compliance
Lightning Source LLC
Chambersburg PA
CBHW021138230426
43667CB00005B/161
* 9 7 8 1 8 3 9 9 9 3 7 1 8 *